36 AND COUNTING...

KERRY'S FOOTBALL STORY TO 2009

36 AND COUNTING…

KERRY'S FOOTBALL STORY TO 2009

NIALL FLYNN

Order this book online at www.trafford.com
or email orders@trafford.com

Most Trafford titles are also available at major online book retailers.

Printed in Victoria, BC, Canada.

ISBN: 978-1-4269-2070-7 (Soft)
ISBN: 978-1-4269-2069-1 (Hard)

Library of Congress Control Number: 2009940714

*Our mission is to efficiently provide the world's finest, most comprehensive
book publishing service, enabling every author to experience success.
To find out how to publish your book, your way, and have it available
worldwide, visit us online at www.trafford.com*

Trafford rev. 11/12/2009

www.trafford.com

North America & international
toll-free: 1 888 232 4444 (USA & Canada)
phone: 250 383 6864 ♦ fax: 812 355 4082

ACKNOWLEDGEMENTS

As this work grew from humble beginnings, my family time became less and less. To my wife, Mary, and children James, Catherine, and Joey, I give my deepest thanks for allowing me to pursue this endeavour. Their assistance in proof-reading and cross-checking the data is also appreciated.

The main portions of research involved newspapers and various publications to assist in verifying data. The work of PF (Paddy Foley) as correspondent for *The Kerryman* has been invaluable. His reporting of our games interwove the facts of the game as they developed with his insight into the match analysis. PF's book published in the 1940's *"Kerry's Football Story"* is really the forerunner of this book and provides some of the inspiration for the title. Local papers such as *The Cork Examiner, The Clare Champion* and *The Limerick Leader* provided great information. The common link between all these papers is the County Library of each county. Articles were researched and mailed or scanned to me almost immediately, even from outside Kerry. These people are a shining light for all public servants. I especially want to thank the staff of our Kerry County Library in Killarney for allowing me the days to review the material stored. Their courtesy and tolerance is genuinely appreciated.

Honourable mentions must also go to:

My father, Jimmy, for all he has done and one wonderful piece of advice: Never bet against Kerry.
Marjorie and Nicky, and all the O'Sullivan clan in Bishopstown for their encouragement.
Title guidance was precise from Kerry's newest fan, Vance Webb in Houston, Texas.
James Lundon for steering the project along from the beginning.
Derrynane's Mike Curran for the cover work - a truly inspiring piece of art.
And those who offered an answer to a question or a correction to an entry - the legendary Mike Casey (Spa), Diarmuid Murphy, Mike O'Donoghue (Spa), Pat O'Shea (Dr. Crokes), Mike Quirke (Castlemaine and Dublin), and Firies clubmen John O'Donoghue and Michael Allen.

Weeshie Fogarty, the radio voice of Kerry football via the internet for all the Kingdom's exiles, for his continuous support and motivation to make these details available to followers of football everywhere.

One contributor stands above all, Tralee's Tim Slattery. Weeshie Fogarty put me in touch with Tim, who willingly shared all his notes and newspaper accounts of games throughout the years. This repository of information was initially collected by Tim's father and continues to expand with every game. Since I am California-based our communications were mainly via e-mail. Tim confided that he never used email before our inter-continental exchanges on Kerry football matters. Welcome to the technology age, Tim, long may you and your collection prosper.

To Family

The Greatest Team Ever

TABLE OF CONTENTS

FOREWORD

By Weeshie Fogarty

Kerry and its faithful footballer followers world wide will welcome with open arms this magnificent publication, which Firies clubman Niall Flynn has been working on for the past number of years. What you will enjoy between these pages is something that every follower of The Kingdom has been longing for ever since a ball was first kicked in anger.

It's amazing despite being the most successful football county in Ireland that some scribe has not put pen to paper earlier and record for posterity the names and achievements of the long list of Kerry men who have worn the green and gold with such distinction. What Niall has achieved in these pages will prove a veritable treasury of Kerry football history and achievement from the first recorded date when Cork beat Kerry 0-2 to 0-1 in 1889.

In my opinion, he has righted a terrible wrong; that of not remembering our past as it should be. It is without doubt a real labour of love undertaken by a man whose passion for Kerry football and indeed all things Kerry knows no bounds. This magnificent publication is a tribute to all those great men who donned the green and gold for their county through the decades.

Between the covers of this book are the names and achievements, not alone of the Kerry players who have won the coveted Celtic cross on All Ireland final day in Croke Park, but also, and for me more importantly, the names of the unknown and almost-forgotten men who gave their all for the sake of their county without achieving the glory of an All Ireland medal.

The teams, the names, the facts, the figures, the scorers, the opponents, the dates are all brought together here for you in one superb publication for the very first time. What Niall has published is one of the greatest contributions to the story of Kerry football since *The Kerryman's* legendary GAA reporter, Paddy Foley, published his history of Kerry football in 1944. That work was entitled simply "Kerry's Football Story". Niall includes the same words here as a small tribute to PF's account.

Niall's addition of a short summary of news events, both at home and abroad, for each year adds a touch that will educate, recall, and enlighten all of his readers to events long since forgotten. This section of the publication is fascinating in its own right.

I felt greatly honoured when Niall asked me to write the Foreword to this massive work on the history of every Kerry footballer who kicked a ball for his county in the senior football championship. What makes this superb publication even more amazing is the fact that Niall emigrated many years ago to California, where uncovering and cross checking facts and figures was undoubtedly much more difficult than if he was still at home.

I am fully convinced that a copy of this publication will in time rest in every GAA home in Kerry and beyond. On this score it is a must. It will settle many an argument and browsing through its 400 pages or so will pass many an idle hour during those long winter evenings.

Most importantly of all, Niall has now assured that those men who donned the jersey even once with their beloved county have not been forgotten or erased from history's pages but thankfully have been written into the pages of Kerry's amazing football story.

Well done Niall Flynn, you have served your county well. This book is indeed another addition to the Secret of Kerry. You have marked Kerry's contribution to the 125 year history of the Gaelic Athletic Association in one of the most tangible and historic ways possible.

INTRODUCTION

Kerry's football story is well documented...or is it? Despite lengthy searches of articles both online and in printed media, a definitive authority on the facts was hard to come by. Stories, even legends, abound on the topic of Kerry football and its glory, but answers to questions about statistics beyond numbers of All-Ireland medals for the top stars could not be found. Who is the top championship scorer ever? Who scored all the goals? Scoring data is available for each Championship season over the last several years and we are well used to seeing the career numbers for players on television, but where are the comparisons with their predecessors?

This book is a statistical summary of Kerry's Championship games since the GAA was founded in 1884. By the end of 2009, Kerry have played 421 games, from that first game in Mallow on 29 July, 1889, losing to Cork by a point, right through to the 2009 All-Ireland Final in Croke Park, avenging that first defeat yet again.

The scoring data in the first chapter covers 1928 to 2009 only, the era of Sam Maguire being presented to the All-Ireland winners. Tremendous difficulty arises when attempting to cross-check data from prior to 1928, so a decision was made to present data prior to 1928 in a summary format. Teams that won Munster championships and All-Ireland titles are named, but due to the lack of scoring records, especially in early Munster games, the individual scoring statistics are not included.

All of Kerry's Championship games are in an easily read format. Some of our nation's history is covered by an "In the News" report for each year - I'm hoping our history teachers don't take me to task for including some small items while excluding bigger issues.

At the end of the book, where one normally finds an index, is the jewel of the work. It is the Register of Players, where you will find, in alphabetical order, every man to don the green and gold since 1928. Listed beside his name is the year he first appeared, his final year, his total scored if any, and his number of appearances.

Although six games from 1928 to 1946 have incomplete scorer data, with 8-22 unaccounted, when you see that Kerry scored 561 goals and 3575 points since 1928, it is a small shortcoming.

While every effort is made in presenting accurate data, there is no guarantee of it being correct. Anyone who has had the duty of gathering scoring information from the sideline will agree that it is easy to miss a score here and there, especially in high scoring games.

Of course, all the statistics in the world won't help the man on the pitch when starting again in 2010, but I hope you can find some amusement as well as history from what's in this book. A sense of where we have come from in our annual chase for Sam Maguire.

They say that if we ignore history, we are doomed to repeat it. Maybe we can modify that statement by saying that when it comes to Kerry football, it is only by studying our history that we can hope to repeat it.

Here's to our heroes, the 383 men who have appeared in the green and gold from 1928 to 2009. No book will ever come close to relaying the true spirit of Kerry football, but I present the details of who played and who scored to serve as the framework upon which our legends are built.

Enjoy. Ciarraí Abú.

While this book concentrates on championship football, it would be remiss of any account to ignore our hurlers and our Ladies' teams. Long may they continue to uphold the spirit of the Kingdom.

Hurling

All-Ireland titles: Three

Senior:

1891 (21-a-side): P. Carroll, F. Crowley, J. Crowley, T. Dunne, M. Fitzmaurice, M. Kelly, P. Kirby, D. Kissane, J. Mahony, M. McCarthy, T. McCarthy, T.E. McCarthy, J. McDonnell, J. Murphy, J. O'Sullivan, M. O'Sullivan, J. Quane, P. Quane, M. Riordan, P. Rourke, P. Wynne

Junior:

1961: J. O'Donovan, N. Sheehy, N. Quill, T. Kirby, M. Hennessy, R. McElligott, K. Dermody, S. Lovett, S. Healy, J. Barry, T. Hennessy, P. Sullivan, J. Culloty, W. McCarthy, E. Sullivan

1972: A. Casey, B. Fitzgerald, E. Fitzgerald, W. Kenny, E. Canty, T. Cronin, T. Hussey, J. Bunyan, P. Finnegan, C. Nolan, T. Kenny, P. Costello, J. McCarthy, P. Donegan, J. Flanagan. Sub: M. Fitzgerald

Ladies Football

All Ireland Senior Champions - 11 - 1976, 1982, 1983, 1984, 1985, 1986, 1987, 1988, 1989, 1990, 1993

Division 1 National League - 12 - 1980, 1981, 1982, 1983, 1984, 1985, 1987, 1988, 1989, 1990, 1991, 1992

All Ireland Minor Champions - 3 - 1980, 1981, 1995

Senior Munster Champions - 13 - 1976, 1977, 1982, 1983, 1984, 1985, 1986, 1987, 1988, 1989, 1990, 1993, 2003

Individual Scoring Records
from 1928 to 2009
and Scoring Analysis since 1889

We have become well used to looking at the career statistics of players in recent times. Of the 313 games played from 1928 to 2009, some scorer data is missing from 6 games prior to 1946. This gap does not come into play in any of the top categories, but it is unfortunate that the players who scored cannot get the full credit for their efforts.

These lists should give plenty of room for thought. Comparisons across the generations cannot tell the full story since training methods, quality of opposition, and indeed quality of team mates, varied over the years, but the reader can reach their own conclusions on the relative merits of the players.

Total Scoring (goals and points combined):

1. Mike Sheehy 292 points (29-205)
2. Maurice Fitzgerald 241 (12-205)
3. Colm Cooper 210 (15-165)
4. Dara Ó'Cinneide 182 (11-149)
5. Pat Spillane 180 (19-123)
6. Mike Frank Russell 154 (8-130)
7. Mick O'Dwyer 147 (6-129)
8. Mick O'Connell 124 (1-121)
9. Eoin Liston 110 (20-50)
10. John Egan 101 (14-59)
11. Brendan Lynch 96 (3-87)
12. John Crowley 89 (12-53)
13. Jack O'Shea 88 (11-55)
14. Eoin Brosnan 87 (15-42)
15. Tadghie Lyne 80 (5-65)
16. Ger Power 76 (14-34)
17. Paudie Sheehy 74 (6-56)
18. Murt Kelly 73 (7-52)
19. Bryan Sheehan 71 (0-71)
20. Tom Gega O'Connor 68 (7-47)
21. Declan O'Sullivan 65 (7-44)

Goal Scoring:

Mike Sheehy scored 29 goals
Eoin Liston 20
Pat Spillane 19
Eoin Brosnan and Colm Cooper 15 each
John Egan and Ger Power 14 each
Maurice Fitzgerald and John Crowley 12 each
Dara Ó'Cinneide, Jack O'Shea and John Joe Landers 11 each
Charlie O'Sullivan 10

Mike Sheehy's 29 Goals

Cork 7; Waterford 5; Dublin, Derry and Monaghan 3 each; Tipperary 2; Clare, Offaly, Roscommon, Galway, Tyrone, Armagh 1 each.

Mike scored 3 goals in a game twice and two goals in a game 6 times.

Points only:

1. Maurice Fitzgerald and Mike Sheehy 205 each
3. Colm Cooper 165
4. Dara Ó'Cinneide 149
5. Mike Frank Russell 130
6. Mick O'Dwyer 129
7. Pat Spillane 123
8. Mick O'Connell 121
9. Brendan Lynch 87
10. Bryan Sheehan 71
11. Tadghie Lyne 65
12. John Egan 59
13. Paudie Sheehy 56
14. Jack O'Shea 55
15. John Crowley 53
16. Murt Kelly 52
17. Eoin Liston, Jackie Ryan 50 each
19. Tom Gega O'Connor 47
20. Declan O'Sullivan 44

Top Average per Game Scorers (20 game minimum)

1. Mike Sheehy 5.96
2. Maurice Fitzgerald 5.36

3. Colm Cooper 3.89
4. Dara Ó'Cinneide 3.37
5. Tadghie Lyne 3.33
6. Pat Spillane 3.21
7. Mick O'Dwyer 3.06
8. Brendan Lynch 3.00
9. Eoin Liston 2.82
10. Mike Frank Russell 2.75

Goals-only in One Game

4 Charlie O'Sullivan Limerick 1936;
3 Martin Regan Tipperary 1931; Sean McCarthy Cork 1937; Frank O'Keeffe Clare 1947; Willie Bruddy O'Donnell Clare 1948; Paudie Sheehy Clare 1953; Mike Sheehy Derry 1976; Eoin Liston Dublin 1978; Pat Spillane Clare 1979; Mike Sheehy Monaghan 1979; Eoin Liston Clare 1981; Eoin Brosnan Longford 2006.

Points-only in One Game

12 Maurice Fitzgerald Limerick 1991;
11 Mike Sheehy Cork 1976;
10 Mick O'Dwyer Cork 1972; Maurice Fitzgerald Cork 1988; Maurice Fitzgerald Tipperary 1998; Maurice Fitzgerald Limerick 1995;

Top Scorer in an Individual Game

16 points Charlie O'Sullivan (4-4) Limerick 1936; Maurice Fitzgerald (2-10) Limerick 1995;

14 points Mike Sheehy (2-8) Waterford 1978; Mike Sheehy (3-5) Monaghan 1979;

12 points Paudie Sheehy (3-3) Clare 1953; Mike Sheehy (3-3) Derry 1976; Mike Sheehy (2-6) Dublin 1979; Eoin Liston (3-3) Clare 1981; Maurice Fitzgerald (0-12) Limerick 1991; Maurice Fitzgerald (2-6) Tipperary 1995;

11 points Willie Bruddy O'Donnell (3-2) Clare 1948; Mike Sheehy (0-11) Cork 1976; Pat Spillane (2-5) Waterford 1978; Mike Sheehy (2-5) Cork 1978; Eoin Liston (3-2) Dublin 1978; Maurice Fitzgerald (1-8) Cork 1992; Dara Ó'Cinneide (2-5) Cork 2000; Colm Cooper (2-5) Limerick 2005; Colm Cooper (1-8) Cork 2008;

10 points   Martin Regan (2-4) Tipperary 1932; Willie Bruddy O'Donnell (2-4) Tipperary 1945; Mick O'Dwyer (0-10) Cork 1972; Brendan Lynch (1-7) Offaly 1972; Pat Spillane (3-1) Clare 1979; Ger Power (2-4) Cork 1979; Mike Sheehy (2-4) Cork 1982; Mike Sheehy (2-4) Tipperary 1983; Maurice Fitzgerald (0-10) Cork 1988; Maurice Fitzgerald (0-10) Tipperary 1998; Dara Ó'Cinneide (1-7) Limerick 2004.

Kerry's Record when scoring (goals and points combined)

Score 19 or more: Of the118 times, won all 118
Score 18: Of the 20 times, won 18 and lost 2 (Cork 1973, Cork 1983)
Score 17: Of the 25 times, won 22, drew 2 (Armagh 2000, Dublin 2001) and lost 1 (Offaly 1982)
Score 16: Of the 27 times, won 20, drew 3, lost 4
Score 15: Of the 18 times, won 17, drew 1
Score 14: Of the 27 times, won 20, drew 1, lost 6
Score 13: Of the 22 times, won 16, drew 3, lost 3
Score 12: Of the 23 times, won 15, drew 2, lost 6
Score 11: Of the 15 times, won 12, drew 1, lost 2
Score 10: Of the 25 times, won 12, drew 4, lost 9
Score 9: Of the 24 times, won 15, drew 4, lost 5
Score 8: Of the 17 times, won 7, drew 3, lost 7
Score 7: Of the 15 times, won 8, drew 2, lost 5
Score 6: Of the 13 times, won 4, drew 2, lost 7
Score 5: Of the 7 times, won 3, lost 4
Score 4: Of the 7 times, won 4, drew 2, lost 1
Score 3: Of the 9 times, won 1, drew 1, lost 7
Score 2: Of the 5 times, drew 1, lost 4
Score 1: Of the 3 times, lost 3
Never been held scoreless in a Championship game.

Summary: Score 15 or more: Kerry win 93.75% of the time.

Kerry's Record when Scoring Goals:

5 or more: In 27 instances of Kerry scoring 5 goals or more in a game, Kerry won all 27 games. Kerry's most goals scored an All-Ireland Final was 5, Dublin 1978
4: Kerry scored 4 goals in 23 games, and won all 23.
3: Kerry scored 3 goals in 54 games, won 52, drew 1 Galway 1919, lost 1 Cork 1983
2: Kerry scored 2 goals in 103 games, won 86, drew 8, lost 9.
1: Kerry scored 1 goal in 114 games, won 80, drew 11, lost 23.
0: Kerry scored no goals in 99 games, won 44, drew 12, lost 43.

Summary: When Kerry scored 3 or more goals, the win rate is 98.1%.
When Kerry score exactly 2 goals, the win rate is 83.5%
When Kerry score exactly 1 goal, the win rate is 70.2%
When Kerry score no goal, the win rate is 44.4%

Kerry's Record when Conceding Goals

Kerry have conceded 5 goals twice and lost both games, Cork 1973 and Limerick 1895
Kerry have conceded 4 goals twice, losing to Galway 1919 but beating Offaly 1980
Kerry have conceded 3 goals 15 times, won 7, drew 2, lost 6
Kerry have conceded 2 goals 65 times, won 42, drew 7, lost 16
Kerry have conceded 1 goal 155 times, won 109, drew 11, lost 35
Kerry have conceded no goal 181 times, won 153, drew 12, lost 16

Summary: Concede 3 or more goals, Kerry win 36.8%
Concede 2, Kerry win 64.6%
Concede 1, Kerry win 70.3%
Concede no goal, Kerry win 84.5%

Goal Scoring Differential Analysis

Combining the above, when Kerry score more goals than their opponents, Kerry have won 213 of 230, with 9 draws, and 8 losses, win rate of 92.6%.

When Kerry score the same number of goals as their opponents, Kerry have won 68 of 109, with 14 draws, and 27 losses, win rate of 62.4%.

When Kerry have conceded more goals than they have scored Kerry have won 31 of 81, with 9 draws, and 41 losses, win rate of 38.3%.

When goal scoring differential is +2 or more (meaning Kerry score at least 2 goals more than their opponent), Kerry have won 132 out 133 times, the exception being a draw in 1956 Munster Final (Kerry 2-2 Cork 0-8). This represents a win rate of 99.3%.

When goal scoring differential is +1, Kerry's record is 81 wins, 8 draws 8 losses, win rate of 83.51%.

When goal scoring differential is 0, Kerry's record is 68 wins, 14 draws, 27 losses, win rate of 62.39%.

When goal scoring differential is -1, Kerry's record is 25 wins, 7 draws, 26 losses, win rate of 42.4%.

When goal scoring differential is -2, Kerry's record is 5 wins, 2 draws, 10 losses, win rate of 29.41%.

When goal scoring differential is -3 or greater, Kerry's record is 1 win, 0 draws, 5 losses, win rate of 16.66%. The one win was against Limerick in 1991 (Kerry 0-23 Limerick 3-12).

1969 and 2009 are the only years Kerry conceded more goals than scored yet won the All-Ireland title. In 1969, Kerry conceded 4 goals and scored one, while in 2009 conceded 7 and scored 6.

Kerry's Record Points-only

17 and more: 46 times; Won 45, Lost 1 (Offaly 1982)
16: 11 times; Won 10, Lost 1 (Cork 1988)
15: 26 times; Won 25, Lost 1 (Cork 1973)
14: 29 times; Won 24, Drew 2, Lost 3 (Cork 1971, Armagh 2002, Tyrone 2008)
13: 20 times; Won 14, Drew 3, Lost 3
12: 19 times; Won 16, Drew 1, Lost 2
11: 25 times; Won 22, Drew 1, Lost 2
10: 29 times; Won 18, Drew 5, Lost 6
9: 24 times; Won 14, Drew 2, Lost 8
8: 32 times; Won 25, Drew 1, Lost 6
7: 31 times; Won 23, Drew 1, Lost 7
6: 35 times; Won 27, Drew 2, Lost 6
5: 19 times; Won 10, Drew 2, Lost 7
4: 27 times; Won 19, Drew 5, Lost 3
3: 28 times; Won 15, Drew 5, Lost 8
2: 12 times; Won 4, Drew 2, Lost 6
1: 7 times; Won 2, Lost 5
0: Lost 1

Summary: Scoring 14 points or more has a win rate of 92.9%

Kerry's Biggest Winning Margins:

36 Points, Clare 1979 (9-21 to 1-9)
33 points, Clare 1946 (9-10 to 0-4)
29 points, Waterford 1974 (7-16 to 0-8)
26 points, Clare 1953 (6-10 to 0-2)
25 points, Waterford 1978 (4-27 to 2-8)
23 points, 3 times: Clare 1981 (4-17 to 1-6) Clare 1919 (6-11 to 2-0) Wicklow 2002 (5-15 to 0-7)

Biggest win in an All-Ireland Final: 18 points, Monaghan 1930 (3-11 to 0-2)

Kerry's Greatest Losing Margins:

17 points, Limerick 1895, 5-6 to 1-1
15 points, Cork 1990, 2-23 to 1-11
12 points, Antrim 1912, 3-5 to 0-2
11 points, Cork 1971 (0-25 to 0-14); Dublin 1934 (3-8 to 0-6); Tipperary 1900 (1-13 to 1-2)
10 points, Mayo 1948 (0-13 to 0-3); Cork 1906 (1-10 to 0-3).

Biggest loss in an All-Ireland Final: 9 points, Offaly in the 1972 Replay.

Top Appearances from 1928-2009

81 - Darragh Ó'Sé
69 - Tomás Ó'Sé
66 - Dan O'Keeffe
65 - Tom O'Sullivan
61 - Seamus Moynihan
56 - Mick O'Connell, Pat Spillane, Mike Frank Russell
54 - Dara Ó'Cinneide, Colm Cooper
53 - Páidí Ó'Sé, Jack O'Shea, Eoin Brosnan, Marc Ó'Sé
52 - Ger Power, Mike McCarthy
49 - Charlie Nelligan, John O'Keeffe, Mike Sheehy
48 - Eamonn Fitzmaurice, Mick O'Dwyer
46 - John Crowley, Denis Ogie Moran
45 - Maurice Fitzgerald
44 - Johnny Culloty, Paddy Kennedy, Joe Keohane
42 - Liam Hassett, Declan O'Sullivan
41 - Tommy Doyle, John Egan, Seamus Murphy, Sean Walsh, Diarmuid Murphy
40 - Paddy Bawn Brosnan, Aidan O'Mahony

Darragh Ó'Sé - Details of an Ironman

81 total appearances, 77 starts with 4 appearances as substitute.

First Appearance: 1994, midfield versus Limerick, scored first point the same day

Total scored: 1 goal (Mayo 2005) and 31 points, good for 42nd position in the all time scorers list since 1928.

Darragh started with 12 different midfield partners in those 77 games. Donal Daly (25), Seamus Scanlon (17) and Willie Kirby (12) lead the way in partnering Darragh.

Every game he started was at midfield.

Family Names

Of the 383 men that appeared in the Kerry jersey from 1928, the most common family names are as follows:

O'Sullivan with 18 different players
O'Shea (including Ó'Sé) with 17
O'Connor, Murphy and Fitzgerald (including 2 MacGearailts) all have 12 each
Walsh has 10.

County by County Records 1884-2009

Summary: Played 421, won 313, drew 32, lost 76, a win rate of 74.35%

Connacht: Played 56, won 39, drew 6, lost 11 - win rate 69.6%
Galway - Played 19, won 10, drew 3, lost 6
Leitrim - Played 1, won 1
London - Played 1, won 1
Mayo - Played 22, won 16, drew 2, lost 4
Roscommon - Played 11, won 9, drew 1, lost 1
Sligo - Played 2, won 2

Leinster: Played 64, won 42, drew 7, lost 15 - win rate 65.6%
Carlow - Played 1, won 1
Dublin - Played 25, won 17, drew 2, lost 6
Kildare - Played 11, won 6, drew 2, lost 3
Kilkenny - Played 0
Laois - Played 3, won 2, drew 1
Longford - Played 3, won 3
Louth - Played 3, won 2, lost 1
Meath - Played 7, won 5, lost 2
Offaly - Played 6, won 3, drew 1, lost 2
Westmeath - Played 0
Wexford - Played 4, won 2, drew 1, lost 1
Wicklow - Played 1, won 1

Munster: Played 261, won 208, drew 15, lost 38 - win rate 79.7%
Clare - Played 43, won 40, drew 1, lost 2
Cork - Played 103, won 65, drew 10, lost 28
Limerick - Played 29, won 27, drew 1, lost 1
Tipperary - Played 57, won 50, drew 2, lost 5
Waterford - Played 29, won 26, drew 1, lost 2

Ulster: Played 40, won 24, drew 4, lost 12 - win rate 60%
Antrim - Played 3, won 2, lost 1
Armagh - Played 6, won 4, drew 1, lost 1
Cavan - Played 12, won 8, drew 2, lost 2
Derry - Played 4, won 3, lost 1
Donegal - Played 0
Down - Played 4, lost 4
Fermanagh - Played 1, won 1
Monaghan - Played 6, won 5, drew 1
Tyrone - Played 4, won 1, lost 3

Replay Records

Summary: 32 drawn games, Kerry won 21 of the replays and lost 11.

Galway - drew 3 - Galway won the replay in 1919 and 1938, Kerry won the 2000 replay
Mayo - drew 2 - Kerry won 1939 replay, Mayo won 1951 replay
Roscommon - drew 1 - Kerry won the replay of 1946

Dublin - drew 2 - Kerry won both replays, 1941 and 2001
Kildare - drew 2 - Kerry won both replays, 1903 and 1926
Laois - drew 1 - Kerry won replay in 1937
Offaly - drew 1 - Offaly won replay in 1972
Wexford - drew 1 - Kerry won replay in 1914

Clare - drew 1 - Kerry won replay in 1950
Cork - drew 10 - Cork won 6 replays (1943, 1956, 1987, 2002, 2006, 2009), while Kerry won 4 replays (1961, 1976, 1982, 2008)
Limerick - drew 1 - Kerry won replay in 2004
Tipperary - drew 2 - Kerry won replay in 1913, Tipperary won replay in 1902
Waterford - drew 1 - Kerry won replay in 1904

Armagh - drew 1 - Kerry won replay in 2000
Cavan - drew 2 - Kerry won both replays, 1937 and 1955
Monaghan - drew 1 - Kerry won replay in 1985

Goalkeepers 1928-2009

Johnny Riordan	10 games, conceded 6 goals (Johnny also played from 1926-1927)
Denis "Rory" O'Connell	1 game, conceded 1
Brendan Reidy	1 game, conceded 0
Dan O'Keeffe	66 games, conceded 57, 24 clean sheets. Note: 1941 won the All-Ireland without conceding a goal in all 4 games
Pat Dennehy	1 game, conceded 3
Tommy Dowling	1 game, conceded 2
Liam Fitzgerald	6 games, conceded 7
Jerh Moloney	1 game, conceded 1
Donal O'Neill	7 games, conceded 6
Johnny Foley	2 games, conceded 1
Gerard Stack	3 games, conceded 4
Garry O'Mahony	7 games, conceded 8
Tim Barrett	1 game, conceded 2
Tom Fitzgerald	2 games, conceded 0
Johnny Culloty	41 games, conceded 44, 12 clean sheets
Eamonn O'Donoghue	2 games, conceded 1
Josie O'Brien	(partial game in 1967) conceded 0
Teddy Bowler	2 games, conceded 5
Eamonn Fitzgerald	7 games, conceded 10
Paudie O'Mahony	15 games, conceded 7, 10 clean sheets Note: 1975 won the All-Ireland without conceding a goal in all 4 games
Charlie Nelligan	49 games, conceded 49, 21 clean sheets
Peter O'Leary	6 games, conceded 5
Brendan Lane	1 game, conceded 0
Peter O'Brien	2 games, conceded 1
Declan O'Keeffe	39 games, conceded 29, 15 clean sheets
Diarmuid Murphy	41 games, conceded 33, 15 clean sheets

Diarmuid Murphy has conceded 3 goals in a game twice, but did not lose either of those games. Diarmuid has most clean sheets in a row in one year - 5 in 2005. Diarmuid has lost games to only two counties to the end of the championship in 2009 - Cork and Tyrone.

Declan O'Keeffe conceded 3 goals in a game just the once, but won the game. Declan has most games in 1 year - 9 in 2002, with four clean sheets in a row the same year.

Charlie Nelligan conceded 3 goals in 3 games (winning only one of the 3) and conceded 4 goals once (1980 semi-final win over Offaly). Charlie has 3 clean sheets in a row twice, in 1982 and 1986.

Paudie O'Mahony has the record 6 clean sheets in a row (all 1975 and start of 1976).

Johnny Culloty conceded 3 goals once, but won the game (1963 Munster Final). Johnny's has 3 clean sheets in a row (1960).

Dan O'Keeffe conceded 3 goals twice, lost one game and drew the other.

1884-1899...It all begins

Summary

Kerry played 10 games, scoring 6-29.

Munster Championship titles: 1 (1892)

All Ireland titles: 0

Summary of Kerry's Games:

1889 Cork 0-2 Kerry 0-1
1890 Kerry 1-9 Limerick 0-0; Cork 1-4 Kerry 0-1 (original game was abandoned).
1891 Cork 2-5 Kerry 0-2.
1892 Kerry 1-6 Waterford 1-3; Munster Final: Kerry 3-6 Cork 0-5; All-Ireland Final: Dublin 1-4 Kerry 0-3.
1895 Limerick 5-6 Kerry 1-1.
1896-1898 Kerry did not enter a team

The following fixtures are not part of the official list:

1890 Munster Final, Kerry v Cork was abandoned;
1893 Munster Final, Kerry conceded a walkover to Cork;
1894 Kerry conceded to Tipperary by refusing to fulfill a refixture of the game (which Kerry won).
1899 Kerry conceded a walkover to Waterford

1884

In the News:

- On Saturday November 1, in Hayes' Hotel, Thurles, Co. Tipperary, Michael Cusack, Maurice Davin and other Gaelic games enthusiasts meet to establish the Gaelic Athletic Association (GAA). The following goals are set out:
  To foster and promote the native Irish pastimes;
  To open athletics to all social classes;
  To aid in the establishment of hurling and football clubs and organise inter-county matches.
- Ballymena, Cushendall and Red Bay Railway are taken over by Belfast and Northern Counties Railway.
- The first woman receives a degree from an Irish university. The degree is granted by the Royal University of Ireland.

1885

In the News:

- The Munster & Leinster Bank begins operations following the collapse of the Munster Bank.
- The Railway Tavern in Belfast is renovated and reopened as the Crown Liquor Saloon.
- Distinctive twin spires are added to St Peter's Cathedral, Belfast, which had been dedicated in 1860.

1886

In the News:

- Protestants in Ulster, known as Unionists, begin to lobby against Irish Home Rule establishing the Ulster Loyal Anti-Repeal Union in Belfast. Prime Minister Gladstone announces his support for Irish Home Rule.
- Gladstone introduces Home Rule Bill for Ireland to the House of Commons.
- Eight Irish Catholics are killed during riots following Protestant celebrations of the defeat of the First Home Bill.
- In a statement to Parliament, Gladstone calls for a general election and, with the dissolution of Parliament, an official election is held a month later.

- Thirty-one Irish Catholics are killed during riots after the Orange Order Parades.
- The first of Irish tenant farmers are evicted during the first year of the Plan of Campaign.
- Secretary of the Treasury H.H. Fowler states his support for Irish Home Rule Bill which in his words would bring about a "real Union - not an act of Parliament Union - but a moral Union, a Union of heart and soul between two Sister Nations".
- Lord Randolph Churchill voices his opposition to the Irish Home Rule Bill with the slogan "Ulster will fight, Ulster will be right".
- The 1886 Tramways Act allows the Board of Works to grant loans to railway companies including £54,400 to the West Clare Railway, one of the first railways in western Ireland.
- Maud Gonne's father passes away leaving her a wealthy inheritance ensuring her financial independence.
- Synge joins the Dublin Naturalist's Field Club.
- Over 50 people are killed in anti-Unionist riots in Belfast, Ulster.
- Charles Cunningham Boycott, supposedly from which the word derived from protests he began, leaves Ireland permanently.
- The first Gaelic Athletic Association match in the United States is held between Kerry and Galway in Boston, Massachusetts.

1887

In the News:

- A Dublin newspaper, *The Union* is founded. The Unionist newspaper's goals were stated in its first edition: "A Journal devoted to the maintenance of the Union in three kingdoms."
- *The Times* publishes a series of articles on "Parnellism and Crime" from March 7, 1887 to April 17, 1888 accusing Charles Stewart Parnell of involvement in illegal activities, in particular, the 1882 Phoenix Park Murders. A special commission, known as the "Times Commission", is proposed by Lord Frederick Cavendish to investigate the allegations, as well as links between the Home Rule party and the Fenians, eventually proving the letters were forged by a Richard Pigott.
- The Irish Crimes Act of 1887 is introduced by Arthur Balfour in response to the boycott of certain landlords by their tenants (led by the National Land League), suspending the right to trial of people suspected of involvement in the boycott. The Crimes Act was passed

in September, despite protests from Liberal and Home Rule Members of Parliament, and would continue until 1890.

- Gladstone delivers his speech "The Irish Question".
- The narrow gauge Clogher Valley Railway opens in Co. Tyrone.
- The highest temperature ever recorded in Ireland, 33.3C (91.9F) at Kilkenny Castle.
- The Mitchelstown massacre - three men killed by police at an Irish National League demonstration.
- Arthur Balfour becomes Chief Secretary, later enacting the policy of "killing Home Rule with kindness".
- The 1887 Land Act, an extension of the Ashbourne Act of 1885, is passed by Parliament.
- The period of rent set by the Land Court is reduced to 3 years.
- According to census records 69,084 emigrate from Ireland to the United States.
- The Plan of Campaign starts its first phase as tenant farmers begin withholding rent from landlords.
- Police attack a Land League march in Kiltimagh, Co. Mayo.
- Newtownbrowne School is opened in Kiltimagh, Co. Mayo.
- The Romanesque doorway of St. Flannan's Cathedral, a late 12th century church in Killaloe, is restored.
- George Roe & Company Distillers becomes the largest distillery in Europe.
- Edward Carson is appointed as counsel to the Attorney-General for Ireland.
- William Ewart Gladstone publishes Handbook of Home Rule.
- Michael Davitt publishes Revival of the Irish woollen Industry. Brief Historical Record: How England Endeavoured to Destroy Irish Manufacture, and how Irish Leaders Propose to Accomplish its Revival
- GAA President Michael Davin resigns.
- The Limerick Commercials win the first All-Ireland Senior Football Championship defeating the Dundalk Young Irelands.
- The first All-Ireland Senior Hurling Championship is held in Birr Co. Offaly between Galway and Tipperary.

1888

In The News:

- The Pan-Celtic Society is founded by William Butler Yeats.
- Pope Leo XIII issues a decree denouncing the "Plan of Campaign" as the Holy Office issued a rescript to the Bishops of Ireland to boycott the Campaign. This is ignored by many.
- The Christian Brothers College is founded in Cork.
- James Joyce enters the Clongowes Wood College as the schools youngest student.
- Irish members of the British House of Commons attempt to introduce an Irish Local Government Bill; however the Bill is opposed by Chief Secretary Arthur Balfour.
- Belfast is awarded city status by Queen Victoria.
- The Belfast Central Library is founded.
- A large flock of 110 Pallas's Sandgrouse, a rare species of birds in Ireland, is recorded. It is one of the last known migrations witnessed in Ireland.
- William Butler Yeats joins the Esoteric Section of Theosophistical Society.
- James Daly sells *Connaught Telegraph* to employee T.H. Gillespie.
- Thomas Lindsay Buick becomes Secretary of the Gladstone branch of the Irish National League.
- Reverend Henry Lett publishes a research paper on several unknown forms of fungi found in Ulster, however this document, as well as other research by Lett, were later lost.
- The Leopardstown Racecourse is established by Captain George Quin becoming the first modern fully enclosed race track

1889

Summary: 29 July in Mallow, Cork 0-2 Kerry 0-1.

In The News:

- Edward Carson becomes the youngest QC in Ireland (aged 35).
- Ballymena and Larne Railway taken over by Belfast and Northern Counties Railway.
- Irish nationalist Charles Stewart Parnell is accused of adultery after Captain Willy O'Shea files for divorce on the grounds his wife Kitty

O'Shea had an affair with Parnell. The scandal would later result in the dismissal of Parnell as leader of the Irish Parliamentary Party.

- A religious group of the Order of Carmelite leave Dublin for the United States at the invitation of the New York Archbishop later establishing the Provence of St. Elias.
- The National Society for the Prevention of Cruelty to Children is founded.
- The Land League builds a house for recently evicted tenant Tom Kelly in Kiltimagh, Co. Mayo.
- Poet William Butler Yeats is introduced by John O'Leary to Irish nationalist Maude Gonne.
- Union leader James Connolly is married to Lillie Reynolds in Dublin. Connolly later deserts the British Army and flees to Perth, Scotland.
- Industrialist Horace Plunkett returns to Ireland after his father's death.
- The Tropical Ravine House in Belfast Botanic Gardens is built by head gardener Charles McKimm.
- Foundation stone laid for the Albert Bridge, Belfast by Queen Victoria's grandson, Prince Albert Victor.
- The hierarchy of the Catholic Church, including Archbishop Logue, condemn the GAA for its violence and demoralising influences as well as charging the association as a recruiting ground of radical nationalist organizations.
- Golf is first played at the Dooks Golf Club near Killorglin, Co. Kerry.

1890

Summary: Played two championship games.

3 August 1890 in Tralee, Kerry 1-9 Limerick 0-0; 29 September fixture against Cork was abandoned, Refixed for Banteer on 20 October, Cork 1-4 Kerry 0-1.

In the News:

- The newly covered St George's Market in Belfast is opened to the public.
- Captain Willie O'Shea divorces his wife, Kitty O'Shea, and wins custody of their children. Charles Stewart Parnell is named as the

co-respondent. Despite his personal problems Parnell is re-elected as leader of the Irish Parliamentary Party.
- Prime Minister William Ewart Gladstone announces that Home Rule for Ireland is impossible as long as Parnell remains as leader of the Party.
- After five days of discussion and argument about Parnell's leadership, 44 members of the Irish Parliamentary Party walk out of the meeting and withdraw from the party. Parnell is left with only 28 supporters.
- Albert Bridge, Belfast is completed.
- The Royal Society of Antiquaries of Ireland is founded.
- A study finds that the most common Irish surnames are Murphy, Kelly, O'Sullivan and Walshe.

1891

Summary: Played one championship games.

2 September 1891 in Killarney, Cork 2-5 Kerry 0-2.

In the News:

- In June, Charles Stewart Parnell marries Kitty O'Shea in Sussex. On 6 October, however, Parnell dies, and up to 200,000 people attend the funeral of the Uncrowned King of Ireland.
- The Balfour Land Act makes more funds available for land purchase and sets up the Congested Districts Board for Ireland.
- Parnellites form the Irish National Federation and win seats in Sligo and Carlow.
- The *Irish Daily Independent* newspaper is founded. It becomes the *Irish Independent* in 1905.
- James Stephens, founder of the Irish Republican Brotherhood, returns home to Ireland after 25 years in exile.
- Michael Davitt, standing as an anti-Parnellite candidate, is defeated by John Redmond in a Waterford by-election.
- All-Ireland Senior Hurling Championship Final: Kerry 2-3 Wexford 1-5. It is Kerry's only hurling senior championship victory.

1892

Summary: Played three championship games, won 1ˢᵗ Munster title.

In Mallow, Kerry 1-6 Waterford 1-3; Munster Final in Killarney on 30 October, Kerry 3-6 Cork 0-5; All-Ireland Final, Dublin 1-4 Kerry 0-3.

In the News:

- Ulster Unionists hold a huge convention in Belfast at which they solemnly swear that "We will not have Home Rule".
- Edward Carson sworn in as Solicitor-General for Ireland.
- In the General Election, Edward Carson, standing as a Liberal Unionist, is elected to one of two Trinity College, Dublin seats.
- Douglas Hyde lectures to the Irish National Literary Society on "The Necessity for De-anglicising the Irish People". Precursor to founding of Gaelic League.
- The Belfast Labour Party, the first Socialist Party in Ireland, is established in Belfast.
- Free primary schooling and compulsory education up to the age of 14 is introduced through the Irish Education Act.
- Professor John Joly of Trinity College, Dublin invents the first practical colour photographic process.

1893

Summary: Kerry conceded a walkover to Cork.

In the News:

- Prime Minister Gladstone introduces his second Home Rule Bill to the House of Commons, where it is passed, but is later rejected by the House of Lords.
- Edward Carson is called to the English Bar at the Middle Temple.
- Douglas Hyde and Eoin MacNeill establish the Gaelic League.
- The biggest opposition to Home Rule manifests itself in Ulster, particularly amongst Protestants.
- Consecration of St. Mel's Church in Co. Longford takes place. The church had taken 53 years to build.

1894

Summary: Kerry refused to play a refixture ordered against Tipperary. Kerry had won the original game.

In the News:

- The former Prime Minister of the United Kingdom, William Ewart Gladstone, retires from politics. In his career he introduced land reform to Ireland and also attempted to grant Home Rule.
- The first meeting of the Irish Trade Union Congress takes place.
- The Irish Agricultural Organisation Society is established by Horace Plunkett. The new organisation encourages the co-operative movement.

1895

Summary: Played one championship game.

30 November in Mallow, Limerick 5-6 Kerry 1-1.

In the News:

- Oscar Wilde launches a criminal libel case against the Marquess of Queensberry. During the trial he collapses under cross-examination by Edward Carson, and is eventually found guilty and imprisoned for two years on homosexuality charges.
- Grand Opera House in Belfast is opened.
- Kingstown Lifeboat Disaster - the crew of fifteen were lost.
- Michael Davitt enters the British House of Commons as the elected Member of Parliament for South Mayo. He was refused entry on two previous attempts.
- Belfast Botanic Gardens becomes a public park when Belfast Corporation purchases the gardens from the Belfast Botanical and Horticultural Society.
- In the General Election, Edward Carson is re-elected to a Trinity College, Dublin seat and as senior MP becomes a member of the Privy Council of Ireland.

1896

In the News:

- James Connolly founds the Irish Republican Socialist Party.
- John Dillon assumes the leadership of the anti-Parnellite wing of the Home Rule Party.
- An extension is made to Arthur Balfour's Land Act. 1,500 bankrupt estates are made available for sale to tenants.
- Ireland's first motor vehicle laws are introduced.
- The first electric tram runs in the streets of Dublin.

- The Limavady hoard of prehistoric gold objects is discovered by Tom Nicholl while ploughing.
- Ireland's first cinema shows are held at Dan Lowry's Music Hall in Dublin.

1897

In the News:

- The Irish Motor Car and Cycle Company is established.
- Bram Stoker's novel, *Dracula*, is published for the first time.
- Amanda McKittrick Ros publishes *Irene Iddesleigh*.

1898

Summary: Kerry did not play.

In The News:
- James Connolly launches the first issue of the Workers' Republic newsletter.
- Tom Clarke released after serving 15 years in Pentonville Prison.
- The Local Government Act is introduced. It establishes popularly elected local authorities and gives qualified women a vote for the first time.
- The Mary Immaculate College in Limerick is founded to train Catholic national school teachers.
- Dr. John Colohan of Dublin imports the first petrol driven car into Ireland.
- The Gaelic League holds its first feis at Macroom, Co. Cork.
- Work starts on the building of Belfast City Hall.

1899

In The News:
- The foundation stone of St Anne's Cathedral, Belfast is laid by the Countess of Shaftesbury.
- The Second Boer War begins in South Africa. Major John McBride forms an Irish brigade to aid the Boers.
- Michael Davitt withdraws from the British House of Commons in protest of the Boer War.
- The first issue of Arthur Griffith's, "United Irishman", is published.

1900-1909...A new millennium

Summary of the Decade

Kerry played 36 games, scoring 52-267.

Munster Championship titles: 5 (1903, 1904, 1905, 1908, 1909)

All Ireland titles: 3 (1903, 1904, 1909)

The following fixtures are not part of the official list:

1901 Kerry v Cork (refixture ordered);
1909 Kerry v Cork (refixture ordered).

1900
Kerry 2-5 Limerick 0-1;
Kerry 1-3 Waterford 0-5;
Tipperary 1-13 Kerry 1-2.

1901
Cork 0-8 Kerry 0-6.

1902
Kerry 0-4 Waterford 0-3;
Kerry 2-7 Cork 0-3;
Munster Final: Kerry 1-4 Tipperary 1-4;
Replay: Tipperary 1-6 Kerry 1-5.

1903
Kerry 4-8 Waterford 1-3;
Kerry 2-7 Clare 2-0;
Munster Final: Kerry 1-7 Cork 0-3;
All-Ireland semi-final: Kerry 2-7 Mayo 0-4;
All-Ireland Home Final: Kerry 1-4 Kildare 1-3 (Replay ordered);
Refixture: Kerry 1-4 Kildare 0-7 (Draw);
Replay: Kerry 0-8 Kildare 0-2;
All-Ireland Final: Kerry 0-11 London 0-3.

1904
Kerry 1-4 Cork 0-0;
Munster Final: Kerry 0-3 Waterford 0-3 (Draw);
Replay: Kerry 2-3 Waterford 0-2;
All-Ireland semi-final: Kerry 4-10 Cavan 0-1;
All-Ireland Final: Kerry 0-5 Dublin 0-2.

1905
Kerry 5-8 Tipperary 1-4;
Kerry 1-7 Cork 0-5;
Munster Final: Kerry 2-10 Limerick 1-6;
All-Ireland semi-final: Kerry 2-10 Roscommon 1-3;
All-Ireland Final: Kildare 1-7 Kerry 0-5.

1906
Kerry 2-8 Clare 0-1;
Kerry 0-7 Tipperary 1-3;
Munster Final: Cork 1-10 Kerry 0-3.

1907
Kerry 4-6 Clare 0-2;
Cork 1-9 Kerry 0-6.

1908
Kerry 0-11 Clare 0-3;
Munster Final: Kerry 0-7 Waterford 0-2;
All-Ireland semi-final: Kerry 2-4 Mayo 0-1;
All-Ireland Home Final: Dublin 0-10 Kerry 0-3.

1909
Kerry 2-10 Tipperary 0-5;
Kerry 2-18 Limerick 1-2;
Munster Final Refixture: Kerry 1-6 Cork 0-6;
All-Ireland semi-final: Kerry 2-12 Mayo 0-6;
All-Ireland Final: Kerry 1-9 Louth 0-6.

1900

Summary: Played three championship games, lost Munster Final.

Kerry 2-5 Limerick 0-1, Kerry 1-3 Waterford 0-5, 11 May 1902, Tipperary 1-13 Kerry 1-2.

In the News:

- Three lion cubs reared by an Irish red setter go on view at Dublin Zoo.
- The different sections of the Nationalist Party meet in the Mansion House's Oak Room to promote national unity.
- Unofficial figures show that the Dublin Fusiliers suffered the most in the Second Boer War.
- The 45th Company of the Imperial Yeomanry leave Dublin for service in South Africa.
- Queen Victoria arrives at Kingstown and travels to Dublin where she is greeted by the Lord Mayor and members of the Corporation. 52,000 children greet Queen Victoria at the Phoenix Park in Dublin.
- At a meeting in Loughrea, Douglas Hyde complains of the rapid Anglicisation of the country and the loss of the language.
- The rift in the Irish Parliamentary Party is healed as John Dillon and John Redmond share a platform for the first time in 10 years.
- The British War Office issues a list of Irish prisoners from the 1st Battalion Royal Irish Fusiliers. It names 473 men from 8 companies.
- Oscar Wilde, dramatist and wit, dies in poverty in Paris aged 46.
- Edward Carson becomes Solicitor General for England and Wales and is knighted.

1901

Summary: Played one championship game.

5 September 1902, Cork 0-8 Kerry 0-6.

In the News:

- The centenary of the Act of Union is celebrated by British forces in Ireland.
- Despite some opposition, Drogheda Corporation votes to confer the freedom of the town on President Kruger of the Boers.

- Queen Victoria dies in London. In Dublin theatres are closed and the blinds are drawn at the General Post Office. Banks, public offices, theatres and music halls are closed again in Dublin for the funeral.
- In a state ceremony at Dublin Castle, Edward VII is proclaimed King of Ireland.
- Thomas O'Donnell, a Nationalist Member of Parliament, is stopped by the speaker from addressing the British House of Commons in Irish.
- The census return shows the population of the entire island is 4.5 million people. Catholics outnumber Anglicans and Presbyterians by almost three to one.
- The steam ship, Celtic, is launched at the Harland and Wolff shipyard in Belfast. She is now the largest ship in the world and will sail between Liverpool and New York.

1902

Summary: Played four championship games.

10 May 1903, Kerry 0-4 Waterford 0-3; 10 August 1903, Kerry 2-7 Cork 0-3; Munster Final on 4 October, Kerry 1-4 Tipperary 1-4 (Draw); Replay on 1 November 1903, Tipperary 1-6 Kerry 1-5.

In the News:
- Waterford Corporation passes a motion to confer the freedom of the city on John Redmond.
- The Great National Convention takes place in the Round Room of the Rotunda in Dublin. Motions are passed regarding coercion, the Irish language and evicted tenants.
- John Redmond is awarded the freedom of Dublin.
- The centenary of the Christian Brothers is celebrated with High Mass in the Pro-Cathedral.
- Archbishop Thomas Croke dies at the age of 78. He was the first patron of the Gaelic Athletic Association and was a supporter of the Gaelic League and the Land League.
- Dunraven land conference starts.
- Irish Literary Theatre becomes Irish National Theatre Society.

1903

Summary: Played eight championship games, won Munster title for 2nd time, won All-Ireland title for 1st time.

12 June 1904, Kerry 4-8 Waterford 1-3; 7 August 1904, Kerry 2-7 Clare 2-0; Munster Final on 31 October 1904, Kerry 1-7 Cork 0-3; All-Ireland semi-final on 17 May 1905, Kerry 2-7 Mayo 0-4; All-Ireland Home Final on 23 July 1905, Kerry 1-4 Kildare 1-3 (Replay ordered); Refixture on 27 August 1905, Kerry 1-4 Kildare 0-7 (Draw); Replay on 15 October 1905, Kerry 0-8 Kildare 0-2; Final on 12 November 1905, Kerry 0-11 London 0-3.

London (which was conveniently declared the fifth province of Ireland and given a bye to the All-Ireland Final) had Sam Maguire as captain in the 1903 campaign. The All-Ireland Senior Football Championship trophy is named in his honour.

In the News:

- The Norwegian ship, Remittent, is towed into quarantine in Queenstown (Cóbh). The entire crew are suffering from beriberi.
- The proposed canonisation of Oliver Plunkett is discussed in Rome.
- A meeting at the Mansion House enthusiastically welcomes a movement to establish St. Patrick's Day as a national holiday.
- Charles Gavan Duffy is buried at Glasnevin Cemetery in Dublin. He is laid to rest near others who took part in the 1848 Rising.
- The Lord-Lieutenant announces that King Edward VII and Queen Alexandra intend to visit Ireland within the coming year.
- Extracts from the annual report of the British Army show that there are 35,717 Irishmen in its service.
- University of Dublin announces that it will award degrees to women.
- The Wyndham Land Act is passed in the British House of Commons. It offers special incentives to landlords to sell their entire estates.
- Irish painter Henry Jones Thaddeus is granted permission to paint the first portrait of Pope Pius X.
- The 2nd battalion of the Dublin Fusiliers is welcomed home after nearly 20 years of foreign service.
- The well-known Irish optician, Patrick Cahill, who had the sole privilege of supplying the late Pope Leo XIII with spectacles, will also supply Pope Pius X.
- Pigeon House generating station in Dublin starts producing electricity

1904

Summary: Played five championship games, won Munster title for 3rd time, won 2nd All-Ireland title.

29 October 1905, Kerry 1-4 Cork 0-0; Munster Final on 10 December 1905, Kerry 0-3 Waterford 0-3; Replay on 7 January 1906, Kerry 2-3 Waterford 0-2; All-Ireland semi-final on 6 May 1906, Kerry 4-10 Cavan 0-1; All-Ireland Final on 1 July 1906, Kerry 0-5 Dublin 0-2.

In the News:

- King Edward VII and his Queen arrive in Kingstown. The royal couple attends the Punchestown Races. The King and Queen then travel to Waterford where they stay at Lismore Castle, the home of the Duke of Devonshire.
- The nave of St Anne's Cathedral, Belfast is consecrated.
- Construction of Government Buildings, Merrion Street starts (finishes 1922).
- 16 June is Bloomsday: James Joyce meets Nora Barnacle on this day and later sets his novel *Ulysses* on this day.
- The Irish National Theatre Society (Abbey Theatre) opens to the public for the first time. They witness a play by W.B. Yeats and Lady Gregory.
- James Joyce's *Eveline* was first published.
- Arthur Griffith's *The Resurrection of Hungary* was published.

1905

Summary: Played five championship games, won Munster title for 4th time.

27 August 1905, Kerry 5-8 Tipperary 1-4; 21 January 1907, Kerry 1-7 Cork 0-5; Munster Final on 8 April 1907, Kerry 2-10 Limerick 1-6; All-Ireland semi-final on 2 September 1906, Kerry 2-10 Roscommon 1-3; All-Ireland Final, Kildare 1-7 Kerry 0-5.

In the News:

- The Lillebonne, the largest vessel ever constructed in Dublin, is successfully launched in the North Wall Yard.
- The obligation of the Post Office in regard to letters addressed in Irish is raised in the British House of Commons. The debate arises

because the GPO in Dublin returned parcels addressed in Irish by the Gaelic League.

- Statistics for Ireland in 1904 show that nearly 37,000 people emigrated. Since 1851 almost 4 million people have left the island.
- The Drunkenness (Ireland) Bill is debated in the British House of Commons. Irish Members of Parliament criticise the bill on the grounds that it is offensive.
- On 28 November Sinn Féin is founded.
- Church House, Belfast is built, home to the General Assembly of the Presbyterian Church in Ireland.

1906

Summary: Played three championship games.

12 May 1907, Kerry 2-8 Clare 0-1; Kerry 0-7 Tipperary 1-3; Munster Final on 19 August 1907, Cork 1-10 Kerry 0-3.

In the News:

- Irish Parliamentary Party Member of Parliament, William O'Brien, calls on nationalists to extract the maximum concessions for Ireland from every English government.
- The 25th annual soccer match between Ireland and England takes place in Belfast. Ireland has yet to beat the 'old enemy' in the competition. Val Harris becomes the first Dubliner to play for Ireland.
- Temperance reformers meet with the Lord-Lieutenant. They want Sunday closing for all public houses, earlier closing on Saturdays and a reduction of licences throughout the country.
- Land reform campaigner Michael Davitt dies aged 60.
- The Catholic Hierarchy rules out any scheme for mixed education at Trinity College, Dublin.
- Douglas Hyde is awarded the freedom of Dublin.
- A Parisian court cannot grant a divorce to Maud Gonne and John MacBride. A separation is granted and she is given custody of their son, Seán MacBride.
- Belfast and Northern Counties Railway taken over by Midland Railway (of England).
- Royal Victoria Hospital, Belfast is completed, laying claim to being the first air conditioned building in the world.
- Work on the building of Belfast City Hall is completed.

1907

Summary: Played two championship games.

15 March 1908, Kerry 4-6 Clare 0-2; 29 March 1908, Cork 1-9 Kerry 0-6.

In the News:
- A new system of rail cars running from Amien Street in Dublin to Howth is introduced.
- The first motor show, under the auspices of the Irish Automobile Club, opens in the RDS Dublin.
- The Sunday provisions of the new Licensing Act come into operation in Dublin and four other cities. Sunday opening hours will be from 2pm to 5pm.
- The first performance of John Millington Synge's play *The Playboy of the Western World* at the Abbey Theatre in Dublin triggers a week of rioting. In a public debate at the Abbey Theatre the poet William Butler Yeats denies trying to suppress audience distaste during a performance.
- Irish State Jewels, valued at £50,000, are stolen from the safe in Dublin Castle.
- A large rally is held in Belfast City Hall in support of the ongoing Dockers and Carters Strike.
- An Irish Parliamentary Party meeting in the Mansion House is disrupted by Sinn Féin who hold a demonstration outside.
- The Marconi transatlantic wireless telegraphy service between Galway and Canada is opened. Messages are exchanged without a hitch.
- The Irish International Exhibition ends after six months. An estimated 3 million people visited it, including a large number from abroad.

1908

Summary: Played four championship games, won Munster title for 5th time.

26 July, Kerry 0-11 Clare 0-3; Munster Final on 6 December, Kerry 0-7 Waterford 0-2; All-Ireland semi-final on 14 February 1909, Kerry 2-4 Mayo 0-1; All-Ireland Home Final on 21 February 1909, Dublin 0-10 Kerry 0-3.

In The News:

- The British House of Commons votes in favour of the Irish Universities Bill. This ultimately leads to the establishment of the National University of Ireland and Queen's University of Belfast.
- Work begins on a monument to Charles Stewart Parnell in Upper Sackville Street, Dublin.
- Pádraig Pearse opens Scoil Eanna (St. Enda's) school for boys in Cullenswood House, Ranelagh. It would be later moved to the Hermitage, Rathfarnham.
- Irish Women's Franchise League was formed with Hanna Sheehy-Skeffington as secretary.
- Formation of the Irish Transport Workers' Union with James Larkin as general secretary.

1909

Summary: Played five championship games, won Munster title for 6th time, won 3rd All-Ireland title.

4 July, Kerry 2-10 Tipperary 0-5; 1 August, Kerry 2-18 Limerick 1-2; Munster Final Refixture on 7 November, Kerry 1-6 Cork 0-6; All-Ireland semi-final on 21 November, Kerry 2-12 Mayo 0-6; All-Ireland Final on 5 December, Kerry 1-9 Louth 0-6.

In The News:

- The Royal University of Ireland is dissolved.
- In the large hall of the National University in Dublin, Ernest Shackleton delivers a lecture entitled "Nearest the South Pole".
- Harry Ferguson becomes the first person to fly in Ireland, when he takes off in a monoplane he had designed and built himself.
- Mater Infirmorum Hospital in Belfast is officially recognised as a university teaching hospital.
- John Millington Synge, author and playwright, dies in Dublin aged 38.
- The famous tenor, Enrico Caruso, performs at the Theatre Royal in Dublin.

1910-1919...As we fought for Freedom

Summary of the Decade

Kerry played 36 games, scoring 64-137.

Munster Championship titles: 6 (1910, 1912, 1913, 1914, 1915, 1919)

All Ireland titles: 2 (1913, 1914)

1910
Kerry 2-13 Waterford 0-1;
Kerry 3-1 Clare 0-0;
Munster Final: Kerry 0-4 Cork 0-2;
All-Ireland semi-final: Kerry 1-7 Mayo 0-4. Kerry refused to travel to the All-Ireland Final versus Louth due to a dispute with the Great Southern and Western Railroad regarding travel facilities for the team and supporters.

1911
Kerry 2-4 Limerick 1-1;
Waterford 1-2 Kerry 1-0.

1912
Kerry 2-3 Cork 0-1;
Kerry 1-4 Waterford 0-1;
Munster Final: Kerry 0-3 Clare 0-1;
All-Ireland semi-final: Antrim 3-5 Kerry 0-2.

1913
Kerry 2-2 Clare 0-1;
Kerry 0-2 Tipperary 0-2;
Replay: Kerry 0-5 Tipperary 1-0;
Munster Final: Kerry 1-6 Cork 0-1;
All-Ireland semi-final: Kerry 1-8 Galway 0-1;
All-Ireland Final: Kerry 2-2 Wexford 0-3.

1914
Kerry 3-6 Clare 2-0;
Kerry 2-2 Tipperary 0-2;
Munster Final: Kerry 0-5 Cork 0-1;
All-Ireland semi-final: Kerry 2-4 Roscommon 0-1:
All-Ireland Final: Kerry 1-3 Wexford 2-0;
Replay: Kerry 2-3 Wexford 0-6.

1915
Kerry 4-3 Limerick 0-2;
Kerry 1-6 Tipperary 0-2;
Munster Final: Kerry 4-3 Clare 0-1;
All-Ireland semi-final: Kerry 2-3 Roscommon 1-1;
All-Ireland Final: Wexford 2-4 Kerry 2-1.

1916
Kerry 2-2 Tipperary 0-1.
Kerry then withdrew from the Munster Championship when unable to resolve a financial dispute with Central Council.

1917
Kerry did not participate in the Munster Championship, conceding a walkover to Tipperary.

1918
Kerry 5-3 Clare 1-3;
Tipperary 1-1 Kerry 0-1.

1919
Kerry 2-4 Tipperary 2-3;
Kerry 3-2 Waterford 0-0;
Munster Final: Kerry 6-11 Clare 2-0;
All-Ireland semi-final: Kerry 3-3 Galway 2-6;
Replay: Galway 4-2 Kerry 2-2.

1910

Summary: Played four championship games, won 7th Munster title.

12 June, Kerry 2-13 Waterford 0-1; 2 October, Kerry 3-1 Clare 0-0; Munster Final on 29 October, Kerry 0-4 Cork 0-2; All-Ireland semi-final on 21 August, Kerry 1-7 Mayo 0-4. Kerry refused to travel to the All-Ireland Final versus Louth due to a dispute with the Great Southern and Western Railroad regarding travel facilities for the team and supporters

Note the Munster Final was held after the All-Ireland semi-final...Kerry being nominated by the Munster Council to represent the province in the All-Ireland series, which was considered a completely separate competition.

In the News:

- Sinéad Flanagan marries Éamon de Valera in Dublin.
- Irish Unionist MPs at Westminster elect Sir Edward Carson as party leader, replacing Walter Long.
- St Patrick's College, Maynooth becomes a recognised college of the National University of Ireland.
- The Aero Club of Ireland holds its inaugural aviation meeting at Leopardstown Racecourse.
- Edward Carson and James Campbell are re-elected unopposed as Unionist representatives for Trinity College, Dublin.
- Irish Countrywomen's Association founded.
- In May, Anne Horniman withdraws financial support from the Abbey Theatre, in protest because the Theatre refused to close on the death of King Edward VII, who had died the previous day.

1911

Summary: Played two championship games.

2 July in Limerick, Kerry 2-4 Limerick 1-1; 27 August in Mallow, Waterford 1-2 Kerry 1-0.

No Killarney players featured on the county team due to the entire club being suspended for 6 months arising from walking off the field in a county championship match versus Tralee on 19 March.

In the News:

- Protestant church leaders condemn the Ne Temere Papal decree on mixed marriages.
- The RMS Titanic's hull is launched at the Harland & Wolff shipyard in Belfast. It is the largest steamship afloat.
- As King George V is crowned in London a Sinn Féin meeting at the Customs House in Dublin condemns Irish participation in the coronation ceremonies.
- King George V and Queen Mary officially open the College of Science in Merrion Square, Dublin.
- A statue of Charles Stewart Parnell is hoisted onto its pedestal in Sackville Street, Dublin.
- Dublin County Council votes in favour of using Greenwich Mean Time. The councillors hear that Irish time, being 25 minutes behind Greenwich, is a great handicap for trade.
- The Parliament Act 1911 removes the House of Lords's power regarding budgets and restricts their power over other bills to a two-year suspensive veto. This Act makes Home Rule a possibility in the future.
- 70,000 unionists and Orangemen march from Belfast to Craigavon House to protest against Home Rule.
- The monument to Charles Stewart Parnell is officially unveiled in Upper Sackville Street, Dublin.
- Bellevue Pleasure Gardens, a public park and recreational area, is opened on the slopes of Cavehill, Belfast.

1912

Summary: Played four championship games, won 8th Munster title.

23 June in Tralee, Kerry 2-3 Cork 0-1; 15 September in Fermo, Kerry 1-4 Waterford 0-1; Munster Final in Ennis on 10 October, Kerry 0-3 Clare 0-1; All-Ireland semi-final at Jones' Road on 25 August, Antrim 3-5 Kerry 0-2.

In the News:

- 250,000 Orangemen converge on Balmoral Showground, declaring that under no circumstances will they accept Home Rule.
- Prime Minister of the United Kingdom, Herbert Asquith, introduces the Home Rule Bill in the British House of Commons.
- A convention of Sinn Féin delegates led by Arthur Griffith opposes the Home Rule Bill.

- The RMS Titanic, the largest vessel in the world, built in Belfast and making its last stop at Cóbh, collides with an iceberg and sinks within a few hours.
- A serious outbreak of foot and mouth disease occurs in Co. Dublin, Co. Meath, Co. Kildare and Co. Wicklow. Cattle are slaughtered in Mullingar when the disease hits the area.
- Andrew Bonar Law makes a defiant speech at Blenheim Palace against Home Rule.
- Ulster Covenant to resist Home Rule is signed by almost 250,000 men throughout Ulster. 229,000 women sign a parallel declaration.

1913

Summary: Played six championship games, won Munster title for 9th time, won All-Ireland title for 4th time.

25 May in Ennis, Kerry 2-2 Clare 0-1; 31 August in Cork, Kerry 0-2 Tipperary 0-2; Replay in Fermoy on 12 October, Kerry 0-5 Tipperary 1-0; Munster Final on 26 October in Cork, Kerry 1-6 Cork 0-1; All-Ireland semi-final on 9 November in Portlaoise, Kerry 1-8 Galway 0-1; All-Ireland Final on 14 December at Jones' Road, Kerry 2-2 Wexford 0-3. **All-Ireland winning team:** D. Mullins, C. Clifford, T. Costelloe, D. Doyle, R. Fitzgerald, P. Healy, P. Kenneally, J. Lawlor, M. McCarthy, C. Murphy, J. O'Mahony, P. O'Shea, J. Rice, T. Rice, J. Skinner

In the News:

- At Westminster the House of Lords rejects the Home Rule Bill by 326 to 69.
- The Home Rule Bill is once again carried in the House of Commons, despite attempts by Andrew Bonar Law to obstruct it.
- There is social unrest in Dublin as members of James Larkin's Irish Transport and General Workers' Union begin strike action.
- Protest by locked-out workers lead to serious riots in Dublin. Shops are looted and attempts are made to tear up tram lines.
- A meeting of 400 employers with William Martin Murphy pledges not to employ any persons who continue to be members of the Irish Transport & General Workers' Union.
- A large meeting in Dublin's Sackville Street asserts the rights of free speech, trade union representation and demands an enquiry into police conduct.

- In Newry, Edward Carson says that a Provisional Government will be established in Ulster if Home Rule is introduced. Meanwhile in Dublin, labour unrest grows with a march of 5,000 through the city.
- 12,000 Ulster Volunteers parade at the Royal Ulster Agricultural Society's show grounds at Balmoral in protest at the Home Rule Bill.
- In Dublin the food ship, The Hare, arrives bringing forty tons of food that was raised by British trade unionists.
- An official report on the lockout suggests that workers should be reinstated without having to give a pledge not to join the ITGWU.
- 4,000 men and women march through Dublin in support of James Larkin and the Transport Union.
- James Larkin of the ITGWU is sentenced to seven months in prison for seditious language.
- The Dublin Volunteer Corps enrolls over 2,000 men. They declare they will preserve the "civil and religious liberties" of Protestants outside Ulster in the event of Home Rule.
- The Irish Citizen Army is launched at a meeting of the Dublin Civic League in Dublin. The army is founded by James Connolly to protect workers in the general lockout.
- The Irish Volunteers are formed at a meeting attended by 4,000 men in Dublin's Rotunda Rink.
- Andrew Bonar Law addresses a huge unionist rally in the Theatre Royal in Dublin, declaring that if Home Rule is introduced Ulster will resist and will have the support of his party.

1914

Summary: Played six championship games, won Munster title for 10th time, won 5th All-Ireland title.

15 June in Ennis, Kerry 3-6 Clare 2-0; 13 September in Dungarvan, Kerry 2-2 Tipperary 0-2; Munster Final in Tralee, on 4 October, Kerry 0-5 Cork 0-1; All-Ireland semi-final at Portlaoise on 6 September, Kerry 2-4 Roscommon 0-1; All-Ireland Final at Croke Park on 1 November, Kerry 1-3 Wexford 2-0; Replay at Croke Park on 29 November, Kerry 2-3 Wexford 0-6. **All-Ireland winning team:** D. Mullins, P. Breen, C. Clifford, T. Costelloe, D. Doyle, R. Fitzgerald, P. Healy, J. Lawlor, M. McCarthy, C. Murphy, J. O'Mahony, P. O'Shea, J. Rice, T. Rice, J. Skinner.

In the News:

- Edward Carson inspects a parade of the East Belfast Regiment of the Ulster Volunteers.
- Three outbreaks of foot and mouth disease are confirmed in Co. Cork.
- The British Prime Minister proposes to allow the Ulster counties to hold a vote on whether or not to join a Home Rule parliament in Dublin.
- The second reading of the Home Rule Bill is carried in Westminster.
- 35,000 rifles and over 3 million rounds of ammunition are landed at Larne, Bangor and two other ports for the UVF. The equipment is quickly distributed around Ulster.
- The Government of Ireland Bill is introduced into the House of Lords. It allows Ulster counties to vote on whether or not they want to come under Dublin's jurisdiction. The wishes of Fermanagh and Tyrone are eventually ignored.
- The Provisional Government of Ulster meets for the first time in the Ulster Hall. It vows "to keep Ulster in trust" for the British Empire.
- A conference is opened at Buckingham Palace by the King. It is hoped that unionists and nationalists attending will break the impasse over Home Rule.
- The Buckingham Palace conference ends in failure. Nationalists and unionists present couldn't agree in principle or detail.
- Erskine Childers and his wife sail into Howth and land 2,500 guns for the Irish Volunteers.
- The Government of Ireland (Amendment) Bill is postponed indefinitely due to the worsening European situation.

1915

Summary: Played five championship games, won Munster title for 11th time.

Kerry 4-3 Limerick 0-2; Kerry 1-6 Tipperary 0-2; Munster Final: Kerry 4-3 Clare 0-1;
All-Ireland semi-final: Kerry 2-3 Roscommon 1-1; All-Ireland Final: Wexford 2-4 Kerry 2-1.

In the News:

- 25,000 National Volunteers assemble at the Phoenix Park. John Redmond takes the salute from under the statue of Charles Stewart Parnell on Sackville Street.
- At the National Volunteers convention at the Mansion House John Redmond praises their response to World War I.
- The RMS Lusitania is torpedoed by German submarines about eight miles off the coast of Kinsale, Co. Cork while en route from New York to Liverpool. 1,195 lives are lost.
- The British Prime Minister appoints a national wartime coalition of 12 Liberals, 8 Unionists and 1 Labour member. In Dublin, the Irish Parliamentary Party approves John Redmond's decision not to join.
- Republicans, led by Pádraig Pearse, take over the Gaelic League at its Dundalk conference. Douglas Hyde resigns as its President.
- Jeremiah O'Donovan Rossa is buried in Glasnevin Cemetery in Dublin, and Pádraig Pearse delivers the graveside oration.

1916

Summary: Played one championship game and then withdrew from the Munster Championship when unable to resolve a financial dispute with Central Council.

9 July in Cork, Kerry 2-2 Tipperary 0-1.

In the News:

- Michael Collins quits his job in London and returns to Ireland in January.
- John Redmond is re-elected Chairman of the Irish Parliamentary Party in Dublin.
- A week long Derry Feis opens in the city.
- Roger Casement and two others are arrested at Banna Strand, Co. Kerry for landing arms and ammunition.
- On April 22 Eoin MacNeill, Chief of Staff of the Irish Volunteers, cancels all manoeuvres of Volunteers planned for the following day.
- Easter Sunday (April 23): The military council of the Irish Republican Brotherhood meets at Liberty Hall and decides to begin the planned insurrection at noon the next day. The Proclamation of the Republic is signed by the seven leaders.
- On April 24 The Easter Rising begins. The Irish Volunteers and the Irish Citizen Army occupy the GPO, City Hall, the College

of Surgeons, the Four Courts, Jacob's Factory, Boland's Mills, the South Dublin Union, and the Mendicity Institution. At noon Pádraig Pearse reads the proclamation on the steps of the General Post Office, Dublin.

- On April 25 Martial law is declared in Dublin for a period of one month.
- April 26 - Francis Sheehy-Skeffington, Thomas Dickson and Patrick McIntyre are summarily executed at Portobello Barracks.
- April 27 - Major-General John Maxwell arrives in Dublin to take control. 12,000 British troops are now in Dublin and the city centre is cordoned off.
- April 29 - At 3.45pm, Pádraig Pearse, James Connolly and Thomas MacDonagh surrender unconditionally as the Easter Rising collapses.
- May 1 - The Easter Rising collapses. Sir John Maxwell, Commander-in-Chief of the British forces, announces that all involved in the insurrection have surrendered.
- May 3 - Following their courts martial, Pádraig Pearse, Thomas MacDonagh and Thomas J. Clarke are executed at Kilmainham Gaol.
- May 4 - The executions continue. Joseph Plunkett, Michael O'Hanrahan, Edward Daly and Willie Pearse are executed for their part in the Rising. The Chief Secretary of Ireland, Augustine Birrell, resigns.
- May 5 - John MacBride, another leader of the Rising, is executed today. W. T. Cosgrave is sentenced to death; however, this is later commuted to penal servitude for life.
- May 8 - Another four leaders of the Easter Rising are executed. They are Eamon Ceannt, Con Colbert, Michael Mallin and Seán Heuston.
- May 11 - During a debate in Westminster on the Irish crisis, John Dillon of the Irish Parliamentary Party calls on the British government to end the executions of the Easter Rising leaders.
- May 12 - Two more leaders, Seán MacDiarmada and James Connolly, are executed. Connolly, who was wounded in the fighting, is strapped to a chair and shot. Meanwhile Prime Minister H. H. Asquith arrives in Dublin for a week-long visit.
- May 17 - Thomas O'Dwyer, Bishop of Limerick, refuses a request to discipline two of his curates who expressed republican sympathies. He reminds General Maxwell that he had shown no mercy to those who surrendered.

- Daylight Saving Time begins in May for the very first time as people in Britain and Ireland put their clocks forward one hour. The purpose is to reduce the number of evening hours to save fuel.
- June 26 - Roger Casement goes on trial at the Royal Courts of Justice on a charge of treason. He has been stripped of his knighthood.
- July 1 - The Battle of the Somme begins. The 36th Ulster Division sustains 5,000 casualties on the first day.
- July 23 - Thousands attend an open-air meeting at the Phoenix Park in Dublin to discuss the British government's Irish partition proposals. It is the first open-air meeting since martial law was proclaimed.
- August 3 - Roger Casement is hanged at Pentonville Prison for high treason.
- There is a large audience at the Bohemian Theatre in Dublin for the first screening of the Film Company of Ireland's first film, "O'Neill of the Glen".
- August 19 - *The Irish Times* publishes a 264-page handbook detailing the events of the Easter Rising.
- John Redmond demands the abolition of martial law, the release of suspected persons, and that Irish prisoners be treated as political prisoners.
- November 18 - Battle of the Somme ends after 141 days; stopped by foul weather and with thousands of Irish casualties
- December 21 - In the British House of Commons, it is announced that all Irish prisoners are to be released.
- December 25 - The last group of Irish prisoners, 460 men, arrive from Reading Gaol to Dublin. Seán T. O'Kelly and Arthur Griffith are among those released.

1917

Summary: Kerry did not participate in the Munster Championship, conceding a walkover to Tipperary.

In the News:

- Count George Noble Plunkett, father of Joseph Mary Plunkett, wins Roscommon North on abstentionist Sinn Féin platform.
- David Lloyd-George announces that Britain is ready to confer self-government to the parts of Ireland that wants it. He adds the north-eastern part will not be "coerced".
- In the British House of Commons, J. P. Farrell proposes that Ireland be excluded from the operation of the National Services Act.

- A motion to reduce the salary of the British Prime Minister by £100 is introduced in the British House of Commons. It is a protest against the refusal to publish the proceedings of the 1916 Rising courts martial.
- Sinn Féin candidate, Joseph McGuinness, wins a by-election in South-Longford against the Irish Parliamentary Party's candidate McKenna. It is a political disaster for John Redmond and his Party.
- British Prime Minister, David Lloyd-George, announces that he wants immediate Home Rule for the 26 counties. Six north-eastern counties are to be excluded for a period of 5 years.
- Oiler Batoum sunk by U-boat 6 miles south of Fastnet Rock.
- Prisoners taken during the Easter Rising arrive at Dún Laoghaire by mail boat.
- Éamon de Valera of Sinn Féin beats Patrick Lynch, a Home Rule candidate, in the East-Clare by-election. One Dublin Castle official calls it "the most important election that has ever taken place, or ever will, in Irish history".
- The Round Room in the Mansion House is filled to capacity as the leaders of Sinn Féin demand the bodies of the Easter Rising leaders so that they can be given a Christian burial.
- Large crowds assemble at College Green in Dublin as the Irish Convention meets for the first time.
- 1,700 Sinn Féin delegates attend a convention in the Mansion House and see De Valera replace Arthur Griffith as the president of Sinn Féin.

1918

Summary: Played two championship games.

25 August in Limerick, Kerry 5-3 Clare 1-3; 22 September in Cork, Tipperary 1-1 Kerry 0-1.

In The News:

- Count Plunkett, Seán T. O'Kelly and others protest at the forcible feeding of Sinn Féin prisoners in Mountjoy Jail.
- In Skibbereen, Co. Cork, Ernest Blythe is arrested for non-compliance with a military rule directing him to reside in Ulster.
- In the House of Commons in Westminster, tributes are paid to John Redmond, Irish Nationalist leader, who died in London.

- The Military Service Bill, which includes conscription in Ireland, becomes law. A conference of nationalist parties, Sinn Féin and labour movements meets in Dublin to organise an all-Ireland opposition to conscription. The Irish Parliamentary Party also holds a meeting in Dublin to oppose conscription. 15,000 people attend an anti-conscription meeting in Co. Roscommon. John Dillon, leader of the Irish Parliamentary Party and Éamon de Valera of Sinn Féin share the platform in a united cause. A special anti-conscription convention is held in Dublin. It condemns the deportations of many Sinn Féin members.
- In July the Lord-Lieutenant issues a proclamation banning Sinn Féin, the Irish Volunteers, the Gaelic League and Cumann na mBan.
- The Irish mail boat, RMS Leinster, was sunk in October by a German submarine with the loss of 500 lives.
- At 5:00am on November 11 an armistice dictated by the Allies is signed by the Germans. Six hours later World War I officially ends. A total of 140,000 Irishmen were killed during the war.
- Ireland voices a united invitation to US President Woodrow Wilson to visit.
- December 28 - Sinn Féin have a landslide victory in the general election, winning 73 of the 105 seats in Ireland. The Irish Parliamentary Party is nearly wiped out.
- December 30 - The *Irish Independent* strongly criticises Countess Markiewicz, the first female Member of Parliament elected to Westminster.
- 105 Irish MPs were elected at the 1918 United Kingdom general election. Sinn Féin emerged as the largest party, but refused to attend the British House of Commons in Westminster. Instead the Sinn Féin MPs (soon to be known as Teachtaí Dála) vowed to establish their own parliament known as Dáil Éireann, which met for the first time on 21 January 1919 in Mansion House in Dublin. The other Irish MPs from the Irish Parliamentary Party and the Irish Unionist Party refused to attend. The majority of Sinn Féin's MPs were imprisoned at the time, so only 27 elected representatives attended the initial meeting of the First Dáil which lasted 892 days. Kerry's First Dáil members were: Piaras Béaslaí, Kerry East; James Crowley, Kerry North; Finian Lynch, Kerry South; and Austin Stack, Kerry West.

1919

Summary: Played five championship games, won Munster title for 12th time, lost All-Ireland semi final.

25 May in Cork, Kerry 2-4 Tipperary 2-3; 6 July in Tralee, Kerry 3-2 Waterford 0-0; Munster Final on 3 August in Ennis, Kerry 6-11 Clare 2-0; 24 August in Croke Park, Kerry 3-3 Galway 2-6; Replay on 14 September in Croke Park, Galway 4-2 Kerry 2-2.

In The News:

- On 21 January Dáil Éireann meets for the very first time in the Round Room of the Mansion House, Dublin. An independent Irish Republic is declared. In the first shots of the Anglo-Irish War, two Royal Irish Constabulary (RIC) men are killed in Tipperary.
- Éamon de Valera, the leader of Sinn Féin, and two other prisoners escape from Lincoln Prison in England. The prison break was personally arranged by Michael Collins and Harry Boland.
- Fifty-two members of Sinn Féin attend the second meeting of Dáil Éireann. Seán T. O'Kelly is elected Ceann Comhairle and Éamon de Valera is elected Príomh Aire.
- 1,000 delegates from all over Ireland attend the Sinn Féin Ard-Fheis in Dublin. Éamon de Valera is elected President of the organisation.
- Sinn Féin proposes an Executive Council of the Irish National Alliance to challenge the right of any foreign parliament to make laws for Ireland.
- Irish Republican Army volunteers, Dan Breen and Seán Treacy, are injured while rescuing Seán Hogan from custody in Co. Limerick.
- Captain Alcock and Lieutenant Brown arrive in Clifden, Co. Galway, following their 1,900 mile transatlantic flight.
- In September, Dáil Éireann is declared illegal. There are raids on Sinn Féin centres and Ernest Blythe is arrested.
- Labour leader James Larkin is arrested in New York. He is charged with circulating a publication advocating the forcible overthrow of the government.

1920-1929...Civil War

Summary of the Decade

Kerry played 33 games, scoring 59-172.

Munster Championship titles: 6 (1923, 1924, 1925, 1926, 1927, 1929)

All Ireland titles: 3 (1924, 1926, 1929)

1920
Kerry 2-6 Cork 0-4;
Munster Final: Tipperary 2-2 Kerry 0-2.

1921
Kerry withdrew from the Munster Championship, conceding a walkover to Limerick.

1922
No Munster Championship held. Tipperary were nominated to represent Munster in the All-Ireland semi-final, but withdrew, giving Mayo a walk-over. Mayo subsequently lost the final to Dublin.

1923
Kerry 4-5 Limerick 2-3;
Kerry 3-4 Cork 0-3;
Munster Final: Kerry 0-5 Tipperary 0-3;
All-Ireland semi-final: Kerry 1-3 Cavan 1-2;
All-Ireland Final: Dublin 1-5 Kerry 1-3.

1924
Kerry 5-3 Tipperary 1-5;
Kerry 4-3 Cork 2-1;
Munster Final: Kerry 3-7 Clare 2-2;
All-Ireland semi-final: Kerry 1-4 Mayo 0-1;
All-Ireland Final: Kerry 0-4 Dublin 0-3.

1925

Kerry 3-1 Tipperary 0-4;
Kerry 3-8 Cork 1-0;
Munster Final: Kerry 5-5 Clare 0-0;
All-Ireland semi-final: Kerry 1-7 Cavan 2-3.
In 1925, Kerry were found to have used an illegal player versus Cavan and were subsequently disqualified from the competition. Cavan were also disqualified on a counter-objection. Mayo were nominated by the Connacht Council to represent Connacht in the All-Ireland semi-final, in which they beat Wexford. In the subsequent Connacht Final, Galway beat Mayo. After much deliberation, Galway were declared All-Ireland champions by Central Council.

1926

Kerry 0-6 Clare 1-1;
Kerry 1-9 Cork 2-1;
Munster Final: Kerry 0-11 Tipperary 1-4;
All-Ireland semi-final: Kerry 1-6 Cavan 0-1;
All-Ireland Final: Kerry 1-3 Kildare 0-6;
Replay: Kerry 1-4 Kildare 0-4.

1927

Kerry 1-7 Cork 0-1;
Kerry 2-6 Tipperary 1-1;
Munster Final: Kerry 4-4 Clare 1-3;
All-Ireland semi-final: Kerry 0-4 Leitrim 0-2;
All-Ireland Final: Kildare 0-5 Kerry 0-3.

1928

Kerry 3-4 Clare 0-5;
Tipperary 1-7 Kerry 2-3.

1929

Kerry 1-7 Cork 1-3;
Munster Final: Kerry 1-14 Clare 1-2;
All-Ireland semi-final: Kerry 3-8 Mayo 1-1;
All-Ireland Final: Kerry 1-8 Kildare 1-5.

1920

Summary: Played two championship games.

20 June 1920 in Cork, Kerry 2-6 Cork 0-4; Munster Final held on 9 April 1922 in Cork, Tipperary 2-2 Kerry 0-2.

All GAA games were suspended after Bloody Sunday (21 November 1920) when a game at Croke Park was fired upon by the Auxiliary Division of the RIC. Tipperary player Michael Hogan was shot and killed. His name and memory lives on at Croke Park as the Hogan Stand.

The suspension of games explains the almost two-year delay in playing the Munster Final. Tipperary went on to win the 1920 All-Ireland title by beating Dublin on 11 June 1922 by 1-6 to 0-2.

In the News:

- In February, the text of the Home Rule Bill to be introduced in the British House of Commons is published. It provides for the establishment of a 128-member parliament in Dublin and a 52-member parliament in Belfast.
- On 20 March Cork's Lord Mayor, Thomas MacCurtain, is murdered when armed RIC (Royal Irish Constabulary) men broke into his house. Two days later, thousands gather to pay their respects, with over 8,000 IRA Volunteers lining the route to St. Finbarr's Cemetery.
- In May, Viscount Fitzalan is sworn in as the Lord-Lieutenant. He is the first Catholic to hold the viceroyalty since the reign of King James II.
- In Rome, Pope Benedict XV beatifies Oliver Plunkett.
- Following his arrest in August, the Lord Mayor of Cork, Terence MacSwiney goes on hunger strike in England's Brixton Prison. After 74 days of hunger strike, Mayor MacSwiney dies. He is buried in St. Finbarr's Cemetery, with Arthur Griffith delivering the graveside oration.
- September sees disturbances in Mallow, Co. Cork, when a raid on a military barracks by Liam Lynch and Ernie O'Malley is followed by a sack of the town by British soldiers
- The day after Mayor MacSwiney is buried, an 18-year-old medical student from Cork, Kevin Barry, is executed in Mountjoy Prison for the killing of a British soldier. A protest hunger strike starts in Cork

Jail, but is called off after the Sinn Fein President, Arthur Griffith, intervenes.

- Bloody Sunday - 21 November. The IRA, on the instructions of Michael Collins, shoot dead 14 British undercover agents in Dublin, mostly in their homes. Later that day the Auxiliary Division of the RIC open fire on a crowd at a GAA football match in Croke Park, killing 12 people and wounding 60. Three men are shot that night in Dublin Castle while allegedly trying to escape.
- In late November, the flying column of the 3rd Cork Brigade IRA, led by Tom Barry, ambushes and kills 16 Auxiliaries at Kilmichael, Co. Cork which led to a system of martial law and official reprisals.
- In early December, British forces set fire to some five acres of the centre of Cork City, including the City Hall, in a reprisal attack.

1921

Summary: Kerry withdrew from the Munster Championship, conceding a walkover to Limerick.

In the News:

- In Brighton, England, the widow of Charles Stewart Parnell, Katherine Parnell dies aged 76.
- In the Dáil, Éamon de Valera accuses the delegation to London of having ignored its instructions. Arthur Griffith accuses de Valera of knowing at the time that a Republic could not be achieved.
- As nominations close in the elections for both Northern and Southern parliaments, Sinn Féin takes 124 of the 128 seats available in the Southern parliament. All are returned unopposed and deemed elected.
- Members of the 2nd Dáil (8 Sinn Fein TD's for Co. Kerry and West Limerick) are: Piaras Béaslaí; Finian Lynch; Austin Stack; Patrick Cahill; Con Collins; James Crowley; Thomas O'Donoghue; Edmund Roche.
- The British Army surrounds the Customs House in May in Dublin as it is attacked and set on fire.
- In June, the 40 elected unionist Members of Parliaments gather in Belfast City Hall. James Craig is elected as the first Prime Minister of Northern Ireland. The new Northern Ireland Parliament at Stormont is opened by King George V.
- In July, James Craig refuses to attend a peace conference in Dublin because the invitation by President Éamon de Valera was addressed to

him personally instead of to the Prime Minister of Northern Ireland. At the Peace Conference in the Mansion House, Dublin, President de Valera accepts an invitation to meet the Prime Minister of the United Kingdom, David Lloyd George, in London.

- Under the terms of the truce which becomes effective at noon on July 11, the British Army agrees that there will be no provocative display of forces or incoming troops. The Irish Republican Army agrees that attacks on Crown forces will cease.

- Following the election for the Southern Ireland Parliament in August, Sinn Féin Members of Parliaments assemble at the Mansion House as the Second Dáil.

- The Northern Cabinet agrees that Stormont Castle will be the permanent site of the Northern Houses of Parliament.

- In September, David Lloyd George's final offer is delivered to Éamon de Valera. Sinn Féin is invited to discuss the proposals which would grant limited sovereignty within the British Empire. Dáil Éireann selects five delegates to negotiate agreement with Lloyd George in London. The delegates include Michael Collins and Arthur Griffith.

- On October 8, the Irish delegation leaves for London to discuss the Treaty. Large crowds greet the Irish delegation at Euston Station in London. Arthur Griffith tells the crowd that Éamon de Valera will not travel to London.

- By December 6, agreement is reached in the Treaty negotiations in London. The main points of the agreement include the creation of an Irish Free State within the Commonwealth, an Oath of Allegiance to the Crown and the British naval services will be able to avail of certain Irish ports.

- On December 16, the British House of Commons accepts the Articles of Agreement. The House of Lords also votes to accept the Treaty by a large majority.

1922

Summary: No Munster Championship held. Tipperary were nominated to represent Munster in the All-Ireland semi-final, but withdrew, giving Mayo a walk-over. Mayo subsequently lost the final to Dublin.

In the News:

- The first edition of the newspaper *Poblacht na hÉireann* is published. It is established by republican opponents to the Anglo-Irish Treaty who declare their fealty to the Irish Republic.
- On January 6, the terms of the Anglo-Irish Treaty are published. Éamon de Valera offers his resignation as President. The following day, Dáil Éireann votes on the Treaty following Arthur Griffith's motion for approval. The result is 64 in favour and 57 against.
- On January 9, Éamon de Valera fails to be re-elected as President of Irish Republic. Arthur Griffith is elected President of the Provisional Government. Michael Collins becomes Minister for Finance. Éamon de Valera and 56 of his supporters walk out of Dáil Éireann.
- On January 16, Dublin Castle is handed over to Michael Collins.
- On January 30, the first meeting of the committee to draft a constitution for the Irish Free State takes place under the chairmanship of Michael Collins.
- The first edition of *Iris Oifigiúil* is published; it is the newspaper of record of the state and replaces the *Dublin Gazette*-founded November 7, 1706 with the last issue dated January 27, 1922.
- The formal handing over of Beggar's Bush Barracks takes place in Dublin on February 1. This marks the first act of British withdrawal from Ireland.
- At the opening of the British parliament in Westminster, King George V says that the world is anxiously awaiting the final establishment of the Irish Free State.
- The Treaty Bill is introduced in the British House of Commons. It provides for the dissolution of the "Southern Ireland" parliament and the election of a parliament to which the Provisional Government will be responsible.
- At the launch of the Republican Party on February 12, Éamon de Valera says that the Treaty denies the sovereignty of the Irish people.
- Existing British postage stamps issued with overprint *Rialtas Sealadach na hÉireann 1922*.
- In April, the British Government orders the release of all Irish prisoners in British prisons convicted of seditious offences.
- The Irish Hierarchy implores the people of Ireland to accept the Treaty and to make the best of the freedom which it brings.
- A May conference at the Mansion House between both sections of the Irish Republican Army secures a three-day truce.

- The final group of British troops leave the Curragh Army Camp in mid-May.
- A "Pact" between de Valera and Collins provides that Sinn Féin contest election as a single party.
- In June at Windsor Castle, King George V receives the colours of the six Irish regiments that are to be disbanded - the Royal Irish Regiment, the Connaught Rangers, the South Irish Horse, the Prince of Wales Leinster Regiment, the Royal Munster Fusiliers and the Royal Dublin Fusiliers.
- Pro-treaty candidates receive 75 percent of the vote in the Irish general election, held on June 16, 1922. Members of the 3rd Dáil (8 TD's for Co. Kerry and West Limerick) are: Piaras Béaslaí (Sinn Féin Pro-Treaty); Patrick Cahill (Sinn Féin Anti-Treaty); Con Collins (Sinn Féin Anti-Treaty); James Crowley (Sinn Féin Pro-Treaty); Finian Lynch (Sinn Féin Pro-Treaty); Thomas O'Donoghue (Sinn Féin Anti-Treaty); Edmund Roche (Sinn Féin Anti-Treaty); Austin Stack (Sinn Féin Anti-Treaty).
- On June 30, an official bulletin announces that anti-treaty forces have stormed the Four Courts and take 33 prisoners.
- Foundation of the Irish Air Corps, with one Biplane; by the end of the year the IAC consists of 10 aircraft and 400 men.
- Cathal Brugha refuses to surrender in July and is badly wounded as he tries to escape from the Hamman Hotel in Dublin.
- On July 13, the government appoints a War Council, comprising Michael Collins, Richard Mulcahy and Eoin O'Duffy, to direct military operations against the Irregulars.
- July 16 sees 300 Irregulars captured in Dundalk, Co. Louth by the National Army. 70 more surrender in Co. Sligo and the last stronghold of the Irregulars in Co. Donegal is captured.
- 105 Irregular prisoners escape from Dundalk Jail on July 27.
- On July 31, Éamon de Valera's Private Secretary, Harry Boland, is seriously wounded while resisting arrest in a hotel room in Dublin.
- On August 12, Arthur Griffith dies suddenly in Dublin. He founded Sinn Féin, was a supporter of national self-reliance and led the Treaty negotiations in 1921. His funeral takes place at Glasnevin Cemetery in Dublin. W. T. Cosgrave delivers the graveside oration.
- August 17 sees Dublin Castle being formally handed over to the Irish Republican Army as the last British Army troops leave.
- On August 22, Michael Collins is killed in an ambush at Béal na Bláth, Co. Cork. In his 32 years of life he fought during the Easter Rising in 1916, was a member of the delegation that negotiated the

Treaty in 1921 and at the time of his death he was Commander-in-Chief of the government forces. All businesses closed as a mark of respect on his funeral-day. Richard Mulcahy delivers the graveside oration.

- In September, the first meeting of the Provisional Parliament, or the Third Dáil, takes place at Leinster House. W. T. Cosgrave is elected President of Dáil Éireann and Chairman of the Provisional Government.
- W. T. Cosgrave introduces the Constitution of Saorstát Éireann Bill to enable the implementation of the Treaty between Great Britain and Ireland.
- In late November, Erskine Childers is executed for the unlawful possession of a gun. The gun was presented to him by Michael Collins in 1920 as a gift.
- Twelve months after the signing of the Treaty the Irish Free State officially comes into existence.
- The first domestically designed 2d postage stamp issued depicting a map of Ireland and inscribed *Éire*.
- Existing British postage stamps issued with overprint *Saorstát Éireann 1922*.
- In December, Pope Pius XI sends a message to the government of the Irish Free State praying for a *happy era of peace and prosperity.*
- The Oireachtas meets for the first time in December. The Governor-General, T.M. Healy, delivers the first address to both houses. A message from King George V is also read out.

1923

Summary: Played five championship games, won Munster title for 13th time.

29 July in Limerick, Kerry 4-5 Limerick 2-3; 2 September in Cork, Kerry 3-4 Cork 0-3; Munster Final on 14 October in Tralee, Kerry 0-5 Tipperary 0-3; All-Ireland semi-final on 27 April 1924 in Croke Park, Kerry 1-3 Cavan 1-2; All-Ireland Final on 28 September 1924 in Croke Park, Dublin 1-5 Kerry 1-3.

In the News:

- Beechpark, the residence of President W. T. Cosgrave in Dublin, is set on fire.
- An order is signed creating the Revenue Commissioners.

- The Minister for Education, Eoin MacNeill, announces that Irish is to become a subject for examination in the Civil Service.
- An amnesty for IRA Irregulars expires on February 18. It was introduced by the Minister for Home Affairs, Kevin O'Higgins.
- Liam Lynch, Chief of Staff of the Irregulars, is wounded and captured in April. His subsequent death in Clonmel is also announced by the army.
- On April 14, ex-Kerry footballer and All-Ireland winning captain, Austin Stack is captured by Free State troops at the foot of the Knockmealdown Mountains.
- Thousands turn up to greet Jim Larkin as he returns to Ireland after a nine year absence.
- On May 28, the government releases two captured documents issued by the IRA on May 24. The letters, signed by Éamon de Valera and Frank Aiken, call for the dumping of arms and the ending of armed struggle. The Civil War is officially over.
- Éamon de Valera appeals to the American Association for the Recognition of the Irish Republic for $100,000 to fight the upcoming general election.
- Éamon de Valera is arrested at an election meeting in Ennis, Co. Clare in mid-August.
- In September, 33 members present themselves at Leinster House for the swearing in of the new Dáil. No anti-Treaty republicans attend. The Fourth Dáil meets for the first time at Leinster House. Michael Hayes is elected Ceann Comhairle and W. T. Cosgrave is elected President of the Executive Council.
- Members of the 4th Dáil (7 TD's for All of Co. Kerry) are: Patrick Cahill (Sinn Fein); James Crowley (Cumann na nGaedhael); Finian Lynch (Cumann na nGaedhael); Thomas McEllistrim (Sinn Fein); Thomas O'Donoghue (Sinn Fein); John O'Sullivan (Cumann na nGaedhael); Austin Stack (Sinn Fein).
- The Mallow Viaduct over the River Blackwater is officially re-opened by President W. T. Cosgrave.
- The Nobel Prize for Literature is awarded to poet and playwright William Butler Yeats.
- The Royal Bank of Ireland bought the Irish Free State business of the Belfast Banking Company, which in turn bought the Northern Ireland business of the Royal Bank of Ireland.

1924

Summary: Played five championship games, won Munster title for 14th time, won 6th All-Ireland title.

11 May in Clonmel, Kerry 5-3 Tipperary 1-5; 7 September in Cork, Kerry 4-3 Cork 2-1; Munster Final on 12 October in Limerick, Kerry 3-7 Clare 2-2; All-Ireland semi-final, Kerry 1-4 Mayo 0-1; All-Ireland Final Kerry 0-4 Dublin 0-3. **All-Ireland Final winning team:** J. Sheehy, Jas Bailey, Jn. Bailey, J. Barrett, C. Brosnan, W. Landers, J. Moriarty, J. Murphy, R. Prenderville, P. Russell, J. Ryan, J.J. Sheehy, R. Stack, P. Sullivan, J. Walsh

In the News:

- The last internee at Kilmainham Gaol, Ernie O'Malley, is transferred to St. Bricin's Hospital.
- Sinn Féin commemorates the anniversary of the events of the Easter Rising in 1916.
- No agreement is reached at the Boundary Conference in London. The government now sets up a Boundary Commission to examine the border between the Irish Free State and Northern Ireland. James Craig refuses to nominate a Northern Ireland representative to the Boundary Commission.
- A new licensing Bill is introduced by the Minister for Justice, Kevin O'Higgins. Pubs are allowed open between 9am and 10pm and the sale of alcohol is limited to those over the age of 18.
- The Minister for Education, Eoin MacNeill, announces that the teaching of Irish is to be made compulsory in all schools.
- Ireland's first rodeo opens at Croke Park.
- In October, Éamon de Valera is arrested at Newry Town Hall after he defied an order preventing him from speaking in Northern Ireland.
- The President of the Executive Council, W. T. Cosgrave, announces an amnesty for criminal acts committed during the Civil War in connection with the attempt to overthrow the lawfully established government.

1925

Summary: Played four championship games, won Munster title for 15th time.

28 June in Cork, Kerry 3-1 Tipperary 0-4; 16 August in Tralee, Kerry 3-8 Cork 1-0; Munster Final on 20 September in Killarney, Kerry 5-5 Clare 0-0;

Munster Final winning team: J. Sheehy, J. McCarthy, J. Barrett, P. Clifford, J. Moriarty, J. Walsh, P. Russell, B. Stack, T. Mahony, C. Brosnan, J. Ryan, J.J. Sheehy, John Bailey, James Bailey, D. O'Connell.

All-Ireland semi-final on August 23 in Tralee, Kerry 1-7 Cavan 2-3. Kerry were found to have used an illegal player versus Cavan and were subsequently disqualified from the competition. Cavan were also disqualified on a counter-objection. Mayo were nominated by the Connacht Council to represent Connacht in the All-Ireland semi-final, in which they beat Wexford. In the subsequent Connacht Final, Galway beat Mayo. After much deliberation, Galway were declared All-Ireland champions by Central Council.

In the News:

- In the Dáil a resolution is passed making it illegal for any citizen to secure a divorce with the right to re-marry in the State.
- The Prime Minister of Northern Ireland, James Craig, announces the impending dissolution of the parliament. He says the election will be fought on the Boundary Commission.
- At a meeting of the Boundary Commission in Co. Down, witnesses from Newry and Kilkeel support being included in the Irish Free State.
- The Dublin Metropolitan Police merges with the Civic Guard under a new Act. The new organisation will be known as An Garda Síochána, literally meaning "Guardians of the Peace".
- The Dáil accepts the government's motion on the Shannon Power Scheme. Messrs Siemens-Schuchert will be the contractors.
- The Shannon Electricity Bill is passed in Dáil Éireann. £5.2 million is needed to finance the scheme.
- It is announced that Alexander Hull & Co. Building Contractors are to re-build the General Post Office, Dublin at a cost of £50,000.
- In Dublin, Oonagh Keogh becomes the world's first female member of a stock exchange.
- Annie Walsh became the last woman to be executed in Ireland; she had murdered her husband.
- A settlement on the boundary question is presented in London. Controversially, the commission recommends no change to the border.

1926

Summary: Played six championship games, won Munster title for 16th time, won 7th All-Ireland title.

7 May in Miltown Malbay, Kerry 0-6 Clare 1-1; 18 July in Listowel, Kerry 1-9 Cork 2-1; Munster Final on 25 July in Cork, Kerry 0-11 Tipperary 1-4; **Munster Final winning team:** J. Sheehy, P. Clifford, J. Barrett, J. Murphy, P. Russell, J. Walsh, J. Moriarty, B.Stack, C. Brosnan, P. Farren, T. Mahony, J. Ryan, J.J. Sheehy, James Bailey, John Bailey.
All-Ireland semi-final on 8 August in Croke Park, Kerry 1-6 Cavan 0-1; All-Ireland Final on 5 September in Croke Park, Kerry 1-3 Kildare 0-6; Replay on 17 October in Croke Park, Kerry 1-4 Kildare 0-4.
All-Ireland Final winning team: J. Riordan, P. Clifford, J. Barrett, J. Walsh, P. Russell, J. Moriarty, J. Slattery, C. Brosnan, B. Stack, J. Ryan, J.J. Sheehy, D. O'Connell, T. Mahony, James Bailey, W. Gorman.

In the News:

- Dr. Douglas Hyde officially opens the Irish Free State broadcasting service, 2RN, in Dublin. It will later become RTE Radio 1.
- The country's first Aeroplane Club is formed in Dublin.
- The Minister for Finance, Ernest Blythe, introduces a Bill providing for the issue of silver, nickel and bronze coins for Saorstát Éireann.
- The Northern Ireland Minister for Agriculture meets his Free State counterpart, Patrick Hogan. The meeting paves the way for co-operation in securing better animal health for livestock.
- A play by Sean O'Casey, *The Plough and the Stars*, is marred by ugly scenes in the crowd. One man from the audience strikes one of the actresses.
- On March 11, Éamon de Valera resigns as President of Sinn Féin at its Árd-Fheis when one of his proposals was defeated.
- An elderly Irishwoman, Violet Gibson, shoots the Italian Prime Minister, Benito Mussolini, in Rome.
- Dublin city commissioners decide to remove Nelson's Pillar on O'Connell Street. However, this decision needs the approval of the Oireachtas.
- On May 16 at La Scala Theatre in Dublin a new political party is formed. "Fianna Fáil - the Republican Party" is launched by leading republicans including Éamon de Valera and Seán Lemass.

- The Irish pilgrimage to the battlefields of France and Flanders leaves in August. Celtic crosses are to be unveiled in memory of the members of the 16th Irish Division who died during World War I.
- 48 people burned to death in Dromcolliher, Co. Limerick.
- President W. T. Cosgrave introduces the Public Safety (Emergency Powers) Bill following the killing of two unarmed gardaí.
- George Bernard Shaw, having initially refused to accept the prize money for the Nobel Prize for Literature, will now accept the money but return it to the Nobel Trust.
- Éamon de Valera addresses the first Fianna Fáil Árd-Fheis in Dublin.
- The population of the Irish Free State is 2,972,000.
- The population of Northern Ireland is 1,257,000.

1927

Summary: Played five championship games, won Munster title for 17th time.

8 May in Cork Athletic Grounds, Kerry 1-7 Cork 0-1; 14 August in Dungarvan, Kerry 2-6 Tipperary 1-1; Munster Final on 11 September in Kilrush, Kerry 4-4 Clare 1-3; **Munster Final winning team:** J. Riordan, J. Walsh, J. Barrett, P. Clifford, J. Sullivan, P. Sullivan, R. Aherne, C. Brosnan, B. Stack, D. O'Connell, J.J. Sheehy, J.J. Landers, T. Mahony, James Bailey, E. Sweeney.
All-Ireland semi-final on 28 August in Tuam, Kerry 0-4 Leitrim 0-2; All-Ireland Final on 25 September in Croke Park, Kildare 0-5 Kerry 0-3.

In the News:

- Dan Breen proposes a Bill in the Dáil that Article 17 of the Irish Free State Constitution be removed. President W. T. Cosgrave opposes the removal of the Oath of Allegiance.
- Delegates at the annual conference of the Farmers' Party reject proposals to merge with Cumann na nGaedhael.
- Celtic Park in Belfast is opened. It is the first greyhound track in Ireland.
- In a radio broadcast, the leader of Fianna Fáil, Éamon de Valera, says that the results of the general election prove that the people of Ireland want to get rid of the Oath of Allegiance.
- Kevin O'Higgins, Minister for Justice, is assassinated by the anti-Treaty Irish Republican Army in July.

- Constance Georgine, Countess Markiewicz, dies aged 59. She was an officer in the Irish Citizen Army, taking part in the Easter Rising. She was the first woman elected to the British House of Commons, though she did not take her seat.
- Ireland's first automatic telephone exchange is opened in Dublin.
- John Dillon, former nationalist Member of Parliament and last leader of the Irish Parliamentary Party, dies aged 76 in London.
- Following changes to the electoral laws, Fianna Fáil Teachtaí Dála arrive at Leinster House for the first time. They take the Oath of Allegiance, dismissing it as an "empty formula".
- The Electricity Supply Board (ESB) is established as an offshoot of the Shannon Scheme.
- The Agricultural Credit Corporation is set up to encourage investment in agriculture.
- 1927 saw two General Elections.
- Kerry winners in the June Election of the 5th Dáil (7 TD's for all of the County): James Crowley (Cumann na nGaedhael); Finian Lynch (Cumann na nGaedhael); Thomas McEllistrim (Fianna Fáil); William O'Leary (Fianna Fáil); Thomas O'Reilly (Fianna Fáil); John O'Sullivan (Cumann na nGaedhael); Austin Stack (Sinn Fein).
- The September election to the 6th Dáil (again 7 TD's for all of the County) saw the same winners: James Crowley (Cumann na nGaedhael); Finian Lynch (Cumann na nGaedhael); Thomas McEllistrim (Fianna Fáil); William O'Leary (Fianna Fáil); Thomas O'Reilly (Fianna Fáil); John O'Sullivan (Cumann na nGaedhael); Austin Stack (Sinn Fein).

1928

Summary: Played two championship games.

Game 1 - versus Clare in Kilrush on June 10. Final Score: Kerry 3-4; Clare 0-5

Johnny Riordan

Jack Walsh   Dan Ryan   Jas. O'Sullivan

Paud O'Sullivan   Roger Aherne   Con Brosnan

Bob Stack   Paul Russell (0-3)

John Joe Sheehy   Dan Joe Conway   Paddy Whitty (0-1)

Denis "Rory" O'Connell   Jack O'Connor (1-0)   William O'Sullivan

Kerry also scored two "rushing" goals where the actual scorer was not identifiable.

No substitutes used.

Game 2 - versus Tipperary in Tipperary Town on July 8. Final Score: Tipperary 1-7; Kerry 2-3

Johnny Riordan

Jack Walsh   Joe Barrett   Jas. O'Sullivan

Paddy Whitty   Dan Ryan   Paul Russell (0-1)

Bob Stack   Con Brosnan

Jackie Ryan   John Joe Sheehy (1-2)   Eamonn Fitzgerald

Ned Sweeney (1-0)   James Bailey   John Joe Landers

Substitute: Denis "Rory" O'Connell for Johnny Riordan

Scorers for the Year: John Joe Sheehy (1-2), Paul Russell (0-4), Ned Sweeney (1-0), Jack O'Connor (1-0), Paddy Whitty (0-1), plus "rushing" (2-0).

Total Scored: 5-7

Appearances:

2 - Johnny Riordan, Jack Walsh, Dan Ryan, Jas. O'Sullivan, Bob Stack, Con Brosnan, Denis "Rory" O'Connell, Paul Russell, John Joe Sheehy, Paddy Whitty.

1 - Paud O'Sullivan, Roger Aherne, Dan Joe Conway, Jack O'Connor, William O'Sullivan, Joe Barrett, Jackie Ryan, Eamonn Fitzgerald, Ned Sweeney, James Bailey, John Joe Landers.

1928 - GAA Winners:

All-Irelands: Senior Football: Kildare **Minor Football:** Did not start until 1929.

National Leagues: Football: Kerry   Hurling: Tipperary

Senior Hurling: Cork

Kerry Co. Champions: Football: Boherbee   Hurling: Rock Street

1928 - In The News:

- The Sam Maguire is first presented as the trophy awarded to the winners of the All-Ireland Football Championship. It is still the most sought after sporting award in the land.
  Sam Maguire (1879 - 1927), Protestant and Patriot, an Irish Republican and Gaelic footballer, was born in the townland of Mallabraca near the town of Dunmanway in West Cork. Sam had four brothers and two sisters. Willie was the eldest then Mary, Jack , Dick, Paul (who married a Roman Catholic and whose son became a Roman Catholic priest), Sam and Elizabeth. The Maguires farmed 200 acres of land. Sam went to school in Dunmanway and then to the national school in Ardfield. This is the same school Michael Collins later attended.

  After he took a job in the British Civil Service in London, Maguire joined and captained the successful London Hibernians Gaelic football team to several All-Ireland finals between 1900 and 1904, captaining London in the 1903 final, which was Kerry's first title. In 1907 Sam went into the administration of the London GAA, becoming the Chairman of the London County Board and a regular delegate to the Annual Congress of the GAA. He later became a trustee of Croke Park. Coincidentally, Vice-Chairman of the London

County Board was Liam McCarthy who gave his name to the All-Ireland Senior Hurling Championship Cup.

He is also remembered in the political sphere for recruiting the nationalist leader, Michael Collins, to the Irish Republican Brotherhood in 1909. Sam worked for the Irish Republican Brotherhood in London until 1921. He returned to Dublin in 1921 and got a job in the newly established Irish civil service, but because of his political opinions he quickly clashed with his superiors and was dismissed.

Sam Maguire died of tuberculosis on February 6, 1927, aged 48 and is buried in the cemetery of Saint Mary's in Dunmanway. A Celtic cross was raised over his grave with a simple inscription:

Erected to the memory of Samuel Maguire, Mallabraca who died 6th February 1927 by the people of Dunmanway and his numerous friends throughout Ireland and England in recognition of his love for his country.

On September 15, 2002, a statue of Sam Maguire was unveiled as the centrepiece of a new €500,000 town plaza in Dunmanway.

The Sam Maguire Cup was designed on the Ardagh Chalice and was presented to the Gaelic Athletic Association in 1928 in his honour after his death in 1927. The cup cost £300 in 1928. It was made by Hopkins and Hopkins of O'Connell's Bridge after it had been commissioned by the committee under the chairmanship of Dr. Pat McCartan. The Ardagh Chalice was found in 1868 near the village of Ardagh, Co. Limerick. The large, two-handled silver cup, decorated with gold, gilt bronze, brass, lead pewter and enamel, was assembled from 354 separate pieces. The chalice is believed to come from the 8th century and is on display at the National Museum of Ireland.

Kildare was the first county to win the Sam Maguire cup after defeating Cavan 2-6 to 2-5 in 1928. The cup was replaced in 1988.

- In Belfast, members of the nationalist opposition protest at the Ulster Unionist Party government's plan to abolish proportional representation.
- The outgoing Governor-General, T. M. Healy, leaves the Vice-Regal Lodge. His successor is James McNeill.
- William O'Brien, former activist in the Home Rule and land campaigns, dies in London, aged 75.

- The first east-west transatlantic flight leaves Baldonnel Aerodrome in Dublin. Commandant James Fitzmaurice is on board the Bremen. Cheering crowds in New York greet the crew.
- The foundation stone of the new Northern Ireland Parliament Building is laid at Stormont.
- It is suggested that the old Irish flag - that of a gold harp with a blue background - should be carried at the Olympic Games in Amsterdam. However, the Irish tricolour has already been registered as the national flag.
- Amendments to the Court of Justice bill state that certain judges cannot be appointed if they do not have a competent knowledge of the Irish language.
- The Irish Tricolour is raised for the first time at the Olympic Games when Dr. Pat O'Callaghan wins a gold medal for hammer throwing.
- Fifteen countries, including Ireland, sign the Kellog Peace Pact in Paris. The Irish Tricolour flies at the Quai d'Orsay amongst the flags of 50 other nations.
- The United States Secretary of State, Frank Kellogg, visits Dublin on his return journey from the Paris Peace Convention. He is granted the freedom of Dublin.
- The Saorstát Pound (Free State Pound) becomes a reality as the first Irish banknotes circulate for over a century. The first Irish coinage is also circulated in the state to complete the monetary process.
- RMS Celtic, the first ship to exceed 20,000 tons, foundered off Queenstown.
- Irish becomes a compulsory subject for the Intermediate Certificate.
- John McCormack is appointed a Papal Count for his services to music.

1929

Summary: Played four championship games, won 18th Munster title, won 8th All-Ireland title.

Game 1 - versus Cork in Cork on May 26. Final Score: Kerry 1-7; Cork 1-3

Denis "Rory" O'Connell

Dee O'Connor	Joe Barrett	Jack Walsh
Dan Ryan	John Stack (0-1)	Mick Healy

Dan Joe Conway   Con Brosnan

Bob Stack (0-2)	Sammy Locke (0-3)	Paul Russell (0-1)
Ned Sweeney	John Joe Landers(1-0)	James Bailey

No substitutes used.

Game 2 - Munster Final versus Clare in Killarney on July 14. Final Score: Kerry 1-14; Clare 1-2

Johnny Riordan

Dee O'Connor	Joe Barrett	Jack Walsh
Paul Russell	Joe O'Sullivan	Paud O'Sullivan

Bob Stack   Con Brosnan

Jackie Ryan (0-3)	Sammy Locke (0-2)	John Joe Sheehy (0-3)
Ned Sweeney (0-3)	Miko Doyle (0-1)	John Joe Landers (0-1)

Substitute: J. Clifford (1-1) for John Joe Landers

Game 3 - All-Ireland semi-final versus Mayo on August 18. Final Score: Kerry 3-8; Mayo 1-1

Johnny Riordan

Dee O'Connor	Joe Barrett	Jack Walsh
Paul Russell (0-1)	Joe O'Sullivan	Tim O'Donnell

	Bob Stack		Con Brosnan	
Jackie Ryan (0-2)		Miko Doyle (1-4)		John Joe Landers
Ned Sweeney		Micheál Ó'Ruairc (1-0)		John Joe Sheehy (1-1)

No substitutes used.

Game 4 - All-Ireland Final versus Kildare in Croke Park on September 22. Final Score: Kerry 1-8; Kildare 1-5

	Johnny Riordan	
Dee O'Connor	Joe Barrett	Jack Walsh
Paul Russell	Joe O'Sullivan	Tim O'Donnell

	Bob Stack		Con Brosnan	
Jackie Ryan (0-1)		Miko Doyle		John Joe Landers (0-1)
Ned Sweeney (1-0)		James Bailey		John Joe Sheehy (0-6)

No substitutes used.

Scorers for the Year: John Joe Sheehy (1-10), Miko Doyle (1-5), Jackie Ryan (0-6), Ned Sweeney (1-3), Sammy Locke (0-5), John Joe Landers (1-2), J. Clifford (1-1), Micheál O'Ruairc (1-0), Paul Russell (0-2), Bob Stack (0-2), John Stack (0-1).

Total Scored: 6-37

Appearances:

4 - Dee O'Connor, Joe Barrett, Jack Walsh, Con Brosnan, Bob Stack, Paul Russell, Ned Sweeney, John Joe Landers.

3 - Johnny Riordan, Joe O'Sullivan, Jackie Ryan, John Joe Sheehy, Miko Doyle.

2 - Sammy Locke, James Bailey, Tim O'Donnell.

1 - Denis "Rory" O'Connell, Dan Ryan, John Stack, Mick Healy, Paud O'Sullivan, Dan Joe Conway, J. Clifford, Micheál O'Ruairc.

1929 GAA Winners:

All-Irelands: Senior Football: Kerry **Minor Football:** Clare

National Leagues: Football: Kerry   Hurling: Dublin

Senior Hurling: Cork

Kerry Co. Champions: Football: Boherbee   Hurling: Rock Street

1929 - In The News:

- All cats from abroad, except Great Britain, are to be kept in quarantine for a period of six months to avoid rabies.
- A Belfast court sentences Fianna Fáil leader, Éamon de Valera, to one month in jail for illegally entering Co. Armagh.
- Major-General Seán Mac Eoin, the Blacksmith of Ballinalee, is appointed Chief of Staff of the army.
- The first talking film, "The Singing Fool" starring Al Jolson, opens in the Capitol Theatre in Dublin.
- After his resignation from the army Major-General Seán Mac Eoin receives the Cumann na nGaedheal nomination in the Sligo-Leitrim by-election. On the same day Maud Gonne MacBride is arrested and charged with seditious libel against the State.
- 300,000 people attend the Pontifical High Mass at the Phoenix Park to mark the end of the Catholic Emancipation centenary celebrations.
- The restored General Post Office is officially opened by President W. T. Cosgrave.
- The Shannon hydro-electric scheme at Ardnacrusha, Co. Clare is opened and later in the year is handed over to the ESB (Electricity Supply Board), bringing electricity to Galway and Dublin.
- Proportional Representation is abolished in Northern Ireland.
- The Primary Certificate is introduced, but optional, at end of primary education.

1930-1939...No depression for Kerry footballers

Summary of the Decade

Kerry played 37 games, scoring 78-270, conceding 34-144

Munster Championship titles: 9 (every year except 1935)

All Ireland titles: 5 (1930, 1931, 1932, 1937, 1939)

National League titles: 2 (1930, 1931)

Minor titles: 3 (1931, 1932, 1933)

Most Appearances: Dan O'Keeffe 31; Miko Doyle 30.

1930
Munster Final: Kerry 3-4 Tipperary 1-2;
All-Ireland semi-final: Kerry 1-9 Mayo 0-4;
All-Ireland Final: Kerry 3-11 Monaghan 0-2.

1931
Munster Final: Kerry 5-8 Tipperary 0-2;
All-Ireland semi-final: Kerry 1-6 Mayo 1-4;
All-Ireland Final: Kerry 1-11 Kildare 0-8.

1932
Kerry 1-11 Limerick 1-3;
Munster Final: Kerry 3-10 Tipperary 1-4;
All-Ireland semi-final: Kerry 1-3 Dublin 1-1;
All-Ireland Final: Kerry 2-7 Mayo 2-4.

1933
Munster Final: Kerry 2-8 Tipperary 1-4;
All-Ireland semi-final: Cavan 1-5 Kerry 0-5.

1934

Kerry 2-6 Cork 0-3;
Kerry 2-8 Tipperary 1-2;
Munster Final: Kerry 1-14 Limerick 1-2;
All-Ireland semi-final: Dublin 3-8 Kerry 0-6.

1935

Kerry did not play.

1936

Kerry 7-7 Limerick 1-4;
Kerry 1-5 Tipperary 0-5;
Munster Final: Kerry 1-11 Clare 2-2;
All-Ireland semi-final: Mayo 1-5 Kerry 0-6.

1937

Kerry 6-7 Cork 0-4;
Kerry 2-11 Tipperary 0-4;
Munster Final: Kerry 4-9 Clare 1-1;
All-Ireland semi-final: Kerry 2-3 Laois 1-6 (Draw);
Replay: Kerry 2-2 Laois 1-4;
All-Ireland Final: Kerry 2-5 Cavan 1-8 (Draw);
Replay: Kerry 4-4 Cavan 1-7.

1938

Kerry 2-6 Clare 0-1;
Kerry 2-6 Tipperary 1-3;
Munster Final: Kerry 4-14 Cork 0-6;
All-Ireland semi-final: Kerry 2-3 Laois 2-4;
All-Ireland Final: Kerry 2-6 Galway 3-3 (Draw);
Replay: Galway 2-4 Kerry 0-7.

1939

Munster Final: Kerry 2-11 Tipperary 0-4;
All-Ireland semi-final: Kerry 0-4 Mayo 0-4 (Draw);
Replay: Kerry 3-8 Mayo 1-4;
All-Ireland Final: Kerry 2-5 Meath 2-3.

1930

Summary: Played three championship games, won Munster title for 19th time, won All-Ireland for the 9th time.

Game 1 - Munster Final versus Tipperary in Tipperary Town on August 10. Final Score: Kerry 3-4; Tipperary 1-2.

Johnny Riordan

Joe Barrett	Paddy Whitty	Jack Walsh
Paul Russell	Joe O'Sullivan	Tim O'Donnell

Bob Stack   Con Brosnan (1-0)

Jackie Ryan (1-1)	Miko Doyle	Eamonn Fitzgerald (0-1)
Ned Sweeney	Denis "Rory" O'Connell	John Joe Sheehy (1-2)

No substitutes used.

Game 2 - All-Ireland semi-final versus Mayo in Roscommon on August 24. Final Score: Kerry 1-9; Mayo 0-4.

Johnny Riordan

Joe Barrett	Paddy Whitty	Jack Walsh
Paul Russell	Joe O'Sullivan	Tim O'Donnell (0-1)

Bob Stack (0-1)   Con Brosnan

Jackie Ryan (0-1)	Miko Doyle	Sammy Locke
Ned Sweeney	Micheál Ó'Ruairc (0-1)	John Joe Sheehy (1-5)

No substitutes used.

Game 3 - All-Ireland Final versus Monaghan in Croke Park on September 28. Final Score: Kerry 3-11; Monaghan 0-2.

Johnny Riordan

Dee O'Connor	Joe Barrett	Jack Walsh
Paul Russell	Joe O'Sullivan	Tim O'Donnell

	Bob Stack	Con Brosnan	

Jackie Ryan (0-3)	Miko Doyle (0-2)	Eamonn Fitzgerald

Ned Sweeney (1-0)	John Joe Landers (2-3)	John Joe Sheehy (0-3)

No substitutes used.

Scorers for the Year: John Joe Sheehy (2-10), John Joe Landers (2-3), Jackie Ryan (1-5), Con Brosnan (1-0), Ned Sweeney (1-0), Miko Doyle (0-2), Tim O'Donnell (0-1), Bob Stack (0-1), Eamonn Fitzgerald (0-1), Micheál Ó'Ruairc (0-1).

Total Scored: 7-24

Appearances:

3 - Johnny Riordan, Joe Barrett, Jack Walsh, Paul Russell, Joe O'Sullivan, Tim O'Donnell, Con Brosnan, Bob Stack, Jackie Ryan, Miko Doyle, Ned Sweeney, John Joe Sheehy.

2 - Paddy Whitty, Eamonn Fitzgerald.

1 - Dee O'Connor, John Joe Landers, Sammy Locke, Denis "Rory" O'Connell, Micheál Ó'Ruairc.

1930 - GAA Winners:

All-Irelands: Senior Football: Kerry **Minor Football:** Dublin

National Leagues: Football: Not Held   Hurling: Cork

Senior Hurling: Tipperary

Kerry Co. Champions: Football: Rock Street Hurling: Championship Not Finished

1930 - In The News:

- Ireland's new Papal Nuncio, Monsignor Robertson, presents his credentials to the Governor-General at the Vice-Regal Lodge in the Phoenix Park.
- A authentic painting by the Dutch artist Rembrandt is found in an Irish cottage.

1931

Summary: Played three championship games, won 20th Munster title, won 10th All-Ireland title.

Game 1 - Munster Final versus Tipperary in Tralee on August 9. Final Score: Kerry 5-8; Tipperary 0-2.

Johnny Riordan

Dee O'Connor	Joe Barrett	Jack Walsh
Tim O'Donnell	Joe O'Sullivan	Paddy Whitty

Bob Stack   Con Brosnan

Eamonn Fitzgerald	Con Geaney	Tim Landers (1-0)
Jackie Ryan (1-0)	Miko Doyle	Martin Regan (3-0)

Unaccounted scores (0-8). No substitutes used.

Game 2 - All-Ireland semi-final versus Mayo in Tuam on August 30. Final Score: Kerry 1-6; Mayo 1-4.

Johnny Riordan

Dee O'Connor	Joe Barrett	Jack Walsh
Joe O'Sullivan	Paul Russell	Tim O'Donnell

Bob Stack (0-1)   Con Brosnan

John Joe Landers	Miko Doyle (0-1)	Eamonn Fitzgerald
Jackie Ryan (1-1)	Paddy Whitty (0-3)	Martin Regan

No substitutes used.

Game 3 - All-Ireland Final versus Kildare in Croke Park on September 27. Final Score: Kerry 1-11; Kildare 0-8.

Dan O'Keeffe

Dee O'Connor	Joe Barrett	Jack Walsh
Paul Russell (1-0)	Joe O'Sullivan	Tim Landers

	Bob Stack		Con Brosnan	
John Joe Landers (0-2)		Miko Doyle (0-1)		Eamonn Fitzgerald
Jackie Ryan (0-6)		Paddy Whitty (0-2)		Martin Regan

No substitutes used.

Scorers for the Year: Jackie Ryan (2-7), Martin Regan (3-0), Paddy Whitty (0-5), Paul Russell (1-0), Tim Landers (1-0), John Joe Landers (0-2), Miko Doyle (0-2), Bob Stack (0-1), plus unaccounted (0-8).

Total Scored: 7-25

Appearances:

3 - Dee O'Connor, Joe Barrett, Jack Walsh, Joe O'Sullivan, Paddy Whitty, Con Brosnan, Bob Stack, Eamonn Fitzgerald, Jackie Ryan, Miko Doyle, Martin Regan.

2 - Johnny Riordan, Paul Russell, Tim O'Donnell, Tim Landers, John Joe Landers.

1 - Dan O'Keeffe, Con Geaney.

1931 GAA Winners:

All-Irelands: Senior Football: Kerry **Minor Football:** Kerry

Kerry's winning minor team: B. Reidy, F. O'Neill, P. Walsh, E. Mahony, D.J. McCarthy, J. O'Keeffe, T. O'Sullivan, J. O'Gorman, P. McMahon, T. Murphy, P. O'Sullivan, M. Buckley, T. Chute, C. O'Sullivan, B. Healy.

National Leagues: Football: Kerry   Hurling: Not Held

Senior Hurling: Kilkenny

Kerry Co. Champions: Football: Rock Street   Hurling: Causeway

1931 - In The News:

- 16 members of the Ennis Dalcassian Gaelic Athletic Association club are expelled for attending a rugby match between Ennis and Nenagh.
- First St. Patrick's Day parade held in the Irish Free State reviewed by Desmond Fitzgerald, Minister of Defense.

- Persistent rainfall causes the banks of the River Lee to burst and flood half the houses in Cork.
- The Irish Youth Hostel Service, An Óige, is established.
- Muintir na Tíre, the rural organisation, is founded by Canon John Hayes.
- Law books return to the rebuilt Four Courts where High Court business resumes. The Four Courts were destroyed during the Civil War.
- The first issue of the *Irish Press*, the newspaper of Fianna Fáil, goes on sale for 1 penny.
- Saor Éire's first National Congress takes place in the Iona Hall in Dublin.
- A derelict aerodrome at Collinstown, North County Dublin is considered a site for a new civil airport.

1932

Summary: Played four championship games, won 21st Munster title, won 11th All-Ireland title.

Game 1-versus Limerick in Newcastlewest on May 22. Final Score: Kerry 1-11; Limerick 1-3.

Dan O'Keeffe

Dee O'Connor	Joe Barrett	Jack Walsh
Mick Healy	Tim Landers	Paddy Whitty
Bob Stack	Con Brosnan	
Con Geaney (0-1)	John Joe Landers (0-3)	Jack Flavin (0-4)
Martin Regan (1-2)	Frank O'Neill	Tim Hayes (0-1)

Substitute: Brendan Reidy for Con Brosnan (Dan O'Keeffe moved to midfield, Reidy into goals).

Game 2 - Munster Final versus Tipperary in Carrick-on-Suir on August 7. Final Score: Kerry 3-10; Tipperary 1-4.

Dan O'Keeffe

Dee O'Connor	Paddy Whitty	Jack Walsh
Paul Russell	Bill Kinnerk	Tim Landers (1-0)
Bob Stack	Miko Doyle	
Con Geaney	John Joe Landers (0-1)	Jack Flavin
Martin Regan (2-4)	Jackie Ryan (0-4)	Con Brosnan (0-1)

No substitutes used.

Game 3 - All-Ireland semi-final versus Dublin in Croke Park on August 21. Final Score: Kerry 1-3; Dublin 1-1.

Dan O'Keeffe

Dee O'Connor	Joe Barrett	Jack Walsh
Paul Russell (1-0)	Joe O'Sullivan	Paddy Whitty

Bob Stack   Miko Doyle

John Joe Landers (0-1)   Con Brosnan   Tim Landers

Martin Regan (0-1)   Jackie Ryan (0-1)   Con Geaney

No substitutes used.

Game 4 - All-Ireland final versus Mayo in Croke Park on September 25. Final Score: Kerry 2-7; Mayo 2-4.

Dan O'Keeffe

Dee O'Connor   Joe Barrett   Jack Walsh

Paul Russell   Joe O'Sullivan   Paddy Whitty

Bob Stack   Johnny Walsh

Con Geaney   Miko Doyle (1-1)   Tim Landers (1-1)

Jackie Ryan (0-4)   Con Brosnan (0-1)   John Joe Landers

No substitutes used.

Scorers for the Year: Martin Regan (3-7), Jackie Ryan (0-9), Tim Landers (2-1), John Joe Landers (0-5), Jack Flavin (0-4), Miko Doyle (1-1), Paul Russell (1-0), Con Brosnan (0-2), Con Ceaney (0-1), Tim Hayes (0-1).

Total Scored: 7-31

Appearances:

4 - Dan O'Keeffe, Dee O'Connor, Jack Walsh, Tim Landers, Paddy Whitty, Con Brosnan, Bob Stack, Con Geaney, John Joe Landers.

3 - Joe Barrett, Paul Russell, Miko Doyle, Jackie Ryan, Martin Regan.

2 - Joe O'Sullivan, Jack Flavin.

1 - Mick Healy, Bill Kinnerk, Frank O'Neill, Tim Hayes, Johnny Walsh, Brendan Reidy.

1932 - GAA Winners:

All-Irelands: Senior Football: Kerry   **Minor Football:** Kerry

Kerry's winning minor team: B. Reidy, F. O'Neill, E. Healy, J. Doyle, P. McMahon, P. Ronan, S. McCarthy, J. O'Sullivan, T. Weir, P. McMahon (Listowel), T. Wrenn, P. Ferriter, M. Brosnan, T. O'Leary, C. O'Sullivan. Sub: P. Lawlor

National Leagues: Football: Kerry   Hurling: Not Held

Senior Hurling: Kilkenny

Kerry Co. Champions: Football: Rock Street   Hurling: Causeway

1932 - In The News:

- Dublin Corporation demands the return of the Hugh Lane pictures from the Tate Gallery in London.
- One of the first actions of the Fianna Fáil government is the release of 23 political prisoners.
- Dublin Corporation is considering removing Nelson's Pillar on O'Connell Street, Dublin on the grounds that it is an obstruction to traffic.
- The Constitution (Removal of Oath) Bill is passed in Dáil Éireann.
- Amelia Earhart, the first woman to fly solo across the Atlantic, lands just outside Derry having taken 14 hours to cross the ocean.
- Éamon de Valera and some members of his government leave for discussions with the British Government concerning the Ottawa Conference.
- The first pictures of the atom-splitting apparatus are released. The machine was constructed by Dr. John Cockcroft and Dr. Ernest Walton of Trinity College, Dublin.
- Ocean liners carrying thousands of pilgrims arrive in Irish ports for the Eucharistic Congress.
- The 31st Eucharistic Congress opens in the Pro-Cathedral in the greatest gathering of Church dignitaries that Ireland has ever seen. Almost a million worshippers attend the Pontifical Mass in the Phoenix Park in the final ceremony of the Eucharistic Congress.
- The Tailteann Games open in Croke Park, Dublin. The games were first organised in 632 BC.
- At the Los Angeles Olympic Games, Bob Tisdell wins the 400-metre hurdles. Another Irishman, Dr. Pat O'Callaghan, wins gold in the hammer-throwing event.
- Cumann na nGaedhael leader, W. T. Cosgrave, criticises Fianna Fáil's policy of retaining the land annuities.

- Éamon de Valera gives his inaugural speech as President of the League of Nations. He criticises complacent resolutions where the demand is for effective action.
- At a Cumann na nGaedhael meeting in Co. Limerick batons are drawn and shots are fired as General Richard Mulcahy tries to address the crowd.
- Unemployed Dubliners march through the streets of Dublin to Leinster House where they hand in a petition to Seán T. O'Kelly.
- The Prince of Wales travels to Belfast for the first time to open the new parliament building at Stormont.
- Domhnall Ua Buachalla succeeds James McNeill as Governor-General of the Irish Free State.
- Dáil Éireann is dissolved by the Governor-General, James McNeill. It brings ten years of Cumann na nGaedhael rule to an end. The 1932 general election was one of the most important general elections held in Ireland in the 20th Century.
- Cumann na nGaedhael fought the general election on its record of providing ten years of stable government. The party brought stability following the chaos of the Irish Civil War, and provided honest government. However, by 1932 this provision of solid government was wearing thin, particularly since the party had no solution to the collapse in trade which followed the depression of the early 1930s. Instead of offering new policies, the party believed that its record in government would be enough to retain power. Cumann na nGaedhael also played the "red card" tactic, describing Fianna Fáil as communists and likening Éamon de Valera to Joseph Stalin.
- In comparison to Cumann na nGaedhael, Fianna Fáil had an elaborate election programme, designed to appeal to a wide section of the electorate. It played down its republicanism to avoid alarm, but provided very popular social and economic policies. The party promised to free IRA prisoners, abolish the Oath of Allegiance and reduce the powers of the Governor-General and the Senate. It also promised the introduction of protectionist policies, industrial development, self-sufficiency and improvements in housing and social security benefits.
- The election campaign was reasonably peaceful between the two ideologically opposed parties. However, during the campaign the government prosecuted de Valera's newly established newspaper, the *Irish Press*. The editor was also brought before a military tribunal. This was seen by many as a major blunder and a serious infringement on the belief of freedom of speech. The "red scare" tactics also seemed

to backfire on the government, who seemed to have little else to offer the electorate.

- When the results were known Fianna Fáil was still 5 seats short of an overall majority, but looked like the only party capable of forming a government. Discussions got underway immediately after the election and an agreement was reached in which the Labour Party would support Fianna Fáil. The party now had the necessary votes to form a minority government.

- On 9 March 1932, the first change of government in the Irish Free State took place. Many in the country and abroad wondered if the true test of democracy would be passed, whether it would be possible for the men who won a civil war only ten years before to hand over power to their opponents. Similar to when the party first entered the Dáil in 1927, a number of Fianna Fáil TDs had guns in their pockets. However, the feared coup d'état did not take place. W. T. Cosgrave was determined to adhere to the principles of democracy that he had practised while in government. Likewise, the army, an Garda Síochána and the civil service all accepted the change of government, despite the fact that they would now be taking orders from men who had been their enemies less than ten years previously. After a brief and uneventful meeting in the Dáil chamber, Éamon de Valera was appointed President of the Executive Council of the Irish Free State by the Governor-General, James McNeill, who had come to Leinster House to make the appointment rather than require de Valera travel to the Viceregal Lodge, formerly a symbol of British rule. Fianna Fáil, the party most closely identified with opposing the existence of the state ten years earlier, were now the party of government. The 1932 general election was also the beginning of a sixteen year period in government for Fianna Fáil, although this minority government would last only 343 days.

- Kerry return the following members to the 7th Dáil (7 TD's for all of the County):
  Frederick Crowley (Fianna Fáil); John Flynn (Fianna Fáil); Eamonn Kissane (Fianna Fáil); Finian Lynch (Cumann na nGaedhael); Thomas McEllistrim (Fianna Fáil); Thomas O'Reilly (Fianna Fáil); John O'Sullivan (Cumann na nGaedhael).

1933

Summary: Played two championship games, won Munster title for 22nd time, lost All-Ireland semi-final.

Game 1 - Munster Final versus Tipperary in Clonmel on August 13. Final Score: Kerry 2-8; Tipperary 1-4.

Dan O'Keeffe

Jack O'Connor   Dee O'Connor   Mick Healy

Paul Russell (1-1)   Miko Doyle   Tim O'Donnell

Bill Landers   Johnny Walsh (0-1)

Con Geaney   Martin Regan (0-1)   Tim Landers (1-0)

John Joe Landers   Jackie Ryan (0-4)   Charlie O'Sullivan (0-1)

No substitutes used.

Game 2 -versus Cavan in Cavan on August 27. Final Score: Cavan 1-5; Kerry 0-5.

Dan O'Keeffe

Dee O'Connor   Paddy Whitty   Joe O'Sullivan

Jack Walsh   Paul Russell (0-1)   Tim O'Donnell

Bill Landers   Miko Doyle (0-1)

Martin Regan   Tim Landers   Johnny Walsh

Con Geaney   Jackie Ryan (0-3)   John Joe Landers

Substitute: Charlie O'Sullivan for Martin Regan.

Scorers for the Year: Jackie Ryan (0-7), Paul Russell (1-2), Tim Landers (1-0), Miko Doyle (0-1), Martin Regan (0-1), Charlie O'Sullivan (0-1), Johnny Walsh (0-1).

Total Scored: 2-13

Appearances:

2 - Dan O'Keeffe, Dee O'Connor, Paul Russell, Miko Doyle, Tim O'Donnell, Bill Landers, Con Geaney, Martin Regan, Tim Landers, John Joe Landers, Jackie Ryan, Charlie O'Sullivan, Johnny Walsh.

1 - Paddy Whitty, Jack O'Connor, Mick Healy, Joe O'Sullivan, Jack Walsh.

1933 - GAA Winners:

All-Irelands: Senior Football: Cavan **Minor Football:** Kerry

Kerry's winning minor team: B. Reidy, M. O'Gorman, M. McCarthy, L. Crowley, S. Sullivan, W. Myers, T. O'Leary, W. Dillon, S. Brosnan, E. Buckley, B. Cronin, D. Griffin, W. Fitzgibbon, P. Kennedy, J. Counihan

National Leagues: Football: Meath   Hurling: Kilkenny

Senior Hurling: Kilkenny

Kerry Co. Champions: Football: Kerins O'Rahillys   Hurling: Lixnaw

1933 - In The News:

- Fianna Fáil, led by Éamon de Valera, win their first overall majority in Dáil Éireann. He is welcomed in his own constituency in Co. Clare where 77 horsemen and 77 torchbearers light 77 tar barrels in honour of the 77 seats won by the party.
- Kerry return the following members to the 8th Dáil (7 TD's for all of the County):
  Frederick Crowley (Fianna Fáil); Denis Daly (Fianna Fáil); John Flynn (Fianna Fáil); Eamonn Kissane (Fianna Fáil); Finian Lynch (Cumann na nGaedhael); Thomas McEllistrim (Fianna Fáil); John O'Sullivan (Cumann na nGaedhael).
- Representatives from the Netherlands and Germany arrive in Galway to inspect the site of a proposed new £3 million airport.
- General Eoin O'Duffy is removed from his post as Commissioner of an Garda Síochána.
- Four people died in a snowstorm that gripped the country in February.
- Éamon de Valera gives a State reception in St. Patrick's Hall of Dublin Castle, the first since the foundation of the state.
- Ireland's first parachute jump, executed by Joseph Gilmore, is successful.

- In Dáil Éireann the Bill to abolish the Oath of Allegiance is passed.
- General Eoin O'Duffy outlines his proposals for remodelling parliament. He favours a system of representatives from vocational and professional groups.
- The Cistercian Abbey at Mount Melleray, Co. Waterford celebrates its centenary.
- The United Ireland Organisation is formed when Cumann na nGaedhael, the National Centre Party and the National Guard agree to merge under the leadership of Eoin O'Duffy. W. T. Cosgrave will lead the party in Dáil Éireann. This movement which has adopted the title "Fine Gael" will contest the general election in October as a political party.
- The Blueshirts are banned by the Fianna Fáil government.

1934

Summary: Played four championship games, won 23rd Munster title, lost the All-Ireland semi-final.

Game 1 - versus Cork in Fermoy on May 27. Final Score: Kerry 2-6; Cork 0-3.

Dan O'Keeffe

Dee O'Connor	Dan Spring	Jack Walsh
M. McKenna	Paul Russell	Johnny Walsh

John Joe Landers   Miko Doyle

Martin Regan	Con Geaney	Bill Kinnerk
Charlie O'Sullivan	Jackie Ryan	Jimmy O'Gorman

Scorers include: Charlie O'Sullivan (1-2) and Jackie Ryan (0-2), leaving (1-2) unaccounted. No substitutes used.

Game 2 - versus Tipperary in Clonmel on July 15. Final Score: Kerry 2-8; Tipperary 1-2.

Dan O'Keeffe

Dee O'Connor	Paddy Whitty	Bill Kinnerk
Paul Russell (0-1)	Joe O'Sullivan	Tim O'Donnell

Con Geaney (0-1)   Miko Doyle (0-1)

Martin Regan	Willie Brick	M. McKenna (1-1)
Charlie O'Sullivan	John Joe Landers	Jackie Ryan (1-4)

No substitutes used.

Game 3 - Munster Final versus Limerick in Listowel on July 29. Final Score: Kerry 1-14; Limerick 1-2.

Dan O'Keeffe

Dee O'Connor	Paddy Whitty	Jack Walsh
Paul Russell	Joe O'Sullivan	Tim O'Donnell

Con Geaney   Miko Doyle

Martin Regan   Willie Brick (1-2)   M. McKenna

Charlie O'Sullivan (0-1)   John Joe Landers(0-4)   Jackie Ryan (0-7)

Substitute: Johnny Walsh for Jack Walsh

Game 4 - All-Ireland semi-final versus Dublin in Tralee on September 9. Final Score: Dublin 3-8; Kerry 0-6.

Dan O'Keeffe

Joe Barrett   Dee O'Connor   Jack Walsh

Paul Russell (0-1)   Joe O'Sullivan   Paddy Whitty

Tim O'Donnell   Miko Doyle (0-1)

Jimmy O'Gorman   Tim Landers   M. McKenna

Martin Regan (0-1)   Jackie Ryan (0-3)   John Joe Landers

No substitutes used.

Scorers for the Year: Jackie Ryan (1-16), Charlie O'Sullivan (1-3), Willie Brick (1-2), M. McKenna (1-1), John Joe Landers (0-4), Paul Russell (0-2), Miko Doyle (0-2), Martin Regan (0-1), Con Geaney (0-1), plus unaccounted (1-2).

Total Scored: 5-34

Appearances:

4 - Dan O'Keeffe, Dee O'Connor, M. McKenna, Paul Russell, John Joe Landers, Miko Doyle, Martin Regan, Jackie Ryan.

3 - Paddy Whitty, Jack Walsh, Joe O'Sullivan, Tim O'Donnell, Con Geaney, Charlie O'Sullivan.

2 - Bill Kinnerk, Willie Brick, Jimmy O'Gorman, Johnny Walsh.

1 - Dan Spring, Joe Barrett, Tim Landers.

1934 - GAA Winners:

All-Irelands: Senior Football: Galway **Minor Football:** Tipperary

National Leagues: Football: Mayo   Hurling: Limerick

Senior Hurling: Limerick

Kerry Co. Champions: Football: Kerins O'Rahillys   Hurling: Not Finished

1934 - In The News:

- Republican Press Ltd. takes a High Court action against the Garda Síochána over the seizure of the *An Phoblacht* newspaper.
- Dublin Corporation debates a letter from the Gaelic League asking for a ban on the broadcast of jazz music on the grounds that it is contrary to the spirit of Christianity and nationality.
- Discussions on the formation of a new Volunteer Force leads to an explosive debate in the Dáil. Civil War events are revisited and there are angry exchanges between deputies.
- The government introduces the Wearing of Uniform (Restriction) Bill 1934. Cumann na nGaedhael opposes what is soon dubbed The Blueshirts Bill.
- 300 pupils from the Christian Brothers schools in Thurles go on strike as a protest against the wearing of blue shirts by a number of their classmates. They parade through town.
- The Wearing of Uniform (Restriction) Bill is carried in the Dáil by 80 votes to 60. W. T. Cosgrave condemns the Bill and predicts its failure.
- The National Athletic and Cycling Association decides to ban women from taking part in events and meetings.
- General Eoin O'Duffy addresses 2,500 Blueshirts in Trim Market Square.
- The Irish Hospitals' Sweepstakes receive a blow when the House of Lords bans general betting and lotteries.
- W.W. McDowell, US Minister to Ireland, dies at a State banquet in his honour at Dublin Castle. He was seated between President Éamon de Valera and Mrs. Sinéad de Valera.
- An application to obtain permission for deposed Soviet leader, Leon Trotsky, to live in Ireland fails.

1935

Summary: Played no championship games. Kerry conceded a walk-over to Tipperary in the Munster Championship as a mark of protest over the internment of prisoners in the Curragh. The County Championships were also not held in 1935, as the County Board ceased to function.

1935 - GAA Winners:

All-Irelands: Senior Football: Cavan **Minor Football:** Mayo

National Leagues: Football: Mayo   Hurling: Limerick

Senior Hurling: Kilkenny

Kerry Co. Champions: Football: Not Held   Hurling: Not Held

1935 - In The News:

- An Anglo-Irish Coal-Cattle Pact is signed between the governments of Britain and the Irish Free State.
- Relics and souvenirs of the 1916 Easter Rising arrive at the National Museum.
- Workmen unearth a statue of Jesus during excavation for road construction in Co. Clare.
- In his Lenten pastoral the Bishop of Galway denounces immodest dress and vulgar films. Membership of Trinity College, Dublin is still forbidden for Catholics and membership of the IRA and Communist organisations remain mortal sins.
- After 17 days the army intervenes in the bus strike at the request of the Minister for Industry and Commerce by providing lorries for transport.
- 72 republicans are arrested and held at the Bridewell Garda Station.
- The National Athletics and Cycling Association is suspended from the International Amateur Athletic Federation for refusing to confine its activities to the Free State side of the border.
- Eleven families from the Connemara Gaeltacht arrive in Co. Meath to set up the Rath Cairn Gaeltacht.
- 5 people are killed and 70 are injured as a result of sectarian rioting in Belfast.
- George William Russell (AE), poet, essayist, artist and economist, dies aged 68.

- Lord Edward Carson, the Dublin-born unionist leader and barrister, is buried in Belfast.
- Foynes in Co. Limerick is chosen to be the European terminal of a transatlantic air service.

1936

Summary: Played four championship games, won 24th Munster title, but lost All-Ireland semi-final.

Game 1 - versus Limerick in Foynes on May 24. Final Score: Kerry 7-7; Limerick 1-4.

Dan O'Keeffe

Bill Kinnerk   Paddy Whitty   Seamus O'Shea

Eddie Hanrahan   Sean Brosnan   Tim O'Donnell

Miko Doyle (0-1)   Murt Kelly

Paddy Kennedy   G. Fitzgerald (0-1)   Jimmy O'Gorman

Charlie O'Sullivan (4-4)   John Joe Landers(2-0)   Tim Landers (1-1)

No substitutes used.

Game 2 - versus Tipperary in Limerick on July 12. Final Score: Kerry 1-5; Tipperary 0-5.

Dan O'Keeffe

Dee O'Connor   Paddy Whitty   Tim O'Donnell (0-1)

Bill Kinnerk   Miko Doyle   Eddie Hanrahan

Sean Brosnan   Dan Spring (0-1)

Paddy Kennedy   Charlie O'Sullivan   Jimmy O'Gorman

Murt Kelly   John Joe Landers (1-0)   Tim Landers (0-3)

No substitutes used.

Game 3 -Munster Final versus Clare in Limerick on July 26. Final Score: Kerry 1-11; Clare 2-2.

Dan O'Keeffe

Bill Kinnerk   Joe Keohane   Paddy Whitty

Murt Kelly   Miko Doyle   Tim O'Donnell

Sean Brosnan (0-1)   Dan Spring

Paddy Kennedy (0-3)   Willie Brick (0-1)   Jimmy O'Gorman

John Joe Landers(1-1)   Charlie O'Sullivan (0-1)   Tim Landers (0-4)

No substitutes used.

Game 4 - All-Ireland semi-final versus Mayo in Roscommon on August 9. Final Score: Mayo 1-5; Kerry 0-6.

Dan O'Keeffe

Bill Kinnerk   T. Kiely   Paddy Whitty

Murt Kelly   Miko Doyle (0-1)   Tim O'Donnell

Paddy Kennedy   Jimmy O'Gorman

G. Fitzgerald (0-1)   Sean Brosnan   John Joe Landers (0-1)

M. Ferriter(0-1)   Dan Spring   Tim Landers (0-2)

No substitutes used.

Scorers for the Year: Charlie O'Sullivan (4-5), John Joe Landers (4-2), Tim Landers (1-10), Paddy Kennedy (0-3), Miko Doyle (0-2), G. Fitzgerald (0-2), Sean Brosnan (0-1), Tim O'Donnell (0-1), Dan Spring (0-1), Willie Brick (0-1), M. Ferriter (0-1).

Total Scored: 9-29

Appearances:

4 - Dan O'Keeffe, Bill Kinnerk, Paddy Whitty, Tim O'Donnell, Miko Doyle, Murt Kelly, Paddy Kennedy, Jimmy O'Gorman, John Joe Landers, Tim Landers, Sean Brosnan.

3 - Dan Spring, Charlie O'Sullivan.

2 - Eddie Hanrahan, G. Fitzgerald.

1 - Dee O'Connor, Seamus O'Shea, Joe Keohane, Willie Brick, T. Kiely, M. Ferriter.

1936 - GAA Winners:

All-Irelands: Senior Football: Mayo   **Minor Football:** Louth

National Leagues: Football: Mayo   Hurling: Limerick

Senior Hurling: Limerick

Kerry Co. Champions: Football: Austin Stacks   Hurling: St. Brendans

1936 - In The News:

- Brian de Valera (21), third son of Éamon de Valera, dies tragically in a horse-riding accident.
- 500 delegates attend the Fine Gael-United Ireland Party Árd-Feis in Dublin. W. T. Cosgrave is once again nominated as its president.
- A dispute between two unions over who makes coffins results in the coffin of an abandoned infant being turned away from Glasnevin Cemetery.
- Aer Lingus makes its first flight. A five-seater plane, Iolar, travels from Baldonnell to Bristol.
- The Dáil passes a motion abolishing the Senate of the Irish Free State.
- The IRA is again declared an illegal organisation by the government.
- General Eoin O'Duffy leads a 600-man bandera to fight for Franco in the Spanish Civil War.

1937

Summary: Played seven championship games, won 25th Munster title, won 12th All-Ireland title.

Game 1 - versus Cork in Killarney on June 13. Final Score: Kerry 6-7; Cork 0-4.

Dan O'Keeffe

Bill Kinnerk   Joe Keohane   Tim O'Donnell

Jer Carmody   Miko Doyle   Jimmy O'Gorman

Paddy Kennedy (0-2)   Johnny Walsh

Tim O'Leary   Charlie O'Sullivan (0-1)   Tommy Murphy

Con Geaney (1-3)   Sean McCarthy (3-0)   Michael O'Gorman (2-1)

No substitutes used.

Game 2 - versus Tipperary in Mitchelstown on July 11. Final Score: Kerry 2-11; Tipperary 0-4.

Brendan Reidy

Bill Kinnerk   Joe Keohane   Tim O'Donnell

Jer Carmody   Miko Doyle   Bill Dillon

Paddy Kennedy (0-2)   Johnny Walsh

Tim O'Leary (0-1)   Charlie O'Sullivan (1-2)   Jimmy O'Gorman (0-1)

Con Geaney (0-1)   Sean McCarthy (0-1)   M. Ferriter (1-3)

No substitutes used.

Game 3 -Munster Final versus Clare in Limerick on July 18. Final Score: Kerry 4-9; Clare 1-1.

Dan O'Keeffe

Bill Kinnerk   Joe Keohane   Tim O'Donnell

Jer Carmody   Miko Doyle   Bill Dillon

Paddy Kennedy

Johnny Walsh

Tim O'Leary (1-3)   Charlie O'Sullivan   Jimmy O'Gorman (0-4)

Con Geaney (0-1)   Sean McCarthy (2-1)   M. Ferriter (1-0)

No substitutes used.

Game 4 - All-Ireland semi-final versus Laois in Cork on August 15. Final Score: Kerry 2-3; Laois 1-6 (Draw).

Dan O'Keeffe

Bill Kinnerk   Joe Keohane   Tim O'Donnell

Jer Carmody   Miko Doyle   Tadgh Healy (0-1)

Bill Dillon   Johnny Walsh (0-1)

M. Ferriter   Murt Kelly   G. Fitzgerald

Con Geaney (1-1)   Sean McCarthy (1-0)   Tim O'Leary

Substitute: Bill Myers for Bill Kinnerk.

Game 5 - All-Ireland semi-final replay versus Laois in Waterford on August 22. Final Score: Kerry 2-2; Laois 1-4.

Dan O'Keeffe

Bill Myers   Joe Keohane   Tim O'Donnell

Bill Kinnerk   Miko Doyle   Bill Dillon

Tadgh Healy   Johnny Walsh

Murt Kelly   Charlie O'Sullivan   Tim Landers (2-1)

John Joe Landers   Sean McCarthy   Mikey Lyne (0-1)

Substitute: Dan Spring for John Joe Landers

Game 6 - All-Ireland Final versus Cavan in Croke Park on September 26. Final Score: Kerry 2-5; Cavan 1-8 (Draw).

Dan O'Keeffe

Bill Kinnerk   Joe Keohane   Bill Myers

Bill Dillon	Miko Doyle	Tadgh Healy
Paddy Kennedy		Johnny Walsh
Sean Brosnan	Charlie O'Sullivan (0-1)	G. Fitzgerald (0-1)
John Joe Landers (2-1)	Tim O'Donnell (0-1)	Tim Landers (0-1)

Substitute: Sean McCarthy

Game 7 - All-Ireland Final replay versus Cavan in Croke Park on October 17. Final Score: Kerry 4-4; Cavan 1-7.

Dan O'Keeffe

Bill Kinnerk	Joe Keohane	Bill Myers
Tim O'Donnell	Bill Dillon	Tadgh Healy
Sean Brosnan		Johnny Walsh
Jack Flavin	Charlie O'Sullivan	Tim Landers (0-4)
John Joe Landers (1-0)	Miko Doyle (1-0)	Tim O'Leary (2-0)

Substitute: Tom Gega O'Connor for Tim O'Donnell

Scorers for the Year: Sean McCarthy (6-2), Tim O'Leary (3-4), Con Geaney (2-6), Tim Landers (2-6), John Joe Landers (3-1), M. Ferriter (2-3), Michael O'Gorman (2-1), Charlie O'Sullivan (1-4), Jimmy O'Gorman (0-5), Paddy Kennedy (0-4), Miko Doyle (1-0), Tim O'Donnell (0-1), Bill Dillon (0-1), Tadgh Healy (0-1), G. Fitzgerald (0-1), Mikey Lyne (0-1).

Total Scored: 22-41

Appearances:

7 - Bill Kinnerk, Johnny Walsh, Joe Keohane, Miko Doyle, Tim O'Donnell.

6 - Bill Dillon, Dan O'Keeffe, Sean McCarthy.

5 - Tim O'Leary.

4 - Charlie O'Sullivan, Bill Myers, Con Geaney, Jer Carmody, Paddy Kennedy, Tadgh Healy.

3 - Jimmy O'Gorman, John Joe Landers, M. Ferriter, Tim Landers.

2 - G. Fitzgerald, Sean Brosnan, Murt Kelly.

1 - Brendan Reidy, Dan Spring, Jack Flavin, Mikey Lyne, Tommy Murphy, Tom Gega O'Connor, Michael O'Gorman.

1937 - GAA Winners:

All-Irelands: Senior Football: Kerry   **Minor Football:** Cavan

National Leagues: Football: Mayo   Hurling: Limerick

Senior Hurling: Tipperary

Kerry Co. Champions: Football: John Mitchels Hurling: Pearses

1937 - In The News:

- The National Council of Women of Ireland is agitating to form a women's police force.
- All political parties and Church leaders gather at the Mansion House to pay tribute to the Chief Rabbi, Dr. Herzog, who is leaving to take up the new post of Chief Rabbi of Palestine.
- Éamon de Valera introduces the new Constitution of Ireland. It recognises the institution of marriage and the family, as well as the special position of the Catholic Church. Éamon de Valera dismisses claims that the Constitution of Ireland provides for a dictatorship.
- A bronze statue of King George II in St. Stephen's Green is blown to pieces.
- An amendment to the Constitution of Ireland proposing membership of the Commonwealth is rejected.
- The Draft Constitution is passed in the Dáil by 62 votes to 48. The Eighth Dáil is also dissolved and a general election is called.
- Fianna Fáil form a minority government, taking 68 of the 138 total seats.
- Kerry return the following members to the 9th Dáil:
  Kerry South: Frederick Crowley (Fianna Fáil); John Healy (Fianna Fáil); Finian Lynch (FG).
  Kerry North: Stephen Fuller (Fianna Fáil); Eamonn Kissane (Fianna Fáil); Tom McEllistrim Sr. (Fianna Fáil); John O'Sullivan (FG).
- Éamon de Valera and Seán Lemass inspect the flying boat Caledonia before its survey flight across the Atlantic Ocean.
- The *Irish Times* newspaper publishes its 25,000th edition.
- Dublin's first automatic traffic signals come into operation at Merrion Square and Clare Street.

- Mrs. Thomas J. Clarke addresses the Fianna Fáil Árd-Fheis. She tells the party that it's moving away from its original values of republicanism.
- The text of a new bill providing a seal of office for the President of Ireland is introduced in Dáil Éireann. The Official Seal of the President of Ireland is photographed for archive purposes.
- The Kelly Line steamer, Annagher, sank at Ballymacormick Point with the loss of 9 crewmen. There was only one survivor.
- The Constitution of Ireland comes into force. A 21-gun salute is fired from the Royal Hospital and the national flag flies over all public buildings.

1938

Summary: Played six championship games, won 26th Munster title, lost All-Ireland final.

Game 1 - versus Clare in Ennis on May 29. Final Score: Kerry 2-6; Clare 0-1.

Dan O'Keeffe

Bill Kinnerk	Joe Keohane	Bill Myers
Tom Gega O'Connor	Bill Casey	Dan Ryan

Paddy Kennedy　　　　　Johnny Walsh (1-1)

Eugene Powell (0-1)	Tommy Murphy	Tim O'Leary
John Joe Landers	Murt Kelly (1-3)	Martin Regan (0-1)

No substitute used.

Game 2 - versus Tipperary in Mitchelstown on July 3. Final Score: Kerry 2-6; Tipperary 1-3.

Dan O'Keeffe

J. Murphy	Joe Keohane	Bill Myers
Ger Teahan	Bill Dillon	Eddie Walsh

Sean Brosnan　　　　　Johnny Walsh

Tony McAuliffe	Charlie O'Sullivan (0-2)	Eugene Powell (0-2)
Con Geaney (0-1)	Tom Gega O'Connor (1-0)	Martin Regan (1-0)

Substitute: Tim O'Leary (0-1)

Game 3 - Munster Final versus Cork in Clonakilty on August 7. Final Score: Kerry 4-14; Cork 0-6.

Dan O'Keeffe

Bill Kinnerk	Joe Keohane	Bill Myers
Tom Gega O'Connor	Bill Dillon	Eddie Walsh

Sean Brosnan (0-2)		Johnny Walsh
Paddy Kennedy (1-1)	Charlie O'Sullivan (0-1)	Tony McAuliffe (1-1)
Martin Regan (0-4)	Miko Doyle (2-1)	Tim O'Leary (0-4)

No substitutes used.

Game 4 - All-Ireland semi-final versus Laois in Croke Park on August 21. Final Score: Kerry 2-6; Laois 2-4.

Dan O'Keeffe

Bill Kinnerk	Joe Keohane	Bill Myers
Tom Gega O'Connor	Bill Dillon	Eddie Walsh
Sean Brosnan		Johnny Walsh
Tony McAuliffe (0-2)	Charlie O'Sullivan (1-1)	Paddy Kennedy (0-1)
Tim O'Leary	Murt Kelly (1-1)	John Joe Landers (0-1)

No substitutes used.

Game 5 - All-Ireland Final versus Galway in Croke Park on September 25. Final Score: Kerry 2-6; Galway 3-3 (Draw).

Dan O'Keeffe

Bill Kinnerk	Joe Keohane	Bill Myers
Bill Dillon	Bill Casey	Tom Gega O'Connor
Sean Brosnan (0-1)		Johnny Walsh
Paddy Kennedy (0-1)	Charlie O'Sullivan	Tony McAuliffe (0-1)
John Joe Landers(1-0)	Miko Doyle (0-2)	Tim O'Leary (1-1)

No substitutes used.

Game 6 - All-Ireland Final replay versus Galway in Croke Park on October 23. Final Score: Galway 2-4; Kerry 0-7.

Dan O'Keeffe

Bill Kinnerk	Paddy Bawn Brosnan	Bill Myers

| Bill Dillon | Bill Casey | Tom Gega O'Connor |

Sean Brosnan (0-3)   Johnny Walsh

| Paddy Kennedy | Charlie O'Sullivan (0-1) | Tony McAuliffe |

| Martin Regan | Miko Doyle (0-3) | Tim O'Leary |

Substitute: John Joe Landers for Sean Brosnan

Scorers for the Year: Miko Doyle (2-6), Murt Kelly (2-4), Tim O'Leary (1-6), Charlie O'Sullivan (1-5), Martin Regan (1-5), Tony McAuliffe (1-4), Sean Brosnan (0-6), Paddy Kennedy (1-3), Johnny Walsh (1-1), John Joe Landers (1-1), Tom Gega O'Connor (1-0), Eugene Powell (0-3), Con Geaney (0-1).

Total Scored: 12-45

Appearances:

6 - Dan O'Keeffe, Bill Myers, Johnny Walsh, Tim O'Leary.

5 - Bill Kinnerk, Joe Keohane, Tom Gega O'Connor, Sean Brosnan, Paddy Kennedy, Tony McAuliffe, Charlie O'Sullivan, Bill Dillon.

4 - John Joe Landers, Martin Regan.

3 - Bill Casey, Eddie Walsh, Miko Doyle.

2 - Eugene Powell, Murt Kelly.

1 - J. Murphy, Ger Teahan, Dan Ryan, Tommy Murphy, Con Geaney, M. O'Connor, Paddy Bawn Brosnan.

1938 - GAA Winners:

All-Irelands: Senior Football: Galway **Minor Football:** Cavan

National Leagues: Football: Mayo   Hurling: Limerick

Senior Hurling: Dublin

Kerry Co. Champions: Football: Dingle   Hurling: Pearses

1938 - In The News:

- The Ford Motor Works in Cork City produces its 25,000th car.

- The Department of Local Government & Public Health reports that cases of typhoid and diphtheria have reduced, although infant deaths have increased.
- Founder of the Gaelic League, Douglas Hyde, is selected unanimously by the two main political parties to serve as the first President of Ireland.
- The text of the Anglo-Irish Agreement is published. The agreement results in the transfer of the ports at Cobh, Berehaven and Lough Swilly in return for a one-off payment of £10 million.
- The government makes an order converting the "Saorstát pound" to the "Irish pound" as part of the new constitutional reforms.
- The new Anti-Partition Party takes eight seats in a unionist-controlled Derry Corporation.
- Three Cork Harbour forts are returned to the Irish Government.
- Dublin Corporation purchases 16 sets of traffic lights.
- The £50,000 20,000-seat Cusack Stand is officially opened at GAA headquarters in Croke Park.
- Éamon de Valera is elected President of the Assembly of the League of Nations in Geneva.
- Britain's last forts in the 26 counties are handed back to the people of Ireland.
- The Gaelic Athletic Association confirms that the President of Ireland, Douglas Hyde, will cease to be a patron of the organisation because of his attendance at an international soccer match.
- Fianna Fáil take 76 of the 138 seats on offer and form a majority government, with Éamon de Valera elected Taoiseach and Sean T. O'Kelly as Tánaiste.
- Kerry return the following members to the 10th Dáil:
  Kerry South: Frederick Crowley (FF); John Flynn (FF); Finian Lynch (FG).
  Kerry North: Stephen Fuller (FF); Eamonn Kissane (FF); Tom McEllistrim Sr. (FF); John O'Sullivan (FG).

1939

Summary: Played four championship games, won 27th Munster final, won 13th All-Ireland title.

Game 1 - Munster Final versus Tipperary in Clonmel on July 23. Final Score: Kerry 2-11; Tipperary 0-4.

Dan O'Keeffe

Joe Keohane   Bill Myers   Eddie Walsh

Bill Dillon   Bill Casey   Tom Gega O'Connor (0-1)

Paddy Kennedy   Johnny Walsh (0-1)

Tony McAuliffe (1-1)   Charlie O'Sullivan (0-1)   Johnny McCarthy

Mikey Lyne (0-3)   Miko Doyle   Murt Kelly (1-4)

Substitute: Paddy Bawn Brosnan for Tony McAuliffe

Game 2 - All-Ireland semi-final versus Mayo in Croke Park on August 13. Final Score: Kerry 0-4; Mayo 0-4 (Draw).

Dan O'Keeffe

Bill Myers   Joe Keohane   Tadgh Healy

Bill Dillon   Tom Gega O'Connor   Eddie Walsh

Sean Brosnan (0-2)   Johnny Walsh

Tony McAuliffe   Charlie O'Sullivan (0-1)   Paddy Kennedy

Murt Kelly (0-1)   Dan Spring   Mikey Lyne

Substitutes: Johnny Moriarty, Mick Raymond

Game 3 - All-Ireland semi-final replay versus Mayo in Croke Park on September 10. Final Score: Kerry 3-8; Mayo 1-4.

Dan O'Keeffe

Bill Myers   Joe Keohane   Tadgh Healy

Bill Dillon   Bill Casey   Eddie Walsh

Paddy Kennedy (0-1)		Tom Gega O'Connor
Jimmy O'Gorman (0-2)	Sean Brosnan (0-1)	Johnny Walsh (1-1)
Tim Landers (0-2)	Dan Spring (1-0)	Charlie O'Sullivan (1-1)

No substitutes used.

Game 4 - All-Ireland Final versus Meath in Croke Park on September 24. Final Score: Kerry 2-5; Meath 2-3.

	Dan O'Keeffe	
Bill Myers	Joe Keohane	Tadgh Healy
Bill Dillon	Bill Casey	Eddie Walsh
Paddy Kennedy	Jimmy O'Gorman	
Murt Kelly (0-2)	Tom Gega O'Connor	Johnny Walsh (0-1)
Charlie O'Sullivan	Dan Spring (2-1)	Tim Landers (0-1)

No substitutes used.

Scorers for the Year: Dan Spring (3-1), Murt Kelly (1-7), Charlie O'Sullivan (1-3), Johnny Walsh (1-3), Tony McAuliffe (1-1), Sean Brosnan (0-3), Mikey Lyne (0-3), Tim Landers (0-3), Jimmy O'Gorman (0-2), Tom Gega O'Connor (0-1), Paddy Kennedy (0-1).

Total Scored: 7-28

Appearances:

4 - Dan O'Keeffe, Joe Keohane, Bill Myers, Eddie Walsh, Bill Dillon, Tom Gega O'Connor, Paddy Kennedy, Johnny Walsh, Charlie O'Sullivan.

3 - Tadgh Healy, Bill Casey, Dan Spring, Murt Kelly.

2 - Sean Brosnan, Jimmy O'Gorman, Tony McAuliffe, Mikey Lyne, Tim Landers.

1 - Johnny McCarthy, Miko Doyle, Paddy Bawn Brosnan, J. Moriarty, Mick Raymond.

1939 - GAA Winners:

All-Irelands: Senior Football: Kerry   **Minor Football:** Roscommon

National Leagues: Football: Mayo   Hurling: Dublin

Senior Hurling: Kilkenny

Kerry Co. Champions: Football: Kerins O'Rahillys   Hurling: Crotta

1939 - In The News:

- The INTO Congress in Galway calls on the government to abolish the ban on married women teachers.
- The Department of External Affairs announces that it recognises the government of General Francisco Franco.
- In his Lenten pastoral, Bishop Daniel Mageean refers to A Protestant Parliament for a Protestant People
- Taoiseach Éamon de Valera attends the consecration of Pope Pius XII in Rome.
- Éamon de Valera is greeted by Benito Mussolini in Rome. A luncheon is held in honour of the Taoiseach.
- Ireland's neutrality is discussed during a Dáil debate on defence estimates. The government considered the implications to the export market to Britain if a neutral stand is taken.
- The Gaelic Athletic Association votes to keep the name of President Douglas Hyde off its list of patrons because he attended another soccer match.
- The Prime Minister of Northern Ireland, Lord Craigavon, dismisses the Dublin government's position of neutrality as cowardly.
- In a speech to Seanad Éireann, Taoiseach Éamon de Valera refers to the dropping of all references to the King and Great Britain from new Irish passports.
- The Prime Minister of Northern Ireland announces that conscription will not be extended to Northern Ireland.
- The Earl of Iveagh presents the Irish Government with his Dublin townhouse.
- The Treason Act 1939 becomes law. A sentence of death may be passed on anyone convicted of levying war against the State.
- A state of emergency is declared by the government in response to events in Europe.
- Taoiseach Éamon de Valera tells the Dáil that Ireland will remain neutral in the European War.
- SS Athenia torpedoed and sunk in the Atlantic Ocean. Knut Nelson (Norway) lands 450 survivors in Galway.

- The Irish-flagged tanker Inverliffey was shelled and sunk by U-38, which then towed the lifeboats away from the blazing oil.
- The Minister for Supplies, Seán Lemass, introduces petrol rationing.
- More than two dozen air-raid sirens, acquired by Dublin Corporation, are tested across the city.
- 1 million rounds of ammunition are stolen from the national arsenal at the Phoenix Park by pro-Nazi elements of the IRA.

1940-1949...The Emergency grips the world

Summary of the Decade

Kerry played 36 games, scoring 80-259, conceding 28-220.

Munster Championship titles: 7 (1940, 1941, 1942, 1944, 1946, 1947, 1948)

All Ireland titles: 3 (1940, 1941, 1946)

National League titles: 0 Minor titles: 1 (1946)

Most Appearances: Dan O'Keeffe 35; Eddie Walsh 31.

1940
Kerry 4-9 Limerick 1-2;
Kerry 4-8 Tipperary 1-5;
Munster Final: Kerry 1-10 Waterford 0-6;
All-Ireland semi-final: Kerry 3-4 Cavan 0-8;
All-Ireland Final: Kerry 0-7 Galway 1-3.

1941
Munster Final: Kerry 2-9 Clare 0-6;
All-Ireland semi-final: Kerry 0-4 Dublin 0-4;
Replay: Kerry 2-9 Dublin 0-3;
All-Ireland Final: Kerry 1-8 Galway 0-7.

1942
Kerry 3-8 Clare 1-3;
Kerry 3-6 Tipperary 1-5;
Munster Final: Kerry 3-7 Cork 0-8;
All-Ireland semi-final: Galway 1-3 Kerry 0-3.

1943
Kerry 0-9 Cork 2-3 (Draw);
Replay: Cork 1-5 Kerry 1-4.

1944
Kerry 4-8 Clare 1-4;
Kerry 3-9 Limerick 0-4;
Munster Final: Kerry 1-6 Tipperary 0-5;
All-Ireland semi-final: Kerry 3-3 Carlow 0-10;
All-Ireland Final Roscommon: 1-9 Kerry 2-4.

1945
Kerry 5-8 Limerick 2-7;
Munster Final: Cork 1-11 Kerry 1-6.

1946
Kerry 1-8 Cork 1-4;
Kerry 1-6 Clare 0-7;
Munster Final: Kerry 2-15 Waterford 2-1;
All-Ireland semi-final: Kerry 2-7 Antrim 0-10;
All-Ireland Final: Kerry 2-4 Roscommon 1-7;
Replay: Kerry 2-8 Roscommon 0-10.

1947
Kerry 9-10 Clare 0-4;
Munster Final: Kerry 3-8 Cork 2-6;
All-Ireland semi-final: Kerry 1-11 Meath 0-5;
All-Ireland Final: Cavan 2-11 Kerry 2-7.

1948
Kerry 6-6 Clare 1-8;
Munster Final: Kerry 2-9 Cork 2-6;
All-Ireland semi-final: Mayo 0-13 Kerry 0-3.

1949
Clare 3-7 Kerry 1-8.

1940

Summary: Played five championship games, won 28th Munster title, won All-Ireland for the 14th time.

Game 1 - versus Limerick in Glin on May 19. Final Score: Kerry 4-9; Limerick 1-2.

Dan O'Keeffe

Bill Myers   Joe Keohane   Tadgh Healy

J B Fitzgerald   Eddie Walsh   Johnny Walsh

Tom Gega O'Connor (0-1)   Paddy Bawn Brosnan

Jimmy O'Gorman (1-1)   Murt Kelly (0-1)   Tony McAuliffe (1-1)

Sean McCarthy   Dan Spring (1-3)   Jimmy O'Gorman (B) (1-2)

No substitutes used.

Game 2 - versus Tipperary in Cork on June 30. Final Score: Kerry 4-8; Tipperary 1-5.

Dan O'Keeffe

Bill Myers   Joe Keohane   Tadgh Healy

Bill Dillon   Bill Casey   Eddie Walsh

Tom Gega O'Connor   Paddy Kennedy

Johnny Walsh (0-1)   Sean Brosnan   Paddy Bawn Brosnan

Murt Kelly (0-2)   Dan Spring (2-2)   Jimmy O'Gorman (B) (2-1)

Substitute: J B Fitzgerald (0-2) for Jack Walsh

Game 3 - Munster Final versus Waterford in Waterford on July 21. Final Score: Kerry 1-10; Waterford 0-6.

Dan O'Keeffe

Bill Myers   Joe Keohane   Tadgh Healy

Bill Dillon   Bill Casey   Eddie Walsh

	Tom Gega O'Connor(0-2)		Paddy Kennedy	
Tony McAuliffe		Sean Brosnan (1-2)		Paddy Bawn Brosnan
Murt Kelly (0-2)		Dan Spring (0-2)	Jimmy O'Gorman (B) (0-2)	

No substitutes used.

Game 4 - All-Ireland semi-final versus Cavan in Croke Park on August 18. Final Score: Kerry 3-4; Cavan 0-8.

Dan O'Keeffe

Bill Myers	Joe Keohane	Tadgh Healy
Bill Dillon	Bill Casey	Eddie Walsh

	Tom Gega O'Connor(0-1)		Paddy Kennedy	
Johnny Walsh (1-1)		Sean Brosnan (0-1)		Paddy Bawn Brosnan
Murt Kelly		Dan Spring	Jimmy O'Gorman (B) (2-1)	

No substitutes used.

Game 5 - All-Ireland Final versus Galway in Croke Park on September 22. Final Score: Kerry 0-7; Galway 1-3.

Dan O'Keeffe

Bill Myers	Joe Keohane	Tadgh Healy
Bill Dillon	Bill Casey	Eddie Walsh

Sean Brosnan		Johnny Walsh	
Jimmy O'Gorman (B)	Tom Gega O'Connor (0-1)		Paddy Kennedy
Murt Kelly (0-2)	Dan Spring (0-1)		Charlie O'Sullivan (0-2)

Substitute: Paddy Bawn Brosnan (0-1) for Dan Spring.

Scorers for the Year: Jimmy O'Gorman (B) (5-7), Dan Spring (3-8), Murt Kelly (0-7), Sean Brosnan (1-3), Tom Gega O'Connor (0-5), Johnny Walsh (1-2), Jimmy O'Gorman (1-1), Tony McAuliffe (1-1), J B Fitzgerald (0-2), Charlie O'Sullivan (0-2).

Total Scored: 12-38

Appearances:

5 - Dan O'Keeffe, Bill Myers, Joe Keohane, Tadgh Healy, Eddie Walsh, Tom Gega O'Connor, Paddy Bawn Brosnan, Murt Kelly, Dan Spring.

4 - Johnny Walsh, Bill Dillon, Bill Casey, Paddy Kennedy, Sean Brosnan, Jimmy O'Gorman (B).

3 - None.

2 - J B Fitzgerald, Jimmy O'Gorman, Tony McAuliffe.

1 - Sean McCarthy, Charlie O'Sullivan.

1940 - GAA Winners:

All-Irelands: Senior Football: Kerry **Minor Football:** Louth

National Leagues: Football: Galway   Hurling: Cork

Senior Hurling: Limerick

Kerry Co. Champions: Football: Dingle Hurling: Banna

1940 - In The News:

- Munster (Capt. R. Paisley) mined and sunk in Irish Sea entering Liverpool.
- Trawler Leukos sunk by gunfire from U-38, NW of Tory Island - 11 dead. (She may have moved between the surfacing U-boat and English trawlers, in the hope that the tricolour would protect her while the English escaped).
- Fire destroys the roof and upper rooms of St. Patrick's College, Maynooth.
- U-38 lands a German spy, Karl Simon, in Dingle. He was promptly arrested and interned for the duration.
- Dublin Institute for Advanced Studies established.
- Minister Frank Aiken encourages everyone to store food and water and to prepare a shelter in case of a direct hit.
- Taoiseach Éamon de Valera announces that the policy of neutrality adopted the previous September will not be reversed.
- Éamon de Valera, in response to Winston Churchill's statement, says that there can be no question of handing over Irish ports for use by British forces while they retain control of Northern Ireland.

- James Craig, the first Prime Minister of Northern Ireland, dies suddenly. He was the longest continually serving Prime Minister in Europe.
- Dr. John Charles McQuaid is consecrated as Archbishop of Dublin.

1941

Summary: Played four championship games, won 29th Munster title, won 15th All-Ireland title.

Game 1 - Munster Final versus Clare in Limerick on July 20. Final Score: Kerry 2-9; Clare 0-6.

Dan O'Keeffe

Bill Myers   Joe Keohane   Tadgh Healy

Bill Dillon   Bill Casey   Eddie Walsh

Sean Brosnan   Paddy Kennedy

Johnny Walsh (0-2)   Tom Gega O'Connor   Paddy Bawn Brosnan (0-1)

Murt Kelly (1-3)   Charlie O'Sullivan (1-3)   Jimmy O'Gorman (B)

No substitutes used.

Game 2 - All-Ireland semi-final versus Dublin in Croke Park on August 10. Final Score: Kerry 0-4; Dublin 0-4 (Draw).

Dan O'Keeffe

Bill Myers   Joe Keohane   Tadgh Healy

Bill Dillon   Bill Casey   Eddie Walsh

Sean Brosnan   Paddy Kennedy

Johnny Walsh   Tom Gega O'Connor   Murt Kelly (0-4)

Jimmy O'Gorman (B)   Charlie O'Sullivan   Paddy Bawn Brosnan

No substitutes used.

Game 3 - All-Ireland semi-final replay versus Dublin in Tralee on August 17. Final Score: Kerry 2-9; Dublin 0-3.

Dan O'Keeffe

Bill Myers   Joe Keohane   Tadgh Healy

Bill Dillon   Bill Casey   Eddie Walsh

Sean Brosnan (0-2)   Paddy Kennedy

Johnny Walsh   Tom Gega O'Connor (1-0)   Paddy Bawn Brosnan (0-1)

Jimmy O'Gorman (B) (0-1)   Murt Kelly (0-5)   Charlie O'Sullivan (1-0)

No substitutes used.

Game 4 - All-Ireland Final versus Galway in Croke Park on September 7. Final Score: Kerry 1-8; Galway 0-7.

Dan O'Keeffe

Bill Myers   Joe Keohane   Tadgh Healy

Bill Dillon   Bill Casey   Eddie Walsh

Sean Brosnan   Paddy Kennedy

Johnny Walsh   Tom Gega O'Connor (1-1)   Paddy Bawn Brosnan (0-2)

Jimmy O'Gorman (B) (0-3)   Murt Kelly (0-2)   Charlie O'Sullivan

Substitutes: Tim Landers for Bill Myers, Mikey Lyne for Jack Walsh

Scorers for the Year: Murt Kelly (1-14), Charlie O'Sullivan (2-3), Tom Gega O'Connor (2-1), Jimmy O'Gorman (B) (0-4), Paddy Bawn Brosnan (0-4), Johnny Walsh (0-2), Sean Brosnan (0-2).

Total Scored: 5-30

Appearances:

4 - Dan O'Keeffe, Bill Myers, Joe Keohane, Tadgh Healy, Bill Dillon, Bill Casey, Eddie Walsh, Sean Brosnan, Paddy Kennedy, Johnny Walsh, Tom Gega O'Connor, Paddy Bawn Brosnan, Murt Kelly, Charlie O'Sullivan, Jimmy O'Gorman (B).

3 - None.

2 - None.

1 - Tim Landers, Mikey Lyne.

1941 GAA Winners:

All-Irelands: Senior Football: Kerry **Minor Football:** Roscommon

National Leagues: Football: Mayo   Hurling: Cork

Senior Hurling: Cork

Kerry Co. Champions: Football: Dingle   Hurling: Crotta

1941 - In The News:

- Three Carlow women are killed in a night of bombing in parts of Leinster.
- The poet and novelist James Joyce dies in Switzerland.
- Part of the old State Chambers in Dublin Castle are destroyed by fire.
- 3,800 animals are slaughtered after the fiftieth case of foot and mouth disease is announced.
- Bread rationing is introduced on March 20.
- Belfast is blitzed, with 1,000 people killed in bombing raids on the city. 71 firemen with 13 fire tenders from Dundalk, Drogheda, Dublin, and Dún Laoghaire cross the border to assist their Belfast colleagues.
- Belfast suffers a third bombing raid during World War II. The Dublin government authorises its emergency services to assist.
- A special sitting of Dáil Éireann unanimously condemns the introduction of conscription in Northern Ireland. Speaking in the British House of Commons, Prime Minister Winston Churchill subsequently rules out the introduction of conscription in the North.
- Charles Stewart Parnell, the uncrowned King of Ireland, is honoured in a huge pageant in Dublin.

1942

Summary: Played four championship games, won 30th Munster title, lost the All-Ireland semi-final.

Game 1 - versus Clare in Ennis on June 14. Final Score: Kerry 3-8; Clare 1-3.

Dan O'Keeffe

Bill Myers	Denis Walsh	Martin McCarthy
Eddie Walsh	Mick Raymond	Johnny Walsh

Willie O'Donnell   Joe Kennington

Jimmy O'Gorman (B)	P. Sexton	Bill Dillon
Paddy Bawn Brosnan	Bill Casey	Jackie Falvey

Scorers includes: O'Gorman (0-1), Dillon (1-1), leaving (2-6) unaccounted.

No substitutes used.

Game 2 - versus Tipperary in Tipperary Town on June 28. Final Score: Kerry 3-6; Tipperary 1-5.

Dan O'Keeffe

Bill Myers	Joe Keohane	Tadgh Healy
Martin Raymond	Bill Casey	Eddie Walsh

Paddy Kennedy (0-1)   Sean Brosnan

Johnny Walsh (0-1)	Willie O'Donnell(1-1)	Joe Kennington
Jimmy O'Gorman (B) (2-1)	Murt Kelly (0-2)	Paddy Bawn Brosnan

No substitutes used.

Game 3 - Munster Final versus Cork in Tralee on July 19. Final Score: Kerry 3-7; Cork 0-8.

Dan O'Keeffe

Bill Myers	Joe Keohane	Tadgh Healy

Ger Teahan	Bill Casey	Eddie Walsh

Sean Brosnan	Joe Kennington

Johnny Walsh	Tom Gega O'Connor (0-1)	Paddy Kennedy

Jimmy O'Gorman (B) (1-3)   Murt Kelly (1-3)   Paddy Bawn Brosnan (1-0)

No substitutes used.

Game 4 - All-Ireland semi-final versus Galway in Croke Park on August 9. Final Score: Galway 1-3; Kerry 0-3.

Dan O'Keeffe

Bill Myers	Joe Keohane	Denis Walsh

Jimmy Pierce	Tadgh Healy	Eddie Walsh

Paddy Kennedy	Mick Raymond

Tom Lawlor	Tom Gega O'Connor	Johnny Walsh

Jimmy O'Gorman (B)	Murt Kelly (0-3)	Joe Kennington

Substitute: Paddy O'Donoghue for Johnny Walsh.

Scorers for the Year: Jimmy O'Gorman (B) (3-5), Murt Kelly (1-8), Willie O'Donnell (1-1), Bill Dillon (1-1), Paddy Bawn Brosnan (1-0), Johnny Walsh (0-1), Paddy Kennedy (0-1), Tom Gega O'Connor (0-1), plus unaccounted (2-6).

Total Scored: 9-24

Appearances:

4 - Dan O'Keeffe, Bill Myers, Eddie Walsh, Johnny Walsh, Joe Kennington, Jimmy O'Gorman (B).

3 - Joe Keohane, Mick Raymond, Paddy Kennedy, Paddy Bawn Brosnan, Bill Casey, Tadgh Healy, Murt Kelly.

2 - Tom Gega O'Connor, Denis Walsh, Willie O'Donnell, Sean Brosnan.

1 - Martin McCarthy, P.Sexton, Bill Dillon, Jackie Falvey, Paddy O'Donoghue, Ger Teahan, Jimmy Pierce, Tom Lawlor.

1942 - GAA Winners:

All-Irelands: Senior Football: Dublin **Minor Football:** Not Held

National Leagues: Football: Not Held   Hurling: Not Held

Senior Hurling: Cork

Kerry Co. Champions: Football: Shannon Rangers   Hurling: Kenmare

1942 - In The News:

- Due to The Emergency the rationing of gas is introduced.
- It is announced that Ireland is to have a new Central Bank replacing the old Currency Commission.
- There are reports of a split in the Irish Labour Party due to the selection of candidates for the forthcoming general election.

1943

Summary: Played two championship games.

Game 1 - versus Cork in Cork on June 6. Final Score: Kerry 0-9; Cork 2-3 (Draw).

Dan O'Keeffe

Eddie Condon	Joe Keohane	Tadgh Healy
Eddie Walsh	Martin McCarthy	Denis Walsh

Pat Holly (0-1)   Jack Walsh

Joe Kennington (0-1)	Murt Kelly (0-5)	Tom Gega O'Connor
Jimmy O'Gorman (B) (0-1)	Paddy Bawn Brosnan	Mikey Lyne (0-1)

No substitutes used.

Game 2 - Replay versus Cork in Cork on July 11. Final Score: Cork 1-5; Kerry 1-4.

Dan O'Keeffe

Bill Myers	Joe Keohane	Tadgh Healy
Martin McCarthy	Bill Casey	Eddie Walsh

Paddy Kennedy (0-1)   Jimmy Pierce

Johnny Walsh (0-1)	Tom Gega O'Connor (1-0)	Johnny Clifford
Murt Kelly (0-2)	Charlie O'Sullivan	Paddy Bawn Brosnan

No substitutes used.

Scorers for the Year: Murt Kelly (0-7), Tom Gega O'Connor (1-0), Paddy Kennedy (0-1), Johnny Walsh (0-1), Pat Holly (0-1), Joe Kennington (0-1), Jimmy O'Gorman (B) (0-1), Mikey Lyne (0-1).

Total Scored: 1-13

Appearances:

2 - Dan O'Keeffe, Joe Keohane, Tadgh Healy, Eddie Walsh, Martin McCarthy, Johnny Walsh, Murt Kelly, Tom Gega O'Connor, Paddy Bawn Brosnan.

1 - Bill Myers, Eddie Condon, Bill Casey, Denis Walsh, Paddy Kennedy, Pat Holly, Jimmy Pierce, Joe Kennington, Johnny Clifford, Jimmy O'Gorman (B), Mikey Lyne, Charlie O'Sullivan.

1943 - GAA Winners:

All-Irelands: Senior Football: Roscommon **Minor Football:** Not Held

National Leagues: Football: Not Held   Hurling: Not Held

Senior Hurling: Cork

Kerry Co. Champions: Football: Dingle   Hurling: Crotta

1943 - In The News:

- The Central Bank of Ireland is established, but it was not given all the powers expected of a central bank.
- 35 children lose their lives to fire in St Joseph's Orphanage, Main Street, Cavan. Verdict criticises the Poor Clare nuns.
- Éamon de Valera and his government celebrate St. Patrick's Day with a céilí in the Great Hall of Dublin Castle.
- Sir Basil Brooke becomes Prime Minister of Northern Ireland.
- In the largest manufacturing campaign in the history of the Irish Sugar Company, 700 employees at the Carlow Sugar Beet Factory will work in three shifts without pause for 18 weeks until all the 230,000 acres (930 km²) of beet is processed.
- Fianna Fáil form a minority government, taking 66 of the 138 total seats.
- Kerry return the following members to the 11th Dáil:
  Kerry South: Frederick Crowley (FF); John Healy (FF); Finian Lynch (FG).
  Kerry North: Patrick Finucane (Clann na Talmhan); Eamonn Kissane (FF); Tom McEllistrim Sr. (FF); Dan Spring (Labour Party).

1944

Summary: Played five championship games, won 31st Munster title, lost the All-Ireland Final.

Game 1 - versus Clare in Tralee on May 14. Final Score: Kerry 4-8; Clare 1-4.

Dan O'Keeffe

Ger Teahan	Tim Brosnan	Eddie Condon
Paddy Cronesberry	Martin McCarthy	Eddie Walsh

J. Fitzgerald   Dan Kavanagh

Eddie Dowling	Jackie Lyne	Johnny Clifford
Dinny Lyne	Phil McCarthy	Paddy Bawn Brosnan

Scorers include: Jackie Lyne (0-2), Johnny Clifford (1-0), Phil McCarthy (1-0), leaving (2-6) unaccounted. No substitutes used.

Game 2 - versus Limerick in Listowel on June 18. Final Score: Kerry 3-9; Limerick 0-4.

Dan O'Keeffe

Tadgh Healy	Ger Teahan	Tim Brosnan
Dinny Lyne	Martin McCarthy	F. O'Connor

J. Fitzgerald (0-2)   Willie O'Donnell (0-3)

Eddie Dowling	Johnny Clifford	Gus Cremin (1-2)
Paddy O'Donoghue (2-1)	Paddy Bawn Brosnan (0-1)	Johnny Moriarty

No substitutes used.

Game 3 - Munster Final versus Tipperary in Limerick on July 9. Final Score: Kerry 1-6; Tipperary 0-5.

Dan O'Keeffe

Tadgh Healy	Joe Keohane	Tim Brosnan
Martin McCarthy	Eddie Condon	Eddie Walsh

Paddy Kennedy (1-0)		Dan Kavanagh
Johnny Clifford	Sean Brosnan (0-2)	Paddy Bawn Brosnan
Jackie Lyne	Murt Kelly (0-3)	Eddie Dunne (0-1)

No substitutes used.

Game 4 - All-Ireland semi-final versus Carlow in Croke Park on August 27. Final Score: Kerry 3-3; Carlow 0-10.

Dan O'Keeffe

Tadgh Healy	Joe Keohane	Tim Brosnan
Martin McCarthy	Eddie Condon	Eddie Walsh

Paddy Kennedy		Sean Brosnan
Johnny Clifford (0-1)	Bill Dillon (1-0)	Dan Kavanagh
Willie O'Donnell(0-1)	Paddy Bawn Brosnan (1-0)	Murt Kelly (1-1)

No substitutes used.

Game 5 - All-Ireland Final versus Roscommon in Croke Park on September 24. Final Score: Roscommon 1-9; Kerry 2-4.

Dan O'Keeffe

Tadgh Healy	Joe Keohane	Tim Brosnan
Bill Dillon (0-1)	Martin McCarthy	Eddie Walsh

Paddy Kennedy (0-2)		Sean Brosnan
Johnny Clifford	Jackie Lyne	Paddy Bawn Brosnan
Dinny Lyne	Murt Kelly (1-1)	Eddie Dunne (1-0)

Substitutes: Dan Kavanagh for Paddy Kennedy, Johnny Walsh for Paddy Bawn Brosnan.

Scorers for the Year: Murt Kelly (2-5), Paddy O'Donoghue (2-1), Gus Cremin (1-2), Paddy Kennedy (1-2), Paddy Bawn Brosnan (1-1), Johnny Clifford (1-1), Bill Dillon (1-1), Eddie Dunne (1-1), Willie O'Donnell (0-4), Phil McCarthy (1-0), Sean Brosnan (0-2), Jackie Lyne (0-2), J. Fitzgerald (0-2) plus unaccounted (2-6).

Total Scored: 13-30

Appearances:

5 - Dan O'Keeffe, Tim Brosnan, Martin McCarthy, Johnny Clifford, Paddy Bawn Brosnan.

4 - Tadgh Healy, Eddie Walsh, Dan Kavanagh.

3 - Joe Keohane, Dinny Lyne, Paddy Kennedy, Sean Brosnan, Murt Kelly, Jackie Lyne, Eddie Condon.

2 - Ger Teahan, J. Fitzgerald, Willie O'Donnell, Eddie Dunne, Eddie Dowling, Bill Dillon.

1 - Paddy Cronesberry, F. O'Connor, Gus Cremin, Phil McCarthy, Paddy O'Donoghue, Johnny Moriarty, Johnny Walsh.

1944 - GAA Winners:

All-Irelands: Senior Football: Roscommon   **Minor Football:**   Not Held

National Leagues: Football: Not Held   Hurling: Not Held

Senior Hurling: Cork

Kerry Co. Champions: Football: Dingle   Hurling: Crotta

1944 - In The News:

- W. T. Cosgrave officially resigns as leader of Fine Gael.
- The United States alleges that Ireland's neutrality is operating in favour of the Axis Powers.
- The British Government bans all travel between Great Britain and Ireland.
- The general election gives the ruling Fianna Fáil a majority of 14 seats, with 75 of the 138 seats.
- Kerry return the following members to the 12th Dáil:
  Kerry South: Frederick Crowley (FF); John Healy (FF); Finian Lynch (FG).
  In the November 1944 by-election Donal O'Donoghue (FF) takes the seat vacated by the appointment of Finian Lynch as a judge. In

the December 1945 by-election Honor Crowley (FF) holds the seat vacated by the death of her husband Frederick Crowley.

Kerry North: Patrick Finucane (Clann na Talmhan); Eamonn Kissane (FF); Tom McEllistrim Sr. (FF); Dan Spring (National Labour Party).

- The Minister for Supplies, Seán Lemass, announces further rationing of electricity.
- Men from Tyrone and Fermanagh form an Anti-Partition League in Dublin.
- The Chief Genealogical Officer issues County Dublin with a coat of arms, the first county to receive such a distinction.
- General Eoin O'Duffy, former leader of the Blueshirts, dies aged 52.

1945

Summary: Played two championship games.

Game 1 - versus Limerick in Limerick on June 10. Final Score: Kerry 5-8; Limerick 2-7.

Dan O'Keeffe

Tadgh Healy	Tim Brosnan	Tom Lawlor

Ger Teahan	Eddie Dowling	Eddie Walsh

Dan Kavanagh (1-1)		Willie Burke

Paddy Kennedy (2-4)	Willie O'Donnell(1-1)	Batt Garvey (0-1)

Dinny Lyne	Eddie Dunne (1-1)	Paddy Bawn Brosnan

Substitute: Derry Burke

Game 2 - Munster Final versus Cork in Killarney on July 8. Final Score: Cork 1-11; Kerry 1-6.

Dan O'Keeffe

Tadgh Healy	Eddie Walsh	Dinny Lyne

Jackie Lyne	Paddy Kennedy	Martin McCarthy

Dan Kavanagh (0-1)		Willie Burke

Albie Conway	Willie O'Donnell	Batt Garvey (0-1)

Tim Landers (1-0)	Tom Gega O'Connor	Mikey Lyne (0-4)

No substitutes used.

Scorers for the Year: Paddy Kennedy (2-4), Dan Kavanagh (1-2), Willie O'Donnell (1-1), Eddie Dunne (1-1), Mikey Lyne (0-4), Tim Landers (1-0), Batt Garvey (0-2).

Total Scored: 6-14

Appearances:

2 - Dan O'Keeffe, Tadgh Healy, Eddie Walsh, Dan Kavanagh, Willie Burke, Paddy Kennedy, Willie O'Donnell, Batt Garvey, Dinny Lyne.

1 - Tim Brosnan, Paddy Bawn Brosnan, Eddie Dowling, Tom Lawlor, Ger Teahan, Eddie Dunne, Derry Burke, Jackie Lyne, Martin McCarthy, Albie Conway, Tim Landers, Tom Gega O'Connor, Mikey Lyne.

1945 - GAA Winners:

All-Irelands: Senior Football: Cork **Minor Football:** Dublin

National Leagues: Football: Not Held Hurling: Not Held

Senior Hurling: Tipperary

Kerry Co. Champions: Football: Shannon Rangers   Hurling: Crotta

1945 - In The News:

- Most traffic in Ireland comes under the control of Córas Iompair Éireann.
- The people of Ireland donate £100,000 to the starving people of Italy.
- In one of the most controversial episodes of his leadership, Taoiseach Éamon de Valera calls on the German Ambassador to express his sympathy following the death of Adolf Hitler.
- Reports of a German surrender bring students of Trinity College, Dublin onto the roof singing the English and French national anthems. A riot ensues following the burning of the Irish tricolour.
- Éamon de Valera replies in a radio broadcast to Winston Churchill's criticism of Irish neutrality.
- Seán T. O'Kelly is inaugurated as the second President of Ireland, defeating Fine Gael's Sean Mac Eoin and an Independent candidate, Patrick McCartan, on the second count.
- Two nationalist MP's take the Oath of Allegiance and enter the Westminster parliament.
- Count John McCormack, the famous tenor, dies in Dublin aged 61.
- Professor Eoin MacNeill dies in Dublin aged 77. He was a founder-member of the Gaelic League and the Irish Volunteers.
- The Nuremberg Trials hear the story of German plans to create a revolution in Ireland during the War.
- In his presidential address President Seán T. O'Kelly asks the youth of Ireland to make a particular effort to restore the Irish language.

1946

Summary: Played six championship games, won 32nd Munster title, won 16th All-Ireland title.

Game 1 - versus Cork in Killarney on June 2. Final Score: Kerry 1-8; Cork 1-4.

Dan O'Keeffe

Dinny Lyne   Paddy Bawn Brosnan   Ger Teahan

Nicholas O'Donoghue   Bill Casey   Eddie Walsh

Teddy O'Connor   Eddie Dowling

Jackie Falvey (0-1)   Charlie O'Connor (0-3)   Batt Garvey (0-1)

Jackie Lyne (0-1)   Paddy Burke (0-2)   Paddy Kennedy

Kerry's goal was an own goal by Cork's goalkeeper. No substitutes used.

Game 2 -versus Clare in Ennis on July 7. Final Score: Kerry 1-6; Clare 0-7.

Dan O'Keeffe

Dinny Lyne   Bill Myers   E. Coughlan

Charlie O'Connor   Bill Casey   Eddie Walsh

Teddy O'Connor   Ger Teahan

Jackie Falvey (0-1)   Willie O'Donnell (0-1)   Batt Garvey

Jackie Lyne (0-1)   Paddy Burke (1-3)   Paddy Kennedy

Substitute: Dan Kavanagh for Willie O'Donnell

Game 3 - Munster Final versus Waterford in Tralee on July 21. Final Score: Kerry 2-15; Waterford 2-1.

Dan O'Keeffe

Dinny Lyne   Tom McElligott   Eddie Walsh

Carl O'Sullivan   Ger Teahan   Batt Garvey

<table>
<tr><td>Teddy O'Connor (0-1)</td><td></td><td>Eddie Dowling</td><td></td></tr>
<tr><td>Jackie Falvey (1-1)</td><td>Dan Kavanagh (0-1)</td><td>Tom Gega O'Connor (0-7)</td></tr>
<tr><td>Jackie Lyne (1-2)</td><td>Paddy Burke (0-2)</td><td>Paddy Kennedy (0-1)</td></tr>
</table>

No substitutes used.

Game 4 - All-Ireland semi-final versus Antrim in Croke Park on August 18. Final Score: Kerry 2-7; Antrim 0-10.

Dan O'Keeffe

Dinny Lyne	Joe Keohane	Eddie Walsh
Ger Teahan	Bill Casey	Teddy O'Connor

Eddie Dowling   Gus Cremin

Willie O'Donnell (1-5)	Paddy Kennedy (0-1)	Batt Garvey (1-0)
Jackie Lyne	Paddy Burke	Dan Kavanagh (0-1)

Substitute: Gerald O'Sullivan for Ger Teahan

Game 5 - All-Ireland Final versus Roscommon in Croke Park on October 6. Final Score: Kerry 2-4; Roscommon 1-7 (Draw).

Dan O'Keeffe

Dinny Lyne	Joe Keohane	Paddy Bawn Brosnan
Teddy O'Connor	Bill Casey	Eddie Walsh

Gus Cremin   Dan Kavanagh

Willie O'Donnell	Paddy Kennedy	Batt Garvey (0-1)
Jackie Lyne	Paddy Burke (1-1)	Tom Gega O'Connor (1-2)

Substitutes: Eddie Dowling for Paddy Kennedy, Brian Kelliher for Jackie Lyne.

Game 6 - All-Ireland Final Replay versus Roscommon in Croke Park on October 21. Final Score: Kerry 2-8; Roscommon 0-10.

Dan O'Keeffe

Dinny Lyne	Joe Keohane	Paddy Bawn Brosnan
Jackie Lyne	Bill Casey	Eddie Walsh

Paddy Kennedy (0-1)   Teddy O'Connor

Jackie Falvey	Tom Gega O'Connor (1-4)	Batt Garvey (0-2)
Frank O'Keeffe	Paddy Burke (1-0)	Dan Kavanagh

Substitute: Gus Cremin (0-1) for Jackie Falvey.

Scorers for the Year: Paddy Burke (3-8), Tom Gega O'Connor (2-13), Willie O'Donnell (1-6), Batt Garvey (1-4), Jackie Lyne (1-4), Jackie Falvey (1-3), Paddy Kennedy (0-3), Charlie O'Connor (0-3), Gus Cremin (0-1), Dan Kavanagh (0-2), Teddy O'Connor (0-1) plus an own goal by Cork.

Total Scored: 10-48

Appearances:

6 - Dan O'Keeffe, Dinny Lyne, Eddie Walsh, Jackie Lyne, Batt Garvey, Paddy Burke, Paddy Kennedy, Teddy O'Connor.

5 - Bill Casey, Dan Kavanagh.

4 - Eddie Dowling, Ger Teahan, Jackie Falvey.

3 - Gus Cremin, Joe Keohane, Paddy Bawn Brosnan, Tom Gega O'Connor, Willie O'Donnell.

2 - Charlie O'Connor.

1 - Brian Kelliher, Bill Myers, E. Coughlan, Frank O'Keeffe, Nicholas O'Donoghue, Tom McElligott, Gerald O'Sullivan, Carl O'Sullivan.

1946 - GAA Winners:

All-Irelands: Senior Football: Kerry   **Minor Football:** Kerry

Kerry's winning minor team: J. Ryan, Jimmy McCarthy, B. O'Sullivan, D. Murphy, S. O'Sullivan, D. Sheehan, J. Fenton, T. Moriarty, T. Ashe, M. Lynch, D. O'Regan, P. O'Sullivan, J. O'Brien, J. Madden, P. Godley

National Leagues: Football: Meath   Hurling: Clare

Niall Flynn

Senior Hurling: Cork

Kerry Co. Champions: Football: Killarney Legion Hurling: Ballyheigue

1946 - In The News:

- William Joyce, alias Lord Haw Haw, is hanged in Wandsworth Prison for treason.
- The Minister for Education, Tomás Ó Deirg, announces that refugee children who arrived in Ireland during the war cannot obtain the Leaving Certificate because of an insufficient knowledge of the Irish language.
- Work starts on a comprehensive Irish-English dictionary.
- A new republican political party, Clann na Poblachta, is formed in Dublin.
- Éamon de Valera's motion to apply for membership of the United Nations is accepted in the Dáil.
- On the first anniversary of the Hiroshima bombing, Captain Bob Lewis, co-pilot of the Enola Gay which dropped the bomb, arrives at Shannon Airport on his first flight as a civil aviation pilot.
- An order is signed removing Ireland from the state of emergency in existence since 1939.
- George Bernard Shaw is honoured by being made a freeman of Dublin.
- 70 primary school teachers protest low pay on the pitch in Croke Park at half-time during the Kerry-Roscommon All-Ireland Football Final.
- Walt Disney arrives in Dublin for a meeting with the Folklore Commission to further his investigation of leprechauns for a forthcoming film.
- The government announces the release of 24 internees, including Brendan Behan.

1947

Summary: Played four championship games, won 33rd Munster title, lost All-Ireland Final.

Game 1 - versus Clare in Limerick on July 6. Final Score: Kerry 9-10; Clare 0-4.

Dan O'Keeffe

Dinny Lyne   Joe Keohane   Paddy Bawn Brosnan

Jackie Lyne   Bill Casey   Eddie Walsh

Paddy Kennedy (1-0)   Teddy O'Connor

Gerald O'Sullivan (1-2)   Willie O'Donnell (1-0)   Batt Garvey (2-0)

Frank O'Keeffe (3-0)   Tom Gega O'Connor (0-7)   Dan Kavanagh (1-1)

No substitutes used.

Game 2 - versus Cork in Cork on July 27. Final Score: Kerry 3-8; Cork 2-6.

Dan O'Keeffe

Jackie Lyne   Joe Keohane   Dinny Lyne

Paddy Bawn Brosnan   Bill Casey   Eddie Walsh

Paddy Kennedy   Teddy O'Connor (0-1)

Gerald O'Sullivan (1-0)   Willie O'Donnell (0-1)   Batt Garvey (0-1)

Frank O'Keeffe (1-0)   Tom Gega O'Connor (0-3)   Dan Kavanagh (1-2)

Subs: Eddie Dowling for Kennedy, Tim Brosnan for Casey, Paddy Kennedy for Kavanagh

Game 3 - versus Meath in Croke Park on August 10. Final Score: Kerry 1-11; Meath 0-5.

Dan O'Keeffe

Dinny Lyne   Joe Keohane   Paddy Bawn Brosnan

Jackie Lyne   Bill Casey   Eddie Walsh

Paddy Kennedy   Teddy O'Connor (0-1)

Gerald O'Sullivan (0-2)   Willie O'Donnell(1-1)   Batt Garvey (0-3)

Frank O'Keeffe   Tom Gega O'Connor (0-2)   Dan Kavanagh (0-1)

Substitutes: Eddie Dowling (0-1) for Paddy Kennedy, Teddy O'Sullivan for Bill Casey

Game 4 - versus Cavan in Polo Grounds, New York on September 14. Final Score: Cavan 2-11; Kerry 2-7.

Dan O'Keeffe

Dinny Lyne   Joe Keohane   Paddy Bawn Brosnan

Jackie Lyne   Bill Casey   Eddie Walsh

Eddie Dowling (1-0)   Teddy O'Connor

Teddy O'Sullivan   Dan Kavanagh   Batt Garvey (1-0)

Frank O'Keeffe   Tom Gega O'Connor (0-6)   Paddy Kennedy (0-1)

Substitutes: Willie O'Donnell for Eddie Dowling, Mick Finucane for Eddie Walsh, Tim Brosnan for Willie O'Donnell, Ger Teahan for Paddy Kennedy.

Scorers for the Year: Tom Gega O'Connor (0-11), Batt Garvey (1-6), Dan Kavanagh (1-3), Gerald O'Sullivan (1-2), Willie O'Donnell (1-2), Eddie Dowling (1-0), Frank O'Keeffe (1-0), Teddy O'Connor (0-2).

Total Scored: 15-36

Appearances:

4 - Dan O'Keeffe, Dinny Lyne, Joe Keohane, Paddy Bawn Brosnan, Jackie Lyne, Bill Casey, Eddie Walsh, Teddy O'Connor, Paddy Kennedy, Willie O'Donnell, Batt Garvey, Frank O'Keeffe, Tom Gega O'Connor, Dan Kavanagh.

3 - Eddie Dowling, Gerald O'Sullivan.

2 -Tim Brosnan, Teddy O'Sullivan.

1 - Mick Finucane, Ger Teahan.

1947 - GAA Winners:

All-Irelands: Senior Football: Cavan   **Minor Football:** Tyrone

National Leagues: Football: Derry   Hurling: Limerick

Senior Hurling: Kilkenny

Kerry Co. Champions: Football: John Mitchels Hurling: Crotta

1947 - In The News:

- The internationally known labour leader, Jim Larkin, dies in Dublin aged 72.
- The 21st anniversary of the founding of Fianna Fáil is celebrated in the Capitol Theatre, Dublin.
- Aer Lingus begins a new direct service between Dublin and Amsterdam.
- The Soviet Union blocks Ireland's entry into the United Nations.
- The All-Ireland Football Final is played in the Polo Grounds in New York, to mark the centenary of the Great Famine of 1847.
- A 60-day transport strike hits Dublin.

1948

Summary: Played three championship games, won 34th Munster title, lost All-Ireland semi-final.

Game 1 - versus Clare in Ballylongford on July 4. Final Score: Kerry 6-6; Clare 1-8.

Dan O'Keeffe

Dinny Lyne	Joe Keohane	Donie Murphy
Jackie Lyne	Bill Casey	Gus Cremin

Tom Spillane (0-1)   Eddie Dowling

Gerald O'Sullivan (1-0)	Willie O'Donnell (3-2)	Batt Garvey (1-2)
Brian Kelliher (1-1)	Derry Burke	Dan Kavanagh

No substitutes used.

Game 2 - Munster Final versus Cork in Killarney on July 25. Final Score: Kerry 2-9; Cork 2-6.

Dan O'Keeffe

Dinny Lyne	Joe Keohane	Paddy Bawn Brosnan
Teddy O'Connor	Jackie Lyne	Teddy O'Sullivan

Tom Spillane   Eddie Dowling

Gerald O'Sullivan	Willie O'Donnell	Batt Garvey (0-1)
Dan Kavanagh (0-1)	Martin McCarthy (1-0)	Tom Gega O'Connor (1-6)

Substitutes: Gus Cremin (0-1) for Eddie Dowling, Derry Burke for Tom Gega O'Connor

Game 3 - All-Ireland semi-final versus Mayo in Croke Park on August 29. Final Score: Mayo 0-13; Kerry 0-3.

Dan O'Keeffe

Dinny Lyne	Joe Keohane	Paddy Bawn Brosnan
Eddie Dowling (0-1)	Jackie Lyne	Teddy O'Connor

Tom Spillane   Gus Cremin

Gerald O'Sullivan   Willie O'Donnell   Batt Garvey

Dan Kavanagh   Martin McCarthy   Tom Gega O'Connor (0-2)

No substitutes used.

Scorers for the Year: Willie O'Donnell (3-2), Tom Gega O'Connor (1-8), Batt Garvey (1-3), Brian Kelliher (1-1), Gerald O'Sullivan (1-0), Martin McCarthy (1-0), Gus Cremin (0-1), Tom Spillane (0-1), Eddie Dowling (0-1), Dan Kavanagh (0-1).

Total Scored: 8-18

Appearances:

3 - Dan O'Keeffe, Dinny Lyne, Joe Keohane, Jackie Lyne, Gus Cremin, Tom Spillane, Eddie Dowling, Gerald O'Sullivan, Willie O'Donnell, Batt Garvey, Dan Kavanagh.

2 - Paddy Bawn Brosnan, Teddy O'Connor, Martin McCarthy, Tom Gega O'Connor, Derry Burke.

1 - Donie Murphy, Bill Casey, Teddy O'Sullivan, Brian Kelliher.

1948 - GAA Winners:

All-Irelands: Senior Football: Cavan **Minor Football:** Tyrone

National Leagues: Football: Cavan   Hurling: Cork

Senior Hurling: Waterford

Kerry Co. Champions: Football: Dingle   Hurling: Kilmoyley

1948 - In The News:

- The Council of State meets for the first time when President Douglas Hyde tests the constitutionality of the Offences Against the State Bill.
- Gas rationing ends in Dublin for the first time since 1942.
- Fianna Fáil had ruled uninterrupted since 1932 with Éamon de Valera as prime minister (titled as President of the Executive Council of the Irish Free State until 1937 and since then as Taoiseach). However,

the 1948 general election left the party six seats short of a majority. Negotiations with the National Labour Party failed when National Labour insisted on a formal coalition; at the time, Fianna Fáil would not enter coalitions with other parties.

- At first, it seemed that de Valera would attempt to govern alone in a minority government. Fianna Fáil had 37 more seats than the next-biggest party, Fine Gael, and thus appeared to be the only party that could possibly form a government. However, to the surprise of most observers, the other parties realized that if they banded together, they would have only one seat fewer than Fianna Fáil, and would be able to form a government with the support of seven independents.

- It was a foregone conclusion that in such a coalition, the Taoiseach would come from Fine Gael, since it was by far the second-largest party. However, Seán MacBride let it be known that he and his party, Clann na Poblachta, would not serve in a government headed by Fine Gael's leader, Richard Mulcahy. Many Irish Republicans had never forgiven Mulcahy for his role in carrying out 77 executions under the government of the Irish Free State in the 1920s during the Irish Civil War. Without MacBride, the other parties would have been nine seats short of the 74 they needed to topple de Valera. Accordingly, Mulcahy bowed out in favour of former Attorney General John A. Costello.

- On 18 February 1948, Costello was elected as the second Taoiseach of the Irish state, consigning de Valera to the opposition benches for the first time in 16 years. Costello found himself as leader of a disparate group of young and old politicians, republicans and Free Staters, conservatives and socialists. The government's survival depended on the skill of Costello as Taoiseach and the independence of various ministers.

- Kerry return the following members to the 13th Dáil:
  Kerry South: Honor Crowley (FF); Patrick Palmer (FG); John Flynn (Independent).
  Kerry North: Patrick Finucane (Clann na Talmhan); Eamonn Kissane (FF); Tom McEllistrim Sr. (FF); Dan Spring (National Labour Party).

- The Minister for Health, Noel Browne, announces his emergency drive against tuberculosis.

- The government asks Aerlínte Éireann to postpone its inaugural transatlantic service due to high costs.

- The Minister for External Affairs, Seán MacBride, recommends an economic or customs union between the two parts of Ireland.

- A fire at Shannon Airport destroys the control tower.
- Seán MacBride represents Ireland at the Marshall Aid conference in Paris.
- Captain EG Hitzen hands over a flag surrendered during the 1916 Easter Rising. He also discusses his capture of Éamon de Valera.
- A 36-foot shark is spotted off the coast of Co. Donegal.
- 500 people attend a 1798 Rebellion commemoration on the hills overlooking Belfast.
- The body of W. B. Yeats is re-buried at Drumcliffe, Co. Sligo.
- Taoiseach John A. Costello is presented with an honorary Doctorate of Law from Fordham University, New York.
- In Ottawa Taoiseach John A. Costello announces the government intends to repeal the 1936 External Relations Act, thus severing the last constitutional link with Britain. In November, the Republic of Ireland Act 1948, which involves the repeal of the External Relations Act, is passed in Dáil Éireann. President Seán T. O'Kelly signs the Republic of Ireland Bill at a ceremony at Áras an Uachtaráin.
- Tánaiste William Norton and the Lord Mayor of Dublin refuse to share a platform with Fianna Fáil deputy Seán MacEntee following controversial remarks he made about partition.

1949

Summary: Played one championship game.

Game 1 - versus Clare in Ennis on June 19. Final Score: Clare 3-7; Kerry 1-8.

Pat Dennehy

Mick Finucane	Jas. Murphy	Teddy O'Connor

Tim Healy	Bill Casey	Teddy O'Sullivan

Eddie Dowling   Tom Moriarty

Jim Brosnan	Gerald O'Sullivan (1-2)	Batt Garvey

Tom Ashe (0-1)	Tom Spillane	Willie O'Donnell (0-5)

No substitutes used.

1949 - GAA Winners:

All-Irelands: Senior Football: Meath **Minor Football:** Armagh

National Leagues: Football: Mayo   Hurling: Tipperary

Senior Hurling: Tipperary

Kerry Co. Champions: Football: Killarney   Hurling: Ardfert

1949 - In The News:
- The Irish Government leases a residence in the Phoenix Park to the United States government for a period of 99 years. It will be the residence of the U.S. Ambassador.
- At midnight on April 17, the 26 counties officially leave the British Commonwealth. A 21-gun salute on O'Connell Bridge, Dublin ushers in the Republic of Ireland.
- Major de Courcy Wheeler, the man who accepted the surrender of Pádraig Pearse in 1916, presents President Seán T. O'Kelly with Pearse's revolver at a special function at Áras an Uachtaráin.
- The British Government passes an act guaranteeing the position of Northern Ireland as part of the United Kingdom as long as a majority of its citizens want it to be. The government also recognises the existence of the Republic of Ireland.

- John A. Costello, Éamon de Valera, William Norton and Seán MacBride share a platform to protest the British government's attitude to the constitutional status of Northern Ireland.
- Princess Elizabeth and the Duke of Edinburgh receive the freedom of Belfast during a visit to the city.
- 80,000 people gather in Croke Park to affirm the pledge as members of the teetotal Pioneer Total Abstinence Society.
- The last Dublin tram runs from Nelson's Pillar to Blackrock.
- Douglas Hyde, first President of Ireland and founder of the Gaelic League, dies in Dublin aged 89.
- Tánaiste William Norton tells the European Consultative Assembly in Strasbourg that Ireland would not agree to a customs union of western European states.
- Street names in any language other than English are prohibited by an Amendment to a Bill passed in the Senate of Northern Ireland.
- Students and professional staff celebrate the centenary of University College Galway.

1950-1959...Ups and Downs of the 50's

Summary of the Decade

Kerry played 34 games, scoring 65-272, conceding 37-188.

Munster Championship titles: 7 (1950, 1951, 1953, 1954, 1955, 1958, 1959)

All-Ireland titles: 3 (1953, 1955, 1959)

National League titles: 1 (1959) **Minor titles:** 1 (1950)

Total Scored: 65-272

Top Scorers: Tadghie Lyne (5-56), Paudie Sheehy (5-38)

Top Points-only scorers: Tadghie Lyne (56), Paudie Sheehy (38)

Top Goals-only scorers: Tadghie Lyne (5), Paudie Sheehy (5)

Most Appearances: Paudie Sheehy (27), Jim Brosnan (24)

1950
Kerry 1-6 Clare 2-3;
Replay: Kerry 6-6 Clare 2-4;
Munster Final: Kerry 2-5 Cork 1-5;
All-Ireland semi-final: Louth 1-7 Kerry 0-8.

1951
Kerry 5-6 Waterford 1-1;
Munster Final: Kerry 1-6 Cork 0-4;
All-Ireland semi-final: Kerry 1-5 Mayo 1-5;
Replay: Mayo 2-5 Kerry 1-5.

1952
Kerry 0-14 Waterford 1-7;
Munster Final: Cork 0-11 Kerry 0-2.

1953
Kerry 6-10 Clare 0-2;
Munster Final: Kerry 2-7 Cork 2-3;
All-Ireland semi-final: Kerry 3-6 Louth 1-6;
All-Ireland Final: Kerry 0-13 Armagh 1-6.

1954
Kerry 3-10 Waterford 1-2;
Munster Final: Kerry 4-9 Cork 2-3;
All-Ireland semi-final: Kerry 2-6 Galway 1-6;
All-Ireland Final: Meath 1-13 Kerry 1-7.

1955
Kerry 3-7 Waterford 0-4;
Munster Final: Kerry 0-14 Cork 2-6;
All-Ireland semi-final: Kerry 2-10 Cavan 1-13;
Replay: Kerry 4-7 Cavan 0-5;
All-Ireland Final: Kerry 0-12 Dublin 1-6.

1956
Kerry 3-7 Tipperary 3-2;
Munster Final: Kerry 2-2 Cork 0-8;
Replay: Cork 1-8 Kerry 1-7.

1957
Waterford 2-5 Kerry 0-10

1958
Kerry 1-6 Tipperary 0-7;
Munster Final: Kerry 2-7 Cork 0-3;
All-Ireland semi-final: Derry 2-6 Kerry 2-5.

1959
Kerry 1-15 Tipperary 1-2;
Munster Final: Kerry 2-15 Cork 2-8;
All-Ireland semi-final: Kerry 1-10 Dublin 2-5;
All-Ireland Final: Kerry 3-7 Galway 1-4.

1950

Summary: Played four championship games, won Munster title for 35th time, lost All-Ireland semi-final.

Game 1 - versus Clare in Tralee on June 18. Final Score: Kerry 1-6; Clare 2-3 (Draw).

Tommy Dowling

Jas. Murphy	Paddy Bawn Brosnan	Paddy Batt Shanahan
Micksie Palmer	Jackie Lyne	Teddy O'Sullivan

Dermot Hanafin   Eddie Dowling

Padraig Murphy	Gerald O'Sullivan (0-1)	DJ McMahon (1-0)
Dan Kavanagh (0-1)	Phil McCarthy (0-1)	Batt Garvey (0-3)

No substitutes used.

Game 2 - Replay versus Clare in Limerick on July 16. Final Score: Kerry 6-6; Clare 2-4.

Liam Fitzgerald

Jas. Murphy	Donie Murphy	Paddy Bawn Brosnan
Mick Finucane	Jackie Lyne	Teddy O'Connor (1-0)

Jim Brosnan   Eddie Dowling

Teddy O'Sullivan (2-3)	Gerald O'Sullivan (0-1)	DJ McMahon
Phil McCarthy	Micksie Palmer (1-0)	Batt Garvey (1-2)

Substitutes: Pat Godley (1-0) for McMahon, Michael O'Connor for G. O'Sullivan.

Game 3 - Munster Final versus Cork in Cork on July 30. Final Score: Kerry 2-5; Cork 1-5.

Liam Fitzgerald

Jas. Murphy	Paddy Bawn Brosnan	Paddy Batt Shanahan
Mick Finucane	Jackie Lyne	Teddy O'Connor (0-1)

Jim Brosnan	Eddie Dowling	
Teddy O'Sullivan (0-2)	Phil McCarthy	Gerald O'Sullivan
Pat Godley (0-1)	Dan Kavanagh (2-1)	Batt Garvey

No substitutes used.

Game 4 - All-Ireland semi-final versus Louth in Croke Park on August 20. Final Score: Louth 1-7; Kerry 0-8.

	Liam Fitzgerald	
Jas. Murphy	Paddy Bawn Brosnan	Donie Murphy
Mick Finucane	Jackie Lyne	Teddy O'Connor
Jim Brosnan	Eddie Dowling	
Teddy O'Sullivan (0-1)	Micksie Palmer (0-1)	Pat Godley
Dan Kavanagh	Phil McCarthy (0-1)	Batt Garvey (0-4)

Substitute: Gerald O'Sullivan (0-1) for Godley.

Scorers for the Year: Teddy O'Sullivan (2-6), Batt Garvey (1-9), Dan Kavanagh (2-2), Pat Godley (1-1), Micksie Palmer (1-1), Teddy O'Connor (1-1), Gerald O'Sullivan (0-3), DJ McMahon (1-0), Phil McCarthy (0-2).

Total Scored: 9-25

Appearances:

4 - Jas. Murphy, Paddy Bawn Brosnan, Jackie Lyne, Eddie Dowling, Gerald O'Sullivan, Phil McCarthy, Batt Garvey, Teddy O'Sullivan.

3 - Liam Fitzgerald, Micksie Palmer, Mick Finucane, Teddy O'Connor, Jim Brosnan, Dan Kavanagh, Pat Godley.

2 - Paddy Batt Shanahan, Donie Murphy, DJ McMahon.

1 - Tommy Dowling, Dermot Hanafin, Padraig Murphy, Michael O'Connor.

1950 - GAA Winners:

All-Irelands: Senior Football: Mayo **Minor Football:** Kerry **Senior Hurling:** Tipperary

National Leagues: Football: Cavan   Hurling: Tipperary

Kerry Co. Champions: Football: Castleisland Hurling: Crotta

Kerry's winning minor team: D. O'Neill, M. Galway, M. Brosnan, J. Collins, T. Murphy, P. O'Donnell, J. Kerins, S. Murphy, P. Sheehy, R. Millar, C. Kennelly, C. O'Riordan, B. Galvin, T. Lawlor, P. Fitzgerald.

1950 - In The News:

- Nationalist Senators and MP's in Northern Ireland ask the government of the Republic to give Northern-elected representatives seats in the Dail and Seanad.
- At a meeting of the European Consultative Assembly in Strasbourg, Irish representatives vote against Winston Churchill's plan for a European Army.
- George Bernard Shaw dies, age 94.

Niall Flynn

1951

Summary: Played four championship games, won 36th Munster title, lost All-Ireland semi-final replay.

Game 1 - versus Waterford in Waterford on July 1. Final Score: Kerry 5-6; Waterford 1-1

Jerh Moloney

| Jas. Murphy | Paddy Bawn Brosnan | Donie Murphy |

Eddie Dowling | Jackie Lyne | Micksie Palmer

Jim Brosnan (0-1) | Dermot Hanafin

Pat Godley (0-3) | JJ Sheehan | Sean O'Connor (2-0)

Frank O'Keeffe (1-1) | Eddie Kennelly (1-0) | Tom Ashe (1-1)

Substitute: Gerald O'Sullivan for Kennelly.

Game 2 -Munster Final versus Cork in Killarney on July 15. Final Score: Kerry 1-6; Cork 0-4.

Liam Fitzgerald

Jas. Murphy | Paddy Bawn Brosnan | Donie Murphy

Eddie Dowling | Jackie Lyne | Micksie Palmer

JJ Sheehan | Dermot Hanafin (1-0)

Jim Brosnan | Tom Ashe (0-3) | Sean O'Connor (0-1)

Pat Godley (0-1) | Gerald O'Sullivan (0-1) | Frank O'Keeffe

Substitute: Paudie Sheehy for O'Keeffe.

Game 3 - All-Ireland semi-final versus Mayo in Croke Park on August 12. Final Score: Kerry 1-5; Mayo 1-5 (Draw).

Liam Fitzgerald

Jas. Murphy | Paddy Bawn Brosnan | Donie Murphy

Sean Murphy | Jackie Lyne | Micksie Palmer

JJ Sheehan (0-1)   Dermot Hanafin (0-1)

Pat Godley (1-0)   Eddie Dowling   Jim Brosnan

Tom Ashe (0-2)   Gerald O'Sullivan (0-1)   Sean O'Connor

Substitute: Tim Healy for Jas. Murphy.

Game 4 - All-Ireland semi-final replay versus Mayo in Croke Park on September 9. Final Score: Mayo 2-5; Kerry 1-5.

Liam Fitzgerald

Jas. Murphy   Paddy Bawn Brosnan   Donie Murphy

Sean Murphy   Jackie Lyne   Micksie Palmer

JJ Sheehan   Dermot Hanafin

Paudie Sheehy   Eddie Dowling (1-1)   Jim Brosnan

Pat Godley   Gerald O'Sullivan (0-1)   Tom Ashe (0-1)

Substitutes: John Dowling for Hanafin, Tim Healy for Jas. Murphy, Sean O'Connor for John Dowling, Willie O'Donnell (0-2) for Godley.

Scorers for the Year: Tom Ashe (1-7), Sean O'Connor (2-1), P. Godley (1-4), Frank O'Keeffe (1-1), Dermot Hanafin (1-1), Eddie Dowling (1-1), Eddie Kennelly (1-0), Gerald O'Sullivan (0-3), Willie O'Donnell (0-2), JJ Sheehan (0-1), Jim Brosnan (0-1).

Total Scored: 8-22

Appearances:

4 - Jas. Murphy, Paddy Bawn Brosnan, Donie Murphy, Eddie Dowling, Jackie Lyne, Micksie Palmer, Jim Brosnan, Dermot Hanafin, Pat Godley, JJ Sheehan, Sean O'Connor, Tom Ashe, Gerald O'Sullivan.

3 - Liam Fitzgerald.

2 - Sean Murphy, Tim Healy, Paudie Sheehy, Frank O'Keeffe.

1 - Jerh Moloney, Eddie Kennelly, Willie O'Donnell, John Dowling.

1951 GAA Winners:

All-Irelands: Senior Football: Mayo **Minor Football:** Roscommon

National Leagues: Football: Meath   Hurling: Galway

Senior Hurling: Tipperary

Kerry Co. Champions: Football: Dick Fitzgeralds   Hurling: Crotta

1951 - In The News:

- Éamon de Valera visits Newry for the first time since he was arrested there in 1924. He also visits Derry.
- The general election of 1951 was caused by a number of crises within the First Inter-Party Government, most notably the so-called Mother and Child Scheme. While the whole affair, which saw the resignation of the Minister for Health, Noel Browne, was not entirely to blame for the collapse of the government, it added to the pressure between the various political parties. There were other problems facing the country such as rising prices, balance of payments problems and two farmer TD's withdrew their support for the government because of rising milk prices.
- Although the first inter-party government was now coming to an end, it had a number of achievements. It proved that the country could be led by a group other than Fianna Fail. It also provided a fresh perspective after sixteen years of unbroken rule by that party. The coalition parties fought the general election on their record on government over the previous three years, while Fianna Fáil argued strongly against coalition governments.
- Of the 147 available seats, Fianna Fail, led by Éamon de Valera, took 68 seats, with Richard Mulcahy's Fine Gael taking 40, while William Norton led Labour to 16, and Joseph Blowick and Sean MacBride led Clann na Talmhan and Clann na Poblachta to 6 and 2 seats respectively. In addition, 14 Independents were returned, plus the outgoing Ceann Comhairle to form the 14th Dail.
- The 1951 election result was inconclusive. Fianna Fáil's support increased by 61,000 votes, however, the party only gained one extra seat. The coalition parties had mixed fortunes. Fine Gael being the big winners, increasing to 40 seats. The Labour Party patched up its differences with the National Labour Party and fought the election together. In spite of this, the party lost seats. Clann na Poblachta

were the big losers of the election, in the space of three years, the party went from being a big political threat to being shattered.

- Fianna Fáil had not won enough seats to govern alone. However, the party was able to form a government with the support of Noel Browne, the sacked Minister for Health, and other Independent deputies. Éamon de Valera was elected Taoiseach on a vote of 74-69.

- Kerry return the following members to the 14th Dáil:

  Kerry South: Honor Crowley (Fianna Fail), John Flynn (FF), and Patrick Palmer (Fine Gael).

  Kerry North: John Lynch (Fine Gael), Patrick Finucane (Independent), Thomas McEllistrim (Fianna Fail) and Dan Spring (Labour).

1952

Summary: Played two championship games, losing in the Munster Final.

Game 1 - versus Waterford in Tralee on July 6. Final Score: Kerry 0-14; Waterford 1-7.

Donal O'Neill

Jas. Murphy	Jackie Lyne	Jerome O'Shea
Sean Murphy	Jerome Spillane	Micksie Palmer

Dermot Hanafin   Brendan O'Shea

Paudie Sheehy (0-4)	Padraig Murphy	Tadghie Lyne (0-3)
Jim Brosnan (0-2)	Sean Kelly (0-5)	Colm Kennelly

No substitutes used.

Game 2 - Munster Final versus Cork in Cork on July 20. Final Score: Cork 0-11; Kerry 0-2.

Donal O'Neill

Jas. Murphy	Paddy Bawn Brosnan	Gerald O'Sullivan
Sean Murphy	Jackie Lyne	Micksie Palmer

Dermot Hanafin   Brendan O'Shea

Paudie Sheehy	JJ Sheehan	Tadghie Lyne
Jim Brosnan (0-1)	Sean Kelly	Tom Ashe

Substitutes: Brendan Galvin (0-1) for Tom Ashe, Colm Kennelly for Sean Murphy, Eddie Dowling for Tadghie Lyne, Teddy O'Connor for Micksie Palmer.

Scorers for the Year: Sean Kelly (0-5), Paudie Sheehy (0-4), Tadghie Lyne (0-3), Jim Brosnan (0-3), B. Galvin (0-1).

Total Scored: 0-16

Appearances:

2 - Donal O'Neill, Jas. Murphy, Jackie Lyne, Sean Murphy, Micksie Palmer, Dermot Hanafin, Brendan O'Shea, Paudie Sheehy, Tadghie Lyne, Jim Brosnan, Sean Kelly, Colm Kennelly.

1 - Paddy Bawn Brosnan, Jerome O'Shea, Gerald O'Sullivan, Jerome Spillane, Eddie Dowling, JJ Sheehan, Padraig Murphy, Tom Ashe, Brendan Galvin, Teddy O'Connor.

1952 - GAA Winners:

All-Irelands: Senior Football: Cavan **Minor Football:** Galway

National Leagues: Football: Cork　　Hurling: Tipperary

Senior Hurling: Cork

Kerry Co. Champions: Football: John Mitchels　　Hurling: Ardfert

1952 - In The News:

- In the presidential election of 1952, the second held since the creation of the office in 1937, the outgoing president, Sean T. O'Kelly decided to seek a second term. No party opposed him, though independent satirist Eoin (the Pope) O'Mahony tried and failed to be nominated. With only one nominated candidate, O'Kelly was re-elected without the need to hold a poll.
- An Aer Lingus aircraft crashed in Wales, killing twenty passengers and the crew. It is the airline's first fatal crash in its fifteen-year history.
- Peig Sayers visits Dublin for the first time in her 81 years.
- The Adoption Bill makes provision for the adoption of orphans and children aged between six months and seven years born outside wedlock.
- Minister for Education, Sean Moylan, announces longer summer holidays for national school children.

1953

Summary: Played four championship games, won 37th Munster title, won All-Ireland for 17th time.

Game 1 - versus Clare in Ennis on July 5. Final Score: Kerry 6-10; Clare 0-2.

Donal O'Neill

Jas. Murphy	Ned Roche	Jerome O'Shea
Colm Kennelly	John Cronin	Micksie Palmer

Gerald O'Sullivan   Brendan O'Shea

Paudie Sheehy (3-3)	Bobby Buckley	Tadghie Lyne (0-2)
Jim Brosnan (0-2)	Sean Kelly (1-2)	Jackie Lyne (2-1)

No substitutes used.

Game 2 - Munster Final versus Cork in Killarney on July 19. Final Score: Kerry 2-7; Cork 2-3.

Donal O'Neill

Jas. Murphy	Ned Roche	Jerome O'Shea
Colm Kennelly	John Cronin	Micksie Palmer

Gerald O'Sullivan   Brendan O'Shea

Paudie Sheehy (0-1)	Sean Murphy	Tadghie Lyne (0-4)
Jim Brosnan (0-1)	Sean Kelly (1-0)	Jackie Lyne (0-1)

Substitutes: Tom Ashe (1-0) for Micksie Palmer, Bobby Buckley for Jackie Lyne.

Game 3 - All-Ireland semi-final versus Louth in Croke Park on August 23. Final Score: Kerry 3-6; Louth 1-6.

Johnny Foley

Jas. Murphy	Ned Roche	Donie Murphy
Colm Kennelly	John Cronin	Sean Murphy

	Brendan O'Shea	Bobby Buckley	

Paudie Sheehy (0-2)	Jim Brosnan	Tadghie Lyne (0-1)
Tom Ashe (2-0)	Sean Kelly (1-1)	Jackie Lyne

Substitutes: Gerald O'Sullivan (0-1) for Jim Brosnan, Micksie Palmer for Colm Kennelly, Mick Brosnan (0-1) for Micksie Palmer, Jim Brosnan for Tom Ashe.

Game 4 - All-Ireland Final versus Armagh in Croke Park on September 27. Final Score: Kerry 0-13; Armagh 1-6.

Johnny Foley

Jas. Murphy	Ned Roche	Donie Murphy
Colm Kennelly	John Cronin	Micksie Palmer

Sean Murphy   Dermot Hanafin

Jim Brosnan (0-4)	JJ Sheehan (0-3)	Tadghie Lyne (0-4)
Tom Ashe (0-1)	Sean Kelly	Jackie Lyne (0-1)

Substitutes: Gerald O'Sullivan for Dermot Hanafin.

Scorers for the Year: Paudie Sheehy (3-6), Sean Kelly (3-3), Tadghie Lyne (0-11), Tom Ashe (3-1), Jackie Lyne (2-3), Jim Brosnan (0-7), JJ Sheehan (0-3), Gerald O'Sullivan (0-1), Mick Brosnan (0-1).

Total Scored: 11-36

Appearances:

4 - Jas. Murphy, Ned Roche, Colm Kennelly, John Cronin, Micksie Palmer, Gerald O'Sullivan, Tadghie Lyne, Jim Brosnan, Sean Kelly, Jackie Lyne.

3 - Brendan O'Shea, Sean Murphy, Paudie Sheehy, Bobby Buckley, Tom Ashe.

2 - Donal O'Neill, Johnny Foley, Jerome O'Shea, Donie Murphy.

1 - Mick Brosnan, JJ Sheehan, Dermot Hanafin.

1953 - GAA Winners:

All-Irelands: Senior Football: Kerry **Minor Football:** Mayo

National Leagues: Football: Dublin   Hurling: Cork

Senior Hurling: Cork

Kerry Co. Champions: Football: Kerins O'Rahillys   Hurling: Kilgarvan

1953 - In The News:

- Sinn Fein decides to contest all 12 constituencies in the next Westminster elections in Northern Ireland, while 3 Independent TD's become members of Fianna Fail.
- Up to 10,000 civil servants march down O'Connell Street in Dublin demanding a just wage. 500 unemployed men march at Kildare Street demanding jobs, not dole. 1,000 unemployed people sit on O'Connell Bridge a few weeks later for 15 minutes in protest.
- Franklin D. Roosevelt asks Congress to support a United Ireland. Kilmainham Gaol is to be preserved as a national monument.
- The Irish Censorship Board bans almost 100 publications on the grounds that they are indecent or obscene.

1954

Summary: Played four championship games, won Munster title for 38th time, but lost the All-Ireland Final.

Game 1 - versus Waterford in Waterford on July 4. Final Score: Kerry 3-10; Waterford 1-2.

Gerard Stack

Jas. Murphy	Ned Roche	Donie Murphy
Sean Murphy	Brendan O'Shea	Micksie Palmer

Tom Moriarty (0-1)   Colm Kennelly (0-1)

Jim Brosnan	JJ Sheehan (0-1)	Paudie Sheehy (0-2)
Bobby Buckley (2-1)	Sean Kelly (0-2)	Jackie Lyne (1-2)

No substitutes used.

Game 2 - Munster Final versus Cork in Cork on July 25. Final Score: Kerry 4-9; Cork 2-3.

Gerard Stack

Micksie Palmer	Ned Roche	Donie Murphy
Sean Murphy	John Cronin	Colm Kennelly

John Dowling   Bobby Buckley

Paudie Sheehy (0-3)	Tom Moriarty (0-1)	Tadghie Lyne (0-1)
Jim Brosnan (2-1)	Sean Kelly (1-2)	Jackie Lyne (1-1)

Substitute: Jerome O'Shea for John Cronin.

Game 3 - All-Ireland semi-final versus Galway in Croke Park on August 15. Final Score: Kerry 2-6; Galway 1-6.

Gerard Stack

John Cronin	Donie Murphy	Micksie Palmer
Sean Murphy	JJ Sheehan	Colm Kennelly

John Dowling		Bobby Buckley
Paudie Sheehy (1-1)	Tom Moriarty	Tadghie Lyne (1-3)
Jim Brosnan (0-1)	Sean Kelly (0-1)	Jackie Lyne

No substitutes used.

Game 4 - All-Ireland Final versus Meath in Croke Park on September 26. Final Score: Meath 1-13; Kerry 1-7.

Garry O'Mahony

Micksie Palmer	Ned Roche	Donie Murphy
Sean Murphy	John Cronin	Colm Kennelly

John Dowling		Tom Moriarty
Bobby Buckley	JJ Sheehan (1-1)	Paudie Sheehy
Jim Brosnan (0-2)	Sean Kelly	Tadghie Lyne (0-4)

No substitutes used.

Scorers for the Year: Tadghie Lyne (1-8), Jim Brosnan (2-4), Jackie Lyne (2-3), Paudie Sheehy (1-6), Sean Kelly (1-5), Bobby Buckley (2-1), JJ Sheehan (1-2), Tom Moriarty (0-2), Colm Kennelly (0-1).

Total Scored: 10-32

Appearances:

4 - Donie Murphy, Sean Murphy, Micksie Palmer, Tom Moriarty, Colm Kennelly, Jim Brosnan, Paudie Sheehy, Bobby Buckley, Sean Kelly.

3 - Gerard Stack, Ned Roche, John Cronin, John Dowling, JJ Sheehan, Tadghie Lyne, Jackie Lyne.

2 - None.

1 - Garry O'Mahony, Jas. Murphy, Brendan O'Shea, Jerome O'Shea.

1954 - GAA Winners:

All-Irelands: Senior Football: Meath **Minor Football:** Dublin

National Leagues: Football: Mayo   Hurling: Tipperary

Senior Hurling: Cork

Kerry Juniors also take All-Ireland honours with the following team: N. Hussey, T. Spillane, J. O'Connor, T. Healy, T. Costelloe, J. Spillane, D. Falvey, E. Fitzgerald, D. Dillon, J. Culloty, T. Collins, S. Lovett, P. Fitzgerald, E. Dowling, B. Galvin.

Kerry Co. Champions: Football: Kerins O'Rahillys   Hurling: Lixnaw

1954 - In The News:

- Government announces that Cork Airport will be built in Ballygarvan, four miles from the city.
- Michael Manning, aged 25, is the last person to be judicially executed in the State.
- Fianna Fail win 65 seats, Fine Gael 50, Labour 18, Clann na Talmhan 5, Clann na Poblachta 3, Independents 5, plus the outgoing Ceann Comhairle. This resulted in the formation of the second Inter-Party Government which led from 1954 to 1957. The combined parties of Fine Gael, Labour, and Clann na Talmhan formed this government, with Fine Gael's John A. Costello as Taoiseach.
- Kerry return the following members to the 15th Dáil:
  Kerry South: Honor Crowley (Fianna Fail), John Flynn (FF), and Patrick Palmer (Fine Gael).
  Kerry North: Johnny Connor (Clann na Poblachta), Patrick Finucane (Clann na Talmhan), Thomas McEllistrim (Fianna Fail), and Dan Spring (Labour).

1955

Summary: Played five championship games, won 39th Munster title, won 18th All-Ireland title.

Game 1 - versus Waterford in Listowel on July 3. Final Score: Kerry 3-7; Waterford 0-4.

Garry O'Mahony

Jerome O'Shea	Ned Roche	Donie Murphy
Colm Kennelly	John Cronin	Tom Spillane

John Dowling   Tom Moriarty

Paudie Sheehy	Bobby Buckley (1-0)	Tadghie Lyne (0-3)
Gerald O'Sullivan (0-1)	Mick Murphy (0-1)	Tom Costelloe (2-2)

No substitutes used.

Game 2-Munster Final versus Cork in Killarney on July 24. Final Score: Kerry 0-14; Cork 2-6.

Garry O'Mahony

Jerome O'Shea	Donie Murphy	Micksie Palmer
Sean Murphy	John Cronin	Bobby Buckley

Dinny O'Shea   John Dowling (0-1)

Paudie Sheehy (0-5)	Tom Moriarty	Tadghie Lyne (0-4)
Gerald O'Sullivan (0-1)	Mick Murphy (0-2)	Dan McAuliffe (0-1)

Substitutes used: Colm Kennelly, Johnny Culloty.

Game 3 - All-Ireland semi-final versus Cavan in Croke Park on August 4. Final Score: Kerry 2-10; Cavan 1-13 (Draw).

Garry O'Mahony

Jerome O'Shea	Ned Roche	Micksie Palmer
Sean Murphy	John Cronin	Bobby Buckley

Dinny O'Shea	John Dowling (0-1)	
Paudie Sheehy	Tom Moriarty (0-1)	Tadghie Lyne (1-6)
Johnny Culloty (0-1)	Mick Murphy (1-0)	Dan McAuliffe (0-1)

Substitutes: Colm Kennelly for Bobby Buckley, Ned Fitzgerald for Tadghie Lyne.

Game 4 - All-Ireland semi-final replay versus Cavan in Croke Park on September 11. Final Score: Kerry 4-7; Cavan 0-5.

Garry O'Mahony

Jerome O'Shea	Ned Roche	Micksie Palmer
Sean Murphy	John Cronin	Colm Kennelly

John Dowling		Dinny O'Shea

Paudie Sheehy (0-2)	JJ Sheehan (1-0)	Tadghie Lyne (0-5)
Johnny Culloty (1-0)	Tom Costelloe	Mick Murphy (2-0)

Substitute: Tom Moriarty for Colm Kennelly.

Game 5 - All-Ireland Final versus Dublin in Croke Park on September 25. Final Score: Kerry 0-12; Dublin 1-6.

Garry O'Mahony

Jerome O'Shea	Ned Roche	Micksie Palmer
Sean Murphy	John Cronin	Tom Moriarty

John Dowling (0-1)		Dinny O'Shea

Paudie Sheehy (0-1)	Tom Costelloe	Tadghie Lyne (0-6)
Johnny Culloty	Mick Murphy (0-1)	Jim Brosnan (0-2)

Substitute: JJ Sheehan (0-1) for Tom Moriarty.

Scorers for the Year: Tadghie Lyne (1-24), Mick Murphy (3-4), Tom Costelloe (2-2), Paudie Sheehy (0-8), JJ Sheehan (1-1), Johnny Culloty (1-1), John Dowling (0-3), Bobby Buckley (1-0), Jim Brosnan (0-2), Dan McAuliffe (0-2), Gerald O'Sullivan (0-2), Tom Moriarty (0-1).

Total Scored: 9-50

Appearances:

5 - Garry O'Mahony, Jerome O'Shea, John Cronin, John Dowling, Tom Moriarty, Paudie Sheehy, Tadghie Lyne, Mick Murphy.

4 - Ned Roche, Micksie Palmer, Colm Kennelly, Sean Murphy, Dinny O'Shea, Johnny Culloty.

3 - Bobby Buckley, Tom Costelloe.

2 - Donie Murphy, Gerald O'Sullivan, Dan McAuliffe, JJ Sheehan.

1 - Tom Spillane, Ned Fitzgerald, Jim Brosnan.

1955 - GAA Winners:

All-Irelands: Senior Football: Kerry **Minor Football:** Dublin

National Leagues: Football: Dublin   Hurling: Tipperary

Senior Hurling: Wexford

Kerry Co. Champions: Football: South Kerry   Hurling: Ballyduff

1955 - In The News:

- 1200 people meet in Dublin to form the National Farmer's Association (NFA), which later merged with four smaller organisations representing specific sectors (including beet growers, horticulture, and fresh milk producers) to form the Irish Farmers Association - the IFA.
- Bord na gCon is set up under the Greyhound Industry Bill.
- Ireland is admitted to the United Nations.

1956

Summary: Played three championship games, won 40th Munster title, lost the All-Ireland semi-final.

Game 1 - versus Tipperary in Tralee on June 24. Final Score: Kerry 3-7; Tipperary 3-2.

Garry O'Mahony

Jerome O'Shea	Ned Roche	Jack Dowling
Bobby Buckley	Tom Moriarty	Dinny O'Shea

John Dowling (0-1)   Mick O'Connell (0-1)

Paudie Sheehy (0-1)	Tom Long	Dan McAuliffe (0-1)
Jim Brosnan (0-1)	John Cronin (2-1)	Tadghie Lyne (1-1)

Substitute: Gerald O'Sullivan for Tom Long.

Game 2 - Munster Final versus Cork in Cork on July 15. Final Score: Kerry 2-2; Cork 0-8 (Draw).

Donal O'Neill

Jerome O'Shea	Ned Roche	Tim Lyons
Sean Murphy	Tom Moriarty	Tom Long

John Dowling (0-1)   Mick O'Connell

Paudie Sheehy	Colm Kennelly	Tadghie Lyne (0-1)
Jim Brosnan (1-0)	John Cronin	Dan McAuliffe

Substitute: Dinny O'Shea (1-0) for Tom Moriarty.

Game 3 - Munster Final Replay versus Cork in Killarney on July 29. Final Score: Cork 1-8; Kerry 1-7.

Donal O'Neill

Jerome O'Shea	Ned Roche	Tim Lyons
Sean Murphy	Tom Long	Colm Kennelly

John Dowling (0-1)		Dinny O'Shea
Mick O'Connell	Bobby Buckley	Tadghie Lyne (0-2)
Jim Brosnan (0-1)	John Cronin (1-0)	Paudie Sheehy (0-3)

Substitutes: Mick Murphy for Colm Kennelly, Tom Moriarty for Tadghie Lyne, Tom Collins for Mick Murphy.

Scorers for the Year: John Cronin (3-1), Tadghie Lyne (1-4), Jim Brosnan (1-2), Paudie Sheehy (0-4), John Dowling (0-3), Dinny O'Shea (1-0), Mick O'Connell (0-1), Dan McAuliffe (0-1).

Total Scored: 6-16

Appearances:

3 - Jerome O'Shea, Ned Roche, Tom Moriarty, Dinny O'Shea, John Dowling, Mick O'Connell, Paudie Sheehy, Tom Long, Jim Brosnan, John Cronin, Tadghie Lyne.

2 - Donal O'Neill, Tim Lyons, Bobby Buckley, Sean Murphy, Colm Kennelly, Dan McAuliffe.

1 - Garry O'Mahony, Jack Dowling, Tom Collins, Mick Murphy, Gerald O'Sullivan.

1956 - GAA Winners:

All-Irelands: Senior Football: Galway **Minor Football:** Dublin

National Leagues: Football: Cork   Hurling: Wexford

Senior Hurling: Wexford

Kerry Co. Champions: Football: South Kerry   Hurling: Kilgarvan

1956 - In The News:

- Senator Owen Sheehy-Skeffington introduces a motion calling for the prohibition of all corporal punishment for girls in Irish national schools.
- The Minister for Education, Richard Mulcahy, introduces the debate on a separate government department for the Gaeltacht.

- President Sean T. O'Kelly opens the first Cork International Film Festival.
- The GAA postpones the All-Ireland Hurling and Football Finals due to an outbreak of polio.
- Petrol rationing will be introduced from January 1 due to the crisis in the Suez.
- At the Olympic Games in Melbourne, Ronnie Delaney wins Ireland's first gold medal for 24 years.

1957

Summary: Played one championship game.

Game 1 - versus Waterford in Waterford on June 2. Final Score: Waterford 2-5; Kerry 0-10.

Tim Barrett

Jerome O'Shea	Ned Roche	Tim Lyons
Mick O'Dwyer	John Dowling	Michael Kerins

Mick O'Connell (0-1)   Tom Long

Paudie Sheehy (0-1)	Ned Fitzgerald (0-3)	Tadghie Lyne (0-2)
Pop Fitzgerald (0-1)	Tom Collins (0-1)	Dan McAuliffe (0-1)

Substitute: Dinny O'Shea for Tom Collins.

1957 - GAA Winners:

All-Irelands: Senior Football: Louth **Minor Football:** Meath

National Leagues: Football: Galway   Hurling: Tipperary

Senior Hurling: Kilkenny

Kerry Co. Champions: Football: Kerins O'Rahillys   Hurling: Ballyduff

1957 - In The News:

- Sean South and Fergal O'Hanlon are both killed in an IRA attack on an RUC barracks in Fermanagh. The two men become part of republican folklore.
- Sir Alfred Chester Beatty becomes the first honourary Irish citizen. Born in New York in 1875, he graduated university as a mining engineer. He made his fortune mining in Colorado, USA, and other mining concerns the world over. He was often called the "King of Copper". A collector from an early age, by the 1940s he built up a remarkable and impressive collection of Oriental art and books. He also owned 19 ancient Egyptian papyri that he gave to the British Museum, including the Chester Beatty Biblical Papyri and the Chester Beatty Medical Papyrus. He moved his collections

to Dublin in 1950. The Chester Beatty Library which houses the collection was moved to Dublin Castle from Shrewsbury Road in 2000. On his death in 1968, he was accorded a state funeral - the only private citizen in Irish history to receive such an honour. He is buried in Glasnevin Cemetery, Dublin.

- Fianna Fail returns to power winning 78 seats of the 147 in the general election. Éamon de Valera is elected Taoiseach.
- Kerry return the following members to the 16th Dáil:
  Kerry South: Honor Crowley (Fianna Fail), Patrick Palmer (Fine Gael), John Joe Rice (Sinn Fein).
  Kerry North: Patrick Finucane (Independent), Thomas McEllistrim (Fianna Fail), Daniel Moloney (Fianna Fail), and Dan Spring (Labour).
- Prize Bonds are introduced, with the Bank of Ireland operating the scheme on behalf of the Minister for Finance.
- Dáil debates the Fethard-on-Sea "Ne Temere" boycott. *Ne Temere* (literally meaning "not rashly" in Latin) was a 1908 decree (named for its opening words) of the Roman Catholic Congregation of the Council regulating the canon law of the Church about marriage for Roman Catholics. The result made official civil marriages difficult for lapsed Catholics in some Church-dominated nations. Also, because a priest could refuse to perform mixed marriages between Roman Catholics and non-Roman Catholics, he could impose conditions such as an obligation for any children to be baptised and brought up as Catholics, and for the non-Catholic partners to submit to religious education with the aim of converting them to Catholicism.
- In May 1957, Fethard-on-Sea, Co. Wexford, found itself embroiled in controversy related to the decree. A Roman Catholic priest, Father Stafford, and his parishioners started a boycott of Protestant-owned local businesses; a Protestant music teacher lost 12 of her 13 pupils and the Catholic teacher of the local Protestant school was forced to resign. The boycott was in response to the actions of a Protestant woman, Sheila Kelly Cloney. Mrs. Cloney had left both her Catholic husband, Sean Cloney, and the village, taking her two daughters, rather than sending them to the local National (Catholic) School as Father Stafford demanded. The boycott received national and international coverage through the summer (some TDs regarded this as a case of kidnapping), before ending that autumn. Sean Cloney himself was boycotted as he continued to frequent the Protestant shops. Eventually, the family was reconciled, with the daughters being home-schooled and not attending either parents' church. In

1998, the diocese's bishop publicly apologised for the boycott. Ne Temere was replaced in 1970 with the more relaxed Matrimonia Mixta.

- The Minister for Health, Sean MacEntee, launches the Voluntary Health Insurance Board.
- The Windscale fire begins with a fire in a graphite core of a reactor at the Windscale Nuclear Power Station and Reprocessing Centre in Cumbria, Northern England, now known as Sellafield. Years later there are claims that the radiation caused cancers and birth defects in Co. Louth.
- The Soviet satellite Sputnik is visible over Dublin for the second time in a month.

1958

Summary: Played three championship games, won 40th Munster final, lost All-Ireland semi-final.

Game 1 - versus Tipperary in Thurles on June 29. Final Score: Kerry 1-6; Tipperary 0-7.

Tom Fitzgerald

Jerome O'Shea   Ned Roche   Tim Lyons

Sean Murphy   Jack Dowling   Mick O'Dwyer (1-1)

Mick O'Connell   Dinny O'Shea

Seamus Murphy   Mick Murphy   Paudie Sheehy (0-1)

Ned Fitzgerald (0-1)   Garry McMahon (0-1)   Tadghie Lyne

Substitutes: Dan McAuliffe (0-1) for Dinny O'Shea, Kevin Coffey for Tadghie Lyne, John Dowling (0-1) for Dan McAuliffe.

Game 2 - Munster Final versus Cork in Cork on July 13. Final Score: Kerry 2-7; Cork 0-3.

Tom Fitzgerald

Jerome O'Shea   Ned Roche   Tim Lyons

Sean Murphy   Jack Dowling   Mick O'Dwyer

John Dowling (0-4)   Seamus Murphy

Kevin Coffey   Mick O'Connell   Paudie Sheehy (0-1)

Garry McMahon (2-2)   Mick Murphy   Niall Sheehy

Substitutes: Tadghie Lyne for Mick O'Connell, Tom Moriarty for Niall Sheehy.

Game 3 - All-Ireland semi-final versus Derry in Croke Park on August 24. Final Score: Derry 2-6; Kerry 2-5.

Donal O'Neill

Jerome O'Shea   Ned Roche   Jack Dowling

Sean Murphy	Tom Moriarty	Mick O'Dwyer
John Dowling		Seamus Murphy
Mick O'Connell	Tom Long	Tadghie Lyne (2-2)
Garry McMahon (0-1)	Mick Murphy	Paudie Sheehy (0-2)

Substitutes: Moss O'Connell for Tom Moriarty, Niall Sheehy for Mick Murphy.

Scorers for the Year: Garry McMahon (2-4), Tadghie Lyne (2-2), John Dowling (0-5), Paudie Sheehy (0-4), Mick O'Dwyer (1-1), Ned Fitzgerald (0-1), Dan McAuliffe (0-1).

Total Scored: 5-18

Appearances:

3 - Jerome O'Shea, Ned Roche, Sean Murphy, Jack Dowling, Mick O'Dwyer, Mick O'Connell, Seamus Murphy, Mick Murphy, Paudie Sheehy, Garry McMahon, Tadghie Lyne, John Dowling.

2 - Tom Fitzgerald, Tim Lyons, Tom Moriarty, Niall Sheehy, Kevin Coffey.

1 - Donal O'Neill, Moss O'Connell, Dinny O'Shea, Tom Long, Ned Fitzgerald, Dan McAuliffe.

1958 - GAA Winners:

All-Irelands: Senior Football: Dublin **Minor Football:** Dublin

National Leagues: Football: Dublin   Hurling: Wexford

Senior Hurling: Tipperary

Kerry Co. Champions: Football: South Kerry   Hurling: Kilgarvan

1958 - In The News:

- Manchester United's team plane crashes in Munich.
- The Minister for Education, Jack Lynch, tells the Dail that the ruling requiring women teachers to retire on marriage is to be revoked.
- Australian Herb Elliott shatters the world record for the mile at Santry Stadium, with a time of 3 minutes 54.5 seconds.

- Pan Am's Boeing 707 becomes the first jetliner to touch down on European soil at Shannon Airport.
- Brendan Behan's *Borstal Boy* is banned by the Censorship of Publications Board.

1959

Summary: Played four championship games, won 41ˢᵗ Munster title, won 19ᵗʰ All-Ireland title.

Game 1 - versus Tipperary in Killarney on July 5. Final Score: Kerry 1-15; Tipperary 1-2.

Johnny Culloty

Jerome O'Shea   Niall Sheehy   Tim Lyons

Mickey Ashe   Kevin Coffey   Moss O'Connell

Mick O'Connell (0-3)   Seamus Murphy (0-2)

Dan McAuliffe (1-4)   Tom Long (0-1)   Paudie Sheehy (0-1)

Dave Geaney   John Dowling (0-2)   Jim Brosnan (0-2)

No substitutes used.

Game 2 - Munster Final versus Cork in Killarney on August 2. Final Score: Kerry 2-15; Cork 2-8.

Johnny Culloty

Jerome O'Shea   Jack Dowling   Tim Lyons

Sean Murphy   Kevin Coffey   Mick O'Dwyer

Mick O'Connell (0-1)   Seamus Murphy (0-1)

Dan McAuliffe (0-7)   Tom Long (0-1)   Paudie Sheehy (1-1)

Dave Geaney (1-1)   John Dowling (0-1)   Jim Brosnan (0-2)

No substitutes used.

Game 3 - All-Ireland semi-final versus Dublin in Croke Park on August 16. Final Score: Kerry 1-10; Dublin 2-5.

Johnny Culloty

Jerome O'Shea   Niall Sheehy   Mick O'Dwyer

Sean Murphy   Kevin Coffey   Moss O'Connell

Mick O'Connell (0-2)   Seamus Murphy

Dan McAuliffe (1-4)   Tom Long (0-1)   Paudie Sheehy (0-3)

Dave Geaney   John Dowling   Jim Brosnan

Substitutes: Tim Lyons for Moss O'Connell, Moss O'Connell for Dave Geaney, Garry McMahon for Jim Brosnan.

Game 4 - All-Ireland Final versus Galway in Croke Park on September 27. Final Score: Kerry 3-7; Galway 1-4.

Johnny Culloty

Jerome O'Shea   Niall Sheehy   Tim Lyons

Sean Murphy   Kevin Coffey   Mick O'Dwyer (0-1)

Mick O'Connell   Seamus Murphy

Dan McAuliffe (2-2)   Tom Long   Paudie Sheehy

Dave Geaney   John Dowling (0-2)   Tadghie Lyne (0-2)

Substitutes: Jack Dowling for Tim Lyons, Moss O'Connell for Mick O'Connell, Garry McMahon (1-0) for Dave Geaney.

Scorers for the Year: Dan McAuliffe (4-17), Paudie Sheehy (1-5), Mick O'Connell (0-6), John Dowling (0-5), Jim Brosnan (0-4), Dave Geaney (1-1), Garry McMahon (1-0), Tom Long (0-3), Seamus Murphy (0-3), Tadghie Lyne (0-2), Mick O'Dwyer (0-1).

Total Scored: 7-47

Appearances:

4 - Johnny Culloty, Jerome O'Shea, Tim Lyons, Kevin Coffey, Mick O'Connell, Seamus Murphy, Dan McAuliffe, Tom Long, Paudie Sheehy, Dave Geaney, John Dowling.

3 - Niall Sheehy, Moss O'Connell, Sean Murphy, Mick O'Dwyer, Jim Brosnan.

2 - Jack Dowling, Garry McMahon.

1 - M. Ashe, Tadghie Lyne.

1959 - GAA Winners:

All-Irelands: Senior Football: Kerry **Minor Football:** Dublin

National Leagues: Football: Kerry   Hurling: Tipperary

Senior Hurling: Waterford

Kerry Co. Champions: Football: John Mitchels   Hurling: Ballyduff

1959 - In The News:

- The Dail debates a motion that Éamon de Valera's position as controlling director of the *Irish Press* could be regarded as incompatible with his duties as Taoiseach. It is not carried.
- The government is considering introduction of a Pay-As-You-Earn system of income tax. The new Department of Transport and Power is established, with Erskine H. Childers as the first Minister.
- Fine Gael's James Dillon wants to abolish compulsory Irish as he feels it is counter-productive.
- The presidential election of 1959 was held on June 17. Fianna Fail's founder and long term leader, Éamon de Valera, then Taoiseach, decided to leave active party politics and seek the presidency. The main opposition party, Fine Gael, decided to run its defeated candidate from 1945, Sean Mac Eoin. Éamon de Valera won by a vote count of 538,003 to 417,536, a 56.3% to 47.6% margin.
- Three men collapse and die at Croke Park during the All-Ireland Hurling Final Replay.
- James Dillon is elected leader of the Fine Gael Party, replacing Richard Mulcahy.
- Twelve new female members of An Garda Siochana, known as banghardaí, pass out of the training depot in the Phoenix Park.

1960-1969…More Down…and Galway too

Summary of the Decade

Kerry played 35 games, scoring 45-432, conceding 39-260.

Munster Championship titles: 8 (1960, 1961, 1962, 1963, 1964, 1965, 1968, 1969)

All Ireland titles: 2 (1962, 1969)

National League titles: 3 (1961, 1963, 1969) **U-21 titles:** 1 (1964)

Minor titles: 2 (1962, 1963)

Top Scorers: Mick O'Connell (1-85), Mick O'Dwyer (3-50)

Top Points-only scorers: Mick O'Connell (85), Mick O'Dwyer (50)

Top Goals-only scorers: Bernie O'Callaghan (5), Tom Long (5)

Most Appearances: Mick O'Connell (33), Johnny Culloty (30), Seamus Murphy (30)

1960
Kerry 0-11 Tipperary 0-3;
Munster Final: Kerry 3-15 Waterford 0-8;
All-Ireland semi-final: Kerry 1-8 Galway 0-8;
All-Ireland Final: Down 2-10 Kerry 0-8.

1961
Kerry 1-13 Clare 1-0;
Munster Final: Kerry 4-8 Cork 0-4;
All-Ireland semi-final: Kerry 2-12 Dublin 0-12;
All-Ireland Final: Kerry 1-12 Roscommon 1-6.

1962
Kerry 2-18 Waterford 2-6;
Munster Final: Kerry 0-10 Cork 1-7;
Replay: Kerry 2-13 Cork 1-4;
All-Ireland semi-final: Down 1-12 Kerry 0-9.

1963
Kerry 5-10 Tipperary 1-6;
Munster Final: Kerry 1-18 Cork 3-7;
All-Ireland semi-final: Galway 1-7 Kerry 0-8.

1964
Kerry 1-14 Tipperary 1-7;
Munster Final: Kerry 2-11 Cork 1-8;
All-Ireland semi-final: Kerry 2-12 Cavan 0-6;
All-Ireland Final: Galway 0-15 Kerry 0-10.

1965
Kerry 2-10 Clare 1-6;
Munster Final: Kerry 2-16 Limerick 2-7;
All-Ireland semi-final: Kerry 4-8 Dublin 2-6;
All-Ireland Final: Galway 0-12 Kerry 0-9.

1966
Kerry 3-16 Tipperary 2-6;
Munster Final: Cork 2-7 Kerry 1-7.

1967
Kerry 1-17 Limerick 1-8;
Munster Final: Cork 0-8 Kerry 0-7.

1968
Kerry 0-17 Tipperary 2-7;
Munster Final: Kerry 1-21 Cork 3-8;
All-Ireland semi-final: Kerry 2-13 Longford 2-11;
All-Ireland Final: Down 2-12 Kerry 1-13.

1969
Kerry 1-18 Waterford 2-7;
Munster Final: Kerry 0-16 Cork 1-4;
All-Ireland semi-final: Kerry 0-14 Mayo 1-10;
All-Ireland Final: Kerry 0-10 Offaly 0-7.

1960

Summary: Played four championship games, won 42nd Munster title, lost All-Ireland Final.

Game 1 - versus Tipperary in Clonmel on July 10. Final Score: Kerry 0-11; Tipperary 0-3.

Johnny Culloty

Jerome O'Shea	Niall Sheehy	Tim Lyons
Pat Dowling	Jack Dowling	Mick O'Dwyer

Kevin Coffey (0-2)　　　　Mick O'Connell (0-1)

Dan McAuliffe (0-1)	Tom Long (0-1)	Paudie Sheehy (0-4)
Dave Geaney	John Dowling (0-2)	Garry McMahon

No substitutes used.

Game 2-Munster Final versus Waterford in Cork on July 24. Score: Kerry 3-15; Waterford 0-8.

Johnny Culloty

Jerome O'Shea	Niall Sheehy	Tim Lyons
Pat Dowling	Kevin Coffey	Mick O'Dwyer

Mick O'Connell (0-3)　　　　JD O'Connor (0-1)

Dave Geaney (0-1)	Tom Long (1-2)	Paudie Sheehy (1-4)
Garry McMahon	John Dowling (1-0)	Seamus Murphy (0-4)

Substitute: Jack Dowling for Tim Lyons.

Game 3 - All-Ireland semi-final versus Galway in Croke Park on August 7. Final Score: Kerry 1-8; Galway 0-8.

Johnny Culloty

Jerome O'Shea	Niall Sheehy	Tim Lyons
Pat Dowling	Kevin Coffey	Mick O'Dwyer

| | Mick O'Connell | | JD O'Connor | |

| Seamus Murphy | | Tom Long (0-1) | | Paudie Sheehy (0-1) |

| Garry McMahon (1-0) | | John Dowling (0-1) | | Tadghie Lyne (0-5) |

Substitutes: Jack Dowling for Niall Sheehy, Jim Brosnan for Pat Dowling.

Game 4 - All-Ireland Final versus Down in Croke Park September 25. Score: Down 2-10; Kerry 0-8.

| | Johnny Culloty | |

| Jerome O'Shea | Niall Sheehy | Tim Lyons |

| Sean Murphy | Kevin Coffey | Mick O'Dwyer |

| Mick O'Connell (0-2) | | JD O'Connor (0-1) |

| Seamus Murphy (0-1) | Tom Long | Paudie Sheehy |

| Garry McMahon | John Dowling | Tadghie Lyne (0-4) |

Substitutes: Jack Dowling for John Dowling, Jim Brosnan for Garry McMahon, Dan McAuliffe for Tadghie Lyne.

Scorers for the Year: Paudie Sheehy (1-9), Tadghie Lyne (0-9), Tom Long (1-4), Mick O'Connell (0-6), John Dowling (1-3), Seamus Murphy (0-5), Garry McMahon (1-0), JD O'Connor (0-2), Kevin Coffey (0-2), Dan McAuliffe (0-1), Dave Geaney (0-1).

Total Scored: 4-42

Appearances:

4 - Johnny Culloty, Jerome O'Shea, Niall Sheehy, Tim Lyons, Jack Dowling, Mick O'Dwyer, Kevin Coffey, Mick O'Connell, Tom Long, Paudie Sheehy, John Dowling, Garry McMahon.

3 - Pat Dowling, JD O'Connor, Seamus Murphy.

2 - Jim Brosnan, Dan McAuliffe, Dave Geaney, Tadghie Lyne, Sean Murphy.

1960 - GAA Winners:

All-Irelands: Senior Football: Down   **Minor Football:** Galway

National Leagues: Football: Down   Hurling: Tipperary

Senior Hurling: Wexford

Kerry Co. Champions: Football: John Mitchels   Hurling: Ballyduff

1960 - In The News:

- The Broadcasting Authority Bill proposes to establish an authority to provide the new national television service. The Television Bill passes its final stage in Seanad Éireann.
- Shipping News: A 103-year old shipping service between Cork and Glasgow ends, while the last barge on the Grand Canal leaves Dublin carrying Guinness to Limerick, ending a 156-year service.
- Irish candidate Frederick Henry Boland receives the support of the United States for the presidency of the General Assembly of the United Nations.
- Figures show that 118 million telephone calls were made in 1959 in the country.
- "Mise Eire" is premiered in Dublin's Regal Rooms cinema.
- Nine Irish soldiers serving with the United Nations are killed in the Congo on 8 November.

1961

Summary: Played four championship games, won 43rd Munster title, lost All-Ireland Final.

Game 1 - versus Clare in Newcastlewest on June 25. Final Score: Kerry 1-13; Clare 1-0.

Johnny Culloty

Jack Dowling   Niall Sheehy   Tim Lyons

Sean Murphy   Kevin Coffey   Tim O'Sullivan

Mick O'Connell   Seamus Murphy

Dan McAuliffe   Tom Long (0-2)   David Geaney (0-4)

Gerry McMahon (1-1)   John Burke (0-1)   Tom Burke (0-5)

No substitutes used.

Game 2 - Munster Final versus Cork in Cork on July 16. Final Score: Kerry 0-10; Cork 1-7 (Draw).

Johnny Culloty

Jack Dowling   Niall Sheehy   Tim Lyons

Sean Murphy   Kevin Coffey   Mick O'Dwyer (0-1)

Mick O'Connell (0-3)   Seamus Murphy (0-1)

Dan McAuliffe (0-2)   Tom Long (0-1)   David Geaney (0-1)

Teddy Dowd   Brian Sheehy   Garry Clifford (0-1)

No substitutes used.

Game 3 - Munster Final Replay versus Cork in Killarney on July 23. Final Score: Kerry 2-13; Cork 1-4.

Johnny Culloty

Jack Dowling   Niall Sheehy   Tim Lyons

Sean Murphy   Kevin Coffey   Mick O'Dwyer (0-1)

Mick O'Connell   Seamus Murphy

Dan McAuliffe (0-7)   Tim O'Sullivan (0-1)   Brian Sheehy (1-0)

Teddy Dowd   John Dowling (0-3)   Garry Clifford (1-1)

No substitutes used.

Game 4 - All-Ireland semi-final versus Down in Croke Park on August 6. Final Score: Down 1-12; Kerry 0-9.

Johnny Culloty

Jerome O'Shea   Niall Sheehy   Tim Lyons

Sean Murphy   Kevin Coffey   Mick O'Dwyer (0-2)

Mick O'Connell   Seamus Murphy

Dan McAuliffe (0-1)   Tim O'Sullivan (0-3)   Brian Sheehy

Teddy Dowd (0-1)   John Dowling   Garry Clifford

Substitutes: Tom Burke (0-2) for Sean Murphy, Toss McKenna for Garry Clifford.

Scorers for the Year: Dan McAuliffe (0-10), Tom Burke (0-7), Dave Geaney (0-5), Garry Clifford (1-2), John Dowling (0-4), Garry McMahon (1-1), Mick O'Dwyer (0-4), Mick O'Connell (0-3), Tim O'Sullivan (0-3), Tom Long (0-3), Brian Sheehy (1-0), Seamus Murphy (0-1), Teddy Dowd (0-1), John Burke (0-1).

Total Scored: 3-45

Appearances:

4 - Johnny Culloty, Niall Sheehy, Tim Lyons, Sean Murphy, Kevin Coffey, Mick O'Connell, Seamus Murphy, Dan McAuliffe.

3 - Jack Dowling, Tim O'Sullivan, Mick O'Dwyer, Teddy Dowd, Brian Sheehy, Garry Clifford.

2 - Tom Long, Dave Geaney, Tom Burke, John Dowling.

1 - Jerome O'Shea, Toss McKenna, Garry McMahon, John Burke.

1961 - GAA Winners:

All-Irelands: Senior Football: Down **Minor Football:** Cork

National Leagues: Football: Kerry   Hurling: Tipperary

Senior Hurling: Tipperary

Kerry Co. Champions: Football: John Mitchels   Hurling: Ballyduff

1961 - In The News:

- Lieutenant-General Seán Mac Eoin takes up his new post as General Commanding Officer of the United Nations.
- John F. Kennedy sworn in as President of the United States. He is the first President of Irish-Catholic descent.
- President Éamon de Valera and Mrs. Sinéad de Valera greet Prince Rainier and Princess Grace at Áras an Uachtaráin.
- Prince Rainier and Princess Grace of Monaco have tea in a three roomed cottage near Newport, Co. Mayo. It was from there that the Princess' grandfather, John Henry Kelly, set off for America almost 100 years ago.
- The last legal execution in Ireland occurs in Belfast - it is of Robert McGladdery for murder.
- Teilifís Éireann goes on air on December 31 as President de Valera inaugurates the new service. The station's first broadcast is a New Year countdown with celebrations at the Gresham Hotel and O'Connell Street, Dublin.
- The general election of 1961 saw the three main parties each with new leaders. Seán Lemass had taken charge of Fianna Fáil in 1959, allowing them to face a general election campaign without Éamon de Valera for the first time. Also in 1959, James Dillon took over at Fine Gael. Brendan Corish assumed the reins of the Labour Party.
- Fianna Fáil took 70 seats, Fine Gael 47, Labour 15, while Independents and others took 12. Fianna Fáil formed a minority government with Seán Lemass as Taoiseach and Seán MacEntee as Tánaiste. Notable ministers are Patrick Hillery (Education), Jack Lynch (Industry & Commerce), and Charles Haughey (Justice).
- Kerry return the following members to the 17th Dáil:
  Kerry South: Honor Crowley (FF); Timothy O'Connor (FF); Patrick Connor (FG).
  Kerry North: Patrick Finucane (Independent); Tom McEllistrim Sr. (FF); Dan Spring (Lab.).

1962

Summary: Played four championship games, won 44th Munster title, won 20th All-Ireland title.

Game 1 - versus Waterford in Listowel on June 24. Final Score: Kerry 2-18; Waterford 2-6.

Johnny Culloty

Alan Conway   Niall Sheehy   Tim Lyons

Sean Óg Sheehy   Noel Lucey   Mick O'Dwyer (0-1)

Mick O'Connell (0-3)   Jimmy Lucey

Dave Geaney (0-3)   Seamus Murphy (0-1)   Seamus Roche (1-0)

Dan McAuliffe (0-4)   Tom Long (1-2)   Paudie Sheehy (0-4)

Substitute: John Healy for Alan Conway.

Game 2 - Munster Final versus Cork in Cork on July 15. Final Score: Kerry 4-8; Cork 0-4.

Johnny Culloty

Donie O'Sullivan   Niall Sheehy   Tim Lyons

Seamus Murphy   Noel Lucey   Mick O'Dwyer

Mick O'Connell (1-1)   Jimmy Lucey (0-1)

Dave Geaney (0-1)   Gene O'Driscoll (1-1)   Sean Óg Sheehy

Dan McAuliffe (1-2)   Tom Long (1-1)   Paudie Sheehy (0-1)

No substitutes used.

Game 3 - All-Ireland semi-final versus Dublin in Croke Park on August 5. Final Score: Kerry 2-12; Dublin 0-10.

Johnny Culloty

Donie O'Sullivan   Niall Sheehy   Tim Lyons

Sean Óg Sheehy   Seamus Murphy   Mick O'Dwyer

Mick O'Connell (0-4)   Jimmy Lucey

Dan McAuliffe   Tim O'Sullivan (0-1)   Jerry O'Riordan

Garry McMahon (1-1)   Tom Long (1-3)   Paudie Sheehy (0-2)

Substitutes: Seamus Roche for Garry McMahon, Dave Geaney (0-1) for Tim O'Sullivan.

Game 4 - All-Ireland Final versus Roscommon in Croke Park on September 23. Final Score: Kerry 1-12; Roscommon 1-6.

Johnny Culloty

Seamus Murphy   Niall Sheehy   Tim Lyons

Sean Óg Sheehy   Noel Lucey   Mick O'Dwyer

Mick O'Connell (0-8)   Jimmy Lucey

Dan McAuliffe   Tim O'Sullivan (0-2)   Jerry O'Riordan

Garry McMahon (1-0)   Tom Long   Paudie Sheehy (0-2)

Substitutes: JJ Barrett for Tim Lyons, Kevin Coffey for Dan McAuliffe.

Scorers for the Year: Mick O'Connell (1-16), Tom Long (3-6), Paudie Sheehy (0-9), Dan McAuliffe (1-6), Garry McMahon (2-1), Dave Geaney (0-5), Gene O'Driscoll (1-1), Tim O'Sullivan (0-3), Seamus Roche (1-0), Mick O'Dwyer (0-1), Jimmy Lucey (0-1), Seamus Murphy (0-1).

Total Scored: 9-50

Appearances:

4 - Johnny Culloty, Niall Sheehy, Tim Lyons, Sean Óg Sheehy, Mick O'Dwyer, Mick O'Connell, Jimmy Lucey, Seamus Murphy, Tom Long, Paudie Sheehy.

3 - Noel Lucey, Dave Geaney.

2 - Donie O'Sullivan, Seamus Roche, Tim O'Sullivan, Dan McAuliffe, Jerry O'Riordan, Garry McMahon.

1 - Alan Conway, JJ Barrett, Kevin Coffey, Gene O'Driscoll, John Healy.

1962 - GAA Winners:

All-Irelands: Senior Football: Kerry **Minor Football:** Kerry

Kerry's Winning Minor Team: S. Fitzgerald, D. Lovett, C. O'Connor, S. Burrowes, T. Fitzgerald, P. O'Donoghue, A. Burrowes, D. O'Sullivan, T. Doyle, S. O'Mahony, A. Barrett, D. O'Shea, S. Flavin, R. O'Donnell, T. Mulvihill. Subs: S. Corridon, T. Kenneally.

National Leagues: Football: Down   Hurling: Kilkenny

Senior Hurling: Tipperary

Kerry Co. Champions: Football: John Mitchels   Hurling: Kilmoyley

1962 - In The News:

- Irish artists visit the Congo to entertain United Nations troops there.
- President and Mrs. de Valera have a private audience with Pope John XXIII in Rome.
- The final train is run on the West Cork railway.
- Gay Byrne presents the very first edition of the Late Late Show.
- Secretary General of the United Nations, U Thant, arrives in Dublin. He pays tribute to Irish soldiers who fought in the Congo.
- Former US President Dwight D. Eisenhower arrives in Belfast on a four-day visit to Ireland.
- Aer Lingus air hostesses receive new uniforms, coloured fern-green and St. Patrick's blue.

1963

Summary: Played three championship games, won 45th Munster title, lost All-Ireland semi-final.

Game 1 - versus Tipperary in Listowel on June 23. Final Score: Kerry 5-10; Tipperary 1-6.

Johnny Culloty

Donie O'Sullivan   Niall Sheehy   Tim Lyons

Seamus Murphy   Noel Lucey   JJ Barrett

Mick O'Connell (0-4)   Jimmy Lucey

Bernie Callaghan (2-3)   Mick O'Dwyer   Sean Óg Sheehy (1-0)

Jerry O'Riordan   Vincent Lucey (1-2)   Seamus Roche

Substitutes: Frank O'Leary (1-1) for Seamus Roche, Pat Aherne for JJ Barrett, Tom Long for Jerry O'Riordan.

Game 2 - Munster Final versus Cork in Killarney on July 14. Final Score: Kerry 1-18; Cork 3-7.

Johnny Culloty

Donie O'Sullivan   Niall Sheehy   Tim Lyons

Kevin Coffey   Noel Lucey   Seamus Murphy

Mick O'Connell (0-4)   Jerry O'Riordan

Bernie Callaghan (0-3)   Mick O'Dwyer (1-3)   Sean Óg Sheehy

Vincent Lucey   Tom Long (0-3)   Frank O'Leary (0-3)

Substitutes: Pat Griffin (0-2) for Vincent Lucey, JJ Barrett for Johnny Culloty.

Game 3 - All-Ireland semi-final versus Galway in Croke Park on August 4. Final Score: Galway 1-7; Kerry 0-8.

Johnny Culloty

Donie O'Sullivan   Niall Sheehy   Tim Lyons

Kevin Coffey	Seamus Murphy	Mick O'Dwyer

Mick O'Connell (0-4)   Jimmy Lucey

Bernie Callaghan	Tim O'Sullivan	Pat Griffin (0-1)

Willie Doran	Tom Long (0-1)	Frank O'Leary (0-2)

Substitutes: Mick Fleming for Tim Lyons, Sean Óg Sheehy for Bernie Callaghan.

Scorers for the Year: Bernie Callaghan (2-6), Mick O'Connell (0-12), Frank O'Leary (1-6), Mick O'Dwyer (1-3), Tom Long (0-4), Vincent Lucey (1-2), Pat Griffin (0-3), Sean Óg Sheehy (1-0).

Total Scored: 6-36

Appearances:

3 - Johnny Culloty, Donie O'Sullivan, Niall Sheehy, Tim Lyons, Seamus Murphy, Mick O'Connell, Bernie Callaghan, Mick O'Dwyer, Frank O'Leary, Tom Long.

2 - Kevin Coffey, Noel Lucey, JJ Barrett, Jimmy Lucey, Sean Óg Sheehy, Pat Griffin, Jerry O'Riordan, Vincent Lucey.

1 - Mick Fleming, Tim O'Sullivan, Seamus Roche, Pat Aherne, Willie Doran.

1963 - GAA Winners:

All-Irelands: Senior Football: Dublin **Minor Football:** Kerry

Kerry's Winning Minor Team: S. Fitzgerald, A. Behan, J. McCarthy, S. Burrowes, T. O'Shea, B. Burrowes, C. O'Riordan, D. O'Sullivan, G. Curran, T. O'Hanlon, A. Spring, J. Saunders, T. Kelleher, H. McKinney, C. Donnelly. Subs: M. O'Sullivan, S. O'Shea.

National Leagues: Football: Kerry   Hurling: Waterford

Senior Hurling: Kilkenny

Kerry Juniors also take All-Ireland honours with this team: A. Guerin, P. Kerins, J. Dowling, P. Sayers, T. Sheehan, M. Morris, J. O'Driscoll, J.

O'Connor, D. O'Sullivan, T. Burke, B. Sheehy, D. O'Shea, T. O'Dowd, J. Burke, D. O'Donnell.

Kerry Co. Champions: Football: John Mitchels   Hurling: Kilmoyley

1963 - In The News:

- Thomas Johnson, first parliamentary leader of the Irish Labour Party, dies aged 91.
- Justice Minister, Charles Haughey, states the government wish to abolish the death penalty.
- A new control tower is opened at Shannon Airport.
- The Minister for Education, Dr. Patrick Hillery, announces plans for comprehensive schools and regional technical colleges.
- Teilifís Éireann closes down immediately after its 9 o'clock news bulletin as a mark of respect to the memory of Pope John XXIII.
- US President John F. Kennedy visits his ancestral home at New Ross, Co. Wexford. He inspects a naval guard of honour and then addresses the crowd. President John F. Kennedy receives a standing ovation as he addresses a joint session of both houses of the Oireachtas and chats with President de Valera at the US Embassy in Dublin before leaving Ireland.
- Taoiseach Seán Lemass is greeted by President John F. Kennedy at the White House.
- Domhnall Ua Buachalla, the last Governor-General of the Irish Free State, dies.
- The Beatles arrive in Dublin for a concert in the Adelphi Cinema.
- President de Valera addresses the nation on the death of U.S. President John F. Kennedy on November 22, and attends the funeral. He is accompanied by cadets who have been invited by Jacqueline Kennedy to form a guard of honour.

1964

Summary: Played four championship games, won 46th Munster title, lost All-Ireland Final.

Game 1 - versus Tipperary in Thurles on June 28. Final Score: Kerry 1-14; Tipperary 1-7.

Johnny Culloty

Mick Morris   Niall Sheehy   Paud O'Donoghue

Denis O'Sullivan   Seamus Murphy   JD O'Connor

Mick O'Connell (0-2)   Mick Fleming (0-1)

Bernie Callaghan (0-9)   Frank O'Leary   Pat Griffin (0-1)

Dom O'Donnell (1-0)   Tom Long   Tony Barrett (0-1)

No substitutes used.

Game 2 - Munster Final versus Cork in Cork on July 19. Final Score: Kerry 2-11; Cork 1-8.

Johnny Culloty

Mick Morris   Niall Sheehy   Paud O'Donoghue

Denis O'Sullivan   Seamus Murphy   JD O'Connor

Mick O'Connell (0-1)   Mick Fleming (0-1)

Bernie Callaghan (0-6)   Tim O'Sullivan   Pat Griffin

Dom O'Donnell (2-1)   Tom Long   Tony Barrett (0-1)

Substitute: Frank O'Leary (0-1) for Tim O'Sullivan.

Game 3 - All-Ireland semi-final versus Cavan in Croke Park on August 23. Final Score: Kerry 2-12; Cavan 0-6.

Johnny Culloty

Mick Morris   Niall Sheehy   Paud O'Donoghue

Denis O'Sullivan   Seamus Murphy   JD O'Connor

	Mick O'Connell		Mick Fleming	

Mick O'Connell   Mick Fleming

Bernie Callaghan (0-5)   Mick O'Dwyer (0-4)   Pat Griffin (0-1)

Dom O'Donnell   Tom Long (1-2)   Tony Barrett (1-0)

Substitutes: Donie O'Sullivan for Mick O'Connell, Kevin Coffey for Seamus Murphy, Dan McAuliffe for Dom O'Donnell.

Game 4 - All-Ireland Final versus Galway in Croke Park on September 27. Final Score: Galway 0-15; Kerry 0-10.

Johnny Culloty

Mick Morris   Niall Sheehy   Paud O'Donoghue

Denis O'Sullivan   Seamus Murphy   JD O'Connor

Mick Fleming   Donie O'Sullivan

Pat Griffin (0-2)   Mick O'Dwyer (0-1)   Mick O'Connell (0-7)

Frank O'Leary   Tom Long   JJ Barrett

Substitutes: John McCarthy for JD O'Connor, Kevin Coffey for John McCarthy, Bernie O'Callaghan for Frank O'Leary.

Scorers for the Year: Bernie Callaghan (0-20), Mick O'Connell (0-10), Dom O'Donnell (3-1), Tony Barrett (1-2), Tom Long (1-2), Mick O'Dwyer (0-5), Pat Griffin (0-4), Mick Fleming (0-2), Frank O'Leary (0-1).

Total Scored: 5-47

Appearances:

4 - Johnny Culloty, Mick Morris, Niall Sheehy, Paud O'Donoghue, Denis O'Sullivan, Seamus Murphy, JD O'Connor, Mick O'Connell, Mick Fleming, Bernie Callaghan, Pat Griffin, Tom Long.

3 - Frank O'Leary, Dom O'Donnell, Tony Barrett.

2 - Donie O'Sullivan, Mick O'Dwyer, Kevin Coffey.

1 - John McCarthy, Tim O'Sullivan, Dan McAuliffe, JJ Barrett.

1964 - GAA Winners:

All-Irelands: Senior Football: Galway **Minor Football:** Offaly **Under-21 Football:** Kerry

National Leagues: Football: Dublin   Hurling: Tipperary

Senior Hurling: Tipperary

Kerry Co. Champions: Football: Shannon Rangers   Hurling: Kilmoyley

1964 - In The News:

- Princess Margaret and Lord Snowdon arrive in Ireland for a seven-day visit.
- The new Garda Síochána training centre is opened in Templemore, Co. Tipperary.
- March 16 - Seán Lemass arrives in London to officially launch "Ireland Week".
- Brendan Behan's funeral takes place in Dublin.
- President de Valera, Taoiseach Seán Lemass and An Tánaiste Seán MacEntee attend the official opening of the US Embassy in Dublin.
- The Fine Gael parliamentary party approves Declan Costello's *Just Society* programme.
- Jill, a two-year-old elephant, arrives at Dublin Airport from India. She is headed to a new home at Dublin Zoo.
- Taoiseach Seán Lemass attends celebrations marking the silver jubilee of the first commercial transatlantic flight.
- The Abbey Theatre, Dublin closes in mourning for playwright Seán O'Casey who has died.
- Lifford and Strabane are connected via a new bridge over the River Foyle.
- The death penalty is abolished for all but the murder of gardaí, diplomats and prison officers.

1965

Summary: Played four championship games, won 47th Munster title, lost All-Ireland Final.

Game 1 - versus Clare in Limerick on June 13. Final Score: Kerry 2-10; Clare 1-6.

Johnny Culloty

Donie O'Sullivan   Mick Morris   Seanie Burrows

Denis O'Sullivan   JD O'Connor   Seamus Murphy

Mick Fleming (0-1)   Jimmy Lucey

Bernie Callaghan (1-3)   Mick O'Connell (0-1)   Dave Geaney (0-1)

JJ Barrett   Vincent Lucey (1-0)   Mick O'Dwyer (0-4)

No substitutes used.

Game 2 - Munster Final versus Limerick in Limerick on July 18. Final Score: Kerry 2-16; Limerick 2-7.

Johnny Culloty

Donie O'Sullivan   Paud O'Donoghue   Mick Morris

Denis O'Sullivan   JD O'Connor   Seamus Murphy

Mick Fleming (0-1)   Jimmy Lucey

Bernie Callaghan (1-1)   Mick O'Connell (0-5)   Seanie Burrows

Vincent Lucey (0-6)   JJ Barrett (1-2)   Mick O'Dwyer (0-1)

Substitute: Derry O'Shea for Jimmy Lucey.

Game 3 - All-Ireland semi-final versus Dublin in Croke Park on August 8. Final Score: Kerry 4-8; Dublin 2-6.

Teddy Bowler

Paud O'Donoghue   Niall Sheehy   Mick Morris

Donie O'Sullivan (0-1)   JD O'Connor   Seamus Murphy

Mick O'Connell (0-1)   Denis O'Sullivan (0-1)

Vincent Lucey	Mick Fleming	Derry O'Shea (1-1)
Pat Griffin	JJ Barrett (0-1)	Bernie Callaghan (1-3)

Substitute: Mick O'Dwyer (2-0) for Mick Fleming.

Game 4 - All-Ireland Final versus Galway in Croke Park on September 26. Final Score: Galway 0-12; Kerry 0-9.

Johnny Culloty

Donie O'Sullivan	Niall Sheehy	Mick Morris
Seamus Murphy	Paud O'Donoghue	JD O'Connor

Mick O'Connell (0-2)   Denis O'Sullivan

Vincent Lucey	Pat Griffin	Derry O'Shea
Bernie Callaghan (0-6)	Mick O'Dwyer (0-1)	JJ Barrett

Substitutes: Dave Geaney for Vincent Lucey, John "Thorny" O'Shea for JJ Barrett.

Scorers for the Year: Bernie Callaghan (3-13), Mick O'Dwyer (2-6), Mick O'Connell (0-9), Vincent Lucey (1-6), JJ Barrett (1-3), Derry O'Shea (1-1), Mick Fleming (0-2), Donie O'Sullivan (0-1), Denis O'Sullivan (0-1), Dave Geaney (0-1).

Total Scored: 8-43

Appearances:

4 - Donie O'Sullivan, Mick Morris, Seamus Murphy, JD O'Connor, Mick O'Connell, Denis O'Sullivan, Vincent Lucey, Bernie Callaghan, Mick O'Dwyer, JJ Barrett.

3 - Johnny Culloty, Paud O'Donoghue, Mick Fleming, Derry O'Shea.

2 - Niall Sheehy, Seanie Burrows, Pat Griffin, Jimmy Lucey, Dave Geaney.

1 - Teddy Bowler, John "Thorny" O'Shea.

1965 - GAA Winners:

All-Irelands: Senior Football: Galway **Minor Football:** Derry **Under-21 Football:** Kildare

National Leagues: Football: Galway   Hurling: Tipperary

Senior Hurling: Tipperary

Kerry Co. Champions: Football: East Kerry   Hurling: Ballyduff

1965 - In The News:

- Taoiseach Seán Lemass travels to Belfast for an historic meeting with the Prime Minister of Northern Ireland, Terence O'Neill.
- Nationalist leader Eddie McAteer visits Taoiseach Seán Lemass in Dublin.
- Roger Casement is honoured with a state funeral in Dublin.
- Changes to the Liturgy of the Mass are introduced throughout the country today. Mass is said in the vernacular for the first time.
- The Northern Minister for Agriculture, Harry West, attends a meeting with his Southern counterpart, Charles Haughey, in Dublin.
- The Gaelic Athletic Association Congress in Dublin decides that the ban on foreign games is to stay in place.
- The first car ferry service between Rosslare, Co. Wexford and Fishguard, Wales officially opens.
- Huge crowds turn out at Drumcliffe Churchyard, Co. Sligo to honour the poet W.B. Yeats on the centenary of his birth.
- Taoiseach Seán Lemass is conferred with an honourary Doctorate of Law at Trinity College, Dublin.
- The death takes place of W. T. Cosgrave, first President of the Executive Council.
- The failure of Fianna Fáil to win a by-election in Cork resulted in Taoiseach Lemass calling a general election. The general election gave Fianna Fáil an extra two seats, and with it an overall majority in the Dáil. Seán Lemass continued as Taoiseach. James Dillon resigned as leader of Fine Gael after the result was announced, with Liam Cosgrave taking over.
- Kerry returned the following members to the 18th Dáil:
  Kerry South: Honor Crowley (FF); Timothy O'Connor (FF); Patrick Connor (FG).
  Kerry North: Patrick Finucane (Independent); Tom McEllistrim Sr. (FF); Dan Spring (Lab.).

1966

Summary: Played two championship games, lost Munster Final.

Game 1 - versus Tipperary in Killarney on June 26. Final Score: Kerry 3-16; Tipperary 2-6.

Johnny Culloty

Donie O'Sullivan   Paud O'Donoghue   Mick Morris

Denis O'Sullivan   JD O'Connor   Tommy O'Callaghan

Mick Fleming   JP Leen

Geaney (0-3)   Mick O'Connell (0-4)   Derry O'Shea (2-4)

Tom Prendergast (1-0)   Pat Griffin (0-1)   Seamus MacGearailt (0-4)

Substitute: Seanie Burrows for Donie O'Sullivan.

Game 2 - Munster Final versus Cork in Killarney on July 17. Final Score: Cork 2-7; Kerry 1-7.

Johnny Culloty

Donie O'Sullivan   Paud O'Donoghue   Mick Morris

Denis O'Sullivan   JD O'Connor   Tommy O'Callaghan

Mick O'Connell (0-1)   Mick Fleming

Pat Moynihan (0-2)   Seamus MacGearailt   Derry O'Shea

Tom Prendergast (0-2)   Pat Griffin (0-1)   PJ Fitzpatrick (0-1)

Substitutes: Tony Barrett (1-0) for PJ Fitzpatrick, Seanie Burrows for Tommy O'Callaghan.

Scorers for the Year: Derry O'Shea (2-4), Mick O'Connell (0-5), Tom Prendergast (1-2), Seamus MacGearailt (0-4), Dave Geaney (0-3), Tony Barrett (1-0), Pat Moynihan (0-2), Pat Griffin (0-2), PJ Fitzpatrick (0-1).

Total Scored: 4-23

Appearances:

2 - Johnny Culloty, Donie O'Sullivan, Paud O'Donoghue, Mick Morris, Denis O'Sullivan, JD O'Connor, Tommy O'Callaghan, Mick Fleming, Mick O'Connell, Derry O'Shea, Tom Prendergast, Pat Griffin, Seamus MacGearailt, Seanie Burrows.

1 - JP Leen, Pat Moynihan, Dave Geaney, PJ Fitzpatrick, Tony Barrett.

1966 - GAA Winners:

All-Irelands: Senior Football: Galway **Minor Football:** Mayo **Under-21 Football:** Roscommon

National Leagues: Football: Longford   Hurling: Kilkenny

Senior Hurling: Cork

Kerry Co. Champions: Football: John Mitchels   Hurling: Ballyduff

1966 - In The News:
- The Bishop of Clonfert protests over the content of The Late Late Show. The bishop took exception when a woman told the host, Gay Byrne, that she didn't wear a nightie on her wedding night.
- A memorial is to be opened at Kilmichael, Co. Cork to commemorate the 1920 ambush.
- Nelson's Pillar in O'Connell Street is blown up to commemorate the 50th anniversary of the Easter Rising.
- The Tricolour flag flown over the GPO in 1916 is handed back by the British to Taoiseach Seán Lemass in London.
- Celebrations take place to mark the 50th anniversary of the Easter Rising. Nine hundred 1916 survivors hear the reading of the Proclamation. President de Valera takes the salute at a military parade.
- President de Valera opens the Garden of Remembrance in Dublin's Parnell Square.
- In Belfast the Easter Rising is commemorated by large republican parades.
- Éamon de Valera, with Charles Haughey as campaign manager, is re-elected President of Ireland. He defeats Tom O'Higgins by 10,500, less than 1% of the vote.
- Minister for Education, Donagh O'Malley, announces a free secondary education scheme.

- Exactly fifteen years after being burned down, the new Abbey Theatre opens.
- An anti-apartheid demonstration takes place outside the National Stadium as the South African Amateur Boxing Team visit.
- Tributes are paid to Seán Lemass who announces his resignation as Taoiseach. He is succeeded by Jack Lynch.
- Kerry South by-election sees John O'Leary (FF) replace Honor Crowley who died.
- Seán T. O'Kelly, second President of Ireland, dies.
- Foundation of Allied Irish Banks Limited (later Allied Irish Banks PLC). AIB acquired three Irish banks - The Munster & Leinster Bank Limited, The Provincial Bank of Ireland Limited and The Royal Bank of Ireland Limited.

1967

Summary: Played two championship games, lost Munster Final.

Game 1 - versus Limerick in Tralee on June 18. Final Score: Kerry 1-17; Limerick 1-8.

Eamonn O'Donoghue

Paud O'Donoghue	Teddy Bowler	Seanie Burrows
Denis O'Sullivan	Mick Morris	Seamus MacGearailt

Mick Fleming   Pat Griffin

John Saunders (0-5)	JD O'Connor (0-2)	Tom Kelliher (0-3)
Tom Prendergast	DJ Crowley (1-0)	John "Thorny" O'Shea (0-7)

No substitutes used.

Game 2 - Munster Final versus Cork in Cork on July 16. Final Score: Cork 0-8; Kerry 0-7.

Eamonn O'Donoghue

Paud O'Donoghue	Teddy Bowler	Seanie Burrows
Denis O'Sullivan	Mick Morris	Seamus MacGearailt

Mick Fleming   Pat Griffin (0-2)

John Saunders	JD O'Connor	Tim Sheehan (0-1)
Tom Prendergast	DJ Crowley (0-1)	John "Thorny" O'Shea (0-3)

Substitute: Josie O'Brien for John "Thorny" O'Shea.

Scorers for the Year: John "Thorny" O'Shea (0-10), John Saunders (0-5), DJ Crowley (1-1), Tom Kelliher (0-3), JD O'Connor (0-2), Pat Griffin (0-2), Tim Sheehan (0-1).

Total Scored: 1-24

Appearances:

2 - Eamonn O'Donoghue, Paud O'Donoghue, Teddy Bowler, Seanie Burrows, Denis O'Sullivan, Mick Morris, Seamus MacGearailt, Mick Fleming, Pat

Griffin, John Saunders, JD O'Connor, Tom Prendergast, DJ Crowley, John "Thorny" O'Shea.

1 - Tom Kelliher, Tim Sheehan, Josie O'Brien.

1967 - GAA Winners:

All-Irelands: Senior Football: Meath **Minor Football:** Cork **Under-21 Football:** Mayo

National Leagues: Football: Galway   Hurling: Tipperary

Senior Hurling: Kilkenny

Kerry Juniors also take All-Ireland honours with this team: A. Fogarty, D. Lovett, D. O'Sullivan, G. McCarthy, D. Crowley, M. Gleeson, P. Aherne, M. O'Shea, M. Aherne, P. O'Connor, P. O'Connell, W. Doran, P. Finnegan, B. Kennedy, P.J. McIntyre. Sub: B. McCarthy.

Kerry Co. Champions: Football: Mid-Kerry   Hurling: Ardfert

1967 - In The News:

- Demonstrations by the National Farmers' Association cause major chaos as farm machinery blocks many roads.
- The Fianna Fáil Party makes a presentation to former Taoiseach Seán Lemass.
- The Minister for Education, Donagh O'Malley, reveals his plan for a single multi-denominational University of Dublin. This would combine University College Dublin and Trinity College, Dublin.
- Jacqueline Kennedy goes racing at the Curragh with Taoiseach Jack Lynch and Mrs. Máirín Lynch.
- Senator Margaret M. Pearse, sister of Pádraig Pearse and Willie Pearse, the executed 1916 leaders, is 89 today. She is greeted by President de Valera.
- Ireland's free post-primary school transport scheme begins. CIÉ brings 38,000 students to 350 schools.
- Taoiseach Jack Lynch returns to Dublin following talks on the European Community with General Charles de Gaulle in Paris.
- The poet Patrick Kavanagh is buried in his native Inniskeen, Co. Monaghan.
- The first independent computer in Ireland opens at Shannon Airport.

- The Minister for Labour, Dr. Patrick Hillery, announces details of a new redundancy payments scheme which takes effect from New Year's Day.

1968

Summary: Played four championship games, won 48th Munster title, lost All-Ireland Final.

Game 1 - versus Tipperary in Clonmel on June 23. Final Score: Kerry 0-17; Tipperary 2-7.

Teddy Bowler

Seamus Murphy	Paud O'Donoghue	Seanie Burrows
Denis O'Sullivan	Tim Sheehan	Donie O'Sullivan (0-1)
	Mick O'Connell (0-2)	Mick Fleming (0-1)
Brendan Lynch (0-2)	Pat Griffin (0-4)	Tom Prendergast (0-1)
PJ McIntyre	DJ Crowley	Mick O'Dwyer (0-6)

Substitute: Seamus MacGearailt for Teddy Bowler.

Game 2 - Munster Final versus Cork in Cork on July 14. Final Score: Kerry 1-21; Cork 3-8.

Teddy Bowler

Seamus Murphy	Paud O'Donoghue	Seanie Burrows
Denis O'Sullivan	Tim Sheehan	Donie O'Sullivan
	Mick O'Connell (0-4)	Mick Fleming
Brendan Lynch (0-4)	Pat Griffin (0-4)	Eamonn O'Donoghue (1-1)
Tom Prendergast (0-1)	DJ Crowley	Mick O'Dwyer (0-7)

No substitutes used.

Game 3 - All-Ireland semi-final versus Longford in Croke Park on August 4. Final Score: Kerry 2-13; Longford 2-11.

Johnny Culloty

Seamus Murphy	Paud O'Donoghue	Seanie Burrows
Denis O'Sullivan	Micheál Ó'Sé	Donie O'Sullivan

Mick O'Connell (0-1)   Mick Fleming

Brendan Lynch (0-4)   Pat Griffin (1-4)   Eamonn O'Donoghue (0-1)

Dom O'Donnell (1-0)   DJ Crowley (0-2)   Mick O'Dwyer (0-1)

Substitutes: Declan Lovett for Seanie Burrows, Pat Moynihan for Mick Fleming.

Game 4 - All-Ireland Final versus Down in Croke Park on September 22. Final Score: Down 2-12; Kerry 1-13.

Johnny Culloty

Seamus Murphy   Paud O'Donoghue   Seanie Burrows

Denis O'Sullivan   Mick Morris   Donie O'Sullivan

Mick O'Connell (0-2)   Mick Fleming

Brendan Lynch (1-2)   Pat Griffin (0-3)   Eamonn O'Donoghue

Tom Prendergast   DJ Crowley (0-1)   Mick O'Dwyer (0-5)

Substitutes: Seamus MacGearailt for Seanie Burrows, Pat Moynihan for Tom Prendergast.

Scorers for the Year: Mick O'Dwyer (0-19), Pat Griffin (1-15), Brendan Lynch (1-12), Mick O'Connell (0-9), Eamonn O'Donoghue (1-2), Dom O'Donnell (1-0), DJ Crowley (0-3), Tom Prendergast (0-2), Donie O'Sullivan (0-1), Mick Fleming (0-1).

Total Scored: 4-64

Appearances:

4 - Seamus Murphy, Paud O'Donoghue, Seanie Burrows, Denis O'Sullivan, Donie O'Sullivan, Mick O'Connell, Mick Fleming, Brendan Lynch, Pat Griffin, DJ Crowley, Mick O'Dwyer.

3 - Tom Prendergast, Eamonn O'Donoghue.

2 - Teddy Bowler, Johnny Culloty, Seamus MacGearailt, Tim Sheehan, Pat Moynihan.

1 - Micheál Ó'Sé, Mick Morris, Dom O'Donnell, PJ McIntyre, Declan Lovett.

1968 - GAA Winners:

All-Irelands: Senior Football: Down **Minor Football:** Cork **Under-21 Football:** Derry

National Leagues: Football: Down   Hurling: Tipperary

Senior Hurling: Wexford

Kerry Co. Champions: Football: East Kerry   Hurling: Crotta

1968 - In The News:

- Taoiseach Jack Lynch and Northern Ireland Prime Minister Terence O'Neill meet for talks in Dublin.
- Minister for Education Donogh O'Malley collapses and dies while campaigning in Co. Clare.
- A seat to commemorate the poet Patrick Kavanagh is unveiled alongside the Grand Canal in Dublin.
- An Aer Lingus aircraft, *St Phelim,* plunges into the Irish Sea off the Tuskar Rock killing all 57 passengers.
- President de Valera opens the John F. Kennedy Memorial Park in New Ross, Co. Wexford.
- Ireland mourns the loss of Senator Robert Kennedy who was assassinated. Dáil Éireann pays tribute and a book of condolence is opened.
- George Best is star attraction as Manchester United beat Waterford City 3-1 at Lansdowne Road.
- Police in Derry baton-charge a Northern Ireland civil rights march.
- 20 new traffic wardens are introduced on Dublin's streets.
- The New University of Ulster is opened in Coleraine.
- According to the Economic and Social Research Institute, 60% of undergraduates in this country will emigrate on graduation.

1969

Summary: Played four championship games, won 49th Munster title, won 21st All-Ireland title.

Game 1 - versus Waterford in Dungarvan on June 15. Final Score: Kerry 1-18; Waterford 2-7.

Johnny Culloty

Seamus Murphy   Paud O'Donoghue   Seamus MacGearailt

Donie O'Sullivan   Mick Morris   Micheál Ó'Sé

Mick O'Connell (0-4)   DJ Crowley (0-2)

Brendan Lynch (0-3)   Pat Moynihan (0-5)   Eamonn O'Donoghue

Dom O'Donnell   Mick Fleming (1-1)   Mick O'Dwyer (0-2)

Substitute: Tom Prendergast (0-1) for Dom O'Donnell.

Game 2 - Munster Final versus Cork in Cork on July 20. Final Score: Kerry 0-16; Cork 1-4.

Johnny Culloty

Seamus Murphy   Paud O'Donoghue   Seamus MacGearailt

Donie O'Sullivan   Mick Morris   Tom Prendergast

Mick O'Connell (0-6)   DJ Crowley (0-1)

Brendan Lynch (0-2)   Pat Griffin (0-2)   Eamonn O'Donoghue (0-1)

Mick Gleeson (0-1)   Liam Higgins (0-1)   Mick O'Dwyer (0-2)

Substitute: Mick Fleming for Mick Morris.

Game 3 - All-Ireland semi-final versus Mayo in Croke Park on August 10. Final Score: Kerry 0-14; Mayo 1-10.

Johnny Culloty

Seamus Murphy   Paud O'Donoghue   Seamus MacGearailt

Tom Prendergast   Donie O'Sullivan   Micheál Ó'Sé

Mick O'Connell (0-3)   DJ Crowley

Eamonn O'Donoghue(0-1) Pat Griffin (0-2)   Brendan Lynch (0-2)

Mick Gleeson (0-1)   Liam Higgins   Mick O'Dwyer (0-5)

Substitute: Mick Fleming for Donie O'Sullivan.

Game 4 - All-Ireland Final versus Offaly in Croke Park on September 28. Final Score: Kerry 0-10; Offaly 0-7.

Johnny Culloty

Seamus Murphy   Paud O'Donoghue   Seamus MacGearailt

Tom Prendergast   Mick Morris   Micheál Ó'Sé

Mick O'Connell (0-2)   DJ Crowley (0-2)

Brendan Lynch (0-1)   Pat Griffin   Eamonn O'Donoghue

Mick Gleeson (0-2)   Liam Higgins (0-1)   Mick O'Dwyer (0-2)

No substitutes used.

Scorers for the Year: Mick O'Connell (0-15), Mick O'Dwyer (0-11), Brendan Lynch (0-8), Pat Moynihan (0-5), DJ Crowley (0-5), Pat Griffin (0-4), Mick Gleeson (0-4), Mick Fleming (1-1), Eamonn O'Donoghue (0-2), Liam Higgins (0-2), Tom Prendergast (0-1).

Total Scored: 1-58

Appearances:

4 - Johnny Culloty, Seamus Murphy, Paud O'Donoghue, Seamus MacGearailt, Mick O'Connell, DJ Crowley, Brendan Lynch, Eamonn O'Donoghue, Mick O'Dwyer, Tom Prendergast.

3 - Mick Morris, Donie O'Sullivan, Micheál Ó'Sé, Pat Griffin, Mick Gleeson, Mick Fleming, Liam Higgins.

2 - None

1 - Pat Moynihan, Dom O'Donnell.

1969 - GAA Winners:

All-Irelands: Senior Football: Kerry **Minor Football:** Cork **Under-21 Football:** Antrim

National Leagues: Football: Kerry Hurling: Cork

Senior Hurling: Kilkenny

Kerry Co. Champions: Football: East Kerry Hurling: Killarney

1969 - In The News:

- The People's Democracy civil rights march leaves Belfast for Derry.
- Militant loyalists, including off-duty B-Specials, attack the civil rights marchers in Derry.
- The Lichfield Report is issued - it proposes the creation of a "University of Limerick" which will be "orientated towards technological subjects".
- Ireland receives its first loan from the World Bank.
- Civil rights demonstrations take place all over Northern Ireland. Bernadette Devlin, the 21-year-old student and civil rights campaigner, wins the Mid-Ulster by-election. She is the youngest female MP ever.
- Prime Minister of Northern Ireland, Terence O'Neill, resigns with Major James Chichester-Clark replacing him.
- Minister for Finance Charles Haughey announces tax exemptions for painters, sculptors, writers and composers on earnings gained from works of cultural merit.
- Former French President General Charles de Gaulle and his wife are greeted by President de Valera at Áras an Uachtaráin.
- Neil Armstrong becomes the first person to set foot on the moon. President de Valera sends President Nixon a telegram of congratulations and admiration.
- The halfpenny is withdrawn from circulation as the country moves towards decimalisation.
- A huge protest rally over events in Northern Ireland is held outside the GPO. The crowd demands that the Irish Army cross the border.
- Taoiseach Jack Lynch makes a state visit to the Lebanon.
- Belfast experiences the worst sectarian rioting since 1935 on August 5.
- As the siege of the Bogside in Derry continues, Taoiseach Jack Lynch makes a speech on Irish television on August 13. He says that the

Irish government "can no longer stand by" and demands a United Nations peace-keeping force for Northern Ireland.

- August 15 sees a night of shooting and burning in Belfast. In Dublin a Sinn Féin protest meeting calls for the boycott of British goods, Irish government protection of the people of Northern Ireland and United Nations intervention.

- British soldiers are deployed into particularly violent areas of Belfast on August 16.

- Members of Garda Síochána clash with protesters on O'Connell Street, Dublin, on August 17 as a march against the Northern Ireland situation heads for the British embassy.

- On August 27, the B-Specials begin to hand in their guns following the decision by Lieutenant-General Freeland to disband them. The current British Home Secretary, James Callaghan, visits Belfast.

- The Hunt Committee Report, issued in October, recommends an unarmed civil police force in Northern Ireland.

- Fianna Fáil pays tribute to Seán Lemass as his forty-five years of public life come to an end.

- Samuel Beckett is awarded the Nobel Prize in Literature.

- The June general election of 1969 saw two new leaders of the two main parties fight their first general election - Jack Lynch of Fianna Fáil and Fine Gael's Liam Cosgrave. Brendan Corish was fighting his third general election as leader of the Labour Party. Fianna Fáil had been in power since 1957 and, in spite of media predictions, the party was still very popular with the voters. The leader of the party, Jack Lynch, proved to be the party's biggest electoral asset. His quiet, easy-going and reassuring style, coupled with the catchy slogan "Let's back Jack!" attracted many new voters to Fianna Fáil. The party had introduced many innovative pieces of legislation during the 1960s and was now looking for a fresh mandate. A deeply divided opposition also helped Fianna Fáil as Fine Gael had internal divisions. There was tension between the older conservative members who wanted to keep the party as it was and the younger deputies who wanted to move the party to the left. One of the party's policies proposed to abolish compulsory Irish for State examinations and civil service jobs. The Labour Party, on the other hand, was predicted to make massive gains after firmly ruling out a pre-election pact with Fine Gael. The party had fielded a number of new, high-profile candidates, including Justin Keating, Conor Cruise O'Brien, and Noel Browneand the slogan "The Seventies will be Socialist" was very catchy and popular.

However, Labour were foiled by Fianna Fáil playing the "red card", linking them with communism.

- Fianna Fáil took 74 seats, Fine Gael 50, Labour 18, and 2 Others resulting in Fianna Fáil forming a government with Jack Lynch as Taoiseach and Erskine Childers as Tánaiste.
- Kerry return the following members to the 19th Dáil:
Kerry South: John O'Leary (FF); Timothy O'Connor (FF); Michael Begley (FG).
Kerry North: Gerard Lynch (FG); Tom McEllistrim Jr. (FF); Dan Spring (Labour).

1970-1979... We march into Europe

Summary of the Decade

Kerry played 35 games, scoring 84-531, conceding 34-353.

Munster Championship titles: 7 (1970, 1972, 1975, 1976, 1977, 1978, 1979)

All Ireland titles: 4 (1970, 1975, 1978, 1979)

National League titles: 5 (1971, 1972, 1973, 1974, 1977)

U-21 titles: 4 (1973, 1975, 1976, 1977) **Minor titles: 1** (1975)

Top Scorers: Mike Sheehy (17-88), Pat Spillane (12-48), Mick O'Dwyer (2-78)

Top Points-only scorers: Mike Sheehy (88), Mick O'Dwyer (78)

Top Goals-only scorers: Mike Sheehy (17), Pat Spillane (12)

Most Appearances: John O'Keeffe (34), Paudie Lynch (27)

1970
Kerry 2-19 Limerick 2-5;
Munster Final: Kerry 2-22 Cork 2-9;
All-Ireland semi-final: Kerry 0-23 Derry 0-10;
All-Ireland Final: Kerry 2-19 Meath 0-18.

1971
Kerry 1-14 Tipperary 1-7;
Munster Final: Cork 0-25 Kerry 0-14.

1972
Kerry 1-12 Tipperary 0-9;
Munster Final: Kerry 2-21 Cork 2-15;
All-Ireland semi-final: Kerry 1-22 Roscommon 1-12;
All-Ireland Final: Kerry 1-13 Offaly 1-13;
Replay: Offaly 1-19 Kerry 0-13.

1973

Kerry 3-11 Tipperary 0-5;
Munster Final: Cork 5-12 Kerry 1-15.

1974

Kerry 7-16 Waterford 0-8;
Munster Final: Cork 1-11 Kerry 0-7.

1975

Kerry 3-13 Tipperary 0-9;
Munster Final: Kerry 1-14 Cork 0-7;
All-Ireland semi-final: Kerry 3-13 Sligo 0-5;
All-Ireland Final: Kerry 2-12 Dublin 0-11.

1976

Kerry 3-17 Waterford 0-6;
Munster Final: Kerry 0-10 Cork 0-10;
Replay: Kerry 3-20 Cork 2-19;
All-Ireland semi-final: Kerry 5-14 Derry 1-10;
All-Ireland Final: Dublin 3-8 Kerry 0-10.

1977

Kerry 3-14 Tipperary 0-9;
Munster Final: Kerry 3-15 Cork 0-9;
All-Ireland semi-final: Dublin 3-12 Kerry 1-13.

1978

Kerry 4-27 Waterford 2-8;
Munster Final: Kerry 3-14 Cork 3-7;
All-Ireland semi-final: Kerry 3-11 Roscommon 0-8;
All-Ireland Final: Kerry 5-11 Dublin 0-9.

1979

Kerry 9-21 Clare 1-9;
Munster Final: Kerry 2-14 Cork 2-4;
All-Ireland semi-final: Kerry 5-14 Monaghan 0-7;
All-Ireland Final: Kerry 3-13 Dublin 1-8.

1970

Summary: Played four championship games, won 50th Munster title, won 22nd All-Ireland title.

Game 1 - versus Limerick in Askeaton on July 5. Final Score: Kerry 2-19; Limerick 2-5.

Johnny Culloty

Seamus Murphy	Paud O'Donoghue	Donie O'Sullivan
Tom Prendergast	John O'Keeffe	Micheál Ó'Sé

Mick O'Connell (0-1)　　　　DJ Crowley

Brendan Lynch (0-6)	Pat Griffin (0-3)	Eamon O'Donoghue (0-3)
Mick Gleeson (2-0)	Liam Higgins (0-2)	Mick O'Dwyer (0-4)

No substitutes used.

Game 2 - Munster Final versus Cork in Killarney on July 26. Final Score: Kerry 2-22; Cork 2-9.

Johnny Culloty

Seamus Murphy	Paud O'Donoghue	Donie O'Sullivan
Tom Prendergast	John O'Keeffe	Micheál Ó'Sé

Mick O'Connell (0-5)　　　　DJ Crowley (0-3)

Brendan Lynch (0-4)	Pat Griffin (1-1)	Eamon O'Donoghue
Mick Gleeson	Liam Higgins (1-1)	Mick O'Dwyer (0-8)

Substitute: Mick Fleming for Mick O'Connell.

Game 3 - All-Ireland semi-final versus Derry in Croke Park on August 23. Final Score: Kerry 0-23; Derry 0-10.

Johnny Culloty

Seamus Murphy	Paud O'Donoghue	Donie O'Sullivan
Tom Prendergast	John O'Keeffe (0-1)	Micheál Ó'Sé

	Mick O'Connell (0-1)	DJ Crowley (0-1)
Brendan Lynch (0-4)	Pat Griffin (0-5)	Eamon O'Donoghue
Mick Gleeson	Liam Higgins (0-2)	Mick O'Dwyer (0-9)

Substitute: PJ Burns for Mick O'Connell.

Game 4 - All-Ireland Final versus Meath in Croke Park on September 27. Final Score: Kerry 2-19; Meath 0-18.

Johnny Culloty

Seamus Murphy	Paud O'Donoghue	Donie O'Sullivan
Tom Prendergast	John O'Keeffe	Micheál Ó'Sé
Mick O'Connell (0-2)		DJ Crowley (1-0)
Brendan Lynch (0-6)	Pat Griffin (0-2)	Eamon O'Donoghue (0-2)
Mick Gleeson (1-1)	Liam Higgins (0-2)	Mick O'Dwyer (0-4)

Substitute: Seamus MacGearailt for Donie O'Sullivan.

Scorers for the Year: Mick O'Dwyer (0-25), Brendan Lynch (0-20), Pat Griffin (1-11), Mick Gleeson (3-1), Liam Higgins (1-7), Mick O'Connell (0-9), DJ Crowley (1-4), Eamon O'Donoghue (0-5), John O'Keeffe (0-1).

Total Scored: 6-83

Appearances:

4 - Johnny Culloty, Seamus Murphy, Paud O'Donoghue, Donie O'Sullivan, Tom Prendergast, John O'Keeffe, Micheál Ó'Sé, Mick O'Connell, DJ Crowley, Brendan Lynch, Pat Griffin, Eamon O'Donoghue, Mick Gleeson, Liam Higgins, Mick O'Dwyer.

3 - None

2 - None

1 - Mick Fleming, PJ Burns, Seamus MacGearailt.

1970 - GAA Winners:

All-Irelands: Senior Football: Kerry **Minor Football:** Galway **Under-21 Football:** Cork

National Leagues: Football: Mayo   Hurling: Cork

Senior Hurling: Cork

Kerry Co. Champions: Football: East Kerry   Hurling: Kilmoyley

1970 - In The News:

- Huge anti-apartheid demonstrations take place as Ireland play South Africa in rugby.
- Éamon and Sinéad de Valera celebrate their 60th wedding anniversary.
- Sinn Féin splits into Provisional and Official wings over a disagreement on abstentionism.
- Garda Richard Fallon is murdered on duty in Dublin. The first Garda killed in the South during the troubles.
- Rev. Ian Paisley won a by-election to the House of Commons of Northern Ireland in April.
- The Alliance Party is founded in Northern Ireland.
- On April 22, Taoiseach Jack Lynch presents the budget in the absence of the Minister for Finance, Charles Haughey, who was injured, supposedly in a riding accident.
- On May 4, The Minister for Justice, Micheál Ó Móráin, resigns from the government citing ill-health. The Taoiseach states in the Dáil on 7-May, "I wish to state that Deputy Ó Móráin's condition is not unassociated with the shock he suffered as a result of the killing of Garda Fallon".
- On May 6, the Minister for Finance, Charles Haughey, and the Minister for Agriculture, Neil Blaney, are asked to resign by Taoiseach Jack Lynch. He accuses them of the attempted illegal importation of arms for use by the Provisional IRA. Kevin Boland, the Minister for Local Government, resigns in sympathy with them.
- Captain James Kelly, Albert Luykx and John Kelly are arrested on May 27. They are charged with conspiracy to import arms.
- May 28 sees Charles Haughey and Neil Blaney appearing in Dublin's Bridewell Court charged, along with Albert Luykx and Capt. Kelly, with conspiracy to import arms.

- Kevin Boland is expelled from the Fianna Fáil parliamentary party on June 4.
- Bishops meeting at Maynooth lift the ban on Catholic attendance at Trinity College, Dublin.
- Neil Blaney is cleared of arms conspiracy charges on July 2.
- On July 5, after a special cabinet meeting, the government demands a ban on all parades in Northern Ireland and the disarmament of civilians.
- The Galway-Aran Islands air service is launched. A return air-fare costs £5.
- A new political party, the Social Democratic and Labour Party, is founded in Northern Ireland under the leadership of Gerry Fitt on August 21.
- The New University of Ulster is presented with a Royal Charter by Elizabeth II.
- In October, US President Richard Nixon arrives in Ireland. He is greeted by Taoiseach Jack Lynch. Meanwhile in Dublin an anti-Vietnam War protest takes place. Mrs. Nixon visits relatives and her ancestral home in Co. Mayo. Another protest takes place outside the U.S. Embassy in Dublin.
- On October 23 Charles Haughey, James Kelly, Albert Luykx and John Kelly are acquitted in the Arms Conspiracy Trial.
- In late October Taoiseach Jack Lynch, questioned on his return from the United States, says that there will be no change in fundamental Fianna Fáil policy regarding Northern Ireland.
- Aer Lingus takes delivery of its first Boeing 747 (Jumbo Jet), its largest aircraft to date.
- The first Regional Technical Colleges open in Ireland.
- "All Kinds of Everything" sung by Dana (music and text by Derry Lindsay and Jackie Smith), wins Eurovision Song Contest for Ireland.
- "Ryan's Daughter", David Lean's movie, filmed largely in Ireland, is released.
- Nijinsky wins the Irish Derby.
- **Arkle** (19 April 1957 - 31 May 1970) the most famous Irish racehorse dies. The bay gelding was bred at Ballymacoll Stud, Co. Meath by Mrs. Mary Alison Baker of Malahow House, near Naul, Co. Dublin. Owned by Anne Grosvenor, Duchess of Westminster, Arkle was trained by Tom Dreaper at Greenogue, Kilsallaghan in Co. Dublin, Ireland and well ridden for the entirety of steeplechasing career by the famous Pat Taaffe.

Arkle became the first racehorse in Britain to capture public attention outside racing circles. He was regarded as the greatest steeplechaser of all time. Despite his career being cut short by injury, he still won three Cheltenham Gold Cups and a host of other top prizes.

The racing authorities in Ireland took the unprecedented step in the Irish Grand National of devising two weight systems - one to be used when Arkle was running and one when he wasn't. Arkle won the 1964 race by only one length but he carried two and half stones (35 lbs) more than his rivals.

Arkle had a strange quirk in that he crossed his forelegs when jumping a fence, a style used to win 27 of his 35 starts from distances at 1m 6f up to 3m 5f. Legendary racing commentator Peter O'Sullivan has called Arkle a freak of nature - something unlikely to be seen again.

In December 1966, Arkle raced in the King George VI Chase at Kempton Park and struck the guard rail with a hoof when jumping the open ditch, which resulted in a fractured pedal bone. Despite this, he completed the race and finished second. He was in plaster for 4 months, and though he made a good enough recovery to go back into training, he never ran again. He was retired and ridden as a hack by his owner and then succumbed to what has been variously described as advanced arthritis, or possibly brucellosis, and was put down at the early age of 13.

Arkle became a national legend in Ireland. His strength was jokingly claimed to come from drinking Guinness twice a day. At one point the slogan "Arkle for President" was written on a wall in Dublin. Often referred to simply as "Himself", the story goes that he received items of fan mail addressed to "Himself, Ireland". Former Nottinghamshire and England cricketer Derek Randall, known for his exceptional pace while fielding, was nicknamed "Arkle". The government owned Irish National Stud, at Tully, Co. Kildare, has the skeleton of Arkle on display in its museum.

1971

Summary: Played two championship games, lost Munster Final.

Game 1 - versus Tipperary in Killarney on June 13. Final Score: Kerry 1-14; Tipperary 1-7.

Johnny Culloty

Donie O'Sullivan	Paud O'Donoghue	Derry Crowley
Tom Prendergast	John O'Keeffe (0-1)	Micheál Ó'Sé

Mick O'Connell   DJ Crowley (0-1)

Brendan Lynch (0-4)	Pat Griffin (0-1)	Eamon O'Donoghue
Mick Gleeson (0-1)	Liam Higgins	Mick O'Dwyer (1-6)

No substitutes used.

Game 2 - Munster Final versus Cork in Cork on July 18. Final Score: Cork 0-25; Kerry 0-14.

Johnny Culloty

Donie O'Sullivan	Paud O'Donoghue	Seamus MacGearailt
Tom Prendergast	John O'Keeffe	Micheál Ó'Sé

Mick O'Connell (0-2)   DJ Crowley

Brendan Lynch (0-2)	Pat Griffin	Eamon O'Donoghue (0-1)
Mick Gleeson (0-2)	Liam Higgins	Mick O'Dwyer (0-7)

Substitutes: Paudie Lynch for Pat Griffin, Mickey O'Sullivan for Eamon O'Donoghue, Donal Kavanagh for Brendan Lynch.

Scorers for the Year: Mick O'Dwyer (1-13), Brendan Lynch (0-6), Mick Gleeson (0-3), Mick O'Connell (0-2), John O'Keeffe (0-1), DJ Crowley (0-1), Pat Griffin (0-1), Eamon O'Donoghue (0-1).

Total Scored: 1-28

Appearances:

2 - Johnny Culloty, Donie O'Sullivan, Paud O'Donoghue, Tom Prendergast, John O'Keeffe, Micheál Ó'Sé, Mick O'Connell, DJ Crowley, Brendan Lynch, Pat Griffin, Eamon O'Donoghue, Mick Gleeson, Liam Higgins, Mick O'Dwyer.

1 - Derry Crowley, Seamus MacGearailt, Paudie Lynch, Mickey O'Sullivan, Donal Kavanagh.

1971 - GAA Winners:

All-Irelands: Senior Football: Offaly **Minor Football:** Mayo **Under-21 Football:** Cork

National Leagues: Football: Kerry   Hurling: Limerick

Senior Hurling: Tipperary

Kerry Co. Champions: Football: Mid-Kerry   Hurling: Kilmoyley

1971 Football All-Stars:

P.J.Smyth (Galway), Johnny Carey (Mayo), Jack Cosgrove (Galway), **Donie O'Sullivan (Kerry),** Eugene Mulligan (Offaly), Nicholas Clavin (Offaly), Pat Reynolds (Meath), Liam Sammon (Galway), Willie Bryan (Offaly), Tony McTague (Offaly), Ray Cummins (Cork), Mickey Kearns (Sligo), Andy McCallin (Antrim), Sean O'Neill (Down), Seamus Leydon (Galway).

1971 - In The News:

- The Eurovision Song Contest is held in Dublin. Presented by Bernadette Ní Ghallchóir, it is the first colour broadcast by RTÉ.
- The GAA votes to lift its ban on members participating in "foreign games" such as soccer, rugby and cricket.
- Seán Lemass, Taoiseach from 1959 to 1966, dies in Dublin aged 71. He was active during the 1916 Easter Rising, the War of Independence and the Civil War.
- Members of the Irish Women's Liberation Movement return to Dublin by train from Belfast bringing contraceptives as a protest against the law banning their importation.
- The Social Democratic and Labour Party (SDLP) announces that it is withdrawing from Stormont.

- Internment without trial is introduced in Northern Ireland. Over 300 republicans are "lifted" in pre-dawn raids. Some Loyalists are later arrested.
- British troops begin clearing operations in Belfast following the worst rioting in years in August. Taoiseach Jack Lynch calls for an end to the Stormont administration.
- A rally takes place in Dublin in September in support of a campaign of civil disobedience in Northern Ireland.
- The government defeats a motion of no confidence in Minister for Defence, Jim Gibbons.
- Neil Blaney and Paudge Brennan are expelled from the Fianna Fáil parliamentary party.
- Taoiseach Jack Lynch has talks with British Prime Minister Harold Wilson in Dublin in November.
- A bomb in McGurk's Bar in Belfast kills 15 people on December 4.

1972

Summary: Played five championship games, won 51st Munster title, lost All-Ireland Final.

Game 1 - versus Tipperary in Clonmel on June 11. Final Score: Kerry 1-12; Tipperary 0-9.

Eamonn Fitzgerald

Donie O'Sullivan   Paud O'Donoghue   Derry Crowley

Mickey O'Sullivan   Paudie Lynch   Micheál Ó'Sé

Mick O'Connell (0-3)   John O'Keeffe

Jackie Walsh   Donal Kavanagh   Eamon O'Donoghue (0-2)

Mick Gleeson (0-1)   Liam Higgins (1-2)   Mick O'Dwyer (0-3)

Substitutes: Brendan Lynch (0-1) for Jackie Walsh, John Saunders for Brendan Lynch.

Game 2 -Munster Final versus Cork in Killarney on July 16. Final Score: Kerry 2-21; Cork 2-15.

Eamonn Fitzgerald

Donie O'Sullivan   Paud O'Donoghue   Seamus MacGearailt

Tom Prendergast   Micheál Ó'Sé   Paudie Lynch

Mick O'Connell (0-2)   John O'Keeffe (0-2)

Brendan Lynch (0-2)   Donal Kavanagh (1-0)   Eamon O'Donoghue

Mick Gleeson (1-1)   Liam Higgins (0-4)   Mick O'Dwyer (0-10)

Substitutes: Derry Crowley for Donie O'Sullivan, Pat Griffin for Eamon O'Donoghue.

Game 3 - All-Ireland semi-final versus Roscommon in Croke Park on August 13. Final Score: Kerry 1-22; Roscommon 1-12.

Eamonn Fitzgerald

Donie O'Sullivan   Paud O'Donoghue   Seamus MacGearailt

Tom Prendergast(0-1)	Micheál Ó'Sé	Paudie Lynch

Mick O'Connell (0-4)   John O'Keeffe

Brendan Lynch (0-4)	Donal Kavanagh (1-0)	Eamon O'Donoghue
Mick Gleeson (0-2)	Liam Higgins (0-3)	Mick O'Dwyer (0-8)

No substitutes used.

Game 4 - All-Ireland Final versus Offaly in Croke Park on September 24. Final Score: Kerry 1-13; Offaly 1-13.

Eamonn Fitzgerald

Donie O'Sullivan	Paud O'Donoghue	Seamus MacGearailt
Tom Prendergast	Micheál Ó'Sé	Paudie Lynch

Mick O'Connell (0-1)   John O'Keeffe

Brendan Lynch (1-7)	Donal Kavanagh	Eamon O'Donoghue
Mick Gleeson	Liam Higgins	Mick O'Dwyer (0-5)

Substitutes: Pat Griffin for Liam Higgins, Derry Crowley for Seamus MacGearailt.

Game 5 - All-Ireland Final Replay versus Offaly in Croke Park on October 15. Final Score: Offaly 1-19; Kerry 0-13.

Eamonn Fitzgerald

Donie O'Sullivan	Paud O'Donoghue	Seamus MacGearailt
Tom Prendergast	Micheál Ó'Sé	Paudie Lynch

Mick O'Connell (0-7)   John O'Keeffe

Brendan Lynch (0-2)	Donal Kavanagh	Eamon O'Donoghue
Mick Gleeson	Liam Higgins (0-2)	Mick O'Dwyer (0-2)

Substitutes: Derry Crowley for Seamus MacGearailt, Pat Griffin for Mick Gleeson, Jackie Walsh for Brendan Lynch.

Scorers for the Year: Mick O'Dwyer (0-28), Brendan Lynch (1-16), Mick O'Connell (0-17), Liam Higgins (1-11), Mick Gleeson (1-4), Donal Kavanagh

(2-0), John O'Keeffe (0-2), Eamon O'Donoghue (0-2), Tom Prendergast (0-1).

Total Scored: 5-81

Appearances:

5 - Eamonn Fitzgerald, Donie O'Sullivan, Paud O'Donoghue, Micheál Ó'Sé, Paudie Lynch, Mick O'Connell, John O'Keeffe, Brendan Lynch, Donal Kavanagh, Eamon O'Donoghue, Mick Gleeson, Liam Higgins, Mick O'Dwyer.

4 - Derry Crowley, Seamus MacGearailt, Tom Prendergast.

3 - Pat Griffin.

2 - Jackie Walsh.

1 - Mickey O'Sullivan, John Saunders.

1972 - GAA Winners:

All-Irelands: Senior Football: Offaly **Minor Football:** Cork   **Under-21 Football:** Galway

National Leagues: Football: Kerry   Hurling: Cork

Senior Hurling: Kilkenny

Kerry Co. Champions: Football: Shannon Rangers   Hurling: Ballyduff

1972 Football All-Stars:

Martin Furlong (Offaly), Mick Ryan (Offaly), Paddy McCormack (Offaly), **Donie O'Sullivan (Kerry),** Brian McEniff (Donegal), Tommy Joe Gilmore (Galway), Kevin Jer O'Sullivan (Cork), Willie Bryan (Offaly), **Mick O'Connell (Kerry),** Johnny Cooney (Offaly), Kevin Kilmurray (Offaly), Tony McTague (Offaly), Mickey Freyne (Roscommon), Sean O'Neill (Down), Paddy Moriarty (Armagh).

1972 - In The News:

* Taoiseach Jack Lynch and Minister for External Affairs Patrick Hillery sign the Treaty of Accession to the European Communities.

- January 30 is Bloody Sunday: 13 unarmed civilians are shot dead in Derry as British soldiers open fire on a banned civil rights march.
- Taoiseach Jack Lynch announces a national day of mourning following the events in Derry.
- Rioting takes place in Dublin. The British Embassy is burned in Merrion Square.
- The IRA announces a ceasefire on February 10.
- On February 12 William Craig launches the Ulster Vanguard Movement in Lisburn.
- The National Anti-EEC Committee organises a march along O'Connell Street.
- Huge crowds turn out to see Pelé and his club, Santos, play at Dalymount Park.
- Raidió na Gaeltachta goes on the air in April.
- The government launches its European Economic Community referendum campaign.
- RTC Carlow becomes the first Regional Technical College to install a computer – at a cost of £10,000, it will be used for business and engineering courses. It uses the Fortran and RPG languages.
- The referendum on Ireland's membership of the EEC is almost five to one in favour.
- An Garda Síochána celebrates its 50th anniversary.
- Russian composer Dmitri Shostakovich is presented with an honourary D.Mus. degree at a ceremony in Trinity College, Dublin.
- Over 2,000 refugees from Northern Ireland spend the marching season south of the border.
- July 21 is Bloody Friday: 9 people die and over 100 are injured in a series of IRA explosions in Belfast city centre.
- July's Operation Motorman: British troops invade no-go areas in Belfast, Derry and Newry.
- On August 20 commemorations are held at Béal na Bláth, Co. Cork, to mark the 50th anniversary of the death of Michael Collins.
- President Éamon de Valera signs documents covering Ireland's entry into the EEC.
- William Trevor's collection of stories, *The Ballroom of Romance,* is published.
- Gilbert O'Sullivan's song "Alone Again (Naturally)" hits the No. 1 spot in the US singles chart.
- Mary Peters becomes the first Irish woman to win a gold medal at the Olympics.
- Alex.Higgins wins the World Professional Snooker Championship.

1973

Summary: Played two championship games, lost Munster Final.

Game 1 - versus Tipperary in Tralee on June 17. Final Score: Kerry 3-11; Tipperary 0-5.

Eamonn Fitzgerald

Donie O'Sullivan	Paud O'Donoghue	Jim Deenihan
Tom Prendergast	Derry Crowley	Ger O'Keeffe

Donal Kavanagh (0-1)   John O'Keeffe (0-1)

Brendan Lynch (0-1)	Mickey O'Sullivan (2-1)	Eamon O'Donoghue
John Egan (0-1)	Mick O'Dwyer (1-6)	Jackie Walsh

Substitutes: Liam Higgins for Brendan Lynch, Ger Power for Ger O'Keeffe.

Game 2 - Munster Final versus Cork in Cork on July 15. Final Score: Cork 5-12; Kerry 1-15.

Eamonn Fitzgerald

Donie O'Sullivan	Paud O'Donoghue	Jim Deenihan
Tom Prendergast	Derry Crowley	Ger O'Keeffe

John O'Keeffe (0-1)   Donal Kavanagh (1-0)

Brendan Lynch (0-3)	Mickey O'Sullivan	Eamon O'Donoghue (0-1)
John Egan (0-3)	Mick O'Dwyer (0-6)	Jackie Walsh (0-1)

Substitutes: Liam Higgins for Mickey O'Sullivan, Micheál Ó'Sé for Tom Prendergast, Mick Gleeson for Eamon O'Donoghue.

Scorers for the Year: Mick O'Dwyer (1-12), Mickey O'Sullivan (2-1), Donal Kavanagh (1-1), Brendan Lynch (0-4), John Egan (0-4), John O'Keeffe (0-2), Eamon O'Donoghue (0-1), Jackie Walsh (0-1).

Total Scored: 4-26

Appearances:

2 - Eamonn Fitzgerald, Donie O'Sullivan, Paud O'Donoghue, Jim Deenihan, Tom Prendergast, Derry Crowley, Ger O'Keeffe, John O'Keeffe, Donal Kavanagh, Brendan Lynch, Mickey O'Sullivan, Eamon O'Donoghue, Liam Higgins, John Egan, Mick O'Dwyer, Jackie Walsh.

1 - Ger Power, Micheál Ó'Sé, Mick Gleeson.

1973 - GAA Winners:

All-Irelands: Senior Football: Cork **Minor Football:** Tyrone   **Under-21 Football:** Kerry

Winning Under-21 Team: P. O'Mahony, B. Harmon, J. Deenihan, B. O'Shea, G. O'Keeffe, G. Power, K. O'Donoghue, J. Long, P. Lynch, J. Coffey, M. O'Sullivan, P. Ó'Sé, M. O'Shea, J. Egan, M. Sheehy. Subs: M. Ferris, N. Brosnan.

National Leagues: Football: Kerry   Hurling: Wexford

Senior Hurling: Limerick

Kerry Co. Champions: Football: Austin Stacks   Hurling: Ballyduff

1973 Football All-Stars:

Billy Morgan (Cork), Frank Cogan (Cork), Mick Ryan (Offaly), Brian Murphy (Cork), Liam O'Neill (Galway), Tommy Joe Gilmore (Galway), Kevin Jer O'Sullivan (Cork), **John O'Keeffe (Kerry),** Dinny Long (Cork), Johnny Cooney (Offaly), Kevin Kilmurray (Offaly), Liam Sammon (Galway), Jimmy Barry Murphy (Cork), Ray Cummins (Cork), Anthony McGurk (Derry).

1973 - In The News:

- Ireland joins the European Community along with Britain and Denmark.
- Patrick Hillery is appointed Social Affairs Commissioner in the European Economic Community.
- On February 28 the National Coalition of Fine Gael and the Labour Party win the general election, ending 16 years of Fianna Fáil government. Fine Gael's 54 seats added to Labour's 19 gave the Coalition 73 of the 144 available seats. Fianna Fáil actually gained votes on the previous 1969 election, but lost six seats to end with 68.

Two Independents and the outgoing Ceann Comhairle round out the 20ᵗʰ Dail.

- Kerry return the following members to the 20ᵗʰ Dáil:
  Kerry South: John O'Leary (FF); Timothy O'Connor (FF); Michael Begley (FG).
  Kerry North: Gerard Lynch (FG); Tom McEllistrim Jr. (FF); Dan Spring (Lab.).
- Liam Cosgrave is elected Taoiseach with Labour's Brendan Corish serving as Tánaiste.
- The funeral takes place of the former Archbishop of Dublin, Dr. John Charles McQuaid.
- In the presidential election voters go to the poll to find a successor to President Éamon de Valera. Erskine H. Childers is the victor defeating Tom O'Higgins by a margin of just over 48,000 votes, 52% to 48%.
- Éamon de Valera retires from office aged 90. He travels to Boland's Mills where he was positioned during the Easter Rising. The motorcade then proceeds to Talbot Lodge in Blackrock where he will spend his retirement.
- The funeral takes place in July of the Blacksmith of Ballinalee, General Seán Mac Eoin.
- The government lifts colour restrictions on RTÉ transmissions.
- Mountjoy Prison helicopter escape. Three Provisional IRA prisoners escape from Mountjoy Prison after a hijacked helicopter lands in the prison yard.
- The Sunningdale Agreement is signed by British Prime Minister Ted Heath, Taoiseach Liam Cosgrave, Brian Faulkner, Gerry Fitt and Oliver Napier.
- Hugh Leonard's play "Da" is staged for the first time.

1974

Summary: Played two championship games, lost Munster Final.

Game 1 - versus Waterford in Killarney on June 16. Final Score: Kerry 7-16; Waterford 0-8.

Paudie O'Mahony

Donie O'Sullivan   Paud O'Donoghue   Derry Crowley

Páidí Ó'Sé   Paudie Lynch   Ger O'Keeffe

John O'Keeffe (0-2)   John Long (0-1)

Eamon O'Donoghue (0-2)   Mickey O'Sullivan (1-3)   Ger Power (0-1)

John Egan (2-0)   Seamus MacGearailt (2-3)   Mike Sheehy (2-3)

Substitutes: Brendan Lynch (0-1) for Ger Power, Pat Griffin for Mickey O'Sullivan, Jim Deenihan for Páidí Ó'Sé.

Game 2 - Munster Final versus Cork in Killarney on July 14. Final Score: Cork 1-11; Kerry 0-7.

Paudie O'Mahony

Donie O'Sullivan   Paud O'Donoghue   Derry Crowley

Páidí Ó'Sé   John O'Keeffe   Ger O'Keeffe

Paudie Lynch (0-1)   John Long

Eamon O'Donoghue (0-1) Mickey O'Sullivan (0-4)   Ger Power

John Egan   Seamus MacGearailt   Mike Sheehy (0-1)

Substitutes: Brendan Lynch for Eamon O'Donoghue, Jackie Walsh for Seamus MacGearailt, Mick O'Connell for Jackie Walsh.

Scorers for the Year: Mike Sheehy (2-4), Mickey O'Sullivan (1-7), Seamus MacGearailt(2-3), John Egan (2-0), Eamon O'Donoghue (0-3), John O'Keeffe (0-2), Paudie Lynch (0-1), John Long (0-1), Brendan Lynch (0-1), Ger Power (0-1).

Total Scored: 7-23

Appearances:

2 - Paudie O'Mahony, Donie O'Sullivan, Paud O'Donoghue, Derry Crowley, Páidí Ó'Sé , John O'Keeffe, Ger O'Keeffe, Paudie Lynch, John Long, Eamon O'Donoghue, Mickey O'Sullivan, Ger Power, John Egan, Seamus MacGearailt, Mike Sheehy, Brendan Lynch.

1 - Pat Griffin, Jim Deenihan, Jackie Walsh, Mick O'Connell.

1974 - GAA Winners:

All-Irelands: Senior Football: Dublin **Minor Football:** Cork   **Under-21 Football:** Mayo

National Leagues: Football: Kerry   Hurling: Cork

Senior Hurling: Kilkenny

Kerry Co. Champions: Football: Kenmare   Hurling: Abbeydorney

1974 Football All-Stars:

Paddy Cullen (Dublin), Donal Monaghan (Donegal), Sean Doherty (Dublin), Robbie Kelleher (Dublin), Paddy Reilly (Dublin), Barnes Murphy (Sligo), Johnny Hughes (Galway), Dermot Earley (Roscommon), **Paudie Lynch (Kerry),** Tom Naughton (Galway), Declan Barron (Cork), David Hickey (Dublin), Jimmy Barry Murphy (Cork), Jimmy Keaveney (Dublin), Johnny Tobin (Galway).

1974 - In The News:

- The ESB announces that Carnsore Point on the Wexford coast will be the site of its nuclear power station.
- The great hall of University College Dublin is to become a 900-seat concert hall and home of the RTÉ Symphony Orchestra.
- Northern Ireland grinds to a halt as the Ulster Workers' Council calls a strike following the defeat of an anti-Sunningdale Agreement motion. The strike lasts a week in May.
- 31 people die and 150 are injured in four car bomb explosions in Dublin and Monaghan by loyalists on May 17. They are widely suspected of receiving technical assistance from British security forces.
- The five-month old Northern Ireland Executive collapses.

- Anatoli Kaplin, the first Soviet Ambassador to Ireland, visits President Childers at Áras an Uachtaráin.
- The National Coalition's Contraceptive Bill is defeated in a vote in Dáil Éireann. Taoiseach Liam Cosgrave is one of seven Fine Gael TDs who vote against their own bill.
- Jack Lynch says that Fianna Fáil would not support any proposal to repeal Articles 2 and 3 of the Constitution.
- Seán MacBride, former Minister for External Affairs, is to share in the Nobel Prize for Peace.
- Powerscourt House in Enniskerry is destroyed by fire.
- President Erskine H. Childers, fourth President of Ireland, dies suddenly on November 17, aged 69. He had served less than 17 months of his 7 year term.
- Cearbhall Ó'Dálaigh is sworn in as the fifth President of Ireland on December 19. With no other candidates being nominated, an election was not necessary.

1975

Summary: Played four championship games, won 52nd Munster title, won 23rd All-Ireland title.

Game 1 - versus Tipperary in Clonmel on June 15. Final Score: Kerry 3-13; Tipperary 0-9.

Paudie O'Mahony

Páidí Ó'Sé   Ger O'Keeffe   Batt O'Shea

Mickey O'Sullivan   Tim Kennelly   Ger Power

Ger O'Driscoll   Denis Ogie Moran

Brendan Lynch (0-5)   Pat McCarthy   Pat Spillane (0-3)

John Egan (2-3)   Ray Prendiville (1-0)   Mike Sheehy (0-2)

Substitutes: John Bunyan for Ger O'Driscoll, Jim Deenihan for Batt O'Shea.

Game 2 - Munster Final versus Cork in Killarney on July 21. Final Score: Kerry 1-14; Cork 0-7.

Paudie O'Mahony

Ger O'Keeffe   John O'Keeffe   Jim Deenihan

Páidí Ó'Sé   Tim Kennelly   Ger Power

Paudie Lynch   Pat McCarthy (0-1)

Brendan Lynch (0-4)   Mike Sheehy (0-3)   Mickey O'Sullivan (0-1)

John Egan (0-2)   John Bunyan   Pat Spillane (1-1)

Substitutes: Denis Ogie Moran (0-1) for Paudie Lynch, Ger O'Driscoll (0-1) for Brendan Lynch.

Game 3 - All-Ireland semi-final versus Sligo in Croke Park on August 10. Final Score: Kerry 3-13; Sligo 0-5.

Paudie O'Mahony

Ger O'Keeffe   John O'Keeffe   Jim Deenihan

Páidí Ó'Sé	Tim Kennelly	Ger Power (0-1)
Paudie Lynch (0-4)		Pat McCarthy
Brendan Lynch (0-2)	Mike Sheehy	Mickey O'Sullivan (0-1)
John Egan (2-2)	John Bunyan	Pat Spillane (1-1)

Substitutes: Ger O'Driscoll (0-2) for Mike Sheehy, Denis Ogie Moran for Ger O'Driscoll.

Game 4 - All-Ireland Final versus Dublin in Croke Park on September 28. Final Score: Kerry 2-12; Dublin 0-11.

	Paudie O'Mahony	
Ger O'Keeffe	John O'Keeffe	Jim Deenihan
Páidí Ó'Sé	Tim Kennelly	Ger Power
Paudie Lynch		Pat McCarthy
Brendan Lynch (0-3)	Denis Ogie Moran (0-2)	Mickey O'Sullivan
John Egan (1-0)	Mike Sheehy (0-4)	Pat Spillane (0-3)

Substitute: Ger O'Driscoll (1-0) for Mickey O'Sullivan.

Scorers for the Year: John Egan (5-7), Pat Spillane (2-8), Brendan Lynch (0-14), Mike Sheehy (0-9), Ger O'Driscoll (1-3), Paudie Lynch (0-4), Ray Prendiville (1-0), Denis Ogie Moran (0-3), Mickey O'Sullivan (0-2), Ger Power (0-1), Pat McCarthy (0-1).

Total Scored: 9-52

Appearances:

4 - Paudie O'Mahony, Ger O'Keeffe, Jim Deenihan, Páidí Ó'Sé, Tim Kennelly, Ger Power, Pat McCarthy, Brendan Lynch, Denis Ogie Moran, Mickey O'Sullivan, John Egan, Mike Sheehy, Pat Spillane, Ger O'Driscoll.

3 - John O'Keeffe, Paudie Lynch, John Bunyan.

2 - None

1 - Batt O'Shea, Ray Prendiville.

1975 - GAA Winners:

All-Irelands: Senior Football: Kerry **Minor Football:** Kerry **Under-21 Football:** Kerry

Kerry's Winning Minor Team: C. Nelligan, V. O'Connor, M. O'Sullivan, M. Colgan, JJ O'Connor, M. Spillane, G. Casey, S. Walsh, N. O'Donovan, F. Scannell, J. Mulvihill, R. Bunyan, C. O'Connor, J. O'Shea, P. Sheehan.

Kerry's Winning Under-21 Team: C. Nelligan, K. O'Donoghue, P. Ó'Sé, G. Leahy, M. Spillane, T. Kennelly, D. Moran, G. O'Driscoll, S. Walsh, B. Walsh, M. Sheehy, D. Murphy, T. Doyle, J. O'Shea, P. Spillane.

National Leagues: Football: Meath   Hurling: Galway

Senior Hurling: Kilkenny

Kerry Co. Champions: Football: Austin Stacks   Hurling: St. Brendans

1975 Football All-Stars:

Paudie O'Mahony (Kerry), Gay O'Driscoll (Dublin), **John O'Keeffe (Kerry),** Robbie Kelleher (Dublin), Peter Stevenson (Derry), Anthony McGurk (Derry), **Ger Power (Kerry),** Dinny Long (Cork), Colm McAlarney (Down), Gerry McElhinney (Derry), Ken Rennicks (Meath), **Mickey O'Sullivan (Kerry), John Egan (Kerry),** Matt Kerrigan (Meath), Anton O'Toole (Dublin).

1975 - In The News:

- Sinéad Bean de Valera dies in Dublin, aged 96.
- Charles Haughey is brought back onto the Fianna Fáil front bench.
- Aer Lingus hostesses get a new uniform.
- Mary Immaculate College, Limerick and Our Lady of Mercy College, Carysfort become recognised colleges of the National University of Ireland.
- Dr. Danny O'Hare is made acting director of the National Institute for Higher Education, Dublin.
- Three members of the Miami Showband are killed in an Ulster Volunteer Force attack as they return from a dance in Co. Down.
- Éamon de Valera dies on August 29 in Dublin, aged 92. His life has spanned the history of the Irish State. He was a leader of the Easter Rising in 1916. He served as Taoiseach for 21 years and President for 14 years. The government announces a day of mourning.

- Dutch industrialist Dr. Tiede Herrema who owns a factory in Limerick, is kidnapped on October 3. Dr. Herrema is located with his kidnappers in Monasterevin, Co. Kildare on October 21, but remains in captivity until the siege ends on November 18.
- Oliver Plunkett, the 17th-century Archbishop of Armagh, is canonised by Pope Paul VI in Rome.
- George Best plays a League of Ireland match for Cork Celtic against Drogheda.
- The Druid Theatre Company is founded in Galway by Garry Hynes, Mick Lally and Marie Mullen.
- John Ryan's memoir "Remembering How We Stood" and Paul Durkan's collection of poems "O Westport in the Light of Asia Minor" are published.

1976

Summary: Played five championship games, won 53rd Munster title, lost All-Ireland Final.

Game 1 - versus Waterford in Dungarvan on June 20. Final Score: Kerry 3-17; Waterford 0-6.

Paudie O'Mahony

Ger O'Keeffe   John O'Keeffe   Jim Deenihan

Páidí Ó'Sé   Tim Kennelly   Ger Power

Paudie Lynch   Pat McCarthy

Brendan Lynch (1-2)   Denis Ogie Moran (0-2)   Mickey O'Sullivan (0-2)

John Egan (0-2)   Mike Sheehy (1-4)   Pat Spillane (1-5)

Substitute: Sean Walsh for Denis Ogie Moran.

Game 2 - Munster Final versus Cork in Cork on July 11. Final Score: Kerry 0-10; Cork 0-10.

Paudie O'Mahony

Ger O'Keeffe   John O'Keeffe   Jim Deenihan

Páidí Ó'Sé   Tim Kennelly   Ger Power

Paudie Lynch   Pat McCarthy (0-2)

Brendan Lynch   Denis Ogie Moran   Mickey O'Sullivan

John Egan   Mike Sheehy (0-5)   Pat Spillane (0-2)

Substitutes: Sean Walsh (0-1) for Brendan Lynch, Jackie Walsh for Mickey O'Sullivan.

Game 3 - Munster Final Replay versus Cork in Cork on July 25. Final Score: Kerry 3-20; Cork 2-19.

Paudie O'Mahony

Tim Kennelly   John O'Keeffe   Jim Deenihan

Páidí Ó'Sé   Ger O'Keeffe   Ger Power

Paudie Lynch   Pat McCarthy

Denis Ogie Moran   Mickey O'Sullivan (1-2)   Pat Spillane (1-3)

Brendan Lynch   Mike Sheehy (0-11)   John Egan (0-1)

Substitute: Sean Walsh (1-3) for Mickey O'Sullivan.

Game 4 - All-Ireland semi-final versus Derry in Croke Park on August 8. Final Score: Kerry 5-14; Derry 1-10.

Paudie O'Mahony

Ger O'Keeffe   John O'Keeffe   Jim Deenihan

Páidí Ó'Sé   Tim Kennelly (0-1)   Ger Power

Paudie Lynch   Pat McCarthy

Mickey O'Sullivan (0-1) Denis Ogie Moran (0-1)   Pat Spillane (0-2)

Brendan Lynch (0-3)   Mike Sheehy (3-3)   John Egan (0-2)

Substitutes: Sean Walsh (1-1) for Pat McCarthy, Ger O'Driscoll (1-0) for Brendan Lynch.

Game 5 - All-Ireland Final versus Dublin in Croke Park on September 26. Final Score: Dublin 3-8; Kerry 0-10.

Paudie O'Mahony

Ger O'Keeffe   John O'Keeffe   Jim Deenihan

Páidí Ó'Sé   Tim Kennelly   Ger Power

Paudie Lynch   Pat McCarthy

Denis Ogie Moran (0-2)   Mike Sheehy (0-3)   Mickey O'Sullivan (0-1)

Brendan Lynch (0-1)   John Egan (0-1)   Pat Spillane (0-2)

Substitutes: Charlie Nelligan for Paudie O'Mahony, Ger O'Driscoll for Mickey O'Sullivan.

Scorers for the Year: Mike Sheehy (4-26), Pat Spillane (2-14), Sean Walsh (2-5), Mickey O'Sullivan (1-6), Brendan Lynch (1-6), John Egan (0-6), Denis Ogie Moran (0-5), Ger O'Driscoll (1-0), Pat McCarthy (0-2), Tim Kennelly (0-1).

Total Scored: 11-71

Appearances:

5 - Paudie O'Mahony, Ger O'Keeffe, John O'Keeffe, Jim Deenihan, Páidí Ó'Sé, Tim Kennelly, Ger Power, Paudie Lynch, Pat McCarthy, Denis Ogie Moran, Mike Sheehy, Mickey O'Sullivan, Brendan Lynch, John Egan, Pat Spillane.

4 - Sean Walsh.

3 - None

2 - Ger O'Driscoll.

1 - Charlie Nelligan.

1976 - GAA Winners:

All-Irelands: Senior Football: Dublin **Minor Football:** Galway **Under-21 Football:** Kerry

Kerry's Winning Under-21 Team: C. Nelligan, M. Colgan, P. Ó'Sé, G. Leahy, M. Spillane, D. Moran, V. O'Connor, S. Walsh, J. O'Shea, N. O'Donovan, P. Spillane, G. Murphy, B. Walsh, G. O'Sullivan, P. Foley.

National Leagues: Football: Dublin   Hurling: Kilkenny

Senior Hurling: Cork

Kerry Co. Champions: Football: Austin Stacks   Hurling: Ballyduff

1976 Football All-Stars:

Paddy Cullen (Dublin), **Ger O'Keeffe (Kerry), John O'Keeffe (Kerry),** Brian Murphy (Cork), Johnny Hughes (Galway), Kevin Moran (Dublin), **Ger Power (Kerry),** Brian Mullins (Dublin), Dave McCarthy (Cork), Anton O'Toole (Dublin), Tony Hanahoe (Dublin), David Hickey (Dublin), Bobby Doyle (Dublin), **Mike Sheehy (Kerry), Pat Spillane (Kerry).**

1976 - In The News:

- Former Taoiseach John A. Costello dies in Dublin, aged 84.
- Taoiseach and Mrs. Cosgrave are greeted by President and Mrs. Ford at the White House.

- A large quantity of money is stolen from a CIE train at Sallins, Co. Kildare.
- The last passenger train runs on the Limerick-Claremorris line ending a 80-year north-south link along the western seaboard.
- Tim Severin, in the boat *Brendan,* sets off to trace the route of the legendary sixth century Irish monk from Dingle to America.
- June 29 sees the highest temperature recorded in Ireland this century, 32.5C (90.5F) at Boora, Co. Offaly.
- On July 15, four prisoners escape when bombs explode in the Special Criminal Court, Dublin.
- Christopher Ewart-Biggs, UK ambassador, and a civil servant, Judith Cooke, are killed by a landmine at Sandyford, Co. Dublin.
- President Cearbhall Ó'Dálaigh consults with the Council of State for four hours on whether to refer the Emergency Powers legislation to the Supreme Court. On October 22, President Ó'Dálaigh resigns following the "thundering disgrace" remark from the Minister for Defence, Paddy Donegan.
- A new £5 note is introduced with the image of the 9th century philosopher Johannes Scotus Eriugena.
- November 20 is National Peace Day, and marked with marches, church services and bell ringing.
- Dr. Patrick Hillery is inaugurated as the sixth President of Ireland in St. Patrick's Hall, Dublin Castle. No election was necessary as Dr. Hillery was the only nominee.

1977

Summary: Played three championship games, won 54th Munster title, lost All-Ireland semi-final.

Game 1 - versus Tipperary in Tralee on June 3. Final Score: Kerry 3-14; Tipperary 0-9.

Paudie O'Mahony

Jim Deenihan	Paudie Lynch	Ger O'Keeffe
Denis Ogie Moran	Tim Kennelly	Ger Power (0-1)

Páidí Ó'Sé (0-3)   Jack O'Shea

Sean Walsh (0-3)	John Long	Pat Spillane (1-0)
Barry Walsh (2-3)	John O'Keeffe (0-1)	John Egan (0-3)

Substitute: Anthony O'Keeffe for Denis Ogie Moran.

Game 2 - Munster Final versus Cork in Killarney on July 24. Final Score: Kerry 3-15; Cork 0-9.

Paudie O'Mahony

Jim Deenihan	John O'Keeffe	Ger O'Keeffe
Denis Ogie Moran	Tim Kennelly	Ger Power

Páidí Ó'Sé   Jack O'Shea (0-2)

John Egan (1-0)	Paudie Lynch (0-1)	Pat Spillane (1-3)
Barry Walsh (0-5)	Sean Walsh (1-1)	Mike Sheehy (0-3)

No substitutes used.

Game 3 - All-Ireland semi-final versus Dublin in Croke Park on August 21. Final Score: Dublin 3-12; Kerry 1-13.

Paudie O'Mahony

Jim Deenihan	John O'Keeffe	Ger O'Keeffe (0-1)
Denis Ogie Moran	Tim Kennelly	Ger Power

Páidí Ó'Sé   Jack O'Shea

John Egan (0-2)   Paudie Lynch (0-1)   Pat Spillane

Barry Walsh   Sean Walsh (1-2)   Mike Sheehy (0-7)

Substitutes: Tommy Doyle for Barry Walsh, Pat McCarthy for Jack O'Shea.

Scorers for the Year: Barry Walsh (2-8), Sean Walsh (2-6), Mike Sheehy (0-10), Pat Spillane (2-3), John Egan (1-5), Páidí Ó'Sé (0-3), Jack O'Shea (0-2), Paudie Lynch (0-2), John O'Keeffe (0-1), Ger O'Keeffe (0-1), Ger Power (0-1).

Total Scored: 7-42

Appearances:

3 - Paudie O'Mahony, Jim Deenihan, John O'Keeffe, Ger O'Keeffe, Denis Ogie Moran, Tim Kennelly, Ger Power, Páidí Ó'Sé , Jack O'Shea, John Egan, Paudie Lynch, Pat Spillane, Barry Walsh, Sean Walsh.

2 - Mike Sheehy.

1 - John Long, Anthony O'Keeffe, Tommy Doyle, Pat McCarthy.

1977 - GAA Winners:

All-Irelands: Senior Football: Dublin **Minor Football:** Down   **Under-21 Football:** Kerry

Kerry's Winning Under-21 Team: C. Nelligan, M. Keane, V. O'Connor, M. Spillane, D. (Ogie) Moran, J. Mulvihill, G. Casey, J. O'Shea, E. Liston, T. Doyle, S. Walsh, P. Foley, D. Moran, T. Bridgman, D. Coffey. Sub: G. O'Sullivan for D. Moran.

National Leagues: Football: Kerry   Hurling: Clare

Senior Hurling: Cork

Kerry Co. Champions: Football: Shannon Rangers   Hurling: Ballyduff

1977 Football All-Stars:

Paddy Cullen (Dublin), Gay O'Driscoll (Dublin), Pat Lindsay (Roscommon), Robbie Kelleher (Dublin), Tommy Drumm (Dublin), Paddy Moriarty (Armagh), Pat O'Neill (Dublin), Brian Mullins (Dublin), Joe Kernan

(Armagh), Anton O'Toole (Dublin), Jimmy Smith (Armagh), **Pat Spillane (Kerry),** Bobby Doyle (Dublin), Jimmy Keaveney (Dublin), **John Egan (Kerry).**

1977 - In The News:

- A crater on the planet Mercury is named after the Irish poet W.B. Yeats.
- On May 29, a massive peace rally takes place in Belfast organized by Betty Williams, Mairéad Corrigan and Ciarán McKeown.
- Fianna Fáil wins the 1977 general election with over 50% of the votes and a 20-seat majority. The 21st Dáil elects Jack Lynch as Taoiseach. The ruling Fine Gael-Labour Party coalition looked set to defy political history by winning an unprecedented second term. This belief was further augmented following the so-called "Tullymander" of parliamentary constituencies. This refers to the Minister for Local Government, James Tully, and his scheme of redrawing every constituency in the country in an effort to maximise the vote for the coalition partners. For instance, in Dublin there were thirteen three-seat constituencies. It was hoped that the coalition partners would win two of the seats, leaving Fianna Fáil with only one seat. A similar tactic was used in rural areas where the party was at its strongest. As a result of this, Fianna Fáil and its leader, Jack Lynch, believed that they couldn't win the general election. The party drew up a manifesto which offered the electorate a string of financial and economic "sweeteners", encouraging them to vote for Fianna Fáil. Some of the promises that were offered included the abolition of rates on houses, the abolition of car tax and the promise of reducing unemployment to under 100,000. Lynch agreed to the manifesto because he believed that the party needed something dramatic if it were to win the election. This was not the case. The Fianna Fáil campaign was based on the American model. Lynch travelled the length and breadth of the country, accompanied by his followers. His popularity was at its highest, and it soon became clear that the manifesto was unnecessary. Lynch's popularity alone was Fianna Fáil's biggest electoral asset. The party slogan, "Bring Back Jack", also played on Lynch's huge appeal. The campaign swung in Fianna Fáil's favour by polling day. In contrast to Fianna Fáil, the government parties of Fine Gael and the Labour Party fought the general election on their record in government. The redrawing of the constituency boundaries also gave them hope for success, however they offered little else to the electorate

apart from the policies they had been pursuing for the previous four years. While towards the end of the campaign Fianna Fáil were expected to win the general election, nobody predicted the scale of that victory. An unprecedented twenty-seat majority in Dáil Éireann for Fianna Fáil saw the National Coalition swept from power in the biggest political hurricane in Irish history. Only Éamon de Valera had ever done better, but only once out of 13 elections. Following the election defeat the leaders of Fine Gael and the Labour Party, Liam Cosgrave and Brendan Corish, resigned as leaders of their respective parties, the first occasion in which a defeated Taoiseach or Tánaiste had done so. "Tullymandering" was widely blamed for the scale of the coalition's defeat as the constituency boundaries had given them many seats that would be lost on only a small drop in their share of the vote. The new government established an independent commission to carry out future boundary revisions.

- Fianna Fáil hold 84 seats, Fine Gael 43, while Labour drop 2 to 16. 4 Independents plus the Ceann Comhairle round out the 148 seats, which is an increase from the 144 seats of previous elections.
- Kerry return the following members to the 21st Dáil:
  Kerry South: John O'Leary (FF); Timothy O'Connor (FF); Michael Begley (FG).
  Kerry North: Kit Ahern (FF); Tom McEllistrim Jr. (FF); Dan Spring (Lab.).
- The Royal College of Surgeons in Ireland is granted recognition as a recognised college of the National University of Ireland.
- Irish horses are prevented from entering the United States because of an outbreak of venereal disease in Irish, British and French horses.
- In Ennis, Co. Clare the Christian Brothers celebrate their 150th anniversary.
- The Peace Movement founders, Mairéad Corrigan and Betty Williams, win the Nobel Prize for Peace.
- The National Council for Educational Awards is given degree awarding status.

1978

Summary: Played four championship games, won 55th Munster title, won 24th All-Ireland title.

Game 1 - versus Waterford in Killarney on June 18. Final Score: Kerry 4-27; Waterford 2-8.

Charlie Nelligan

Jim Deenihan	John O'Keeffe	Denis Ogie Moran
Páidí Ó'Sé	Tim Kennelly	Paudie Lynch

Jack O'Shea   John Mulvihill (0-2)

Ger Power (0-3)	Tommy Doyle (0-3)	Pat Spillane (2-5)
John Egan (0-5)	Sean Walsh	Mike Sheehy (2-8)

Substitute: Mickey O'Sullivan (0-1) for Sean Walsh.

Game 2 - Munster Final versus Cork in Cork on July 16. Final Score: Kerry 3-14; Cork 3-7.

Charlie Nelligan

Paudie Lynch	John O'Keeffe	Jim Deenihan
Páidí Ó'Sé (0-1)	Tim Kennelly	Denis Ogie Moran

Jack O'Shea   Sean Walsh

Ger Power (1-0)	Tommy Doyle (0-2)	Pat Spillane (0-4)
Mike Sheehy (2-5)	Eoin Liston	John Egan (0-2)

Substitute: Pat McCarthy.

Game 3 - All-Ireland semi-final versus Roscommon in Croke Park on August 13. Final Score: Kerry 3-11; Roscommon 0-8.

Charlie Nelligan

Paudie Lynch	John O'Keeffe	Jim Deenihan
Páidí Ó'Sé	Tim Kennelly	Denis Ogie Moran

	Jack O'Shea (0-1)		Sean Walsh	
Ger Power (1-2)		Tommy Doyle		Pat Spillane (1-2)
John Egan (0-1)		Eoin Liston (0-1)		Mike Sheehy (0-4)

Substitutes: Pat McCarthy for Tommy Doyle, Mickey O'Sullivan for Pat McCarthy, Pat O'Mahony (1-0) for Denis Ogie Moran.

Game 4 - All-Ireland Final versus Dublin in Croke Park on September 24. Final Score: Kerry 5-11; Dublin 0-9.

	Charlie Nelligan	
Jim Deenihan	John O'Keeffe	Mick Spillane
Páidí Ó'Sé	Tim Kennelly	Paudie Lynch

	Jack O'Shea (0-1)		Sean Walsh	
Ger Power (0-1)		Denis Ogie Moran		Pat Spillane (0-1)
Mike Sheehy (1-4)		Eoin Liston (3-2)		John Egan (1-2)

Substitute: Paudie O'Mahony for Jim Deenihan.

Scorers for the Year: Mike Sheehy (5-21), Pat Spillane (3-12), John Egan (1-10), Eoin Liston (3-3), Ger Power (2-6), Tommy Doyle (0-5), Pat O'Mahony (1-0), Jack O'Shea (0-2), John Mulvihill (0-2), Páidí Ó'Sé (0-1), Mickey O'Sullivan (0-1).

Total Scored: 15-63

Appearances:

4 - Charlie Nelligan, Jim Deenihan, John O'Keeffe, Páidí Ó'Sé, Tim Kennelly, Paudie Lynch, Jack O'Shea, Sean Walsh, Ger Power, Denis Ogie Moran, Pat Spillane, Mike Sheehy, John Egan.

3 - Eoin Liston, Tommy Doyle.

2 - Pat McCarthy, Mickey O'Sullivan.

1 - Paudie O'Mahony, Mick Spillane, Pat O'Mahony, John Mulvihill.

1978 - GAA Winners:

All-Irelands: Senior Football: Kerry **Minor Football:** Mayo   **Under-21 Football:** Roscommon

National Leagues: Football: Dublin   Hurling: Clare

Senior Hurling: Cork

Kerry Co. Champions: Football: Feale Rangers   Hurling: Ballyduff

1978 Football All-Stars:

Ollie Crinnigan (Kildare), Harry Keegan (Roscommon), **John O'Keeffe (Kerry),** Robbie Kelleher (Dublin), Tommy Drumm (Dublin), Ollie Brady (Cavan), **Paudie Lynch (Kerry),** Colm McAlarney (Down), Matt Connor (Offaly), **Ger Power (Kerry),** Declan Barron (Cork), **Pat Spillane (Kerry), Mike Sheehy (Kerry),** Jimmy Keaveney (Dublin), **John Egan (Kerry).**

1978 - In The News:

- The European Court of Human Rights finds Britain guilty of inhuman and degrading treatment of republican internees in Northern Ireland.
- The government dismiss the Garda Commissioner Edmund Garvey. No explanation is given.
- John Giles resigns as manager of the Republic of Ireland national football team.
- The state funeral of former President Cearbhall Ó'Dálaigh takes place in Sneem, Co. Kerry.
- 6,000 people march through Dublin to the Wood Quay site to protest the building of civic offices on the Viking site.
- David Cooke of the Alliance Party becomes the first non-unionist Lord Mayor of Belfast.
- Over 5,000 people take part in a rally against a nuclear power station at Carnsore Point, Co. Wexford.
- Dublin Institute of Technology is created on an ad-hoc basis by the City of Dublin VEC.
- Ireland's second national television channel, RTÉ 2, opens with a live broadcast from the Cork Opera House.

1979

Summary: Played four championship games, won 56th Munster title, won 25th All-Ireland title.

Game 1 - versus Clare in Milltown Malbay on July 1. Final Score: Kerry 9-21; Clare 1-9.

Charlie Nelligan

Jim Deenihan	John O'Keeffe	Mick Spillane
Páidí Ó'Sé	Tim Kennelly	Paudie Lynch

Jack O'Shea (0-2)   Vincent O'Connor (1-2)

Ger Power (2-3)	Tommy Doyle (0-5)	Pat Spillane (3-1)
Mike Sheehy (1-4)	Eoin Liston (2-2)	John Egan (0-2)

No substitutes used.

Game 2 - Munster Final versus Cork in Killarney on July 22. Final Score: Kerry 2-14; Cork 2-4.

Charlie Nelligan

Jim Deenihan	John O'Keeffe	Mick Spillane
Páidí Ó'Sé	Tim Kennelly	Paudie Lynch

Jack O'Shea   Vincent O'Connor

Ger Power (2-4)	Tommy Doyle (0-1)	Pat Spillane (0-5)
Mike Sheehy (0-3)	Eoin Liston	John Egan

Substitutes: Denis Ogie Moran for Tommy Doyle, Sean Walsh (0-1) for Denis Ogie Moran.

Game 3 - All-Ireland semi-final versus Monaghan in Croke Park on August 12. Final Score: Kerry 5-14; Monaghan 0-7.

Charlie Nelligan

Jim Deenihan	John O'Keeffe	Mick Spillane
Páidí Ó'Sé	Tim Kennelly	Paudie Lynch

Jack O'Shea	Vincent O'Connor (0-1)	
Ger Power (1-0)	Sean Walsh (0-2)	Pat Spillane (0-1)
Mike Sheehy (3-5)	Eoin Liston (1-1)	John Egan (0-3)

Substitutes: Denis Ogie Moran (0-1) for Páidí Ó'Sé, Ger O'Keeffe for Jim Deenihan, Tommy Doyle for Eoin Liston.

Game 4 - All-Ireland Final versus Dublin in Croke Park on September 16. Final Score: Kerry 3-13; Dublin 1-8.

	Charlie Nelligan	
Jim Deenihan	John O'Keeffe	Mick Spillane
Páidí Ó'Sé	Tim Kennelly	Paudie Lynch
Jack O'Shea (0-1)		Sean Walsh
Tommy Doyle	Denis Ogie Moran	Pat Spillane (0-4)
Mike Sheehy (2-6)	Eoin Liston (0-1)	John Egan (1-1)

Substitute: Vincent O'Connor for John O'Keeffe.

Scorers for the Year: Mike Sheehy (6-18), Ger Power (5-7), Pat Spillane (3-11), Eoin Liston (3-4), John Egan (1-6), Vincent O'Connor (1-3), Tommy Doyle (0-6), Jack O'Shea (0-3), Sean Walsh (0-3), Denis Ogie Moran (0-1).

Total Scored: 19-62

Appearances:

4 - Charlie Nelligan, Jim Deenihan, John O'Keeffe, Mick Spillane, Páidí Ó'Sé, Tim Kennelly, Paudie Lynch, Jack O'Shea, Vincent O'Connor, Tommy Doyle, Pat Spillane, Mike Sheehy, Eoin Liston, John Egan.

3 - Sean Walsh, Ger Power, Denis Ogie Moran.

2 - None

1 - Ger O'Keeffe.

1979 - GAA Winners:

All-Irelands: Senior Football: Kerry **Minor Football:** Dublin **Under-21 Football:** Down

National Leagues: Football: Roscommon   Hurling: Tipperary

Senior Hurling: Kilkenny

Kerry Co. Champions: Football: Austin Stacks   Hurling: Causeway

1979 Football All-Stars:

Paddy Cullen (Dublin), Eugene Hughes (Monaghan), **John O'Keeffe (Kerry),** Tom Heneghan (Roscommon), Tommy Drumm (Dublin), **Tim Kennelly (Kerry),** Danny Murray (Roscommon), Dermot Earley (Roscommon), Bernard Brogan (Dublin), **Ger Power (Kerry), Sean Walsh (Kerry), Pat Spillane (Kerry), Mike Sheehy (Kerry),** Sean Lowry (Offaly), Joe McGrath (Mayo).

1979 - In The News:

- The lowest temperature recorded in Ireland in the 20th century, -18.8C (-1.8F) at Lullymore, Co. Kildare.
- Fifty people are killed when an explosion destroys the French oil tanker "Betelgeuse", off Whiddy Island, near Bantry, Co. Cork.
- Cork's legendary hurler Christy Ring dies.
- PAYE workers across the country take to the streets to protest the tax system.
- The Republic of Ireland ends its pound's parity with sterling.
- Patrick McGilligan, the last surviving member of the first government, celebrates his 90th birthday in Dublin.
- Petrol shortages due to crisis in the Middle East cause long delays in Ireland.
- Protesters opposed to the building of civic offices on the site of Viking excavations in Wood Quay occupy the area.
- Aer Lingus's first female pilot, Gráinne Cronin, gets her wings.
- In Crossmaglen, Co. Armagh, Gaelic Athletic Association supporters parade silently in protest against the British Army's commandeering of part of the local football pitch. Former Gaelic Athletic Association president Con Murphy addresses the crowd.
- The first group of Vietnamese refugees arrives in Ireland.
- Lord Mountbatten, his 15-year old grandson and 15-year old Paul Maxwell are killed in an explosion on his boat in Co. Sligo. On the

same day, the IRA blow up 18 British soldiers with 2 bombs in the Warrenpoint ambush.

- In September, Pope John Paul II arrives in Ireland for a three day visit. 1.25 million people welcome him at a special Mass in the Phoenix Park. His Holiness speaks to 200,000 people in Drogheda, Co. Louth. The Pope returns to Dublin where an estimated 750,000 people witness his motorcade travel through the city. Pope John Paul II addresses 285,000 people at a youth rally in Galway, before travelling to Knock, Co. Mayo where a further 300,000 people hear him speak. He also visits Clonmacnoise and Galway. On the final day of his visit Pope John Paul II visits the Nunciature at Maynooth College and celebrates Mass before 400,000 people in Limerick. His Holiness then leaves Shannon Airport for the United States.

- Taoiseach Jack Lynch greets European Economic Community heads of government as they arrive for a summit meeting at Dublin Castle.

- Jack Lynch announces his resignation as Taoiseach and leader of Fianna Fáil in December. He has led the party for 13 years, spending 9 years as Taoiseach.

- Charles Haughey is elected leader of Fianna Fáil and is elected Taoiseach by Dáil Éireann.

- 1979 is the worst year ever for industrial disputes in Ireland, costing the economy over 1,460,000 working days.

- John Treacy wins the world cross-country championship for the second time.

1980-1989...The Golden Years turn to famine

Summary of the Decade

Kerry played 34 games, scoring 69-452, conceding 28-318.

Munster Championship titles: 6 (1980, 1981, 1982, 1984, 1985, 1986)

All Ireland titles: 5 (1980, 1981, 1984, 1985, 1986)

National League titles: 2 (1982, 1984)

U-21 titles: None **Minor titles: 2** (1980, 1988)

Top Scorers: Mike Sheehy (12-117), Pat Spillane (7-69)

Top Points-only scorers: Mike Sheehy (117), Pat Spillane (69)

Top Goals-only scorers: Eoin Liston (14), Mike Sheehy (12)

Most Appearances: Charlie Nelligan (34), Jack O'Shea (33), Tommy Doyle (33)

1980
Munster Final: Kerry 3-13 Cork 2-9;
All-Ireland semi-final: Kerry 4-15 Offaly 4-10;
All-Ireland Final: Kerry 1-9 Roscommon 1-6.

1981
Kerry 4-17 Clare 0-6;
Munster Final: Kerry 1-11 Cork 0-3;
All-Ireland semi-final: Kerry 2-19 Mayo 1-6;
All-Ireland Final: Kerry 1-12 Offaly 0-8.

1982
Kerry 1-15 Clare 0-9;
Munster Final: Kerry 0-9 Cork 0-9;
Replay: Kerry 2-18 Cork 0-12;
All-Ireland semi-final: Kerry 3-15 Armagh 1-11;
All-Ireland Final: Offaly 1-15 Kerry 0-17.

1983
Kerry 5-16 Tipperary 2-5;
Munster Final: Cork 3-10 Kerry 3-9.

1984
Kerry 0-23 Tipperary 0-6;
Munster Final: Kerry 3-14 Cork 2-10;
All-Ireland semi-final: Kerry 2-17 Galway 0-11;
All-Ireland Final: Kerry 0-14 Dublin 1-6.

1985
Kerry 2-18 Limerick 0-5;
Munster Final: Kerry 2-11 Cork 0-11;
All-Ireland semi-final: Kerry 1-12 Monaghan 2-9;
Replay: Kerry 2-9 Monaghan 0-10;
All-Ireland Final: Kerry 2-12 Dublin 2-8.

1986
Kerry 5-9 Tipperary 0-12;
Munster Final: Kerry 0-12 Cork 0-8;
All-Ireland semi-final: Kerry 2-13 Meath 0-12;
All-Ireland Final: Kerry 2-15 Tyrone 1-10.

1987
Kerry 3-15 Waterford 2-8;
Munster Final: Kerry 2-7 Cork 1-10;
Replay: Cork 0-13 Kerry 1-5.

1988
Kerry 3-19 Waterford 1-7;
Munster Final: Cork 1-14 Kerry 0-16.

1989
Kerry 6-7 Limerick 1-10;
Munster Final: Cork 1-12 Kerry 1-9.

1980

Summary: Played three championship games, won 57th Munster title, won 26th All-Ireland title.

Game 1 - Munster Final versus Cork in Cork on July 6. Final Score: Kerry 3-13; Cork 0-12.

Charlie Nelligan

Ger O'Keeffe	John O'Keeffe	Mick Spillane
Páidí Ó'Sé	Tim Kennelly	Denis Ogie Moran

Jack O'Shea   Sean Walsh

Ger Power (1-2)	Tommy Doyle (0-1)	Pat Spillane (0-5)
Mike Sheehy (0-3)	Eoin Liston (2-1)	John Egan (0-1)

Substitute: Vincent O'Connor for Sean Walsh.

Game 2 - All Ireland semi-final versus Offaly in Croke Park on August 24. Final Score: Kerry 4-15; Offaly 4-10.

Charlie Nelligan

Ger O'Keeffe	John O'Keeffe	Mick Spillane
Páidí Ó'Sé	Tim Kennelly	Denis Ogie Moran (0-1)

Jack O'Shea   Sean Walsh

Ger Power (0-2)	Tommy Doyle (0-2)	Pat Spillane (2-2)
Mike Sheehy (1-3)	Eoin Liston (0-1)	John Egan (1-4)

Substitute: Jim Deenihan for Sean Walsh.

Game 3 - All-Ireland Final versus Roscommon in Croke Park on September 21. Final Score: Kerry 1-9; Roscommon 1-6.

Charlie Nelligan

Jim Deenihan	John O'Keeffe	Paudie Lynch
Páidí Ó'Sé	Tim Kennelly	Ger O'Keeffe

	Jack O'Shea (0-1)		Sean Walsh	

Ger Power (0-1)   Denis Ogie Moran   Pat Spillane (0-1)

Mike Sheehy (1-6)   Tommy Doyle   John Egan

Substitute: Ger O'Driscoll for Ger Power.

Scorers for the Year: Mike Sheehy (2-12), Pat Spillane (2-8), Eoin Liston (2-2), Ger Power (1-5), John Egan (1-5), Tommy Doyle (0-3), Jack O'Shea (0-1), Denis Ogie Moran (0-1).

Total Scored: 8-37

Appearances:

3 - Charlie Nelligan, Ger O'Keeffe, John O'Keeffe, Páidí Ó'Sé, Tim Kennelly, Denis Ogie Moran, Jack O'Shea, Sean Walsh, Ger Power, Tommy Doyle, Pat Spillane, Mike Sheehy, John Egan.

2 - Jim Deenihan, Mick Spillane, Eoin Liston.

1 - Paudie Lynch, Ger O'Driscoll, Vincent O'Connor.

1980 - GAA Winners:

All-Irelands: Senior Football: Kerry **Minor Football:** Kerry   **Under-21 Football:** Cork

Kerry's Minor Winning Team: R. O'Brien, D. Keane, M. Crowley, M. Counihan, J. O'Sullivan, T. Sheehy, J.T. O'Sullivan, P. O'Donoghue, A. O'Donovan, T. Dee, J. Shannon, L. Kearns, T. Parker, W. Maher, M. McAuliffe. Sub: T. Spillane.

National Leagues: Football: Cork   Hurling: Cork

Senior Hurling: Galway

Kerry Co. Champions: Football: Feale Rangers   Hurling: Causeway

1980 Football All-Stars:

Charlie Nelligan (Kerry), Harry Keegan (Roscommon), Kevin Kehily (Cork), Gerry Connellan (Roscommon), Kevin McCabe (Tyrone), **Tim Kennelly (Kerry),** Danny Murray (Roscommon), **Jack O'Shea (Kerry),** Colm McKinstry (Armagh), **Ger Power (Kerry),** Dinny Allen (Cork), **Pat**

Spillane (Kerry), Matt Connor (Offaly), **Eoin Liston (Kerry), John Egan (Kerry).**

1980 - In The News:

- In January, Taoiseach Charles Haughey addresses the nation on worsening finances.
- CIÉ's first bus lane comes into operation on Parliament Street in Dublin.
- Johnny Logan wins the Eurovision Song Contest with the song "What's Another Year".
- The Derrynaflan Chalice is discovered in a bog.
- Eighteen people die in the Buttevant Rail Disaster, Co. Cork and ten people die in the Central Hotel Fire, Bundoran, Co. Donegal.
- China's first Ambassador to Ireland, Madame Gong Pusheng, arrives in Dublin.
- Justice Mella Carroll is the first woman to reach the position of High Court Judge.
- Over 2,000 people take part in the first RTÉ Radio 2 Dublin City Marathon.
- National Institute for Higher Education, Dublin admits its first 200 students.
- On December 8, Taoiseach Charles Haughey meets with the British Prime Minister, Margaret Thatcher, at Dublin Castle. It is the first visit by a British prime minister since independence.
- Former Taoiseach Jack Lynch is conferred with the freedom of his native city, Cork.

1981

Summary: Played four championship games, won 58th Munster title, won 27th All-Ireland title.

Game 1 - versus Clare in Listowel on June 28. Final Score: Kerry 4-17; Clare 0-6.

Charlie Nelligan

Jim Deenihan   John O'Keeffe   Paudie Lynch

Páidí Ó'Sé (0-1)   Tommy Doyle   Mick Spillane

Jack O'Shea (0-1)   Tom Spillane (0-1)

Ger Power   Denis Ogie Moran (0-1)   Pat Spillane (0-3)

Mike Sheehy (0-6)   Eoin Liston (3-3)   John Egan (1-1)

Substitute: Bernard O'Sullivan for John O'Keeffe.

Game 2 - Munster Final versus Cork in Cork on July 15. Final Score: Kerry 1-11; Cork 0-3.

Charlie Nelligan

Jim Deenihan   John O'Keeffe   Paudie Lynch

Páidí Ó'Sé   Sean Walsh   Mick Spillane

Jack O'Shea (0-1)   Tommy Doyle

Ger Power   Denis Ogie Moran   Pat Spillane (0-3)

Mike Sheehy (1-5)   Eoin Liston (0-1)   John Egan (0-1)

Substitutes: Denis Ogie Moran for Tommy Doyle, Sean Walsh for Denis Ogie Moran.

Game 3 - All-Ireland semi-final versus Mayo in Croke Park on August 9. Final Score: Kerry 2-19; Mayo 1-6.

Charlie Nelligan

Jim Deenihan   John O'Keeffe   Paudie Lynch

Páidí Ó'Sé   Sean Walsh   Mick Spillane

Jack O'Shea (0-1)   Tommy Doyle (0-1)

Ger Power (1-0)   Denis Ogie Moran (0-3)   Pat Spillane (0-3)

Mike Sheehy (0-6)   Eoin Liston (1-2)   John Egan (0-3)

Substitute: Tim Kennelly for Ger Power.

Game 4 - All-Ireland Final versus Offaly in Croke Park on September 20. Final Score: Kerry 1-12; Offaly 0-8.

Charlie Nelligan

Jim Deenihan   John O'Keeffe   Paudie Lynch

Páidí Ó'Sé (0-1)   Tim Kennelly   Mick Spillane

Jack O'Shea (1-0)   Sean Walsh (0-1)

Ger Power (0-1)   Denis Ogie Moran (0-2)   Tommy Doyle (0-1)

Mike Sheehy (0-5)   Eoin Liston   John Egan (0-1)

Substitutes: Pat Spillane, Ger O'Keeffe.

Scorers for the Year: Mike Sheehy (1-22), Eoin Liston (4-6), John Egan (1-6), Pat Spillane (0-9), Jack O'Shea (1-3), Denis Ogie Moran (0-6), Ger Power (1-1), Páidí Ó'Sé (0-2), Tommy Doyle (0-2), Sean Walsh (0-1), Tom Spillane (0-1).

Total Scored: 8-59

Appearances:

4 - Charlie Nelligan, Jim Deenihan, John O'Keeffe, Paudie Lynch, Páidí Ó'Sé, Tommy Doyle, Mick Spillane, Jack O'Shea, Ger Power, Denis Ogie Moran, Mike Sheehy, Eoin Liston, John Egan.

3 - Sean Walsh, Pat Spillane.

2 - Tim Kennelly.

1 - Bernard O'Sullivan, Tom Spillane, Ger O'Keeffe.

1981 - GAA Winners:

All-Irelands: Senior Football: Kerry **Minor Football:** Cork   **Under-21 Football:** Cork

National Leagues: Football: Galway   Hurling: Cork

Senior Hurling: Offaly

Kerry Co. Champions: Football: South Kerry   Hurling: Causeway

1981 Football All-Stars:

Martin Furlong (Offaly), **Jimmy Deenihan (Kerry),** Paddy Kennedy (Down), **Paudie Lynch (Kerry), Páidí Ó'Sé (Kerry),** Richie Connor (Offaly), Seamus McHugh (Galway), **Jack O'Shea (Kerry), Sean Walsh (Kerry),** Barry Brennan (Galway), **Denis Ogie Moran (Kerry), Pat Spillane (Kerry), Mike Sheehy (Kerry), Eoin Liston (Kerry),** Brendan Lowry (Offaly).

1981 - In The News:

- 48 young people die in a fire at the Stardust Ballroom in Artane, Dublin on St. Valentines Day.
- On March 1 Bobby Sands begins a hunger strike at the Long Kesh prison in Belfast.
- The petrol strike ends as 800 tanker drivers resume work.
- Ireland hosts the Eurovision Song Contest, presented by Doireann Ní Bhriain and aired on RTÉ.
- Bobby Sands is elected Member of Parliament (MP) for Fermanagh/ South Tyrone on April 10.
- An Aer Lingus Boeing 737, en route from Dublin to London, is hijacked and ordered to fly to Teheran. The flight is diverted to Paris and the hijacker, Laurence Downey, is arrested.
- Bobby Sands dies on the 66th day of his hunger strike (May 5) in the Maze Prison in Belfast. On May 12 Francis Hughes dies on the 59th day of his hunger strike in Belfast. On May 21 Raymond McCreesh and Patsy O'Hara both die on the 61st day of their hunger strike in the Maze Prison. On July 8 IRA hunger striker Joseph McDonnell is the fifth person to die. On August 1 hunger striker Kevin Lynch dies. On August 2 Kieran Doherty, TD for Cavan-Monaghan, dies on the 73rd day of his hunger strike.
- The Irish Sugar Company announces that it is to close its factory in Tuam, Co. Galway.
- Artist and writer Christy Brown is buried in Dublin.
- The Arklow-bound, Dublin-registered *Union Star* was lost on its maiden voyage off Cornwall. 16 lives were lost, 8 from the *Union Star* and 8 from RNLB *Solomon Browne* who died while attempting rescue.

- Supporters of the Society for the Protection of Unborn Children march in Dublin to demand a referendum for a pro-life amendment to the Constitution.
- Arkle, Ireland's greatest racehorse, is commemorated on a postage stamp.
- The general election of 1981 was the first one of five during the 1980s. The number of seats was increased from 148 to 166 this year. The election also saw three new leaders of the three main parties fight their first general election. Charles Haughey had become Taoiseach and leader of Fianna Fáil at the end of 1979, Garret FitzGerald was the new leader of Fine Gael and Frank Cluskey was in charge of the Labour Party.
- Charles Haughey and Fianna Fáil seemed extremely popular with the electorate. He had wanted to call the general election for early in the year, however a series of events led to the postponement of the election until the summer. By that stage much of the earlier optimism in the party had filtered out. The party still offered a very attractive manifesto, promising the electorate more spending programmes. Fine Gael also put forward a series of tax-cutting plans. Both main party policies seemed completely unrealistic, particularly since the national debt of the country was spiralling out of control.
- When the votes were counted the result was inconclusive. Fianna Fáil lost seats as a result of sympathy to the Anti H-Block candidates and the attractive tax proposals of Fine Gael. It was the worst performance for Fianna Fáil in twenty years. Meanwhile, Labour Party leader Frank Cluskey suffered the loss of his seat, necessitating a leadership change with Michael O'Leary succeeding Cluskey. Fianna Fáil won 77 seats, Fine Gael 65, Labour 15, and 9 went to Others.
- The 22nd Dail comprised a Fine Gael-Labour Party coalition government with Garret FitzGerald becoming the seventh Taoiseach and Michael O'Leary Tánaiste.
- Kerry return the following members to the 22nd Dáil:
  Kerry South: John O'Leary (FF); Michael Begley (FG); Michael Moynihan (Lab.).
  Kerry North: Denis Foley (FF); Tom McEllistrim Jr. (FF); Dick Spring (Lab.).

1982

Summary: Played four championship games, won 59th Munster title, lost All-Ireland Final.

Game 1 - versus Clare in Ennis on June 6. Final Score: Kerry 1-15; Clare 0-9.

Charlie Nelligan

Ger O'Keeffe   John O'Keeffe   Paudie Lynch

Páidí Ó'Sé   Tim Kennelly   Ger Lynch

Tommy Doyle (0-1)   Vincent O'Connor (0-1)

Ger Power (0-2)   Denis Ogie Moran (0-1)   Pat Spillane (0-4)

Mike Sheehy (0-6)   Eoin Liston (1-0)   John Egan

Substitute: John L. McElligott for Ger Power.

Game 2 - Munster Final versus Cork in Cork on July 4. Final Score: Kerry 0-9; Cork 0-9.

Charlie Nelligan

Tim Kennelly   John O'Keeffe   Paudie Lynch

Páidí Ó'Sé   Ger O'Keeffe   Ger Lynch

Jack O'Shea   Sean Walsh (0-3)

Ger Power   Denis Ogie Moran   Tommy Doyle

Mike Sheehy (0-5)   Eoin Liston (0-1)   John Egan

Substitutes: John L. McElligott for Denis Ogie Moran, Mick Spillane for Tim Kennelly, Vincent O'Connor for Jack O'Shea.

Game 3 - Munster Final replay versus Cork in Killarney on August 1. Final Score: Kerry 2-18; Cork 0-12.

Charlie Nelligan

Ger O'Keeffe   John O'Keeffe   Paudie Lynch

Páidí Ó'Sé   Tim Kennelly   Tommy Doyle

Jack O'Shea (0-1)   Sean Walsh

Ger Power   Tom Spillane (0-4)   Denis Ogie Moran (0-4)

Mike Sheehy (2-4)   Eoin Liston (0-4)   John Egan (0-1)

Substitutes: Vincent O'Connor for John O'Keeffe, John L. McElligott for Ger Power.

Game 4 - All-Ireland semi-final versus Armagh in Croke Park on August 15. Final Score: Kerry 3-15; Armagh 1-11.

Charlie Nelligan

Ger O'Keeffe   John O'Keeffe   Paudie Lynch

Páidí Ó'Sé   Tim Kennelly   Tommy Doyle

Jack O'Shea   Sean Walsh (0-1)

Ger Power (0-2)   Tom Spillane (0-2)   Denis Ogie Moran (0-2)

Mike Sheehy (1-4)   Eoin Liston (1-3)   John Egan (1-1)

Substitutes: Mick Spillane for Tommy Doyle, Pat Spillane for Denis Ogie Moran.

Game 5 - All-Ireland Final versus Offaly in Croke Park on September 19. Final Score: Offaly 1-15; Kerry 0-17.

Charlie Nelligan

Ger O'Keeffe   John O'Keeffe   Paudie Lynch

Páidí Ó'Sé (0-2)   Tim Kennelly   Tommy Doyle

Jack O'Shea (0-1)   Sean Walsh (0-2)

Ger Power   Tom Spillane (0-3)   Denis Ogie Moran

Mike Sheehy (0-3)   Eoin Liston (0-2)   John Egan (0-3)

Substitute: Pat Spillane (0-1) for Denis Ogie Moran.

Scorers for the Year: Mike Sheehy (3-22), Eoin Liston (2-10), Tom Spillane (0-9), John Egan (1-5), Denis Ogie Moran (0-7), Sean Walsh (0-6), Pat Spillane (0-5), Ger Power (0-4), Jack O'Shea (0-2), Páidí Ó'Sé (0-2), Tommy Doyle (0-1), Vincent O'Connor (0-1).

Total Scored: 6-74

Appearances:

5 - Charlie Nelligan, Ger O'Keeffe, John O'Keeffe, Paudie Lynch, Páidí Ó'Sé, Tim Kennelly, Tommy Doyle, Ger Power, Denis Ogie Moran, Mike Sheehy, Eoin Liston, John Egan.

4 - Jack O'Shea, Sean Walsh.

3 - John L. McElligott, Vincent O'Connor, Tom Spillane.

2 - Mick Spillane, Ger Lynch, Pat Spillane.

1 - None

1982 - GAA Winners:

All-Irelands: Senior Football: Offaly **Minor Football:** Dublin **Under-21 Football:** Donegal

National Leagues: Football: Kerry Hurling: Kilkenny

Senior Hurling: Kilkenny

Kerry Co. Champions: Football: South Kerry Hurling: Causeway

1982 Football All-Stars:

Martin Furlong (Offaly), Mick Fitzgerald (Offaly), Liam O'Connor (Offaly), Kevin Kehily (Cork), **Páidí Ó'Sé (Kerry),** Sean Lowry (Offaly), Liam Currams (Offaly), **Jack O'Shea (Kerry),** Padraig Dunne (Offaly), Peter McGinnity (Fermanagh), Joe Kernan (Armagh), Matt Connor (Offaly), **Mike Sheehy (Kerry), Eoin Liston (Kerry), John Egan (Kerry).**

1982 - In The News:
- Kildare TD, Charlie McCreevy, is expelled from the Fianna Fáil parliamentary party for criticising Charles Haughey.
- The 23rd Dáil was elected at the first general election of 1982 on 18 February and first met on 9 March when the 18th Government of Ireland was appointed. The 23rd Dáil lasted for 279 days. Charles Haughey was elected Taoiseach and Ray McSharry was Tánaiste.
- The first general election was caused by the sudden collapse of the Fine Gael-Labour Party coalition government when the budget was defeated. The Minister for Finance, John Bruton, attempted to put

VAT on children's shoes, a measure which was rejected by some left-wing Independent TDs. Taoiseach Garret FitzGerald dissolved the Dáil immediately, however, while he was with President Patrick Hillery at Áras an Uachtaráin, a number of Fianna Fáil members attempted to contact the President, to urge him against a dissolution. If he refused a dissolution, FitzGerald would have to resign and Fianna Fáil would be invited to form a government. While the attempt to contact the President was highly unconstitutional, (the President can only take advice from the Taoiseach) a dissolution was granted and the general election campaign began in earnest.

The campaign was largely fought on economic issues. Spending cuts were a reality for whatever party won, but the scale of the cuts were played down by all parties. Fine Gael continued its policies that it had been implementing while in office. The Fianna Fáil leader, Charles Haughey, dismissed the budget cuts when the campaign first began, however, the reality soon became apparent and the party adopted similar policies that involved cuts.

Fianna Fáil emerged as the largest party with 81 of the 166 seats and looked most likely to form a government. However, internal divisions within the party threatened Charles Haughey's nomination for Taoiseach. In the end a leadership challenge did not take place and Haughey was the party's nominee for Taoiseach. Haughey gained the support of the Independent TD, Tony Gregory, the Independent Fianna Fáil TD Neil Blaney and the three Workers Party deputies and was appointed Taoiseach.

- Kerry return the following members to the 23rd Dáil in February:
  Kerry South: John O'Leary (FF); Michael Begley (FG); Michael Moynihan (Lab.).
  Kerry North: Dick Spring (Lab.); Tom McEllistrim Jr. (FF); Denis Foley (FF).
- Corporal punishment is banned in schools in the Republic.
- The country's first crematorium is officially opened at Glasnevin Cemetery, Dublin.
- James Prior launches "rolling devolution" for Northern Ireland.
- Work begins on the Cork-Dublin natural gas pipeline.
- The Irish Government affirms its neutrality in the Falklands conflict between the United Kingdom and Argentina, and opposes EEC sanctions against Argentina (as does Italy).
- Seamus Mallon of the Social Democratic and Labour Party is appointed to Seanad Éireann.

- 20,000 people across the country march in protest at income tax and PRSI changes.
- The Irish Republican Army kills ten servicemen in bomb attacks in Hyde Park and Regent's Park, London.
- The Attorney General, Patrick Connolly, resigns after a wanted double-murderer is found staying on his property; the ensuing scandal is later described as being "grotesque, unbelievable, bizarre and unprecedented" by Taoiseach Charles Haughey.
- On September 14, Ireland mourns the death of Princess Grace of Monaco.
- In October Taoiseach Charles Haughey emerges with a majority of 58 votes to 22 in an open ballot on Charlie McCreevy's motion of no confidence in his leadership.
- Cork Airport celebrates its 21st birthday. The airport has yet to make a profit.
- Desmond O'Malley and Martin O'Donoghue both resign from the Government and from Fianna Fáil in October 1982, following an unsuccessful leadership challenge by O'Malley against Charles Haughey.
- The second general election of 1982 took place just nine months after the first one in February of that year. While it is not the shortest Dáil in Irish history, it is unusual because never before had there been three general elections in eighteen months. This general election was caused by the loss of support of Independents and the Workers Party for the Fianna Fáil government. This was due to the government's insistence on introducing substantial budget cuts which the left-wing TDs could not stomach. While economic issues dominated the campaign the parties were weary in having to fight yet another general election.

  After the votes were counted the result was conclusive. Fine Gael recorded its biggest ever election victory, with their 70 seats coming within five seats of Fianna Fáil; previously Fianna Fáil had been twice as big as Fine Gael. Labour's 16 seats and 5 Others rounded out the 24th Dail. The Labour Party had a new leader with Kerry's own Dick Spring. A programme for government was quickly drawn up and Garret FitzGerald of Fine Gael becomes Taoiseach for the second time. The poor showing for Fianna Fáil resulted in a leadership challenge to Charles Haughey by his opponents within the party. Haughey won the vote of confidence and remained as leader.
- Kerry return the following members to the 24th Dáil in November:

Kerry South: John O'Leary (FF); Michael Begley (FG); Michael Moynihan (Lab.).

Kerry North: Denis Foley (FF); Tom McEllistrim Jr. (FF); Dick Spring (Lab.).

- Former leader of the Labour Party, Michael O'Leary, joins the Fine Gael Party.
- Dublin's Grafton Street officially opens as a pedestrianised street.
- The Irish National Liberation Army kills 17 people in a bomb attack at the Droppin Well Inn, Ballykelly, Co. Derry.
- Ireland's rugby team wins the Triple Crown for the first time since 1949.

1983

Summary: Played two championship games, lost Munster Final.

Game 1 - versus Tipperary in Clonmel on June 26. Final Score: Kerry 5-16; Tipperary 2-5.

Charlie Nelligan

Mick Spillane	John O'Keeffe	Paudie Lynch
Páidí Ó'Sé	Ger O'Keeffe	Ger Lynch

Jack O'Shea (2-1)	Vincent O'Connor

Tommy Doyle (0-2)	Denis Ogie Moran (0-4)	Mike Sheehy (2-4)
Ger Power (0-2)	Sean Walsh (1-1)	John Egan (0-2)

No substitutes used.

Game 2 - Munster Final versus Cork in Cork on July 17. Final Score: Cork 3-10; Kerry 3-9.

Charlie Nelligan

Ger O'Keeffe	John O'Keeffe	Paudie Lynch
Páidí Ó'Sé	Tim Kennelly	Mick Spillane

Jack O'Shea (2-0)	Vincent O'Connor

Ger Power (0-1)	Denis Ogie Moran	Tommy Doyle
Mike Sheehy (0-7)	Eoin Liston	John Egan (0-1)

Substitutes: John L. McElligott for John O'Keeffe, Sean Walsh (1-0) for Ger Power.

Scorers for the Year: Mike Sheehy (2-11), Jack O'Shea (4-1), Sean Walsh (2-1), Denis Ogie Moran (0-4), John Egan (0-3), Ger Power (0-3), Tommy Doyle (0-2).

Total Scored: 8-25

Appearances:

2 - Charlie Nelligan, Mick Spillane, John O'Keeffe, Paudie Lynch, Páidí Ó'Sé, Ger O'Keeffe, Jack O'Shea, Vincent O'Connor, Tommy Doyle, Denis Ogie Moran, Mike Sheehy, Ger Power, Sean Walsh, John Egan.

1 - Tim Kennelly, Ger Lynch, John L. McElligott, Eoin Liston.

1983 - GAA Winners:

All-Irelands: Senior Football: Dublin **Minor Football:** Derry **Under-21 Football:** Mayo

National Leagues: Football: Down   Hurling: Kilkenny

Senior Hurling: Kilkenny

Kerry Juniors also take All-Ireland honours with this team: J. Kennelly, M. Colgan, B. O'Sullivan, P. Brosnan, P. Sheehan, D. Hartnett, J. Stack, G. O'Driscoll, T. O'Connell, J. Walsh, R. O'Donoghue, P. O'Mahony, J. Doyle, J. O'Sullivan, P. Sheehan. Subs: G. Casey, D. Higgins.

Kerry Co. Champions: Football: Killarney   Hurling: Lixnaw

1983 Football All-Stars:

Martin Furlong (Offaly), **Páidí Ó'Sé (Kerry),** Stephen Kinneavy (Galway), John Evans (Cork), Pat Canavan (Dublin), Tommy Drumm (Dublin), Jimmy Kerrigan (Cork), **Jack O'Shea (Kerry),** Liam Austin (Down), Barney Rock (Dublin), Matt Connor (Offaly), Greg Blaney (Down), Martin McHugh (Donegal), Colm O'Rourke (Meath), Joe McNally (Dublin).

1983 - In The News:
- The government confirms that the Gardaí were involved in the bugging of telephones of various politicians and journalists.
- A motion calling for the resignation of Charles Haughey as leader fails after a 12 hour meeting.
- The racehorse Shergar is kidnapped from Ballymany Stud, Co. Kildare.
- The inaugural meeting of Aosdána, an affiliation of creative artists, takes place in the Old Parliament Building, Dublin.
- In the presidential election of 1983, outgoing President Patrick Hillery agreed under enormous political pressure to seek a second term. Though former Nobel Peace Prize and Lenin Peace Prize winner

Seán MacBride made it known in the *Sunday Press* newspaper that he wanted to contest the office, only President Hillery was nominated and was declared re-elected without the need for a poll.

- 2,000 people demonstrate in Dublin against the proposed Pro-Life Amendment Bill.
- The funeral takes place of former Tánaiste Frank Aiken.
- The Bushmills Distillery in Co. Antrim celebrates its 350th anniversary.
- A Mexican jet stranded for five weeks at Mallow Racecourse departs.
- The inaugural meeting of the New Ireland Forum takes place at Dublin Castle.
- Gerry Adams of Sinn Féin is elected the new MP for West Belfast.
- The referendum on the constitutional amendment in relation to abortion is carried by a two to one majority.
- Leading politicians pay tribute to former Tánaiste George Colley as he is laid to rest.
- The first stretch of motorway in the Republic was opened; the 8 km Naas bypass on the N7 national primary route.
- On November 25 Quinnsworth executive Don Tidey is kidnapped outside his home in Dublin. He is rescued in Co. Leitrim on December 16.
- Eamonn Coghlan wins the 5000m gold medal at the World Championships in Helsinki.

1984

Summary: Played four championship games, won 60th Munster title, won 28th All-Ireland title.

Game 1 - versus Tipperary in Tralee on June 10. Final Score: Kerry 0-23; Tipperary 0-6.

Charlie Nelligan

Páidí Ó'Sé	John O'Keeffe	Mick Spillane

Tommy Doyle	Tom Spillane	Ger Lynch

Jack O'Shea (0-1)   Timmy O'Dowd (0-4)

John Kennedy (0-6)	Sean Walsh	Pat Spillane (0-3)

Diarmuid O'Donoghue (0-1)	Eoin Liston (0-4)	Mike Sheehy (0-4)

No substitutes used.

Game 2 - Munster Final versus Cork in Killarney on July 1. Final Score: Kerry 3-14; Cork 2-10.

Charlie Nelligan

Páidí Ó'Sé	Sean Walsh	Mick Spillane

Tommy Doyle	Tom Spillane (0-1)	Ger Lynch

Jack O'Shea (0-1)   Ambrose O'Donovan

John Kennedy (0-4)	Ger Power (0-2)	Pat Spillane (2-1)

Mike Sheehy (0-3)	Eoin Liston (0-1)	Willie Maher (1-0)

Substitutes: Denis Ogie Moran (0-1) for Ger Power, John Egan for Willie Maher.

Game 3 - All-Ireland semi-final versus Galway in Croke Park on August 12. Final Score: Kerry 2-17; Galway 0-11.

Charlie Nelligan

Páidí Ó'Sé	Sean Walsh	Mick Spillane

Tommy Doyle	Tom Spillane (0-1)	Ger Lynch

Jack O'Shea (0-5)		Ambrose O'Donovan (0-1)
John Kennedy (0-1)	Denis Ogie Moran	Pat Spillane (0-3)
Mike Sheehy (1-4)	Eoin Liston	John Egan (1-2)

Substitute: Vincent O'Connor for Sean Walsh.

Game 4 - All-Ireland Final versus Dublin in Croke Park on September 23. Final Score: Kerry 0-14; Dublin 1-6.

	Charlie Nelligan	
Páidí Ó'Sé	Sean Walsh	Mick Spillane
Tommy Doyle	Tom Spillane	Ger Lynch
Jack O'Shea (0-1)		Ambrose O'Donovan
John Kennedy (0-5)	Denis Ogie Moran (0-1)	Pat Spillane (0-4)
Ger Power	Eoin Liston (0-3)	John Egan

Substitute: Timmy O'Dowd for John Egan.

Scorers for the Year: Pat Spillane (2-11), John Kennedy (0-16), Mike Sheehy (1-11), Jack O'Shea (0-8), Eoin Liston (0-8), John Egan (1-2), Timmy O'Dowd (0-4), Willie Maher (1-0), Tom Spillane (0-2), Ger Power (0-2), Denis Ogie Moran (0-2), Ambrose O'Donovan (0-1), Diarmuid O'Donoghue (0-1).

Total Scored: 5-68

Appearances:

4 - Charlie Nelligan, Páidí Ó'Sé, Tommy Doyle, Tom Spillane, Ger Lynch, Jack O'Shea, John Kennedy, Sean Walsh, Pat Spillane, Eoin Liston.

3 - Ambrose O'Donovan, Mike Sheehy, Denis Ogie Moran, John Egan.

2 - Timmy O'Dowd, Ger Power.

1 - John O'Keeffe, Mick Spillane, Vincent O'Connor, Willie Maher, Diarmuid O'Donoghue.

1984 - GAA Winners:

All-Irelands: Senior Football: Kerry **Minor Football:** Dublin **Under-21 Football:** Cork

National Leagues: Football: Kerry   Hurling: Limerick

Senior Hurling: Cork

Kerry Co. Champions: Football: West Kerry   Hurling: Ballyduff

1984 Football All-Stars:

John O'Leary (Dublin), **Páidí Ó'Sé (Kerry),** Mick Lyons (Meath), Seamus McHugh (Galway), **Tommy Doyle (Kerry), Tom Spillane (Kerry),** P.J. Buckley (Dublin), **Jack O'Shea (Kerry),** Eugene McKenna (Tyrone), Barney Rock (Dublin), **Eoin Liston (Kerry), Pat Spillane (Kerry), Mike Sheehy (Kerry),** Frank McGuigan (Tyrone), Dermot McNicholl (Derry).

1984 - In The News:

- Galway City begins celebrations marking its mayoral status granted by King Richard III in 1484.
- Seán MacEntee, founder member of Fianna Fáil and former Tánaiste, dies aged 94. He was the last surviving member of the First Dáil.
- Luke Kelly of The Dubliners dies aged 43.
- Ann Lovett, aged 15, dies after giving birth to a baby boy in a grotto in Granard, Co. Longford.
- Sinn Féin MP Gerry Adams is shot and wounded in Belfast.
- The New Ireland Forum publishes its report presenting three possibilities for discussion: a unitary Irish state, a federal/confederal state and joint sovereignty.
- On May 22 the village of Ballyporeen, Co. Tipperary prepares for the visit of US President Ronald Reagan.
- On June 3 over 10,000 people take part in an anti-Reagan march in Dublin.
- On June 4 President Reagan addresses a joint session of the houses of the Oireachtas.
- European Parliament elections are held in Northern Ireland and the Republic of Ireland.
- Columban missionary Fr. Niall O'Brien, who was imprisoned in the Philippines, is released.
- Workers in Dunnes Store, Henry Street, Dublin refuse to handle South African produce as a protest against apartheid. Later in the

year, they went on strike for 11 weeks in support of a dispute over the handling of South African fruit, and conducted a sit-in at the store.

- The DART rail service between Howth and Bray is introduced.
- In September the Dublin telephone system collapsed due to the network suffering overload as a result of a phone in competition on one of the illegal radio stations.
- The University of Ulster is presented with a Royal Charter by Elizabeth II.
- The IRA kills five people in a bomb attack at the Grand Hotel, Brighton, during the Conservative Party conference.
- Irish Shipping Limited placed into liquidation
- RTÉ's first newsreader, Charles Mitchel, reads his last news bulletin.
- European Economic Community heads of government visit President Hillery and Mrs. Hillery at Áras an Uachtaráin.
- The most sophisticated naval vessel ever built in this country, the £25 million LÉ Eithne is commissioned at the Haulbowline naval base.

1985

Summary: Played five championship games, won 61st Munster title, won 29th All-Ireland title.

Game 1 - versus Limerick in Listowel on June 23. Final Score: Kerry 2-18; Limerick 0-9.

Charlie Nelligan

Páidí Ó'Sé   Sean Walsh   Mick Spillane

Tommy Doyle (0-1)   Tom Spillane   Ger Lynch

Jack O'Shea (2-0)   Ambrose O'Donovan

John Kennedy (0-2)   Denis Ogie Moran (0-3)   Pat Spillane (0-4)

Mike Sheehy (0-7)   Timmy O'Dowd (0-1)   Ger Power

Substitute: John Higgins

Game 2 - Munster Final versus Cork in Cork on July 21. Final Score: Kerry 2-11; Cork 0-11.

Charlie Nelligan

Páidí Ó'Sé   Tom Spillane   Mick Spillane

John Higgins   Tommy Doyle   Ger Lynch

Jack O'Shea (0-1)   Ambrose O'Donovan

John Kennedy (0-1)   Denis Ogie Moran (0-1)   Pat Spillane (0-2)

Mike Sheehy (1-3)   Eoin Liston (1-2)   Ger Power

Substitute: Timmy O'Dowd (0-1) for Ambrose O'Donovan.

Game 3 - All-Ireland semi-final versus Monaghan in Croke Park on August 11. Final Score: Kerry 1-12; Monaghan 2-9 (Draw).

Charlie Nelligan

Páidí Ó'Sé   Tom Spillane   Mick Spillane

John Higgins   Tommy Doyle   Ger Lynch

Jack O'Shea (0-2)		Ambrose O'Donovan (0-1)
John Kennedy	Denis Ogie Moran	Pat Spillane (0-3)
Mike Sheehy (0-4)	Eoin Liston (0-1)	Ger Power (1-0)

Substitutes: Timmy O'Dowd (0-1) for Denis Ogie Moran, Sean Walsh for John Kennedy.

Game 4 - All-Ireland semi-final replay versus Monaghan in Croke Park on August 11. Final Score: Kerry 2-9; Monaghan 0-10.

Charlie Nelligan

Páidí Ó'Sé	Sean Walsh	Mick Spillane
Tommy Doyle	Tom Spillane	Ger Lynch
Jack O'Shea (0-1)		Ambrose O'Donovan
Timmy O'Dowd	Denis Ogie Moran	Pat Spillane (0-3)
Mike Sheehy (0-4)	Eoin Liston (1-0)	Ger Power (1-1)

Substitutes: Dermot Hanafin for Sean Walsh, John Kennedy for Denis Ogie Moran.

Game 5 - All-Ireland Final versus Dublin in Croke Park on September 22. Final Score: Kerry 2-12; Dublin 2-8.

Charlie Nelligan

Páidí Ó'Sé	Sean Walsh	Mick Spillane
Tommy Doyle (0-1)	Tom Spillane	Ger Lynch
Jack O'Shea (1-3)		Ambrose O'Donovan
Timmy O'Dowd (1-1)	Denis Ogie Moran (0-1)	Pat Spillane (0-2)
Mike Sheehy (0-3)	Eoin Liston	Ger Power

Substitute: John Kennedy (0-1) for Ger Power.

Scorers for the Year: Mike Sheehy (1-21), Jack O'Shea (3-7), Pat Spillane (0-14), Eoin Liston (2-3), Ger Power (2-1), Timmy O'Dowd (1-4), Denis Ogie Moran (0-5), John Kennedy (0-4), Tommy Doyle (0-2), Ambrose O'Donovan (0-1).

Total Scored: 9-62

Appearances:

5 - Charlie Nelligan, Páidí Ó'Sé, Mick Spillane, Tommy Doyle, Tom Spillane, Ger Lynch, Jack O'Shea, Ambrose O'Donovan, John Kennedy, Denis Ogie Moran, Pat Spillane, Mike Sheehy, Timmy O'Dowd, Ger Power.

4 - Sean Walsh, Eoin Liston.

3 - John Higgins.

2 - None

1 - Dermot Hanafin.

1985 - GAA Winners:

All-Irelands: Senior Football: Kerry **Minor Football:** Mayo **Under-21 Football:** Cork

National Leagues: Football: Monaghan Hurling: Limerick

Senior Hurling: Offaly

Kerry Co. Champions: Football: West Kerry Hurling: Lixnaw

1985 Football All-Stars:

John O'Leary (Dublin), **Páidí Ó'Sé (Kerry),** Gerry Hargan (Dublin), **Mick Spillane (Kerry), Tommy Doyle (Kerry),** Cathal Murray (Monaghan), Dermot Flanagan (Mayo), **Jack O'Shea (Kerry),** Willie Joe Padden (Mayo), Barney Rock (Dublin), Tommy Conroy (Dublin), **Pat Spillane (Kerry),** Kevin McStay (Mayo), Paul Earley (Roscommon), Eugene Hughes (Monaghan).

1985 - In The News:

- Cork City celebrates 800 years as a chartered city.
- Former minister Desmond O'Malley is expelled from the Fianna Fáil Party.
- The IRA kills nine Royal Ulster Constabulary officers in a mortar attack at Newry station.
- Bob Geldof is honoured for his overseas aid efforts at a civic reception in the Mansion House.

- Gaisce is created by a trust deed under the patronage of the President of Ireland.
- The Ireland national rugby union team wins the Triple Crown and Five Nations Championship at Lansdowne Road. They beat England 13-10.
- Dennis Taylor wins the Embassy World Snooker Championship.
- The Minister for Education, Gemma Hussey, announces a new £20 million project to create the transition year in post-primary schools.
- An Air India Boeing 747 crashes into the sea 190 kilometres off the Irish coast.
- Live Aid is organised by Bob Geldof in London. Ireland is the highest per-capita donor country. President Hillery presents a cheque for £7 million on behalf of the Irish people.
- At Ballinspittle, Co. Cork, two women claim to have seen a statue of the Virgin Mary move. The grotto becomes a place of pilgrimage, with thousands flocking to the village.
- Spike Island Jail in Co. Cork is left in ruins following a riot by prisoners.
- The first heart transplant in Ireland takes place.
- Pleasure Trawler Taurima, owned by Charles Haughey, was wrecked near Mizen Head lighthouse.
- The first commercial flight departs from Knock Airport.
- Taoiseach, Dr. Garret FitzGerald, and the British Prime Minister, Margaret Thatcher, sign the Anglo-Irish Agreement at Hillsborough Castle, Co. Down.
- Mary Harney is expelled from the Fianna Fáil parliamentary party over her support of the Anglo-Irish Agreement.
- Desmond O'Malley founds the Progressive Democrats.
- Barry McGuigan wins the WBA world featherweight boxing championship.

1986

Summary: Played four championship games, won 62nd Munster title, won 30th All-Ireland title.

Game 1 - versus Tipperary in Clonmel on June 15. Final Score: Kerry 5-9; Tipperary 0-12.

Charlie Nelligan

Páidí Ó'Sé	Sean Walsh	John Higgins
Stephen Stack	Tom Spillane	Ger Lynch (0-1)
Jack O'Shea (1-1)		Timmy O'Dowd
John Kennedy (0-2)	Denis Ogie Moran	Pat Spillane (1-2)
Mike Sheehy (0-1)	Eoin Liston (2-2)	Ger Power (1-0)

Subs: Dermot Hanafin for J. O'Shea, Willie Maher for D. Ogie Moran, Domo Lyne for J. Kennedy.

Game 2 - Munster Final versus Cork in Killarney on July 6. Final Score: Kerry 0-12; Cork 0-8.

Charlie Nelligan

Páidí Ó'Sé	Sean Walsh	Mick Spillane
Tommy Doyle (0-1)	Tom Spillane	Ger Lynch
Jack O'Shea (0-2)	Ambrose O'Donovan	
John Kennedy (0-4)	Timmy O'Dowd (0-1)	Pat Spillane
Mike Sheehy (0-4)	Eoin Liston	Ger Power

Substitute: Willie Maher for Pat Spillane.

Game 3 - All-Ireland semi-final versus Meath in Croke Park on August 24. Final Score: Kerry 2-13; Meath 0-12.

Charlie Nelligan

Páidí Ó'Sé	Sean Walsh	Mick Spillane
Tommy Doyle (0-1)	Tom Spillane	Ger Lynch

| Jack O'Shea (0-1) | Ambrose O'Donovan |

| John Kennedy | Denis Ogie Moran (0-1) | Pat Spillane (0-2) |

| Mike Sheehy (0-4) | Eoin Liston (0-3) | Ger Power (1-0) |

Subs: Willie Maher (1-1) for John Kennedy, Timmy O'Dowd for Ambrose O'Donovan, Mick Galwey for Eoin Liston.

Game 4 - All-Ireland Final versus Tyrone in Croke Park on September 21. Final Score: Kerry 2-15; Tyrone 1-10.

                            Charlie Nelligan

| Páidí Ó'Sé | Sean Walsh | Mick Spillane |

| Tommy Doyle | Tom Spillane | Ger Lynch |

| Jack O'Shea | Ambrose O'Donovan |

| Willie Maher | Denis Ogie Moran (0-2) | Pat Spillane (1-4) |

| Mike Sheehy (1-4) | Eoin Liston (0-2) | Ger Power (0-1) |

Substitute: Timmy O'Dowd (0-2) for Ambrose O'Donovan.

Scorers for the Year: Mike Sheehy (1-13), Pat Spillane (2-8), Eoin Liston (2-7), Ger Power (2-1), Jack O'Shea (1-4), John Kennedy (0-6), Willie Maher (1-1), Denis Ogie Moran (0-3), Timmy O'Dowd (0-3), Tommy Doyle (0-2), Ger Lynch (0-1).

Total Scored: 9-49

Appearances:

4 - Charlie Nelligan, Páidí Ó'Sé, Sean Walsh, Tom Spillane, Ger Lynch, Jack O'Shea, Timmy O'Dowd, Pat Spillane, Willie Maher, Mike Sheehy, Eoin Liston, Ger Power.

3 - Mick Spillane, Tommy Doyle, Ambrose O'Donovan, John Kennedy, Denis Ogie Moran.

2 - None

1 - John Higgins, Stephen Stack, Dermot Hanafin, Domo Lyne, Mick Galwey.

1986 - GAA Winners:

All-Irelands: Senior Football: Kerry **Minor Football:** Galway **Under-21 Football:** Cork

National Leagues: Football: Laois Hurling: Kilkenny

Senior Hurling: Cork

Kerry Co. Champions: Football: Austin Stacks Hurling: St. Brendans

1986 Football All-Stars:

Charlie Nelligan (Kerry), Harry Keegan (Roscommon), Mick Lyons (Meath), John Lynch (Tyrone), **Tommy Doyle (Kerry), Tom Spillane (Kerry),** Colm Browne (Laois), Plunkett Donaghy (Tyrone), Liam Irwin (Laois), Ray McCarron (Monaghan), Eugene McKenna (Tyrone), **Pat Spillane (Kerry), Mike Sheehy (Kerry),** Damian O'Hagan (Tyrone), **Ger Power (Kerry).**

1986 - In The News:
- The national offices of the Progressive Democrats are officially opened.
- Phil Lynott, lead singer with Thin Lizzy, dies aged 35.
- Ireland's new soccer team manager, Jack Charlton, takes over.
- Irish citizenship is conferred on Speaker of the United States House of Representatives, Tip O'Neill, for inspiring constitutional nationalists to launch a new initiative for a new Ireland.
- President Hillery and Mrs. Hillery conduct a four-day official visit to Austria. This is the first official visit there by an Irish head of state.
- The Divorce Action Group launches its campaign for the forthcoming referendum.
- Knock Airport, Co. Mayo is officially opened on May 30.
- John Stalker is removed from the "shoot to kill" inquiry.
- Two giant pandas, Ming-Ming and Ping-Ping, arrive at Dublin Zoo.
- An anti-divorce rally takes place in Dublin in June.
- Across the country counting begins in the Divorce Referendum. Tallymen predict a strong rejection. The amendment to the Constitution to allow divorce is defeated by a margin of 63.5% to 35.5%.
- The deputy leader of the Democratic Unionist Party, Peter Robinson MP, is arrested and charged with illegal assembly, after a loyalist mob takes over a village in Co. Monaghan on August 7.

- Dublin Airport opens for the first time on Christmas Day.
- At the United States Embassy in Dublin, visa applications rise by 25%. 30,000 people emigrate during 1986.

1987

Summary: Played three championship games, lost Munster Final.

Game 1 - versus Waterford in Dungarvan on June 21. Final Score: Kerry 3-15; Waterford 2-8.

Charlie Nelligan

Páidí Ó'Sé   Sean Walsh   Mick Spillane

Tommy Doyle   Tom Spillane   Ger Lynch

Jack O'Shea (2-1)   Ambrose O'Donovan

John Kennedy   Denis Ogie Moran (0-4)   Pat Spillane (0-3)

Ger Power (1-1)   Eoin Liston (0-5)   Willie Maher (0-1)

Substitutes: Timmy O'Dowd for John Kennedy, John Higgins for Ger Lynch.

Game 2- Munster Final versus Cork in Cork on July 26. Final Score: Kerry 2-7; Cork 1-10 (Draw).

Charle Nelligan

Páidí Ó'Sé   Sean Walsh   Mick Spillane

Tommy Doyle   Tom Spillane   Ger Lynch

Jack O'Shea (0-2)   Ambrose O'Donovan

Timmy O'Dowd   Denis Ogie Moran (0-1)   Pat Spillane

Mike Sheehy (1-4)   Eoin Liston (1-0)   Ger Power

Substitutes: Dermot Hanafin for Denis Ogie Moran, Mike McAuliffe for Timmy O'Dowd.

Game 3 - Munster Final replay versus Cork in Killarney on August 2. Final Score: Cork 0-13; Kerry 1-5.

Charlie Nelligan

Páidí Ó'Sé   Sean Walsh   Mick Spillane

Tommy Doyle (0-1)   Tom Spillane   Ger Lynch

Dermot Hanafin (1-0)	Ambrose O'Donovan	
John Kennedy	Jack O'Shea (0-2)	Pat Spillane
Mike Sheehy (0-1)	Eoin Liston	Ger Power

Substitutes: Timmy O'Dowd for John Kennedy, Mike McAuliffe for Timmy O'Dowd, Vincent O'Connor (0-1) for Ambrose O'Donovan.

Scorers for the Year: Jack O'Shea (2-5), Mike Sheehy (1-5), Eoin Liston (1-5), Denis Ogie Moran (0-5), Ger Power (1-1), Pat Spillane (0-3), Dermot Hanafin (1-0), Tommy Doyle (0-1), Vincent O'Connor (0-1), Willie Maher (0-1).

Total Scored: 6-27

Appearances:

3 - Charlie Nelligan, Páidí Ó'Sé, Sean Walsh, Mick Spillane, Tommy Doyle, Tom Spillane, Ger Lynch, Jack O'Shea, Ambrose O'Donovan, Timmy O'Dowd, Pat Spillane, Eoin Liston, Ger Power.

2 - Dermot Hanafin, John Kennedy, Denis Ogie Moran, Mike Sheehy, Mike McAuliffe.

1 - John Higgins, Vincent O'Connor, Willie Maher.

1987 - GAA Winners:

All-Irelands: Senior Football: Meath **Minor Football:** Down **Under-21 Football:** Donegal

National Leagues: Football: Dublin Hurling: Galway

Senior Hurling: Galway

Kerry Co. Champions: Football: Kenmare Hurling: Causeway

1987 Football All-Stars:

John Kerins (Cork), Robbie O'Malley (Meath), Colman Corrigan (Cork), Tony Scullion (Derry), Niall Cahalane (Cork), **Tom Spillane (Kerry), Ger Lynch (Kerry),** Gerry McEntee (Meath), Brian McGilligan (Derry), David Beggy (Meath), Larry Tompkins (Cork), Kieran Duff (Dublin), Val Daly (Galway), Brian Stafford (Meath), Bernard Flynn (Meath).

1987 - In The News:

- The general election of 1987 was precipitated by the withdrawal of the Labour Party from the Fine Gael led government on 20 January 1987. The reason was a disagreement over budget proposals. Rather than press on with the government's agenda, the Taoiseach and leader of Fine Gael, Garret FitzGerald, decided to dissolve the Dáil. An unusually long period of four weeks was set for the campaign. It was hoped that the electorate would warm to Fine Gael's budget proposals during the campaign.

  Fianna Fáil's campaign involved the refusal to make any definite commitments, however, they attempted to convince the electorate that the country would be better under them. Charles Haughey's attitude towards Northern Ireland and the Anglo-Irish Agreement were all attacked. However, the campaign was more or less fought on economic issues. The Labour Party decided against any pact before the election. The Progressive Democrats, founded only two years before, surpassed the Labour Party as the third biggest political party in the Dáil. Although the party was made mostly of Fianna Fáil defectors, it also took seats from Fine Gael.

  In spite of the opinion polls suggesting otherwise, Fianna Fáil once again failed to win an overall majority, taking 81 of the 166 seats, against Fine Gael's 50. However, Fianna Fáil was able to govern as a minority government and Charles Haughey was back for his third and final time as Taoiseach, with Brian Lenihan as Tánaiste. The new party, the Progressive Democrats, did exceptionally well on their first outing, taking 14 seats. Fine Gael lost many seats, mostly to the PDs. The Labour Party took only 12 seats, failing to make any huge impact with its leader, Dick Spring, almost losing his seat.

  Former Taoiseach Dr. Garret FitzGerald resigns the leadership of Fine Gael. Alan Dukes succeeds him.
- Kerry returned the following as members of the 25th Dáil:

  Kerry South: John O'Donoghue (FF); John O'Leary (FF); Michael Begley (FG).

  Kerry North: Jimmy Deenihan (FG); Denis Foley (FF); Dick Spring (Lab.).
- The Irish National Lottery is launched, with scratch cards being introduced.
- The SAS kills 8 IRA members and a civilian in an ambush at Loughgall, Co. Tyrone.

- Johnny Logan of Ireland wins the Eurovision Song Contest for a second time with the song "Hold Me Now".
- Voters go to the poll in the referendum on the Single European Act. Nearly 70% vote in favour of the 10th amendment to the constitution.
- Stephen Roche wins the Tour de France.
- 11 civilians are killed in an explosion during a Remembrance Day service in Enniskillen.
- The funeral takes place in Dublin of the broadcaster Eamonn Andrews.
- Beaumont Hospital, Dublin opens to patients.
- U2 release "The Joshua Tree" album to popular international acclaim.

1988

Summary: Played two championship games, lost the Munster Final.

Game 1 - versus Waterford in Tralee on May 29. Final Score: Kerry 3-19; Waterford 1-7.

Charlie Nelligan

Páidí Ó'Sé Tom Spillane Mick Spillane

Tommy Doyle Ambrose O'Donovan Ger Lynch

Jack O'Shea Maurice Fitzgerald (0-6)

Donal McEvoy (1-1) Willie Maher (1-1) Mike McAuliffe (0-4)

Ger Power Pat Spillane (1-6) Gerard Murphy (0-1)

No substitutes used.

Game 2 - Munster Final versus Cork in Cork on July 3. Final Score: Cork 1-14; Kerry 0-16.

Charlie Nelligan

Mick Spillane Tom Spillane Morgan Nix

Tommy Doyle (0-1) Ambrose O'Donovan Ger Lynch

Jack O'Shea (0-1) Dermot Hanafin

Maurice Fitzgerald (0-10) Connie Murphy (0-1) Mike McAuliffe (0-1)

Willie Maher (0-1) Pat Spillane (0-1) Gerard Murphy

Substitutes: Ger Power for Willie Maher, Eoin Liston for Gerard Murphy, Joe Shannon for Dermot Hanafin.

Scorers for the Year: Maurice Fitzgerald (0-16), Pat Spillane (1-7), Willie Maher (1-2), Mike McAuliffe (0-5), Donal McEvoy (1-1), Tommy Doyle (0-1), Jack O'Shea (0-1), Connie Murphy (0-1), Gerard Murphy (0-1).

Total Scored: 3-35

Appearances:

2 - Charlie Nelligan, Tom Spillane, Mick Spillane, Tommy Doyle, Ambrose O'Donovan, Ger Lynch, Jack O'Shea, Maurice Fitzgerald, Willie Maher, Mike McAuliffe, Ger Power, Pat Spillane, Gerard Murphy.

1 - Morgan Nix, Páidí Ó'Sé, Dermot Hanafin, Donal McEvoy, Connie Murphy, Eoin Liston, Joe Shannon.

1988 - GAA Winners:

All-Irelands: Senior Football: Meath **Minor Football:** Kerry **Under-21 Football:** Offaly

Kerry's Minor Winning Team: P. O'Leary, P. Lenihan, N. Savage, J. O'Brien, L. Flaherty, V. Knightley, S. Walsh, E. Stack, F. Ashe, P. Laide, D. Cahill, S. O'Sullivan, C. Geaney, D. Farrell, B. O'Sullivan. Sub: F. Doherty.

National Leagues: Football: Meath   Hurling: Tipperary

Senior Hurling: Galway

Kerry Co. Champions: Football: St. Kierans   Hurling: Ballyduff

1988 Football All-Stars:

Paddy Linden (Monaghan), Robbie O'Malley (Meath), Colman Corrigan (Cork), Mick Kennedy (Dublin), Niall Cahalane (Cork), Noel McCaffrey (Dublin), Martin O'Connell (Meath), Shea Fahy (Cork), Liam Hayes (Meath), **Maurice Fitzgerald (Kerry),** Larry Tompkins (Cork), Kieran Duff (Dublin), Colm O'Rourke (Meath), Brian Stafford (Meath), Eugene Hughes (Monaghan).

1988 - In The News:

- John Hume and Gerry Adams have a surprise meeting in Belfast.
- Former Nobel Prize winner Seán MacBride dies, aged 83.
- The SAS kills three unarmed members of the IRA in Gibraltar.
- It is agreed that a millennium fountain called the Anna Livia Fountain is to be built on O'Connell Street.
- Three men are killed and 70 are wounded in a gun and grenade attack on mourners in Milltown Cemetery during the funerals of three IRA members.

- 5,000 people turn out for an anti-apartheid rally at the GPO in Dublin.
- Tributes are paid to Aran Islands poet Máirtín Ó Direáin at his funeral in Dublin.
- The Irish National Lottery launches its national live draw, "The Lotto".
- The IRA kills six British soldiers in a bomb attack in Lisburn.
- Dublin celebrates its official 1,000th birthday on July 10.
- Nelson Mandela, the jailed anti-apartheid leader, is awarded the freedom of Dublin City.
- The Department of Health launches an information booklet as the number of AIDS cases increases dramatically.
- Leopardstown Racecourse celebrates its 100th birthday.
- Archbishop Thomas Morris resigns as Archbishop of Cashel with Dermot Clifford appointed as his replacement.
- A tax amnesty brings in over £500 million.
- The IRTC is established to regulate radio and television services outside the RTE umbrella.
- Minister for Finance Ray MacSharry is appointed Ireland's new EC Commissioner.
- Ireland's soccer team plays in Euro 88 but does not qualify from group play. The team beats England, draws with USSR and loses to Holland, the eventual tournament winners.

1989

Summary: Played two championship games, lost Munster Final.

Game 1 - versus Limerick in Askeaton on June 18. Final Score: Kerry 6-7; Limerick 1-10.

Charlie Nelligan

Ken Savage	Liam Hartnett	Morgan Nix
Tom Spillane (1-0)	Ambrose O'Donovan	Connie Murphy
Jack O'Shea		Mick Galwey
John Kennedy	Maurice Fitzgerald (1-2)	Timmy Fleming (1-2)
Mike McAuliffe (1-0)	Eoin Liston (1-1)	Pat Spillane (0-2)

Substitutes: Tommy Doyle for Liam Hartnett, Willie Maher (1-0) for John Kennedy, Pa Dennehy for Mike McAuliffe.

Game 2 - Munster Final versus Cork in Killarney on July 23. Final Score: Cork 1-12; Kerry 1-9.

Charlie Nelligan

Ken Savage	Ambrose O'Donovan (1-0)	Mick Spillane
Connie Murphy	Tommy Doyle	Morgan Nix
Jack O'Shea		Tom Spillane
Timmy Fleming	Maurice Fitzgerald (0-6)	Joe Shannon
Willie Maher	Eoin Liston (0-1)	Pat Spillane (0-2)

Substitutes: Anthony Gleeson for Mick Spillane, Mike McAuliffe for Joe Shannon, Pa Dennehy for Willie Maher.

Scorers for the Year: Maurice Fitzgerald (1-8), Eoin Liston (1-2), Timmy Fleming (1-2), Pat Spillane (0-4), Tom Spillane (1-0), Ambrose O'Donovan (1-0), Mike McAuliffe (1-0), Willie Maher (1-0).

Total Scored: 7-16

Appearances:

2 - Charlie Nelligan, Ken Savage, Morgan Nix, Tom Spillane, Ambrose O'Donovan, Connie Murphy, Tommy Doyle, Jack O'Shea, Maurice Fitzgerald, Timmy Fleming, Mike McAuliffe, Eoin Liston, Pat Spillane, Willie Maher, Pa Dennehy.

1 - Liam Hartnett, Mick Spillane, Mick Galwey, John Kennedy, Joe Shannon, Anthony Gleeson.

1989 - GAA Winners:

All-Irelands: Senior Football: Cork **Minor Football:** Derry   **Under-21 Football:** Cork

National Leagues: Football: Cork   Hurling: Galway

Senior Hurling: Tipperary

Kerry Co. Champions: Football: Laune Rangers   Hurling: Ballyduff

1989 Football All-Stars:

Gabriel Irwin (Mayo), Jimmy Browne (Mayo), Gerry Hargan (Dublin), Dermot Flanagan (Mayo), **Connie Murphy (Kerry),** Conor Counihan (Cork), Tony Davis (Cork), Teddy McCarthy (Cork), Willie Joe Padden (Mayo), Dave Barry (Cork), Larry Tompkins (Cork), Noel Durkin (Mayo), Paul McGrath (Cork), Eugene McKenna (Tyrone), Tony McManus (Roscommon).

1989 - In The News:

- Dundalk, Co. Louth celebrates its 1200 year heritage.
- Belfast solicitor Pat Finucane is shot dead by loyalists.
- Three Irish soldiers on United Nations duty are killed in a landmine explosion in southern Lebanon.
- Belfast-born Alex Higgins beats Stephen Hendry to win the British Benson and Hedges snooker championship.
- The Windmill Lane Consortium says that if it gets the franchise it will be on the air within 9 to 12 months with its station TV3.
- Ray McAnally, one of the country's most versatile actors, dies suddenly.
- On June 22 an order is signed creating the University of Limerick, the first university founded since the foundation of the state; later in the day Dublin City University is created.

- The general election of 1989 was precipitated by the defeat of the minority Fianna Fáil government in a private members motion regarding the provision of funds for AIDS sufferers. While a general election was not necessary as the defeat was only seen as something that was an embarrassment for the government, the Dáil was dissolved nonetheless.

Charles Haughey, the leader of Fianna Fáil, called the general election for another reason. Opinion polls had shown that the party's strong performance in government had increased their popularity and the possibility of an overall majority could be on the cards. Rumours that the general election was called so that certain Fianna Fáil members could raise money for themselves were also doing the rounds at the time. While these rumours were dismissed at the time, it was revealed over ten years later that Ray Burke, Pádraig Flynn and Haughey himself had received substantial personal donations during the campaign.

While it was thought that the general election would catch the opposition parties on the hop they coordinated themselves and cooperated very quickly. Cuts in the health service became the dominant issue in spite of the good reputation the government had for managing the economy. Alan Dukes, the leader of Fine Gael, was fighting his first general election as leader. His "Tallaght Strategy" had kept Fianna Fáil in power for the two years since 1987, however now his head was on the block as he had to prove that he was a worthy leader.

Although the general election was held on the same day as the elections to the European Parliament, turnout was only 68.5%. Perhaps the electorate were weary of elections, particularly since this was the fifth general election to be held in Ireland in the 1980s. While Fianna Fáil had hoped to achieve an overall majority, the party actually lost seats with a total of 77. The result was a disaster for Fianna Fáil, particularly when the election was so unnecessary. Fine Gael made a small gain to 55, but nothing substantial. The Progressive Democrats also did badly losing over half their deputies, with 6 remaining. The Labour Party (15 seats)and the Workers Party (7 seats) gained working class votes from Fianna Fáil, but failed to make the big breakthrough, while Sinn Féin polled even worse than its 1987 result. The Green Party won its first seat when Roger Garland was elected for Dublin South. 5 Others made up the 166 deputies.

Forming a government proved to be extremely difficult. Many in Fianna Fáil had hoped that the minority government could continue where it left off, particularly if the "Tallaght Strategy" continued. However, Fine Gael refused to support the government and so a deadlock developed. The prospect of forming a government seemed remote, so much so that Charles Haughey was forced to formally resign as Taoiseach. For the first time in Irish history a Taoiseach and a government had not been appointed when the new Dáil met. However, twenty-seven days after the general election Fianna Fáil entered into a coalition government for the first time with the Progressive Democrats. Charles Haughey resumed as Taoiseach with Brian Lenihan as Tánaiste. Two Progressive Democrats hold Ministerial positions - Desmond O'Malley (Industry and Commerce) and Bobby Molloy (Energy).

- Kerry returned the following as members of the 26th Dáil:
  Kerry South: John O'Donoghue (FF); John O'Leary (FF); Michael Moynihan (Lab.).
  Kerry North: Jimmy Deenihan (FG); Tom McEllistrim Jr. (FF); Dick Spring (Lab.).
- 10,000 people march from Dublin city centre to the British Embassy calling for British withdrawal from Northern Ireland.
- Century Radio goes on the air for the first time.
- Three of the Guildford Four are released in London. Paul Hill is immediately re-arrested.
- Aer Rianta's 5,000,000[th] passenger is presented with a holiday to Florida.

1990-1999...Building something greater?

Summary of the Decade

Kerry played 29 games, scoring 44-388, conceding 25-319.

Munster Championship titles: 4 (1991, 1996, 1997, 1998)

All Ireland titles: 1 (1997)

National League titles: 1 (1997) **U-21 titles: 4** (1990, 1995, 1996, 1998)

Minor titles: 1 (1994)

Top Scorers: Maurice Fitzgerald (10-170), John Crowley (7-16)

Top Points-only scorers: Maurice Fitzgerald (170), Dara Ó'Cinneide (26)

Top Goals-only scorers: Maurice Fitzgerald (10), John Crowley (7)

Most Appearances: Maurice Fitzgerald (29), Eamonn Breen (25)

1990
Kerry 1-23 Clare 0-13;
Munster Final: Cork 2-23 Kerry 1-11.

1991
Kerry 5-16 Clare 2-12;
Kerry 1-10 Cork 0-11;
Munster Final: Kerry 0-23 Limerick 3-12;
All-Ireland semi-final: Down 2-9 Kerry 0-8.

1992
Kerry 2-14 Cork 0-10;
Kerry 1-14 Limerick 1-11;
Munster Final: Clare 2-10 Kerry 0-12.

1993
Cork 1-10 Kerry 0-10.

1994

Kerry 2-19 Limerick 0-8;
Munster Final: Cork 1-13 Kerry 2-8.

1995

Kerry 3-17 Limerick 0-8;
Kerry 7-12 Tipperary 1-13;
Munster Final: Cork 0-15; Kerry 0-9.

1996

Kerry 2-15 Tipperary 1-7;
Kerry 3-16 Waterford 0-8;
Munster Final: Kerry 0-14 Cork 0-11;
All-Ireland semi-final: Mayo 2-13 Kerry 1-10.

1997

Kerry 2-12 Tipperary 1-10;
Munster Final: Kerry 1-13 Clare 0-11;
All-Ireland semi-final: Kerry 1-17 Cavan 1-10;
All-Ireland Final: Kerry 0-13 Mayo 1-7.

1998

Kerry 1-14 Cork 1-11;
Munster Final: Kerry 0-17 Tipperary 1-10;
All-Ireland semi-final: Kildare 0-13 Kerry 1-9.

1999

Kerry 1-11 Tipperary 0-8;
Kerry 3-17 Clare 0-12;
Munster Final: Cork 2-10 Kerry 2-4.

1990

Summary: Played two championship games, lost Munster Final.

Game 1 - versus Clare in Listowel on May 27. Final Score: Kerry 1-23; Clare 0-13.

Charlie Nelligan

Donal McCarthy (0-1)	Kieran Culhane	Connie Murphy
Pat Slattery	Ambrose O'Donovan	Tom Spillane
Maurice Fitzgerald (0-9)	Joe Shannon (0-2)	
Pa Laide (0-2)	Pat McKenna (0-2)	Jack O'Shea (0-1)
Sean McElligott (0-4)	Pat Spillane	Sean Geaney (1-2)

Substitute: Noel O'Mahony for Fitzgerald.

Game 2 - Munster Final versus Cork in Cork on July 6. Final Score: Cork 2-23; Kerry 1-11.

Charlie Nelligan

Stephen Stack	Morgan Nix	Connie Murphy
Pat Slattery	Ambrose O'Donovan	Tom Spillane (0-1)
Maurice Fitzgerald (1-5)	Joe Shannon	
Pa Laide (0-1)	Eamonn Breen	Jack O'Shea (0-1)
Sean McElligott (0-1)	Eoin Liston	Sean Geaney

Substitutes: Pat Spillane (0-2) for Shannon, David Farrell for Liston, Sean Burke for Slattery.

Scorers for the Year: Maurice Fitzgerald (1-14), Sean McElligott (0-5), Sean Geaney (1-2), Pa Laide (0-3), Joe Shannon (0-2), Pat McKenna (0-2), Jack O'Shea (0-2), Pat Spillane (0-2), Donal McCarthy (0-1), Tom Spillane (0-1).

Total Scored: 2-34

Appearances:

2 - Charlie Nelligan, Connie Murphy, Pat Slattery, Ambrose O'Donovan, Tom Spillane, Maurice Fitzgerald, Joe Shannon, Pa Laide, Jack O'Shea, Sean McElligott, Pat Spillane, Sean Geaney.

1 - Donal McCarthy, Kieran Culhane, Pat McKenna, Noel O'Mahony, Stephen Stack, Morgan Nix, Eamonn Breen, Eoin Liston, David Farrell, Sean Burke.

1990 - GAA Winners:

All-Irelands: Senior Football: Cork   **Minor   Football:**   Meath
Under-21 Football: Kerry

Kerry's Winning Under-21 Team: P. O'Leary, J. O'Brien, S. Burke, L. O'Flaherty, P. Slattery, V. Knightley, E. Breen, M. Fitzgerald, N. O'Mahony, P. Laide, P. McKenna, G. O'Driscoll, P. Dennehy, D. Farrell, W. O'Sullivan. Sub: P. Griffin.

National Leagues: Football: Meath   Hurling: Kilkenny

Senior Hurling: Cork

Kerry Co. Champions: Football: West Kerry   Hurling: St. Brendans

1990 Football All-Stars:

John Kearns (Cork), Robbie O'Malley (Meath), Steven O'Brien (Cork), Terry Ferguson (Meath), Michael Slocum (Cork), Conor Counihan (Cork), Martin O'Connell (Meath), Shay Fahy (Cork), Mickey Quinn (Leitrim), David Beggy (Meath), Val Daly (Galway), Joyce McMullan (Donegal), Paul McGrath (Cork), Kevin O'Brien (Wicklow), James McCartan (Down).

1990 - In The News:

- The Northern Ireland Fair Employment Act becomes law.
- There is all-party support for the government bill to abolish the death penalty for capital murder and replace it with lengthy prison sentences.
- Circulation begins of the IR£1 coin as a replacement for the note of the same denomination.
- Deputy President of the ANC, Nelson Mandela, addresses a joint session of both houses of the Oireachtas.

- Brian Keenan is released after 1,574 days in captivity in Beirut.
- September 28 - Centenary of People's Park, Dún Laoghaire celebrated
- An Tánaiste and Minister for Defence Brian Lenihan is sacked from the government over the telephone call controversy.
- Labour candidate Mary Robinson is elected the seventh President of Ireland, beating Brian Lenihan and Austin Currie. She replaces Dr. Patrick Hillery who served the maximum 14 years in office.
- In Italia 90, Ireland's soccer team play in the World Cup tournament for the first time. After draws with England, Egypt and Holland, the team advances from Group play. Ireland beats Romania on penalties before losing 1-0 to Italy in the quarter final.

1991

Summary: Played four championship games, won 63rd Munster title, lost All-Ireland semi-final.

Game 1 - versus Clare in Ennis on May 26. Final Score: Kerry 5-16; Clare 2-12.

Charlie Nelligan

John O'Connell	Kieran Culhane	Niall Savage
Liam O'Flaherty	Connie Murphy (1-0)	Sean Burke

Timmy Fleming (0-1)   Noel O'Mahony

Jack O'Shea (0-4)	Willie Maher (0-3)	Maurice Fitzgerald (0-7)
Pa Dennehy (1-0)	David Farrell (2-1)	Pat Spillane

Substitutes: Eamonn Breen for O'Connell, Murt Moriarty (1-0) for O'Mahony, Morgan Nix for Savage.

Game 2 - versus Cork in Killarney on June 16. Final Score: Kerry 1-10; Cork 0-11.

Charlie Nelligan

Liam O'Flaherty	Kieran Culhane	Stephen Stack
Sean Burke	Connie Murphy	Morgan Nix

Ambrose O'Donovan (0-1)   Noel O'Mahony

Jack O'Shea (0-1)	Timmy Fleming (0-1)	Maurice Fitzgerald (0-5)
John Cronin (1-1)	Pat Spillane	Pa Dennehy (0-1)

Substitutes: Murt Moriarty for Cronin, David Farrell for Fleming.

Game 3 - Munster Final versus Limerick in Limerick on July 21. Final Score: Kerry 0-23; Limerick 3-12.

Charlie Nelligan

JB O'Brien	Kieran Culhane	Stephen Stack
Sean Burke	Connie Murphy	Morgan Nix

Ambrose O'Donovan (0-1)   Noel O'Mahony

John Cronin (0-3)   Pat Spillane (0-2)   Jack O'Shea (0-3)

Pa Dennehy (0-2)   Maurice Fitzgerald (0-12)   Timmy Fleming

Substitutess: Sean Geaney for Fleming, Willie Maher for Nix, David Farrell for O'Mahony.

Game 4 - All-Ireland semi-final versus Down in Croke Park on August 11. Final Score: Down 2-9; Kerry 0-8.

Charlie Nelligan

Stephen Stack   Tom Spillane   Kieran Culhane

Sean Burke   Connie Murphy   Morgan Nix

Ambrose O'Donovan (0-1)   Noel O'Mahony

John Cronin   Pat Spillane (0-2)   Jack O'Shea

Pa Dennehy   Maurice Fitzgerald (0-5)   Timmy Fleming

Substitutes: Domo Lyne for Murphy, David Farrell for Cronin.

Scorers for the Year: Maurice Fitzgerald (0-29), Jack O'Shea (0-8), David Farrell (2-1), John Cronin (1-4), Pa Dennehy (1-3), Pat Spillane (0-4), Murt Moriarty (1-0), Connie Murphy (1-0), Ambrose O'Donovan (0-3), Willie Maher (0-3), Timmy Fleming (0-2).

Total Scored: 6-57

Appearances:

4 - Charlie Nelligan, Kieran Culhane, Connie Murphy, Sean Burke, Timmy Fleming, Noel O'Mahony, Jack O'Shea, Maurice Fitzgerald, Pa Dennehy, David Farrell, Pat Spillane, Morgan Nix.

3 - Stephen Stack, Ambrose O'Donovan, John Cronin.

2 - Liam O'Flaherty, Willie Maher, Murt Moriarty.

1 - John O'Connell, Niall Savage, Eamonn Breen, JB O'Brien, Sean Geaney, Domo Lyne, Tom Spillane.

1991 - GAA Winners:

All-Irelands: Senior Football: Down **Minor Football:** Cork **Under-21 Football:** Tyrone

National Leagues: Football: Dublin   Hurling: Offaly

Senior Hurling: Tipperary

Kerry Juniors also take All-Ireland honours with this team: K. Moran, T. Hanifin, L. Burns, T. Dennehy, R. O'Dwyer, V. Knightley, P. Dillane, F. Ashe, T. Harrington, D. Moynihan, G. O'Driscoll, J. Kennedy, M. McAuliffe, T. Brosnan, S. O'Sullivan. Subs: S. Tuohy, J. Murphy, T. Evans.

Kerry Co. Champions: Football: Dr. Crokes   Hurling: Ballyduff

1991 Football All-Stars:

Michael McQuillan (Meath), Mick Deegan (Dublin), Conor Deegan (Down), Enon Gavin (Roscommon), Tommy Carr (Dublin), Keith Barr (Dublin), Martin O'Connell (Meath), Barry Breen (Down), Martin Lynch (Kildare), Ross Carr (Down), Greg Blaney (Down), Tommy Dowd (Meath), Colm O'Rourke (Meath), Brian Stafford (Meath), Bernard Flynn (Meath).

1991 - In The News:

- Limerick City celebrates 300 years of the Treaty of Limerick.
- The Irish Government and the EC Commission meet in Dublin to officially launch the Irish EC Presidency.
- There is controversy as the government allows US war planes to refuel at Shannon Airport.
- The new Government Buildings in the renovated College of Science are officially opened.
- The IRA fires mortar bombs at 10 Downing Street in London.
- After being wrongfully jailed for 16 years, the Birmingham Six are freed.
- Dublin is officially inaugurated as the European City of Culture.
- The wrongful convictions of the Maguire Seven are overturned.
- Kildare TD Seán Power proposes a no-confidence motion in Charles Haughey's leadership. The Minister for Finance, Albert Reynolds, is sacked from the government over his intention to support the no-confidence motion.
- Jim McDaid, the new Defence Minister, resigns following criticism from the opposition over his attendance at an IRA funeral.

1992

Summary: Played three championship games, lost Munster Final.

Game 1 - versus Cork in Cork on May 24. Final Score: Kerry 2-14; Cork 0-10.

Peter O'Leary

Stephen Stack	Anthony Gleeson	Eamonn Breen
Sean Burke	Connie Murphy	Liam O'Flaherty

Noel O'Mahony   Ambrose O'Donovan (0-1)

Pa Laide (0-1)	Timmy Fleming (0-2)	Maurice Fitzgerald (1-8)
John Cronin (0-1)	Jack O'Shea (0-1)	Billy O'Shea (1-0)

Substitute: Billy O'Sullivan for Laide.

Game 2 - versus Limerick in Limerick on June 21. Final Score: Kerry 1-14; Limerick 1-11.

Peter O'Leary

Stephen Stack	Anthony Gleeson	Liam O'Flaherty
Sean Burke	Connie Murphy	Eamonn Breen

Noel O'Mahony   Ambrose O'Donovan

Pa Laide (0-1)	Timmy Fleming	Maurice Fitzgerald (0-5)
Karl O'Dwyer (0-4)	Jack O'Shea (0-4)	Billy O'Shea (1-0)

Substitutes: Dermot Hanafin for O'Mahony, Sean Geaney for Laide.

Game 3 - Munster Final versus Clare in Limerick on July 19. Final Score: Clare 2-10; Kerry 0-12.

Peter O'Leary

Stephen Stack	Anthony Gleeson	Eamonn Breen
Liam O'Flaherty	Sean Burke	Connie Murphy (0-1)

Noel O'Mahony (0-1)   Seamus Moynihan

Sean Geaney	Timmy Fleming (0-1)	Maurice Fitzgerald (0-7)
Karl O'Dwyer	Jack O'Shea (0-1)	Billy O'Shea (0-1)

Substitutes: Ambrose O'Donovan for O'Dwyer, Pa Laide for Geaney, Noel O'Leary for O'Mahony.

Scorers for the Year: Maurice Fitzgerald (1-20), Billy O'Shea (2-1), Jack O'Shea (0-6), Karl O'Dwyer (0-4), Pa Laide (0-2), Timmy Fleming (0-2), Eamonn Breen (0-1), Connie Murphy (0-1), Noel O'Mahony (0-1), Ambrose O'Donovan (0-1), John Cronin (0-1).

Total Scored: 3-40

Appearances:

3 - Peter O'Leary, Stephen Stack, Anthony Gleeson, Eamonn Breen, Sean Burke, Connie Murphy, Liam O'Flaherty, Noel O'Mahony, Ambrose O'Donovan, Pa Laide, Timmy Fleming, Maurice Fitzgerald, Jack O'Shea, Billy O'Shea.

2 - Karl O'Dwyer, Sean Geaney.

1 - John Cronin, Billy O'Sullivan, Dermot Hanafin, Seamus Moynihan, Noel O'Leary.

1992 - GAA Winners:

All-Irelands: Senior Football: Donegal   **Minor Football:** Meath **Under-21 Football:** Tyrone

National Leagues: Football: Derry   Hurling: Limerick

Senior Hurling: Kilkenny

Kerry Co. Champions: Football: Mid-Kerry   Hurling: Ballyheigue

1992 Football All-Stars:

Gary Walsh (Donegal), Seamus Clancy (Clare), Matt Gallagher (Donegal), Tony Scullion (Derry), Paul Curran (Dublin), Martin Gavigan (Donegal), Eamon Heery (Dublin), Anthony Molloy (Donegal), T.J. Kilgallon (Mayo), Anthony Tohill (Derry), Martin McHugh (Donegal), James McHugh (Donegal), Tony Boyle (Donegal), Vinny Murphy (Dublin), Enda Gormley (Derry).

1992 - In The News:

- Peter Brooke offers to resign as Secretary of State for Northern Ireland following criticism of his singing on The Late Late Show only hours after an IRA bomb explodes.
- Charles Haughey resigns as Taoiseach and as leader of Fianna Fáil.
- Mary Robinson becomes the first President of Ireland to visit Belfast. On the same day an off-duty RUC officer in Belfast kills three people in a Sinn Féin office before committing suicide.
- The High Court prevents a 14-year old rape victim from going to Britain for an abortion. Eventually the Supreme Court lift the High Court ruling.
- Proinsias De Rossa leads a breakaway group from the Workers Party to form what would shortly become Democratic Left. The majority of the breakaway group, including De Rossa, would later join the Irish Labour Party.
- 250 years after the first performance of Handel's Messiah in Dublin, the Academy of St. Martin in the Fields performs the oratario at the Point Theatre.
- Bishop Eamon Casey of Galway resigns following the revelation that he is the father of a teenage boy.
- Linda Martin wins the Eurovision Song Contest for Ireland.
- Christy O'Connor Jnr. wins the British Masters golf tournament.
- A referendum in the Republic approves the Maastricht Treaty on European Union: 69.1% in favour; 30.9% against.
- The IRA destroys Belfast's forensic science laboratory with a huge bomb.
- The government loses a confidence motion and the Dáil is dissolved. Two former Taoisigh, Charles Haughey and Garret FitzGerald, announce their retirement from politics.
- Unemployment reaches record levels with 290,000 people out of work.
- Michael Carruth wins Ireland's first gold medal in 36 years at the Olympic Games in Barcelona. Wayne McCullough wins a silver medal.
- The general election of 1992 was precipitated by the collapse of the Fianna Fáil-Progressive Democrats coalition government. Allegations of dishonesty at the Beef Tribunal forced Desmond O'Malley and his party to part ways with Albert Reynolds's Fianna Fáil. Both Albert Reynolds and John Bruton of Fine Gael were fighting their first general election as leader of their respective parties. For Reynolds it

would be his only election as leader. The campaign went very poorly for Fianna Fáil with Reynolds's support dropping by 20%.

The big winner of the campaign was Dick Spring and the Labour Party. They distanced themselves completely from Fine Gael and fought an independent line. During the campaign Spring made very little comment about what the party would do after the election, however, he did say that if the Labour Party was part of a coalition he would have to be granted a turn as Taoiseach.

Fianna Fáil had its worst performance since 1927, winning less than 40% of the vote. Fine Gael, in spite of predictions of success, actually lost 10 seats. The Labour Party recorded its best ever result and effectively held the balance of power. As mathematically a "Rainbow Coalition" was out of the question, Spring had to enter into coalition with Fianna Fáil, or force another election. The coalition deal proved very unpopular with many of Labour's supporters, because Dick Spring had campaigned heavily against Fianna Fáil and particularly Albert Reynolds. As a result of the coalition, Albert Reynolds was elected Taoiseach with over 100 votes, the biggest majority by any Taoiseach in modern Irish history with Dick Spring as Tánaiste. The election also saw Moosajee Bhamjee (Labour Party) become the first Muslim TD.

Seat distribution: Fianna Fáil 68, Fine Gael 45, Labour 33, PD's 10, Democratic Left 4, Independents 6.

• Kerry returned the following as members of the 27th Dáil:

Kerry South: John O'Donoghue (FF); Breda Moynihan-Cronin; (Lab.); John O'Leary (FF).

Kerry North: Jimmy Deenihan (FG); Denis Foley (FF); Dick Spring (Lab.).

1993

Summary: Played one championship game.

Game 1 - versus Cork in Killarney on June 20. Final Score: Cork 1-10; Kerry 0-10.

Peter O'Leary

Connie Murphy   Kieran Culhane   Morgan Nix

Seamus Moynihan   Sean Burke   Liam O'Flaherty

Dermot Hanafin (0-1)   Bernard McElligott

Maurice Fitzgerald (0-7)   Eamonn Breen (0-1)   Timmy Fleming

Billy O'Shea   Eoin Liston   Karl O'Dwyer (0-1)

Substitutes: Noel O'Mahony for McElligott, Conor Kearney for Liston, Pa Dennehy for Murphy.

1993 - GAA Winners:

All-Irelands: Senior Football: Derry **Minor Football:** Cork   **Under-21 Football:** Meath

National Leagues: Football: Dublin   Hurling: Cork

Senior Hurling: Kilkenny

Kerry Co. Champions: Football: Laune Rangers   Hurling: Ballyduff

1993 Football All-Stars:

John O'Leary (Dublin), John Joe Doherty (Donegal), Dermot Deasy (Dublin), Tony Scullion (Derry), Johnny McGurk (Derry), Henry Downey (Derry), Gary Coleman (Derry), Anthony Tohill (Derry), Brian McGilligan (Derry), Kevin O'Neill (Mayo), Joe Kavanagh (Cork), Charlie Redmond (Dublin), Colin Corkery (Cork), Ger Houlihan (Armagh), Enda Gormley (Derry).

1993 - In The News:

- The Single European Market comes into effect.
- The GAA gets planning permission for the redevelopment of Croke Park.

- Niamh Kavanagh wins the Eurovision Song Contest for Ireland.
- Mother Teresa meets President Robinson at Áras an Uachtaráin.
- Dáil Éireann passes a bill to decriminalise homosexuality.
- The Beef Tribunal ends after 226 days.

1994

Summary: Played two championship games.

Game 1 - versus Limerick in Killarney on May 22. Final Score: Kerry 2-19; Limerick 0-8.

Brendan Lane

Mike Hassett	Anthony Gleeson	Sean Burke

Seamus Moynihan (0-2)	Connie Murphy	Eamonn Breen (0-1)

Noel O'Mahony (0-2)   Darragh Ó'Sé (0-1)

Bingo O'Driscoll (0-2)	Timmy Fleming (0-1)	Billy O'Shea (0-1)

Pa Laide(1-2)	Maurice Fitzgerald (0-5)	Sean Geaney (1-2)

No substitutes used.

Game 2 - versus Cork in Cork on June 26. Final Score: Cork 1-13; Kerry 2-8.

Peter O'Leary

Sean Burke	Anthony Gleeson	Mike Hassett

Seamus Moynihan	Connie Murphy	Eamonn Breen

Conor Kearney   Liam O'Flaherty (0-1)

Bingo O'Driscoll (0-2)	Timmy Fleming (0-2)	Billy O'Shea

Pa Laide	Maurice Fitzgerald (1-3)	Sean Geaney (1-0)

Substitute: Sean McElligott for Kearney.

Scorers for the Year: Maurice Fitzgerald (1-8), Sean Geaney (2-2), Pa Laide (1-2), Bingo O'Driscoll (0-4), Timmy Fleming (0-3), Seamus Moynihan (0-2), Noel O'Mahony (0-2), Eamonn Breen (0-1), Darragh Ó'Sé (0-1), Liam O'Flaherty (0-1), Billy O'Shea (0-1).

Total Scored: 4-27

Appearances:

2 - Mike Hassett, Anthony Gleeson, Sean Burke, Seamus Moynihan, Connie Murphy, Eamonn Breen, Bingo O'Driscoll, Timmy Fleming, Billy O'Shea, Pa Laide, Maurice Fitzgerald, Sean Geaney.

1 - Brendan Lane, Peter O'Leary, Noel O'Mahony, Darragh Ó'Sé, Conor Kearney, Liam O'Flaherty, Sean McElligott.

1994 - GAA Winners:

All-Irelands: Senior Football: Down **Minor Football:** Kerry **Under-21 Football:** Cork

Kerry's Winning Minor Team: B. Murphy, K. O'Driscoll, B. O'Shea, S. O'Mahony, T. Fleming, T. McCarthy, F. O'Connor, D. O'Dwyer, G. O'Keeffe, J. Ferriter, L. Brosnan, G. Lynch, J. O'Shea, P. Sullivan, G. Murphy. Sub: M.F. Russell.

National Leagues: Football: Meath   Hurling: Tipperary

Senior Hurling: Offaly

Kerry Juniors also take All-Ireland honours with this team: D. O'Keeffe, P. Lenihan, L. Burns, J. O'Brien, J. Stack, K. Scanlon, S. Stack, D. Daly, D. Ó'Cinneide, J. Crowley, M. Keating, D. Moynihan, S. Murphy, S. Fitzgerald, P. O'Donoghue. Sub: J. Daly, J. Walsh, C. O'Donnell.

Kerry Co. Champions: Football: Austin Stacks   Hurling: Ballyduff

1994 Football All-Stars:

John O'Leary (Dublin), Michael Magill (Down), Séamus Quinn (Leitrim), Paul Higgins (Down), Graham Geraghty (Meath), Steven O'Brien (Cork), D.J. Kane (Down), Jack Sheedy (Dublin), Greg McCartan (Down), Peter Canavan (Tyrone), Greg Blaney (Down), James McCartan (Down), Micky Linden (Down), Tommy Dowd (Meath), Charlie Redmond (Dublin).

1994 - In The News:

- The Central Bank issues a new £5 note.
- Ireland wins the 39th Eurovision Song Contest with the song "Rock 'n' Roll Kids".
- Jack Charlton is awarded the freedom of Dublin City.

- Irish D-Day veterans join Allied leaders at a 50th commemoration on Omaha Beach.
- The Minister for Education, Niamh Bhreathnach, pledges the introduction of free third-level education for everyone over the next three years.
- The IRA announces a complete cessation of military operations.
- Transition Year is introduced to secondary schools countrywide.
- Taoiseach Albert Reynolds, John Hume and Gerry Adams hold their historic meeting at Government Buildings. All three pledge their commitment to the democratic idea.
- Taoiseach Albert Reynolds and members of the government wait at Shannon Airport to greet Russian President Boris Yeltsin. He fails to leave the aircraft to meet them.
- Loyalist paramilitary groups announce a ceasefire six weeks after the IRA.
- The inaugural session of the Forum for Peace and Reconciliation takes place in St. Patrick's Hall, Dublin Castle.
- In the World Cup Soccer Finals in the United States, the Republic of Ireland gets to the last 16 before losing 2-0 to the Netherlands, but on the way picks up its first World Cup finals win, a 1-0 victory vs. Italy.
- The Fianna Fáil-Labour coalition collapses. However, the Dáil is not dissolved.
- Bertie Ahern is elected leader of Fianna Fáil.
- The 24th Government was formed by Fine Gael, the Labour Party and Democratic Left. This was the first time in Irish political history that a party (Labour) had left a governing coalition and gone into government with opposition parties without a general election.
- Fine Gael's John Bruton became Taoiseach with Dick Spring as Tánaiste.

1995

Summary: Played three championship games, lost Munster Final.

Game 1 - versus Limerick in Limerick on May 28. Final Score: Kerry 3-17; Limerick 0-8.

Peter O'Leary

Mike Hassett   Anthony Gleeson   Barry O'Shea

Seamus Moynihan   Bernard McElligott   Eamonn Breen

Liam O'Flaherty   Conor Kearney

Bingo O'Driscoll (0-1)   Darren Aherne (1-1)   John Crowley (0-1)

Billy O'Shea (0-1)   Maurice Fitzgerald (2-10)   Dara Ó'Cinneide (0-2)

Substitutes: Darragh Ó'Sé (0-1) for O'Flaherty, Morgan Nix for Breen.

Game 2 - versus Tipperary in Tralee on June 25. Final Score: Kerry 7-12; Tipperary 1-13.

Peter O'Brien

Barry O'Shea   Anthony Gleeson   Mike Hassett

Seamus Moynihan   Sean Burke   Eamonn Breen (0-2)

Liam O'Flaherty   Darragh Ó'Sé

Bingo O'Driscoll (1-0)   Liam Hassett (1-2)   John Crowley (2-1)

Billy O'Shea   Maurice Fitzgerald (2-6)   Dara Ó'Cinneide (1-0)

Substitutes: Gene Farrell (0-1) for Darragh Ó'Sé, Morgan Nix for Gleeson.

Game 3 - Munster Final versus Cork in Killarney on July 23. Final Score: Cork 0-15; Kerry 1-9.

Peter O'Brien

Mike Hassett (0-1)   Sean Burke   Morgan Nix

Dara Ó'Cinneide   Seamus Moynihan   Eamonn Breen (1-0)

Conor Kearney   Liam O'Flaherty

Bingo O'Driscoll (0-1)   Liam Hassett   John Crowley

Billy O'Shea   Maurice Fitzgerald (0-4)   Gene Farrell (0-2)

Substitutes: Darragh Ó'Sé for Kearney, Anthony Gleeson for Mike Hassett, Pa Dennehy (0-1) for Farrell.

Scorers for the Year: Maurice Fitzgerald (4-20), John Crowley (2-2), Eamonn Breen (1-2), Dara Ó'Cinneide (1-2), Bingo O'Driscoll (1-2), Liam Hassett (1-2), Darren Aherne (1-1), Gene Farrell (0-3), Mike Hassett (0-1), Darragh Ó'Sé (0-1), Billy O'Shea (0-1), Pa Dennehy (0-1).

Total Scored: 11-38

Appearances:

3 - Mike Hassett, Anthony Gleeson, Morgan Nix, Seamus Moynihan, Eamonn Breen, Dara Ó'Cinneide, Liam O'Flaherty, Darragh Ó'Sé, Bingo O'Driscoll, John Crowley, Billy O'Shea, Maurice Fitzgerald.

2 - Peter O'Brien, Barry O'Shea, Sean Burke, Conor Kearney, Liam Hassett, Gene Farrell.

1 - Peter O'Leary, Bernard McElligott, Darren Aherne, Pa Dennehy.

1995 - GAA Winners:

All-Irelands: Senior Football: Dublin **Minor Football:** Westmeath **Under-21 Football:** Kerry

Kerry's Winning Under-21 Team: D. Murphy, N. Mangan, B. McCarthy, B. O'Shea, K. Burns, M. Hassett, C. McCarthy, D. Ó'Sé, D. Daly, D. O'Dwyer, J. Crowley, M. Moynihan, J. Ferriter, L. Hassett, D. O'Cinneide. Subs: K. O'Driscoll, C. Drummond, D. Dennehy.

National Leagues: Football: Derry   Hurling: Kilkenny

Senior Hurling: Clare

Kerry Co. Champions: Football: Laune Rangers   Hurling: Ballyduff

1995 Football All-Stars:

John O'Leary (Dublin), Tony Scullion (Derry), Mark O'Connor (Cork), Fay Devlin (Tyrone), Paul Curran (Dublin), Keith Barr (Dublin), Steven O'Brien

(Cork), Brian Stynes (Dublin), Anthony Tohill (Derry), Ja Fallon (Galway), Dessie Farrell (Dublin), Paul Clarke (Dublin), Tommy Dowd (Meath), Peter Canavan (Tyrone), Charlie Redmond (Dublin).

1995 - In The News:

- Taoiseach John Bruton and Gerry Adams hold their first formal discussions.
- President Mary Robinson addresses a joint session of the Houses of the Oireachtas.
- English soccer hooligans riot at Lansdowne Road during a friendly match between the Republic of Ireland and England. The match is abandoned when Ireland were 1-0 up. There was over 70 injuries, most of them were English. The English fans were escorted out of Dublin by members of the Irish Army.
- Taoiseach John Bruton and British Prime Minister John Major launch the framework document regarding Northern Ireland.
- Sir Patrick Mayhew, Northern Ireland Secretary, sets out the conditions for Sinn Féin to join all-party talks, including the actual decommissioning of some arms.
- Dublin boxer Stephen Collins beats world champion Chris Eubank to win the WBO super middleweight championship title.
- Queen Elizabeth II and the Duke of Edinburgh make a visit to Northern Ireland. On the same day U.S. President Bill Clinton approves a visa for Gerry Adams to enter the United States.
- The last edition of the *Irish Press* is published on May 25.
- The Prince of Wales has his first official visit to Dublin.
- Gerry Adams tells a rally in Belfast in August that the IRA haven't gone away.
- David Trimble becomes leader of the Ulster Unionist Party.
- The Cabinet agrees on wording of the Constitutional Amendment on divorce.
- Fianna Fáil TD Brian Lenihan dies aged 64.
- Neil Blaney, the longest serving member in the Dáil, is buried on the Fanad Peninsula in Co. Donegal.
- South Africa's deputy-President FW de Klerk addresses the Forum for Peace and Reconciliation at Dublin Castle.
- In a referendum, the people of the Republic vote narrowly to allow divorce.
- 80,000 cheer President Bill Clinton at College Green in Dublin. Afterwards he attends a state dinner at Dublin Castle.

- Plans for a £200 million light rail transit system in Dublin are announced. Eventually to be called Luas, it is to connect the city centre with Howth, Blackrock and Bray when complete.
- December 21 - Jack Charlton retires as manager of the Republic of Ireland national soccer team.

1996

Summary: Played four championship games, won 64th Munster title, lost All-Ireland semi-final.

Game 1 - versus Tipperary in Clonmel on May 19. Final Score: Kerry 2-15; Tipperary 1-7.

Declan O'Keeffe

John O'Driscoll	Anthony Gleeson	Mike Hassett
Charlie McCarthy (0-1)	Sean Burke	Eamonn Breen

Darragh Ó'Sé   John O'Connell

Bingo O'Driscoll (0-2)	Liam Hassett	Billy O'Shea (0-2)
Gene Farrell (0-2)	Maurice Fitzgerald	Dara Ó'Cinneide (1-6)

Substitutes: Killian Burns for Gleeson, John Crowley (1-2) for O'Connell

Game 2 - versus Waterford in Dungarvan on June 22. Final Score: Kerry 3-16; Waterford 0-8.

Declan O'Keeffe

Stephen Stack	Mike Hassett	Killian Burns
Charlie McCarthy	John O'Connell	Eamonn Breen (0-1)

Darragh Ó'Sé   Donal Daly (0-3)

Bingo O'Driscoll (1-0)	Maurice Fitzgerald (2-2)	Billy O'Shea (0-1)
Gene Farrell	Liam Hassett (0-3)	Dara Ó'Cinneide (0-6)

Subs: Liam O'Flaherty for O'Connell, Seamus Moynihan for McCarthy, Denis O'Dwyer for Billy O'Shea.

Game 3 - Munster Final versus Cork in Cork on July 21. Final Score: Kerry 0-14; Cork 0-11.

Declan O'Keeffe

Killian Burns (0-1)	Mike Hassett	Stephen Stack
Charlie McCarthy	Sean Burke	Eamonn Breen (0-1)

Darragh Ó'Sé   Seamus Moynihan

Bingo O'Driscoll (0-2)   Maurice Fitzgerald (0-5)   Billy O'Shea (0-2)

Gene Farrell   Liam Hassett (0-1)   Dara Ó'Cinneide (0-2)

Substitutes: John Crowley for Burke, Donal Daly for Farrell, Sean Geaney for O'Driscoll.

Game 4 - All-Ireland semi-final versus Mayo in Croke Park on August 1. Final Score: Mayo 2-13; Kerry 1-10.

Declan O'Keeffe

Stephen Stack   Mike Hassett   Charlie McCarthy

Killian Burns   Sean Burke (1-0)   Eamonn Breen (0-1)

Darragh Ó'Sé   Seamus Moynihan

John Crowley   Maurice Fitzgerald (0-8)   Billy O'Shea

Gene Farrell   Liam Hassett   Dara Ó'Cinneide (0-1)

Substitutes: John O'Driscoll for McCarthy, Brian Clarke for Hassett, Denis O'Dwyer for Crowley.

Scorers for the Year: Maurice Fitzgerald (2-15), Dara Ó'Cinneide (1-15), Bingo O'Driscoll (1-4), John Crowley (1-2), Billy O'Shea (0-5), Liam Hassett (0-4), Eamonn Breen (0-3), Sean Burke (1-0), Donal Daly (0-3), Gene Farrell (0-2), Killian Burns (0-1), Charlie McCarthy (0-1).

Total Scored: 6-55

Appearances:

4 - Declan O'Keeffe, Killian Burns, Charlie McCarthy, Eamonn Breen, Darragh Ó'Sé, Liam Hassett, Billy O'Shea, Maurice Fitzgerald, Gene Farrell, Dara Ó'Cinneide, Mike Hassett.

3 - Stephen Stack, Sean Burke, Seamus Moynihan, Bingo O'Driscoll, John Crowley.

2 - John O'Driscoll, Donal Daly, Denis O'Dwyer, John O'Connell.

1 - Anthony Gleeson, Liam O'Flaherty, Sean Geaney, Brian Clarke.

1996 - GAA Winners:

All-Irelands: Senior Football: Meath **Minor Football:** Laois **Under-21 Football:** Kerry

Kerry's Winning Under-21 Team: D. Murphy, K. O'Driscoll, B. McCarthy, M. O'Shea, K. Burns, C. Drummond, E. Fitzmaurice, D. Ó'Sé, W. Kirby, D. O'Dwyer, L. Hassett, D. O'Cinneide, J. O'Shea, B. Clarke, M.F. Russell. Subs: J. Brennan, R. O Raghelaigh, J. Ferriter.

National Leagues: Football: Derry   Hurling: Galway

Senior Hurling: Wexford

Kerry Co. Champions: Football: Laune Rangers   Hurling: Ballyheigue

1996 Football All-Stars:

Finbar McConnell (Tyrone), Kenneth Mortimer (Mayo), Darren Fay (Meath), Martin O'Connell (Meath), Pat Holmes (Mayo), James Nallen (Mayo), Paul Curran (Dublin), John McDermott (Meath), Liam McHale (Mayo), Trevor Giles (Meath), Tommy Dowd (Meath), James Horan (Mayo), Joe Brolly (Derry), Peter Canavan (Tyrone), **Maurice Fitzgerald (Kerry).**

1996 - In The News:

- Six principles of democracy and non-violence are proposed, via the Mitchell principles, as conditions for entry to all-party talks in Northern Ireland.
- The FAI appoint Mick McCarthy as the Republic of Ireland national football team manager.
- The IRA ends its ceasefire by exploding a huge bomb at Canary Wharf in London.
- Ireland wins the Eurovision Song Contest for the seventh time with the song *The Voice.*
- President Mary Robinson meets Queen Elizabeth II at Buckingham Palace, London.
- Detective Garda Jerry McCabe is shot dead by the IRA in Adare, Co. Limerick.
- Crime reporter Veronica Guerin is shot in her car in Dublin.
- Ireland's first Irish language television station, Teilifís na Gaeilge (TnaG) launched.
- Michael Collins film opens in Cork and Dublin.

- Michael O'Hehir, legendary broadcaster and sports commentator, dies aged 76.
- It is revealed that Dunnes Stores paid £208,000 for an extension to Minister Michael Lowry's house.
- EU leaders achieve a breakthrough in a dispute over preparations for a single European currency in Dublin.
- Swimmer Michelle Smith wins three gold medals and one bronze medal at the Atlanta Olympic Games.

1997

Summary: Played four championship games, won 65th Munster title, won 31st All-Ireland title.

Game 1 - versus Tipperary in Tralee on June 29. Final Score: Kerry 2-12; Tipperary 1-10.

Declan O'Keeffe

Seamus Moynihan	Barry O'Shea	Morgan O'Shea
Killian Burns (0-1)	Liam O'Flaherty	Eamonn Breen

Darragh Ó'Sé (0-1)   Willie Kirby

Pa Laide	Liam Hassett (0-2)	Denis O'Dwyer (1-0)
John Brennan	Dara Ó'Cinneide	Maurice Fitzgerald (0-7)

Subs: John Crowley (1-1) for Ó'Cinneide, Donal Daly for Kirby, Mike Frank Russell for Brennan.

Game 2-Munster Final versus Clare in Limerick, July 20. Final Score: Kerry 1-13; Clare 0-11.

Declan O'Keeffe

Mike Hassett	Barry O'Shea	Killian Burns
Seamus Moynihan	Liam O'Flaherty	Eamonn Breen

Darragh Ó'Sé   Willie Kirby

Pa Laide(1-2)	Liam Hassett	Denis O'Dwyer (0-1)
Dara Ó'Cinneide (0-2)	Brian Clarke (0-1)	Maurice Fitzgerald (0-5)

Subs: Mike Frank Russell (0-1) for Clarke, Billy O'Shea for Kirby, John Crowley (0-1) for O'Dwyer.

Game 3 - All-Ireland semi-final versus Cavan in Croke Park on August 24. Final Score: Kerry 1-17; Cavan 1-10.

Declan O'Keeffe

Stephen Stack	Barry O'Shea	Sean Burke

Seamus Moynihan   Liam O'Flaherty   Eamonn Breen (0-1)

Darragh Ó'Sé (0-1)   Willie Kirby

Pa Laide(0-1)   Liam Hassett (0-1)   Denis O'Dwyer (0-1)

Dara Ó'Cinneide (0-1)   Brian Clarke (0-1)   Maurice Fitzgerald (0-7)

Subs: Morgan O'Shea for Burke, Billy O'Shea (0-2) for O'Dwyer, Mike Frank Russell (1-1) for Clarke.

Game 4 - All-Ireland Final versus Mayo in Croke Park on September 25. Final Score: Kerry 0-13; Mayo 1-7.

Declan O'Keeffe

Killian Burns   Barry O'Shea   Stephen Stack

Seamus Moynihan   Liam O'Flaherty   Eamonn Breen

Darragh Ó'Sé (0-1)   Willie Kirby

Pa Laide(0-2)   Liam Hassett   Denis O'Dwyer

Billy O'Shea   Dara Ó'Cinneide   Maurice Fitzgerald (0-9)

Substitutes: Donal Daly for Kirby, John Crowley (0-1) for Billy O'Shea, Mike Frank Russell for Ó'Cinneide.

Scorers for the Year: Maurice Fitzgerald (0-28), Pa Laide (1-5), John Crowley (1-3), Denis O'Dwyer (1-2), Mike Frank Russell (1-2), Darragh Ó'Sé (0-3), Liam Hassett (0-3), Dara Ó'Cinneide (0-3), Brian Clarke (0-2), Billy O'Shea (0-2), Eamonn Breen (0-1), Killian Burns (0-1).

Total Scored: 4-55

Appearances:

4 - Declan O'Keeffe, Barry O'Shea, Seamus Moynihan, Liam O'Flaherty, Eamonn Breen, Darragh Ó'Sé, Willie Kirby, Pa Laide, Liam Hassett, Denis O'Dwyer, Dara Ó'Cinneide, Maurice Fitzgerald, Mike Frank Russell.

3 - Killian Burns, Billy O'Shea, John Crowley.

2 - Stephen Stack, Morgan O'Shea, Brian Clarke, Donal Daly.

1 - Sean Burke, Mike Hassett, John Brennan.

Niall Flynn

1997 - GAA Winners:

All-Irelands: Senior Football: Kerry **Minor Football:** Laois **Under-21 Football:** Derry

National Leagues: Football: Kerry   Hurling: Limerick

Senior Hurling: Clare

Kerry Co. Champions: Football: East Kerry   Hurling: Ballyheigue

1997 Football All-Stars:

Declan O'Keeffe (Kerry), Kenneth Mortimer (Mayo), Davy Dalton (Kildare), Cathal Daly (Offaly), **Séamus Moynihan (Kerry),** Glenn Ryan (Kildare), **Eamonn Breen (Kerry),** Pat Fallon (Mayo), Niall Buckley (Kildare), **Pa Laide (Kerry),** Trevor Giles (Meath), Dermot McCabe (Cavan), Joe Brolly (Derry), Brendan Reilly (Meath), **Maurice Fitzgerald (Kerry).**

1997 - In The News:

- Russia seeks to widen its ban on the importation of Irish beef due to BSE.
- The law providing for divorce comes into effect in February.
- President Mary Robinson meets Pope John Paul II in the Vatican.
- The new national independent radio station, Radio Ireland, goes on the air.
- Author Frank McCourt is awarded the Pulitzer Prize for his book, *Angela's Ashes.*
- President Mary Robinson is appointed UN High Commissioner for Human Rights.
- National University of Ireland, Maynooth comes into existence under the Universities Act.
- Taoiseach Bertie Ahern meets Prime Minister Tony Blair for the first time.
- Counsel for Charles Haughey admits he accepted £1.3 million from businessman Ben Dunne.
- The IRA institutes a second ceasefire.
- Mary Robinson resigns as President of Ireland to take up a United Nations post.
- The 1997 general election saw the public offered a choice of two possible coalitions. The existing government coalition of Fine Gael, the Labour Party and Democratic Left - the so-called "Rainbow Coalition". It was opposed by a coalition of Fianna Fáil and the

Progressive Democrats, which most Irish commentators regarded as a centre right coalition.

Following the election none of the major parties had a clear majority. A Fianna Fáil-Progressive Democrats coalition was the result of various negotiations. Four Independent TDs also supported the government, ensuring an overall majority. Bertie Ahern became the tenth Taoiseach while Mary Harney of the Progressive Democrats became Tánaiste.

Seat distribution: Fianna Fáil 77, Fine Gael 54, Labour 17, PD's 4, Democratic Left 4, Green Party 2, Independents 9.

- Kerry return the following to the 28th Dáil:

  Kerry South : John O'Donoghue (FF); Breda Moynihan-Cronin (Lab.); Jackie Healy-Rae (Independent).

  Kerry North: Jimmy Deenihan (FG); Denis Foley (FF); Dick Spring (Lab.).

- Dick Spring resigns as leader of the Labour Party and is replaced by Ruairí Quinn.

- Mary McAleese is inaugurated as the eighth President of Ireland. The Fianna Fáil candidate took over 45% of the vote to win on the second count. Fine Gael's Mary Banotti polled 29.3%, while Independent candidates Dana Rosemary Scallion (13.8%), Adi Roche (7%), and Derek Nally (4.7%) rounded out the nominees.

- The Loyalist Volunteer Force leader, Billy Wright, is shot dead in the Maze prison by members of the Irish National Liberation Army.

1998

Summary: Played three championship games, won 66th Munster title, lost All-Ireland semi-final.

Game 1 - versus Cork in Killarney on July 5. Final Score: Kerry 1-14; Cork 1-11.

Declan O'Keeffe

Tomás Ó'Sé	Barry O'Shea	Stephen Stack
Seamus Moynihan	Liam O'Flaherty	Eamonn Breen

Darragh Ó'Sé   Donal Daly

Pa Laide	Dara Ó'Cinneide (0-1)	Denis O'Dwyer
Mike Frank Russell (0-4)	John Crowley (0-5)	Maurice Fitzgerald (1-4)

Substitutes: Eamonn Fitzmaurice for Tomás Ó'Sé, Liam Brosnan for Laide, Noel Kennelly for Ó'Cinneide.

Game 2 - Munster Final versus Tipperary in Thurles on August 2. Final Score: Kerry 0-17; Tipperary 1-10.

Declan O'Keeffe

Seamus Moynihan	Barry O'Shea	Stephen Stack
Eamonn Fitzmaurice	Liam O'Flaherty	Eamonn Breen

Darragh Ó'Sé   Donal Daly (0-1)

Pa Laide(0-2)	Dara Ó'Cinneide (0-2)	Denis O'Dwyer
Mike Frank Russell (0-1)	John Crowley (0-1)	Maurice Fitzgerald (0-10)

Substitute: Noel Kennelly for O'Dwyer

Game 3 - All-Ireland semi-final versus Kildare in Croke Park on August 30. Final Score: Kildare 0-13; Kerry 1-9.

Declan O'Keeffe

Eamonn Fitzmaurice	Barry O'Shea	Stephen Stack
Seamus Moynihan	Liam O'Flaherty	Eamonn Breen

Darragh Ó'Sé   Donal Daly (0-1)

Pa Laide   Dara Ó'Cinneide (0-2)   Willie Kirby

Mike Frank Russell (0-1)   John Crowley (1-1)   Maurice Fitzgerald (0-4)

Substitutes: Liam Brosnan for Kirby, Denis O'Dwyer for Laide.

Scorers for the Year: Maurice Fitzgerald (1-18), John Crowley (1-7), Mike Frank Russell (0-6), Dara Ó'Cinneide (0-5), Donal Daly (0-2), Pa Laide (0-2).

Total Scored: 2-40

Appearances:

3 - Declan O'Keeffe, Barry O'Shea, Stephen Stack, Eamonn Fitzmaurice, Seamus Moynihan, Liam O'Flaherty, Eamonn Breen, Darragh Ó'Sé, Donal Daly, Pa Laide, Dara Ó'Cinneide, Denis O'Dwyer, Mike Frank Russell, John Crowley, Maurice Fitzgerald.

2 - Liam Brosnan, Noel Kennelly.

1 - Tomás Ó'Sé, Willie Kirby.

1998 - GAA Winners:

All-Irelands: Senior Football: Galway **Minor Football:** Tyrone **Under-21 Football:** Kerry

Kerry's Winning Under-21 Team: D. Moloney, M. McCarthy, T. O'Sullivan, K. Leen, J. Sheehan, T. Ó'Sé, M. Beckett, T. Griffin, E. Fitzmaurice, A. MacGearailt, P. O'Sullivan, L. Brosnan, M.F. Russell, N. Kennelly, B. Scanlon. Subs: I. Twiss, M. Burke.

National Leagues: Football: Offaly   Hurling: Cork

Senior Hurling: Offaly

Kerry Co. Champions: Football: East Kerry   Hurling: Causeway

1998 Football All-Stars:

Martin McNamara (Galway), Brian Lacey (Kildare), Seán Marty Lockhart (Derry), Tomas Mannion (Galway), John Finn (Kildare), Glenn Ryan (Kildare), Sean Óg de Paor (Galway), John McDermott (Meath), Kevin

Walsh (Galway), Michael Donnellan (Galway), Ja Fallon (Galway), Dermot Earley (Kildare), Karl O'Dwyer (Kildare), Pádraic Joyce (Galway), Declan Browne (Tipperary).

1998 - In The News:

- The VECs of the towns of Bray, Drogheda, Sligo, Tralee and Wexford are abolished.
- The Planning Tribunal opens in Dublin Castle in January.
- Republic of Ireland qualifies for entry into the Economic and Monetary Union of the European Union.
- Former Fine Gael Minister Hugh Coveney dies in a fall from a cliff in Co. Cork.
- On Good Friday the British and Irish governments and all the political parties in Northern Ireland (except the Democratic Unionist Party) sign the Belfast Agreement.
- 22 May - The Good Friday Agreement is endorsed in a referendum by people north and south of the border.
- 29 people die in a bomb explosion near the centre of Omagh, Co. Tyrone, caused by the Real IRA.
- TV3 goes on the air.
- Tony Blair becomes the first Prime Minister of the United Kingdom to address the Oireachtas.
- Unemployment falls by 20% with the number of people in work rising by 100,000.
- Members of the Labour Party and Democratic Left agree to merge.
- The Punt is traded for the last time as the Euro currency is launched.
- Actor and comedian Dermot Morgan dies suddenly in London.
- Gay Byrne broadcasts his final radio show from St. Stephen's Green.

1999

Summary: Played three championship games, lost Munster Final.

Game 1 - versus Tipperary in Tralee on May 23. Final Score: Kerry 1-11; Tipperary 0-8.

Declan O'Keeffe

Mike McCarthy   Barry O'Shea   Killian Burns

Tomás Ó'Sé   Seamus Moynihan   Eamonn Breen

Darragh Ó'Sé (0-1)   Donal Daly

John McGlynn (0-1)   Noel Kennelly (0-1)   Dara Ó'Cinneide

Gerard Murphy (1-0)   Aodhán MacGearailt (0-3)   Maurice Fitzgerald (0-4)

Substitutes: Billy O'Shea (0-1) for McGlynn, Brian Clarke for Murphy.

Game 2 - versus Clare in Killarney on June 20. Final Score: Kerry 3-17; Clare 0-12.

Declan O'Keeffe

Mike McCarthy   Barry O'Shea   Killian Burns

Tomás Ó'Sé   Seamus Moynihan   Eamonn Breen (0-1)

Darragh Ó'Sé (0-1)   Donal Daly

John McGlynn (0-3)   Noel Kennelly (0-1)   Dara Ó'Cinneide (1-1)

John Crowley (2-0)   Aodhán MacGearailt (0-4)   Maurice Fitzgerald (0-6)

Substitutes: Billy O'Shea for Fitzgerald, Willie Kirby for D. Ó'Sé, Mike Hassett for Tomás Ó'Sé.

Game 3 - Munster Final versus Cork in Cork on July 17. Final Score: Cork 2-10; Kerry 2-4.

Declan O'Keeffe

Mike McCarthy   Barry O'Shea   Killian Burns

Tomás Ó'Sé   Seamus Moynihan   Eamonn Breen

Darragh Ó'Sé   Donal Daly

John McGlynn (0-1)   Liam Hassett   Dara Ó'Cinneide

John Crowley (0-2)   Aodhán MacGearailt (2-0)   Maurice Fitzgerald

Substitutes: Billy O'Shea for Hassett, Willie Kirby (0-1) for McGlynn, Mike Frank Russell for MacGearailt.

Scorers for the Year: Aodhán MacGearailt (2-7), Maurice Fitzgerald (0-10), John Crowley (2-2), John McGlynn (0-5), Dara Ó'Cinneide (1-1), Gerard Murphy (1-0), Darragh Ó'Sé (0-2), Noel Kennelly (0-2), Eamonn Breen (0-1), Billy O'Shea (0-1), Willie Kirby (0-1).

Total Scored: 6-32

Appearances:

3 - Declan O'Keeffe, Mike McCarthy, Barry O'Shea, Killian Burns, Tomás Ó'Sé, Seamus Moynihan, Eamonn Breen, Darragh Ó'Sé, Donal Daly, John McGlynn, Dara Ó'Cinneide, Aodhán MacGearailt, Maurice Fitzgerald, Billy O'Shea.

2 - Liam Hassett, Noel Kennelly, John Crowley, Willie Kirby.

1 - Gerard Murphy, Brian Clarke, Mike Frank Russell.

1999 - GAA Winners:

All-Irelands: Senior Football: Meath **Minor Football:** Down   **Under-21 Football:** Westmeath

National Leagues: Football: Cork   Hurling: Tipperary

Senior Hurling: Cork

Kerry Co. Champions: Football: East Kerry   Hurling: Lixnaw

1999 Football All-Stars:

Kevin O'Dwyer (Cork), Mark O'Reilly (Meath), Darren Fay (Meath), Anthony Lynch (Cork), Ciaran O'Sullivan (Cork), Kieran McGeeney (Armagh), Paddy Reynolds (Meath), John McDermott (Meath), Ciarán Whelan (Dublin), Diarmuid Marsden (Armagh), Trevor Giles (Meath), James Horan (Mayo), Philip Clifford (Cork), Graham Geraghty (Meath), Ollie Murphy (Meath).

1999 - In The News:

- The Euro makes its debut on European financial markets.
- Derek Hill becomes the eleventh honorary citizen of Ireland.
- New legislation changes the name of the RSI Number to the Personal Public Service Number and expands its use.
- The Irish Land Commission is dissolved.
- Gay Byrne hosts his last Late Late Show after 37 years.
- The electorate of the entire island of Ireland go to the polls to vote on the Good Friday Agreement. People north and south give their overwhelming support to the Agreement.
- President McAleese leads tributes to the former Taoiseach Jack Lynch who died, aged 82.
- Ten designated ministers are appointed to the power-sharing Northern Ireland Assembly.
- The Irish government ratifies changes to Articles 2 and 3 of the Constitution. Direct rule from Westminster in Northern Ireland ends.

2000-2009...Atop the charts again

Summary of the Decade

Kerry played 66 games, scoring 85-927, conceding 53-686.

Munster Championship titles: 6 (2000, 2001, 2003, 2004, 2005, 2007)

All Ireland titles: 5 (2000, 2004, 2006, 2007, 2009)

National League titles: 4 (2004, 2005, 2006, 2009)

U-21 titles: 1 (2008) **Minor titles:** None **Junior titles: 1** (2006)

Top Scorers: Colm Cooper (15-165), Dara Ó'Cinneide (8-123)

Top Points-only scorers: Colm Cooper (165), Dara Ó'Cinneide (123)

Top Goals-only scorers: Eoin Brosnan (15), Colm Cooper (15)

Most Appearances: 65 each by Tomás Ó'Sé (missed the 2001 All-Ireland semi-final loss to Meath), and Tom O'Sullivan (missed the 2002 qualifier win over Wicklow).

2000
Kerry 2-15 Cork 1-13;
Munster Final: Kerry 3-15 Clare 0-8;
All-Ireland semi-final: Kerry 2-11 Armagh 2-11;
Replay: Kerry 2-15 Armagh 1-15 (After Extra Time);
All-Ireland Final: Kerry 0-14 Galway 0-14;
Replay: Kerry 0-17 Galway 1-10.

2001
Kerry 3-17 Tipperary 1-4;
Kerry 1-15 Limerick 0-10;
Munster Final: Kerry 0-19 Cork 1-13;
All-Ireland qrtr-final: Kerry 1-14 Dublin 2-11;
Replay: Kerry 2-12 Dublin 1-12;
All-Ireland semi-final: Meath 2-14 Kerry 0-5.

2002

Kerry 0-14 Limerick 1-7;
Kerry 0-8 Cork 0-8;
Replay: Cork 0-15 Kerry 0-9;
Qualifier: Kerry 5-15 Wicklow 0-7;
Qualifier: Kerry 2-15 Fermanagh 0-4;
Qualifier: Kerry 2-10 Kildare 1-5;
All-Ireland qrtr-final: Kerry 2-17 Galway 1-12;
All-Ireland semi-final: Kerry 3-19 Cork 2-7;
All-Ireland Final: Armagh 1-12 Kerry 0-14.

2003

Kerry 0-25 Tipperary 1-10;
Munster Final: Kerry 1-11 Limerick 0-9;
All-Ireland qrtr-final: Kerry 1-21 Roscommon 3-10;
All-Ireland semi-final: Tyrone 0-13 Kerry 0-6.

2004

Kerry 2-10 Clare 0-9;
Kerry 0-15 Cork 0-7;
Munster Final: Kerry 1-10 Limerick 1-10;
Replay: Kerry 3-10 Limerick 2-9;
All-Ireland qrtr-final: Kerry 1-15 Dublin 1-8;
All-Ireland semi-final: Kerry 1-17 Derry 1-11;
All-Ireland Final: Kerry 1-20 Mayo 2-9.

2005

Kerry 2-22 Tipperary 0-13;
Kerry 2-10 Limerick 0-10;
Munster Final: Kerry 1-11 Cork 0-11;
All-Ireland qrtr-final: Kerry 2-15 Mayo 0-18;
All-Ireland semi-final: Kerry 1-19 Cork 0-9;
All-Ireland Final: Tyrone 1-16 Kerry 2-10.

2006

Kerry 0-16 Waterford 0-8;
Kerry 0-17 Tipperary 1-5;
Munster Final: Kerry 0-10 Cork 0-10;
Replay: Cork 1-12 Kerry 0-9;
Qualifier: Kerry 4-11 Longford 1-11;
All-Ireland qrtr-final: Kerry 3-15 Armagh 1-13;

All-Ireland semi-final: Kerry 0-16 Cork 0-10;
All-Ireland Final: Kerry 4-15 Mayo 3-5.

2007

Kerry 2-15 Waterford 0-4;
Munster Final: Kerry 1-15 Cork 1-13;
All-Ireland qrtr-final: Kerry 1-12 Monaghan 1-11;
All-Ireland semi-final: Kerry 1-15 Dublin 0-16;
All-Ireland Final: Kerry 3-13 Cork 1-9.

2008

Kerry 1-14 Clare 0-5;
Munster Final: Cork 1-16 Kerry 1-11;
Qualifier: Kerry 1-13 Monaghan 0-13;
All-Ireland qrtr-final: Kerry 1-21 Galway 1-16;
All-Ireland semi-final: Kerry 1-13 Cork 3-7;
Replay: Kerry 3-14 Cork 2-13;
All-Ireland Final: Tyrone 1-15 Kerry 0-14.

2009

Kerry 0-13 Cork 1-10;
Replay: Cork 1-17 Kerry 0-12;
Qualifier: Kerry 1-12 Longford 0-11;
Qualifier: Kerry 0-14 Sligo 1-10;
Qualifier: Kerry 2-12 Antrim 0-10;
All-Ireland qrtr-final: Kerry 1-24 Dublin 1-7;
All-Ireland semi-final: Kerry 2-8 Meath 1-7;
All-Ireland Final: Kerry 0-16 Cork 1-9.

2000

Summary: Played six championship games, won 67th Munster title, won 32nd All-Ireland title.

Game 1 - versus Cork in Killarney on June 18. Final Score: Kerry 2-15; Cork 1-13.

Declan O'Keeffe

Killian Burns   Seamus Moynihan   Mike McCarthy

Tom O'Sullivan   Eamonn Fitzmaurice   Tomás Ó'Sé

Darragh Ó'Sé   Donal Daly (0-1)

Aodhán MacGearailt (0-1)   Liam Hassett (0-2)   Noel Kennelly (0-2)

Mike Frank Russell (0-3)   Dara Ó'Cinneide (2-5)   John Crowley (0-1)

Subs: Mike Hassett for Burns, Maurice Fitzgerald for Daly, Denis O'Dwyer for L. Hassett, Enda Galvin for Crowley.

Game 2- Munster Final versus Clare in Limerick on July 16. Final Score: Kerry 3-15; Clare 0-8.

Declan O'Keeffe

Killian Burns   Seamus Moynihan   Mike McCarthy

Tom O'Sullivan   Eamonn Fitzmaurice   Tomás Ó'Sé

Darragh Ó'Sé   Donal Daly

Aodhán MacGearailt (1-3)   Liam Hassett (1-1)   Noel Kennelly (0-2)

Mike Frank Russell (0-2)   Dara Ó'Cinneide (0-4)   John Crowley (1-3)

Subs: Mike Hassett for Moynihan, Maurice Fitzgerald for Ó'Cinneide, Denis O'Dwyer for L. Hassett, Enda Galvin for Kennelly, Tommy Griffin for T. Ó'Sé.

Game 3 - All-Ireland semi-final versus Armagh in Croke Park on August 20. Final Score: Kerry 2-11; Armagh 2-11 (Draw).

Declan O'Keeffe

Killian Burns   Seamus Moynihan   Mike McCarthy

Tom O'Sullivan   Eamonn Fitzmaurice   Tomás Ó'Sé

Darragh Ó'Sé (0-1)   Donal Daly (0-1)

Aodhán MacGearailt (0-1)   Liam Hassett   Noel Kennelly (0-1)

Mike Frank Russell (0-3)   Dara Ó'Cinneide (1-2)   John Crowley (0-1)

Subs: Maurice Fitzgerald (1-1) for L. Hassett, Mike Hassett for Burns, Denis O'Dwyer for MacGearailt, Enda Galvin for Kennelly.

Game 4 - All-Ireland semi-final replay versus Armagh in Croke Park on September 2. Final Score: Kerry 2-15; Armagh 1-15 (After Extra Time).

Declan O'Keeffe

Mike Hassett   Seamus Moynihan   Mike McCarthy

Tom O'Sullivan   Eamonn Fitzmaurice (0-1)   Tomás Ó'Sé

Darragh Ó'Sé (0-1)   Donal Daly (0-1)

Aodhán MacGearailt (0-1)   Denis O'Dwyer   Noel Kennelly (0-1)

Mike Frank Russell (2-3)   Dara Ó'Cinneide (0-3)   John Crowley (0-1)

Subs: Liam Hassett (0-1) for MacGearailt, Maurice Fitzgerald (0-2) for O'Dwyer, Tommy Griffin for O'Sullivan.

Game 5 - All-Ireland Final versus Galway in Croke Park on September 24. Final Score: Kerry 0-14; Galway 0-14 (Draw).

Declan O'Keeffe

Mike Hassett   Seamus Moynihan   Mike McCarthy

Tom O'Sullivan   Eamonn Fitzmaurice   Tomás Ó'Sé

Darragh Ó'Sé (0-1)   Donal Daly

Aodhán MacGearailt   Liam Hassett (0-2)   Noel Kennelly (0-2)

Mike Frank Russell (0-3)   Dara Ó'Cinneide (0-4)   John Crowley (0-2)

Substitutes: Maurice Fitzgerald for Crowley, Denis O'Dwyer for Kennelly.

Game 6 - All-Ireland Final replay versus Galway in Croke Park on October 7. Final Score: Kerry 0-17; Galway 1-10.

Declan O'Keeffe

Mike Hassett   Seamus Moynihan   Mike McCarthy

Tom O'Sullivan   Eamonn Fitzmaurice (0-1)   Tomás Ó'Sé

Darragh Ó'Sé   Donal Daly

Aodhán MacGearailt (0-2)   Liam Hassett (0-4)   Noel Kennelly (0-1)

Mike Frank Russell (0-2)   Dara Ó'Cinneide (0-4)   John Crowley (0-3)

Substitutes: Maurice Fitzgerald for Kennelly, Tommy Griffin for O'Sullivan.

Scorers for the Year: Dara Ó'Cinneide (3-22), Mike Frank Russell (2-16), John Crowley (1-11), Liam Hassett (1-10), Aodhán MacGearailt (1-8), Noel Kennelly (0-9), Maurice Fitzgerald (1-3), Darragh Ó'Sé (0-3), Donal Daly (0-3), Eamonn Fitzmaurice (0-2).

Total Scored: 9-87

Appearances:

6 - Declan O'Keeffe, Mike Hassett, Seamus Moynihan, Mike McCarthy, Tom O'Sullivan, Eamonn Fitzmaurice, Tomás Ó'Sé, Darragh Ó'Sé, Donal Daly, Aodhán MacGearailt, Liam Hassett, Noel Kennelly, Mike Frank Russell, Dara Ó'Cinneide, John Crowley, Maurice Fitzgerald.

5 - Denis O'Dwyer

4 - None

3 - Killian Burns, Enda Galvin, Tommy Griffin.

2 - None

1 - None

2000 - GAA Winners:

All-Irelands: Senior Football: Kerry **Minor Football:** Cork **Under-21 Football:** Tyrone

National Leagues: Football: Derry   Hurling: Galway

Senior Hurling: Kilkenny

Kerry Co. Champions: Football: Dr. Crokes   Hurling: Ballyheigue

2000 Football All-Stars:

Declan O'Keeffe (Kerry), Kieran McKeever (Derry), **Séamus Moynihan (Kerry), Michael McCarthy (Kerry),** Declan Meehan (Galway), Kieran McGeeney (Armagh), Anthony Rainbow (Kildare), Anthony Tohill (Derry), **Darragh Ó'Sé (Kerry),** Michael Donnellan (Galway), **Liam Hassett (Kerry),** Oisin McConville (Armagh), **Mike Frank Russell (Kerry),** Pádraic Joyce (Galway), Derek Savage (Galway).

2000 - In The News:

- John Gilligan's extradition from the UK to Ireland on drug trafficking and murder charges is completed.
- The British government suspends devolution in Northern Ireland from February 11 to May 30.
- The IRA begins decommissioning its weapons.
- President Clinton of the United States arrives in Dublin for what is his last overseas journey as President. He meets Taoiseach Bertie Ahern and the political leaders of Northern Ireland.

2001

Summary: Played six championship games, won 68th Munster title, lost All-Ireland semi-final.

Game 1 - versus Tipperary in Clonmel on May 13. Final Score: Kerry 3-17; Tipperary 1-4.

Declan O'Keeffe

Barry O'Shea	Seamus Moynihan	Mossie Lyons
Tomás Ó'Sé	Eamonn Fitzmaurice	Tom O'Sullivan

Darragh Ó'Sé   Donal Daly

Denis O'Dwyer (0-2)   Maurice Fitzgerald (0-4)   Aodhán MacGearailt (0-1)

Mike Frank Russell (0-3)   Dara Ó'Cinneide (1-2)   John Crowley (1-2)

Substitutes: Noel Kennelly (1-1) for Daly, Eoin Brosnan (0-1) for Ó'Cinneide, Willie Kirby for D. Ó'Sé, Declan Quill (0-1) for Russell, Tommy Griffin for Fitzmaurice.

Game 2 - versus Limerick in Killarney on June 17. Final Score: Kerry 1-15; Limerick 0-10.

Declan O'Keeffe

Mike McCarthy	Seamus Moynihan	Mossie Lyons
Tomás Ó'Sé	Eamonn Fitzmaurice	Tom O'Sullivan

Darragh Ó'Sé (0-1)   Donal Daly

Aodhán MacGearailt   Maurice Fitzgerald (0-3)   Noel Kennelly (0-1)

Mike Frank Russell (1-4)   Dara Ó'Cinneide (0-2)   John Crowley (0-3)

Substitutes: Denis O'Dwyer for Fitzgerald, Willie Kirby (0-1) for Daly, Eoin Brosnan for Kennelly.

Game 3 - Munster Final versus Cork in Cork on July 15. Final Score: Kerry 0-19; Cork 1-13.

Declan O'Keeffe

Mossie Lyons	Seamus Moynihan	Mike McCarthy

Tomás Ó'Sé   Eamonn Fitzmaurice   Tom O'Sullivan

      Darragh Ó'Sé   Donal Daly (0-1)

Aodhán MacGearailt (0-1)   Dara Ó'Cinneide (0-9)   Noel Kennelly (0-1)

Mike Frank Russell (0-2)   Maurice Fitzgerald   John Crowley (0-4)

Subs: Eoin Brosnan (0-1) for Fitzgerald, Denis O'Dwyer for Kennelly, Mike Hassett for Tomás Ó'Sé, Willie Kirby for Daly.

Game 4 - All-Ireland quarter-final versus Dublin in Thurles on August 4. Final Score: Kerry 1-14; Dublin 2-11 (Draw).

                        Declan O'Keeffe

Mossie Lyons   Seamus Moynihan   Mike McCarthy

Tomás Ó'Sé   Eamonn Fitzmaurice   Tom O'Sullivan

      Darragh Ó'Sé   Donal Daly

Eoin Brosnan (0-1)   Noel Kennelly   Aodhán MacGearailt (1-1)

Mike Frank Russell (0-2)   Dara Ó'Cinneide(0-6)   John Crowley (0-3)

Substitutes: Denis O'Dwyer for Kennelly, Mike Hassett for McCarthy, Maurice Fitzgerald (0-1) for Brosnan, Willie Kirby for Daly, Declan Quill for Ó'Cinneide.

Game 5 - All-Ireland quarter-final replay versus Dublin in Thurles on August 11. Final Score: Kerry 2-12; Dublin 1-12.

                        Declan O'Keeffe

Mossie Lyons   Seamus Moynihan   Mike McCarthy

Tomás Ó'Sé   Eamonn Fitzmaurice   Tom O'Sullivan

      Darragh Ó'Sé   Donal Daly

Eoin Brosnan   Noel Kennelly (0-2)   Aodhán MacGearailt

Mike Frank Russell (0-3)   Dara Ó'Cinneide(0-4)   John Crowley (2-2)

Substitutes: Maurice Fitzgerald (0-1) for Brosnan, Willie Kirby for Daly, Declan Quill for Ó'Cinneide.

Game 6 - All-Ireland semi-final versus Meath in Croke Park on September 2. Final Score: Meath 2-14; Kerry 0-5.

Declan O'Keeffe

Mossie Lyons	Seamus Moynihan	Mike McCarthy
Mike Hassett	Eamonn Fitzmaurice	Tom O'Sullivan

Darragh Ó'Sé   Donal Daly

Aodhán MacGearailt	Eoin Brosnan (0-1)	Noel Kennelly
Mike Frank Russell (0-1)	Dara Ó'Cinneide(0-1)	John Crowley (0-1)

Substitutes: Tommy Griffin for Hassett, Maurice Fitzgerald for O'Sullivan, Willie Kirby for Ó'Cinneide, John McGlynn for Daly, Declan Quill (0-1) for MacGearailt.

Scorers for the Year: Dara Ó'Cinneide (1-24), John Crowley (3-15), Mike Frank Russell (1-15), Maurice Fitzgerald (0-9), Noel Kennelly (1-5), Aodhán MacGearailt (1-3), Eoin Brosnan (0-4), Denis O'Dwyer (0-2), Declan Quill (0-2), Darragh Ó'Sé (0-1), Donal Daly (0-1), Willie Kirby (0-1).

Total Scored: 7-82

Appearances:

6 - Declan O'Keeffe, Seamus Moynihan, Mossie Lyons, Eamonn Fitzmaurice, Tom O'Sullivan, Darragh Ó'Sé, Donal Daly, Maurice Fitzgerald, Aodhán MacGearailt, Noel Kennelly, Dara Ó'Cinneide, Eoin Brosnan, Mike Frank Russell, John Crowley, Willie Kirby.

5 - Mike McCarthy, Tomás Ó'Sé.

4 - Declan Quill, Denis O'Dwyer.

3 - Mike Hassett.

2 - Tommy Griffin.

1 - Barry O'Shea, John McGlynn.

2001 - GAA Winners:

All-Irelands: Senior Football: Galway **Minor Football:** Tyrone
Under-21 Football: Tyrone

National Leagues: Football: Mayo   Hurling: Tipperary

Senior Hurling: Tipperary

Kerry Co. Champions: Football: An Gaeltacht   Hurling: Kilmoyley

2001 Football All-Stars:

Cormac Sullivan (Meath), Kieran Fitzgerald (Galway), Darren Fay (Meath), Coman Goggins (Dublin), Declan Meehan (Galway), Francie Grehan (Roscommon), Seán Óg de Paor (Galway), Kevin Walsh (Galway), Rory O'Connell (Westmeath), Evan Kelly (Meath), Stephen O'Neill (Tyrone), Michael Donnellan (Galway), Ollie Murphy (Meath), Pádraic Joyce (Galway), **John Crowley (Kerry).**

2001 - In The News:

- On March 22, Ireland confirms its first case of foot and mouth disease.
- The Irish voters reject the Nice Treaty in a referendum.
- The world is plunged into a state of shock as the 9/11 terrorist attacks take place in New York City and Washington D.C. The people of Ireland extend their sympathies to the people of the United States and hold a national day of mourning as a result. All sports, public functions, and entertainment are cancelled on orders of the government. Schools, businesses, and stores throughout the country are closed. President Mary McAleese said that the events were "an attack on the very foundations of human dignity" and left the people of Ireland "sad, shocked, sickened, grieving, disbelieving, outraged, and frightened all at once."
- The first multiple state funeral is held in honour of 10 Irish Republican Army Volunteers who were executed by the British for their part in the War of Independence.
- The GAA votes to abolish its controversial Rule 21. Members of the British army and the newly established Police Service of Northern Ireland (PSNI) will henceforth be permitted to play.
- Irish euro coins are available in An Post and bank branches in mid-December. These "Starter Packs" contain nineteen coins worth € 6.35 and can be purchased for IR£5.

2002

Summary: Played nine championship games, lost All-Ireland Final.

Game 1 - versus Limerick in Limerick on May 12. Final Score: Kerry 0-14; Limerick 1-7.

Declan O'Keeffe

Marc Ó'Sé   Seamus Moynihan   Mike McCarthy

Tomás Ó'Sé   Eamonn Fitzmaurice   Tom O'Sullivan

Eoin Brosnan   Seamus Scanlon

Aodhán MacGearailt (0-4)   Noel Kennelly (0-2)   Dara Ó'Cinneide (0-1)

Mike Frank Russell (0-4)   John Crowley (0-2)   Colm Cooper (0-1)

Substitutes: Darragh Ó'Sé for Ó'Cinneide, Sean O'Sullivan for Scanlon.

Game 2 - versus Cork in Killarney on June 16. Final Score: Kerry 0-8; Cork 0-8 (Draw).

Declan O'Keeffe

Marc Ó'Sé   Seamus Moynihan   Mike McCarthy

Tomás Ó'Sé   Eamonn Fitzmaurice   Tom O'Sullivan

Darragh Ó'Sé   Seamus Scanlon

Aodhán MacGearailt   Noel Kennelly   Eoin Brosnan

Mike Frank Russell (0-6)   John Crowley (0-1)   Colm Cooper

Substitutes: Barry O'Shea for Scanlon, Dara Ó'Cinneide (0-1) for Cooper, Liam Hassett for Kennelly, Sean O'Sullivan for Brosnan.

Game 3 - Replay versus Cork in Cork on June 23. Final Score: Cork 0-15; Kerry 1-9.

Declan O'Keeffe

Marc Ó'Sé   Tom O'Sullivan   Mike McCarthy

Tomás Ó'Sé   Eamonn Fitzmaurice   Enda Galvin

Darragh Ó'Sé (0-1)   Seamus Moynihan

Declan Quill (0-2)   Dara Ó'Cinneide (0-3)   Colm Cooper (0-1)

Mike Frank Russell (1-1)   Liam Hassett   John Crowley

Substitutes: Mossie Lyons for Galvin, Sean O'Sullivan (0-1) for Hassett, Noel Kennelly for Quill, Eoin Brosnan for Ó'Cinneide, Ian Twiss for Crowley.

Game 4 - Qualifier versus Wicklow in Portlaoise on June 30. Final Score: Kerry 5-15; Wicklow 0-7.

Declan O'Keeffe

Marc Ó'Sé   Seamus Moynihan   Mike McCarthy

Tomás Ó'Sé (1-0)   Eamonn Fitzmaurice   John Sheehan

Darragh Ó'Sé   Donal Daly

Sean O'Sullivan (0-2)   Eoin Brosnan (2-2)   Noel Kennelly

Mike Frank Russell (1-3) Dara Ó'Cinneide (0-3)   Colm Cooper (0-1)

Substitutes: John Crowley (0-1) for Russell, Liam Hassett (1-0) for Kennelly, Seamus Scanlon (0-1) for Darragh Ó'Sé, Ian Twiss (0-2) for Cooper, Barry O'Shea for Moynihan.

Game 5 - Qualifier versus Fermanagh in Portlaoise on July 6. Final Score: Kerry 2-15; Fermanagh 0-4.

Declan O'Keeffe

Marc Ó'Sé   Seamus Moynihan   Mike McCarthy

Tomás Ó'Sé   Eamonn Fitzmaurice   John Sheehan

Darragh Ó'Sé (0-1)   Donal Daly

Sean O'Sullivan (0-2)   Eoin Brosnan (0-3)   Liam Hassett (1-0)

Mike Frank Russell   Dara Ó'Cinneide (0-6)   Colm Cooper (1-0)

Substitutes: Tom O'Sullivan for Fitzmaurice, John Crowley (0-2) for Russell, Ronan O'Connor (0-1) for Cooper, Seamus Scanlon for Sean O'Sullivan, Declan Quill for Ó'Cinneide.

Game 6 - Qualifier versus Kildare in Thurles on July 27. Final Score: Kerry 2-10; Kildare 1-5.

Declan O'Keeffe

Marc Ó'Sé	Seamus Moynihan	Mike McCarthy
Tomás Ó'Sé	Eamonn Fitzmaurice	John Sheehan (0-1)

Darragh Ó'Sé   Donal Daly

Sean O'Sullivan (0-1)	Eoin Brosnan (1-1)	Liam Hassett (0-1)
Mike Frank Russell	Dara Ó'Cinneide (0-4)	Colm Cooper (1-1)

Substitutes: John Crowley (0-1) for Russell, Aodhán MacGearailt for Sean O'Sullivan, Tom O'Sullivan for Fitzmaurice, Ronan O'Connor for Ó'Cinneide, Seamus Scanlon for Daly.

Game 7 - All-Ireland quarter-final versus Galway in Croke Park on August 4. Final Score: Kerry 2-17; Galway 1-12.

Declan O'Keeffe

Marc Ó'Sé	Seamus Moynihan	Mike McCarthy
Tomás Ó'Sé (0-1)	Eamonn Fitzmaurice	John Sheehan (0-1)

Darragh Ó'Sé (0-1)   Donal Daly

Sean O'Sullivan (1-1)	Eoin Brosnan (0-1)	Liam Hassett
Mike Frank Russell (0-4)	Dara Ó'Cinneide (0-3)	Colm Cooper (0-4)

Substitutes: Aodhán MacGearailt (1-1) for Daly, Tom O'Sullivan for Fitzmaurice, John Crowley for Russell.

Game 8 - All-Ireland semi-final versus Cork in Croke Park on August 25. Final Score: Kerry 3-19; Cork 2-7.

Declan O'Keeffe

Marc Ó'Sé	Seamus Moynihan	Mike McCarthy
Tomás Ó'Sé	Eamonn Fitzmaurice	John Sheehan

Darragh Ó'Sé (0-1)   Donal Daly

Sean O'Sullivan (0-1)   Eoin Brosnan (1-0)   Liam Hassett (0-2)

Mike Frank Russell (1-6) Dara Ó'Cinneide (0-3)   Colm Cooper (1-5)

Substitutes: Aodhán MacGearailt (0-1) for Sean O'Sullivan, Tom O'Sullivan for Marc Ó'Sé, John Crowley for Ó'Cinneide, Declan Quill for Hassett, Barry O'Shea for Tomás Ó'Sé.

Game 9 - All-Ireland Final versus Armagh in Croke Park on September 22. Final Score: Armagh 1-12; Kerry 0-14.

Declan O'Keeffe

Marc Ó'Sé   Seamus Moynihan   Mike McCarthy

Tomás Ó'Sé   Eamonn Fitzmaurice (0-1)   John Sheehan

Darragh Ó'Sé   Donal Daly

Sean O'Sullivan   Eoin Brosnan (0-1)   Liam Hassett (0-2)

Mike Frank Russell (0-3) Dara Ó'Cinneide (0-5)   Colm Cooper (0-2)

Substitutes: Aodhán MacGearailt for Sean O'Sullivan, Tom O'Sullivan for Marc Ó'Sé, John Crowley for Hassett, Barry O'Shea for Daly.

Scorers for the Year: Mike Frank Russell (3-27), Dara Ó'Cinneide (0-29), Colm Cooper (3-15), Eoin Brosnan (4-8), Liam Hassett (2-5), Sean O'Sullivan (1-8), Aodhán MacGearailt (1-6), John Crowley (0-7), Tomás Ó'Sé (1-1), Darragh Ó'Sé (0-4), Noel Kennelly (0-2), John Sheehan (0-2), Declan Quill (0-2), Ian Twiss (0-2), Eamonn Fitzmaurice (0-1), Seamus Scanlon (0-1), Ronan O'Connor (0-1).

Total Scored: 15-121

Appearances:

9 - Declan O'Keeffe, Marc Ó'Sé, Seamus Moynihan, Mike McCarthy, Tomás Ó'Sé, Eamonn Fitzmaurice, Darragh Ó'Sé, Eoin Brosnan, Dara Ó'Cinneide, Mike Frank Russell, John Crowley, Colm Cooper, Sean O'Sullivan.

8 - Tom O'Sullivan, Liam Hassett.

7 - None

6 - John Sheehan, Aodhán MacGearailt.

5 - Seamus Scanlon.

4 - Noel Kennelly, Barry O'Shea.

3 - Declan Quill.

2 - Ronan O'Connor.

1 - Enda Galvin, Mossie Lyons.

2002 - GAA Winners:

All-Irelands: Senior Football: Armagh **Minor Football:** Derry **Under-21 Football:** Galway

National Leagues: Football: Tyrone Hurling: Kilkenny

Senior Hurling: Kilkenny

Kerry Co. Champions: Football: Kerins O'Rahillys Hurling: Kilmoyley

2002 Football All-Stars:

Stephen Cluxton (Dublin), Enda McNulty (Armagh), Paddy Christie (Dublin), Anthony Lynch (Cork), Aidan O'Rourke (Armagh), Kieran McGeeney (Armagh), Kevin Cassidy (Donegal), **Darragh Ó'Sé (Kerry),** Paul McGrane (Armagh), Stephen McDonnell (Armagh), Eamonn O'Hara (Sligo), Oisin McConville (Armagh), Peter Canavan (Tyrone), Ray Cosgrove (Dublin), **Colm Cooper (Kerry).**

2002 - In The News:

- The Euro is introduced across the European Union. The people of Ireland adapt without any major confusion.
- Former Soviet leader Mikhail Gorbachev receives the Freedom of Dublin.
- A referendum on a proposal to amend the Constitution to remove the threat of suicide as a ground for legal abortion is narrowly defeated.
- Brendan Comiskey, the Catholic Bishop of Ferns, resigns after criticism of his handling of abuse cases in the diocese.
- The first recruits of the new Police Service of Northern Ireland graduate.
- The Fianna Fáil-Progressive Democrats coalition is re-elected. Fianna Fáil's Bertie Ahern remains Taoiseach and PD Mary Harney remains

Tánaiste. It is the first government to be re-elected since 1969. Electronic voting machines were used in an Irish election for the first time in three constituencies: Meath, Dublin West and Dublin North. The election was considered a success for Fianna Fáil, winning 80 seats, coming within 4 of an overall majority. The only high profile loss was Mary O'Rourke losing her seat in Westmeath.

- Fine Gael hold 31 seats, Labour return with 20 seats, Progressive Democrats 8, Green Party 6, Sinn Fein 5, and 13 are Independents.
- Kerry return the following to the 29th Dáil:
  Kerry South: John O'Donoghue (FF); Breda Moynihan-Cronin (Lab.); Jackie Healy-Rae (Independent).
  Kerry North: Tom McEllistrim (FF); Martin Ferris (Sinn Fein); Jimmy Deenihan (FG).
- Geraldine Kennedy is appointed the first female editor of the *Irish Times*.
- As of midnight on October 14, the Northern Ireland Assembly and the Executive are suspended by order of the Secretary of State.
- Irish voters accept the Nice Treaty in the second referendum held on the issue.

2003

Summary: Played four championship games, won 69th Munster title, lost All-Ireland semi-final.

Game 1 - versus Tipperary in Tralee on June 15. Final Score: Kerry 0-25; Tipperary 1-10.

Declan O'Keeffe

Tom O'Sullivan   Eamonn Fitzmaurice   Mike McCarthy

Tomás Ó'Sé   Seamus Moynihan   John Sheehan

Darragh Ó'Sé (0-1)   Seamus Scanlon (0-1)

Declan Quill (0-3)   Liam Hassett (0-1)   Sean O'Sullivan (0-3)

Colm Cooper (0-5)   Declan O'Sullivan (0-3)   John Crowley (0-2)

Substitutes: Mike Frank Russell (0-4) for Quill, Dara Ó'Cinneide (0-1) for Crowley, Eoin Brosnan (0-1) for Hassett, James Cahalane for Tomás Ó'Sé, Aodhán MacGearailt for Declan O'Sullivan.

Game 2 - Munster Final versus Limerick in Killarney on July 13. Final Score: Kerry 1-11; Limerick 0-9.

Declan O'Keeffe

Tom O'Sullivan   Seamus Moynihan   Mike McCarthy

Tomás Ó'Sé   Eamonn Fitzmaurice   Marc Ó'Sé

Seamus Scanlon   Eoin Brosnan

Liam Hassett (0-2)   Dara Ó'Cinneide (1-6)   Sean O'Sullivan

Colm Cooper (0-1)   Declan O'Sullivan   Mike Frank Russell

Substitutes: Aodhán MacGearailt (0-1) for Russell, John Crowley (0-1) for Cooper, Paul Galvin for Sean O'Sullivan.

Game 3 - All-Ireland quarter-final versus Roscommon in Croke Park on August 4. Final Score: Kerry 1-21; Roscommon 3-10.

Declan O'Keeffe

Tom O'Sullivan   Seamus Moynihan   Mike McCarthy

Tomás Ó'Sé   Eamonn Fitzmaurice   Marc Ó'Sé

Darragh Ó'Sé   Eoin Brosnan

Sean O'Sullivan (0-2)   Dara Ó'Cinneide (0-8)   Liam Hassett (0-2)

Mike Frank Russell (0-2) Declan O'Sullivan (1-2)   Colm Cooper (0-4)

Substitutes: John Sheehan for Marc Ó'Sé, John Crowley (0-1) for Russell, Aodhán MacGearailt for Sean O'Sullivan, Seamus Scanlon for Brosnan.

Game 4 - All-Ireland semi-final versus Tyrone in Croke Park on August 24. Score: Tyrone 0-13; Kerry 0-6.

Declan O'Keeffe

Tom O'Sullivan   Seamus Moynihan   Mike McCarthy

Tomás Ó'Sé   Eamonn Fitzmaurice   John Sheehan

Darragh Ó'Sé   Eoin Brosnan

Sean O'Sullivan   Dara Ó'Cinneide (0-1)   Liam Hassett

Mike Frank Russell   Declan O'Sullivan (0-1)   Colm Cooper (0-1)

Substitutes: Marc Ó'Sé (0-1) for Sheehan, John Crowley for Sean O'Sullivan, Seamus Scanlon for Russell, Declan Quill (0-2) for Ó'Cinneide, Aodhán MacGearailt for Hassett.

Scorers for the Year: Dara Ó'Cinneide (1-16), Colm Cooper (0-11), Declan O'Sullivan (1-6), Mike Frank Russell (0-6), Declan Quill (0-5), Liam Hassett (0-5), Sean O'Sullivan (0-5), John Crowley (0-4), Aodhán MacGearailt (0-1), Marc Ó'Sé (0-1), Darragh Ó'Sé (0-1), Seamus Scanlon (0-1), Eoin Brosnan (0-1).

Total Scored: 2-63

Appearances:

4 - Declan O'Keeffe, Tom O'Sullivan, Eamonn Fitzmaurice, Mike McCarthy, Tomás Ó'Sé, Seamus Moynihan, Seamus Scanlon, Eoin Brosnan, Liam Hassett, Sean O'Sullivan, Colm Cooper, Declan O'Sullivan, John Crowley, Mike Frank Russell, Dara Ó'Cinneide, Aodhán MacGearailt.

3 - Marc Ó'Sé, John Sheehan, Darragh Ó'Sé.

2 - Declan Quill

1 - James Cahalane, Paul Galvin.

2003 - GAA Winners:

All-Irelands: Senior Football: Tyrone **Minor Football:** Laois **Under-21 Football:** Dublin

National Leagues: Football: Tyrone Hurling: Kilkenny

Senior Hurling: Kilkenny

Kerry Co. Champions: Football: An Gaeltacht Hurling: Kilmoyley

2003 Football All-Stars:

Fergal Byron (Laois), Francis Bellew (Armagh), Cormac McAnallen (Tyrone), Joe Higgins (Laois), Conor Gormley (Tyrone), Tom Kelly (Laois), Phillip Jordan (Tyrone), Kevin Walsh (Galway), Sean Cavanagh (Tyrone), Brian Dooher (Tyrone), Brian McGuigan (Tyrone), Declan Browne (Tipperary), Stephen McDonnell (Armagh), Peter Canavan (Tyrone), Adrian Sweeney (Donegal).

2003 - In The News:

- The Spire of Dublin on O'Connell Street is officially completed.
- 100,000 people in Dublin, and 30,000 in Belfast march to express their opposition to the imminent invasion of Iraq.
- President Bush of the United States visits Northern Ireland for discussions with British Prime Minister Tony Blair. He also meets Taoiseach Bertie Ahern and the leaders of the pro-agreement parties.
- The 2003 Special Olympics World Summer Games open in Croke Park, Dublin.
- The remains of Belfast mother Jean McConville are found 31 years after she was abducted and murdered by the Provisional IRA, who accused her of being a British Army agent.
- For the first time the All-Ireland Football Final is contested by two teams from the same province. Tyrone are victorious over Armagh in the first All-Ulster Final.

- The people of Northern Ireland go to the polls in November. The Democratic Unionist Party and Sinn Féin make massive gains at the expense of more moderate unionist and nationalist parties.

Niall Flynn

2004

Summary: Played seven championship games, won 70th Munster title, won 33rd All-Ireland title.

Game 1 - versus Clare in Ennis on May 23. Final Score: Kerry 2-10; Clare 0-9.

Diarmuid Murphy

Tom O'Sullivan   Mike McCarthy   Aidan O'Mahony

Tomás Ó'Sé   Eamonn Fitzmaurice   Seamus Moynihan

Darragh Ó'Sé   Willie Kirby

Paul Galvin   Declan O'Sullivan   Eoin Brosnan (1-4)

Colm Cooper (0-1)   John Crowley (1-0)   Mike Frank Russell (0-5)

Substitutes: Michael Quirke for Crowley, Liam Hassett for Galvin, Marc Ó'Sé for Tomás Ó'Sé, Ronan O'Connor for Quirke.

Game 2 - versus Cork in Killarney on June 13. Final Score: Kerry 0-15; Cork 0-7.

Diarmuid Murphy

Tom O'Sullivan   Mike McCarthy   Aidan O'Mahony

Tomás Ó'Sé (0-1)   Eamonn Fitzmaurice   Seamus Moynihan

Darragh Ó'Sé   Willie Kirby (0-2)

Liam Hassett   Declan O'Sullivan   Eoin Brosnan (0-1)

Colm Cooper (0-3)   John Crowley   Mike Frank Russell (0-7)

Substitutes: Dara Ó'Cinneide (0-1) for Crowley, Paul Galvin for Brosnan, Marc Ó'Sé for O'Mahony.

Game 3 - Munster Final versus Limerick in Limerick on July 4. Final Score: Kerry 1-10; Limerick 1-10.

Diarmuid Murphy

Tom O'Sullivan   Mike McCarthy   Aidan O'Mahony

344

Tomás Ó'Sé   Eamonn Fitzmaurice   Marc Ó'Sé

         Darragh Ó'Sé   Willie Kirby

Liam Hassett   Eoin Brosnan (0-1)   Paul Galvin

Colm Cooper (0-2)   Dara Ó'Cinneide (0-3)   Mike Frank Russell (1-4)

Substitutes: Tommy Griffin for Kirby, John Crowley for Ó'Cinneide, John Sheehan for Fitzmaurice.

Game 4 - Munster Final replay versus Limerick in Killarney on July 11. Final Score: Kerry 3-10; Limerick 2-9.

                        Diarmuid Murphy

Tom O'Sullivan   Mike McCarthy   Aidan O'Mahony

Tomás Ó'Sé (1-0)   Eamonn Fitzmaurice   Marc Ó'Sé

         Darragh Ó'Sé   Eoin Brosnan (1-1)

Paul Galvin (0-1)   Dara Ó'Cinneide (1-7)   Liam Hassett

Colm Cooper   John Crowley   Mike Frank Russell (0-1)

Substitutes: Tommy Griffin for Crowley, Willie Kirby for Hassett.

Game 5 - All-Ireland quarter-final versus Dublin in Croke Park on August 14. Final Score: Kerry 1-15; Dublin 1-8.

                        Diarmuid Murphy

Tom O'Sullivan   Mike McCarthy   Aidan O'Mahony

Tomás Ó'Sé   Eamonn Fitzmaurice   Marc Ó'Sé

         Darragh Ó'Sé   Paddy Kelly

Eoin Brosnan   Declan O'Sullivan (0-1)   Paul Galvin (0-1)

Colm Cooper (0-5)   Dara Ó'Cinneide (1-5)   Mike Frank Russell

Substitutes: Liam Hassett (0-1) for Russell, Willie Kirby (0-2) for Kelly, John Crowley for Declan O'Sullivan, John Sheehan for Tomás Ó'Sé, Sean O'Sullivan for O'Mahony.

Game 6 - All-Ireland semi-final versus Derry in Croke Park on August 29. Final Score: Kerry 1-17; Derry 1-11.

Diarmuid Murphy

Tom O'Sullivan   Mike McCarthy   Marc Ó'Sé

Aidan O'Mahony   Eamonn Fitzmaurice   Tomás Ó'Sé (0-2)

Darragh Ó'Sé (0-1)   Willie Kirby (0-1)

Liam Hassett   Eoin Brosnan (0-1)   Paul Galvin (0-1)

Declan O'Sullivan (1-0)   Dara Ó'Cinneide (0-2)   Colm Cooper (0-6)

Substitutes: Mike Frank Russell (0-2) for Darragh Ó'Sé, Paddy Kelly (0-1) for Hassett, Tommy Griffin for Kirby, John Crowley for Cooper, Declan Quill for Ó'Cinneide.

Game 7 - All-Ireland Final versus Mayo in Croke Park on September 26. Final Score: Kerry 1-20; Mayo 2-9.

Diarmuid Murphy

Aidan O'Mahony   Mike McCarthy   Tom O'Sullivan

Marc Ó'Sé (0-1)   Eamonn Fitzmaurice   Tomás Ó'Sé

Willie Kirby (0-3)   Eoin Brosnan

Liam Hassett   Declan O'Sullivan (0-1)   Paul Galvin (0-1)

Colm Cooper (1-5)   Dara Ó'Cinneide (0-8)   John Crowley

Substitutes: Seamus Moynihan for Hassett, Mike Frank Russell (0-1) for Crowley, Ronan O'Connor for Ó'Cinneide, Paddy Kelly for Galvin, Brendan Guiney for Tomás Ó'Sé.

Scorers for the Year: Dara Ó'Cinneide (2-26), Colm Cooper (1-22), Mike Frank Russell (1-20), Eoin Brosnan (2-8), Willie Kirby (0-8), Tomás Ó'Sé (1-3), Declan O'Sullivan (1-2), Paul Galvin (0-4), John Crowley (1-0), Marc Ó'Sé (0-1), Darragh Ó'Sé (0-1), Paddy Kelly (0-1), Liam Hassett (0-1).

Total Scored: 9-97

Appearances:

7 - Diarmuid Murphy, Aidan O'Mahony, Mike McCarthy, Tom O'Sullivan, Marc Ó'Sé, Eamonn Fitzmaurice, Tomás Ó'Sé, Willie Kirby, Eoin Brosnan, Paul Galvin, Colm Cooper, John Crowley, Mike Frank Russell, Liam Hassett.

6 - Darragh Ó'Sé, Dara Ó'Cinneide.

5 - Declan O'Sullivan.

4 - None

3 - Seamus Moynihan, Paddy Kelly, Tommy Griffin.

2 - John Sheehan, Ronan O'Connor.

1 - Michael Quirke, Sean O'Sullivan, Declan Quill, Brendan Guiney.

2004 - GAA Winners:

All-Irelands: Senior Football: Kerry **Minor Football:** Tyrone **Under-21 Football:** Armagh

National Leagues: Football: Kerry   Hurling: Galway

Senior Hurling: Cork

Kerry Co. Champions: Football: South Kerry   Hurling: Kilmoyley

2004 Football All-Stars:

Diarmuid Murphy (Kerry), Tom O'Sullivan (Kerry), Barry Owens (Fermanagh), **Michael McCarthy (Kerry), Tomás Ó'Sé (Kerry),** James Nallen (Mayo), John Keane (Westmeath), Martin McGrath (Fermanagh), Sean Cavanagh (Tyrone), **Paul Galvin (Kerry),** Ciarán McDonald (Mayo), Dessie Dolan (Westmeath), **Colm Cooper (Kerry),** Enda Muldoon (Derry), Mattie Forde (Wexford).

2004 - In The News:

- Ireland takes over as President of the European Commission.
- Five people are killed in a bus crash at Wellington Quay, Dublin.
- The cooling towers of Rhode Power Station, near Kilbeggan, Co. Westmeath are demolished.

- Ireland's rugby team wins the Triple Crown for the first time since 1985.
- Ireland receives worldwide attention as a smoking ban comes into effect in all pubs, restaurants and work places. The ban is pioneered by the Minister for Health, Micheál Martin.
- 25 heads of government celebrate in Dublin as the European Union admits ten new member-states.
- The Grangegorman Development Bill is published by the Irish Government.
- U.S. President George W. Bush arrives at Shannon Airport for an EU-U.S. summit.
- The Minister for Finance, Charlie McCreevy, is appointed as Ireland's next European Commissioner.
- Irish athlete Cathal Lombard is accused of taking performance enhancing drugs at the Olympic Games.
- The Minister for Agriculture, Joe Walsh, announces his retirement from the Cabinet. He is the longest-serving Agriculture Minister in Europe.
- Cian O'Connor wins a gold medal for Ireland at the Olympic Games in Athens.
- Former Taoiseach John Bruton is appointed EU Ambassador to Washington.
- Mary Coughlan is appointed Ireland's first female Minister for Agriculture.
- The leader of the Democratic Unionist Party, Ian Paisley, makes his first visit to Dublin for political talks with Taoiseach Bertie Ahern.
- Ireland's second national television channel, Network 2, reverts back to its old name of RTÉ Two.
- The Irish Government issue British hostage Ken Bigley with an Irish passport in an effort to secure his release from his Iraqi capturers.
- Taoiseach Bertie Ahern holds discussions with United Nations Secretary-General Kofi Annan in Dublin.
- The International Equestrian Federation confirms that part of the B sample of Waterford Crystal, the horse ridden by Olympic gold medallist Cian O'Connor, has been stolen in England. Banned substances were confirmed in the sample.
- Mary McAleese is inaugurated for a second term as President of Ireland without an election as no other nominations were received.
- Minister for Community, Rural & Gaeltacht Affairs, Éamon Ó Cuív, has a lucky escape when his ministerial car is involved in a head-on collision with another car in Co. Kerry.

- November 16 - Irish-born aid worker, Margaret Hassan, is murdered by her capturers in Iraq.
- Bertie Ahern celebrates 10 years as leader of the Fianna Fáil Party.
- Negotiated proposals to restore the power-sharing institutions to Northern Ireland by March fail to reach finality. The main sticking point was a refusal by the Irish Republican Army to allow photographs be taken of arms decommissioning and a refusal by the Democratic Unionist Party's Ian Paisley to witness disarmament himself.
- In Bogotá, Colombia the Penal Chamber of Bogotá's Supreme Tribunal hands down lengthy jail sentences to Niall Connolly, Martin McCauley and James Monaghan for training Marxist rebels in Colombia. The three are said to have fled the region where they were convicted.
- December 19 - President McAleese convenes a meeting of the Council of State to discuss the Health Amendment II Bill, which was presented by the Health Minister Mary Harney.
- £22 million is stolen in a heist from the Northern Bank in Belfast.
- Taoiseach Bertie Ahern pledges €10 million in aid to the people affected by the tsunami in South-East Asia.
- In the European Parliament election Fine Gael emerge as the largest party eclipsing Fianna Fáil by one seat. Two Independent MEPs are elected. The Labour Party wins one seat and Sinn Féin takes a seat for the first time ever.
- In the local elections, Fianna Fáil's share of the vote falls sharply while all the other opposition parties make gains. Sinn Féin make a huge breakthrough with a record number of councillors being elected.

2005

Summary: Played six championship games, won 71st Munster title, lost All-Ireland Final.

Game 1 - versus Tipperary in Thurles on May 29. Final Score: Kerry 2-22; Tipperary 0-13.

Diarmuid Murphy

Aidan O'Mahony Mike McCarthy Tom O'Sullivan

Tomás Ó'Sé Eamonn Fitzmaurice Marc Ó'Sé (0-1)

Darragh Ó'Sé Willie Kirby

Paul Galvin Eoin Brosnan (1-4) Liam Hassett (0-3)

Colm Cooper (1-5) Declan O'Sullivan Mike Frank Russell (0-8)

Substitutes: Paddy Kelly for Kirby, Bryan Sheehan (0-1) for Galvin, Dara Ó'Cinneide for Declan O'Sullivan, Brendan Guiney for Tomás Ó'Sé, Declan Quill for Cooper.

Game 2 - versus Limerick in Limerick on June 19. Final Score: Kerry 2-10; Limerick 0-10.

Diarmuid Murphy

Marc Ó'Sé Mike McCarthy Tom O'Sullivan

Aidan O'Mahony Eamonn Fitzmaurice (0-1) Tomás Ó'Sé

Darragh Ó'Sé Paddy Kelly

Paul Galvin Eoin Brosnan Liam Hassett (0-1)

Colm Cooper (2-5) Declan O'Sullivan Mike Frank Russell

Substitutes: Dara Ó'Cinneide (0-1) for Russell, Seamus Moynihan (0-1) for Tom O'Sullivan, Willie Kirby for Kelly, Bryan Sheehan (0-1) for Hassett, Declan Quill for Declan O'Sullivan.

Game 3 - Munster Final versus Cork in Cork on July 10. Final Score: Kerry 1-11; Cork 0-11.

Diarmuid Murphy

Aidan O'Mahony   Mike McCarthy   Tom O'Sullivan

Tomás Ó'Sé (0-2)   Seamus Moynihan   Marc Ó'Sé (0-1)

        Darragh Ó'Sé (0-1)   Eoin Brosnan (0-1)

Paul Galvin   Declan O'Sullivan (1-0)   Liam Hassett (0-1)

Colm Cooper (0-2)   Dara Ó'Cinneide (0-2) Mike Frank Russell (0-1)

Substitutes: Willie Kirby for Galvin, Eamonn Fitzmaurice for Marc Ó'Sé, Bryan Sheehan for Declan O'Sullivan, Kieran Donaghy for Hassett, Ronan O'Connor for Brosnan.

Game 4 - All-Ireland quarter-final versus Mayo in Croke Park on August 7. Final Score: Kerry 2-15; Mayo 0-18.

                        Diarmuid Murphy

Marc Ó'Sé (0-1)   Mike McCarthy   Tom O'Sullivan

Tomás Ó'Sé   Seamus Moynihan   Aidan O'Mahony (0-1)

        Darragh Ó'Sé (1-0)   Willie Kirby (0-1)

Liam Hassett (0-1)   Declan O'Sullivan (0-1)   Eoin Brosnan (0-2)

Colm Cooper (1-1)   Dara Ó'Cinneide (0-1) Mike Frank Russell (0-3)

Substitutes: Paul Galvin (0-3) for Hassett, Eamonn Fitzmaurice for Tom O'Sullivan, Bryan Sheehan for Ó'Cinneide, Kieran Donaghy for Darragh Ó'Sé, Declan Quill for Russell.

Game 5 - All-Ireland semi-final versus Cork in Croke Park on August 28. Final Score: Kerry 1-19; Cork 0-9.

                        Diarmuid Murphy

Marc Ó'Sé   Mike McCarthy (0-1)   Tom O'Sullivan

Tomás Ó'Sé (0-1)   Seamus Moynihan   Aidan O'Mahony (0-1)

        Darragh Ó'Sé   Willie Kirby (0-1)

Paul Galvin (0-3)   Eoin Brosnan (1-2)   Liam Hassett (0-1)

Colm Cooper (0-5)   Declan O'Sullivan   Bryan Sheehan (0-2)

Substitutes: Dara Ó'Cinneide (0-1) for Sheehan, Mike Frank Russell (0-1) for Hassett, Eamonn Fitzmaurice for Tomás Ó'Sé, Declan Quill for Cooper, Kieran Donaghy for Kirby.

Game 6 - All-Ireland Final versus Tyrone in Croke Park on September 25. Final Score: Tyrone 1-16; Kerry 2-10.

Diarmuid Murphy

Marc Ó'Sé	Mike McCarthy	Tom O'Sullivan

Tomás Ó'Sé (1-0)	Seamus Moynihan	Aidan O'Mahony

Darragh Ó'Sé (0-2)   Willie Kirby

Paul Galvin	Eoin Brosnan (0-2)	Liam Hassett

Colm Cooper (0-5)	Declan O'Sullivan	Dara Ó'Cinneide (1-1)

Substitutes: Mike Frank Russell for Hassett, Darran O'Sullivan for Ó'Cinneide, Eamonn Fitzmaurice for Moynihan, Bryan Sheehan for Galvin.

Scorers for the Year: Colm Cooper (4-23), Eoin Brosnan (2-11), Mike Frank Russell (0-13), Dara Ó'Cinneide (1-6), Liam Hassett (0-7), Paul Galvin (0-6), Tomás Ó'Sé (1-3), Darragh Ó'Sé (1-3), Declan O'Sullivan (1-1), Bryan Sheehan (0-4), Marc Ó'Sé (0-3), Aidan O'Mahony (0-2), Willie Kirby (0-2), Mike McCarthy (0-1), Seamus Moynihan (0-1), Eamonn Fitzmaurice (0-1).

Total Scored: 10-87

Appearances:

6 - Diarmuid Murphy, Aidan O'Mahony, Mike McCarthy, Tom O'Sullivan, Tomás Ó'Sé, Eamonn Fitzmaurice, Marc Ó'Sé, Darragh Ó'Sé, Willie Kirby, Paul Galvin, Eoin Brosnan, Liam Hassett, Colm Cooper, Declan O'Sullivan, Mike Frank Russell, Bryan Sheehan, Dara Ó'Cinneide.

5 - Seamus Moynihan.

4 - Declan Quill.

3 - Kieran Donaghy.

2 - Paddy Kelly.

1 - Brendan Guiney, Ronan O'Connor, Darran O'Sullivan.

2005 - GAA Winners:

All-Irelands: Senior Football: Tyrone **Minor Football:** Down **Under-21 Football:** Galway

National Leagues: Football: Armagh   Hurling: Kilkenny

Senior Hurling: Cork

Kerry Co. Champions: Football: South Kerry   Hurling: Lixnaw

2005 Football All-Stars:

Diarmuid Murphy (Kerry), Ryan McMenamin (Tyrone), **Michael McCarthy (Kerry),** Andy Mallon (Armagh), **Tomás Ó'Sé (Kerry),** Conor Gormley (Tyrone), Phillip Jordan (Tyrone), Sean Cavanagh (Tyrone), Paul McGrane (Armagh), Brian Dooher (Tyrone), Peter Canavan (Tyrone), Eoin Mulligan (Tyrone), **Colm Cooper (Kerry),** Stephen O'Neill (Tyrone), Stephen McDonnell (Armagh).

2005 - In The News:

- Cork officially becomes the European Capital of Culture for 2005.
- On New Year's Day Littlepace housing estate in Clonee, Co. Meath is struck by a small tornado
- The Irish Farmers Association celebrates its 50th anniversary.
- The Minister for Foreign Affairs, Dermot Ahern TD, begins a visit to the area in South-East Asia that was devastated by the recent tsunami.
- Taoiseach Bertie Ahern conducted a trade mission to China. He is accompanied by one third of the Cabinet, including Micheál Martin, Mary Hanafin, Mary Coughlan and Noel Dempsey.
- The Republic of Ireland officially changes all road signage and regulations to use kilometres per hour (km/h). Distance and speed in Northern Ireland remain in miles per hour.
- Belfast man Robert McCartney is murdered outside a bar in the city by members of the Provisional IRA.
- The former Minister for Justice, Ray Burke, is jailed for six months for tax evasion, as a result of legislation he introduced. He is the first Cabinet minister to be jailed as a result of the tribunals of inquiry.
- Taoiseach Bertie Ahern lays the foundation stone of a new town called Adamstown, just outside Lucan, Co. Dublin.

- Seven people are detained by Gardaí for suspected activities in relation to the bank heist in Belfast in December 2004. £2.3 million sterling is seized in Co. Cork.
- The 100th Sinn Féin Ard-Fheis opens at the Royal Dublin Society in Ballsbridge, Dublin.
- Ireland's oldest sugar factory closes with the loss of several hundred jobs in Carlow.
- Cian O'Connor is stripped of his Olympic gold medal after the sports ruling body find that his horse, Waterford Crystal, had banned substances in its system during the Olympic Games in 2004.
- There is prayer, mourning and remembrance in honour of Pope John Paul II following his death in Rome at 20:37 Irish time on April 2.
- The Minister for Foreign Affairs, Dermot Ahern TD, is appointed one of four special envoys for United Nations reform by the UN Secretary General, Kofi Annan.
- The annual congress of the Gaelic Athletic Association votes to open up Croke Park and allow soccer and rugby to be played there under certain circumstances.
- President McAleese and Taoiseach Bertie Ahern convey messages of congratulations to the newly elected Pope Benedict XVI.
- President Mary McAleese's official state car is involved in a minor road accident in Co. Meath. The President and her driver escape injury.
- Five schoolgirls die and many other people are injured in a collision involving a crowded Bus Éireann school bus and two other vehicles in Co Meath.
- The Irish language is granted official status as a working language within the European Union.
- The M50 motorway is finally completed, 34 years after the route was first envisaged and 17 years after construction began.
- Taoiseach Bertie Ahern meets Pope Benedict XVI for a private audience in Rome.
- In what has been described as an "historic" day, on July 28 the Provisional Irish Republican Army ends its armed campaign and orders all its units to dump arms.
- 45-year-old Limerick woman, Dolores McNamara, scoops €115 million after winning the Euromillions rollover jackpot prize. It is Europe's largest ever lottery jackpot.
- At Lansdowne Road, Dublin the Republic of Ireland lose 1-0 to France in a crucial soccer World Cup qualifier. On the same night at

Windsor Park, Belfast, Northern Ireland beat England 1-0. It is the first time since 1927 that the team has beaten England at home.

- Irish Ferries offers voluntary redundancy packages to its 543 seafaring workers.
- In a move described as "the day the gun was taken out of Irish politics", the head of the Independent International Commission on Decommissioning, General John de Chastelain, says that he is satisfied that the Irish Republican Army has completed the decommissioning of its entire arsenal of weapons.
- Following the failure of the Republic of Ireland to qualify for World Cup 2006 in Germany, Roy Keane announces his retirement from the international game.
- Dr. Tiede Herrema returns to the city of Limerick from which he was kidnapped 30 years ago. Dr. Herrema presents his personal papers relating to the issue to the University of Limerick Library.
- The abducted journalist Rory Carroll is released unharmed after being kidnapped in Iraq on the previous day.
- On the second day of the Fianna Fáil Ard-Fheis in Killarney, news breaks that the former party member and TD, Liam Lawlor, is killed in a car accident in Moscow.
- The Ferns Inquiry on clerical sex abuse in the Diocese of Ferns is published.
- The government launches the biggest national transport plan in the history of the state. The strategy, known as Transport 21, will allow for €34.4 million to be spent on roads, rail and the Dublin metro over a ten year period.
- Roy Keane sensationally leaves Manchester United in a decision that was said to be by mutual consent.
- Abbas Boutrab becomes the first non-republican, non-loyalist to be convicted in the diplock courts of Northern Ireland - he is convicted of having information that could be used to bomb an airliner.
- George Best, the man described as the greatest association football player of his or any generation, dies in London after several months of declining health.
- The Irish-born broadcaster Terry Wogan receives a knighthood from Queen Elizabeth II in London in recognition of his services to broadcasting.
- President Mary McAleese meets Queen Elizabeth II at Hillsborough Castle. It is the first time that the two heads of state meet in Ireland.

- A car carrying a bomb is intercepted by Gardaí and members of Special Branch at the M50 Westlink Toll Bridge. A man arrested is believed to be connected to the continuity IRA.

2006

Summary: Played eight championship games, won 34th All-Ireland title.

Game 1 - versus Waterford in Killarney on May 21. Final Score: Kerry 0-16; Waterford 0-8.

Diarmuid Murphy

Aidan O'Mahony	Marc Ó'Sé	Tom O'Sullivan
Tomás Ó'Sé	Seamus Moynihan	Mossie Lyons

Darragh Ó'Sé   Kieran Donaghy

Paul Galvin (0-2)	Eamonn Fitzmaurice (0-1)	Eoin Brosnan
Colm Cooper (0-2)	Declan O'Sullivan (0-3)	Bryan Sheehan (0-7)

Substitutes: Mike McCarthy for Tomás Ó'Sé, Ronan O'Connor for Fitzmaurice, Darran O'Sullivan for Brosnan, Paul O'Connor (0-1) for Cooper, Tommy Griffin for O'Mahony.

Game 2 - versus Tipperary in Killarney on June 11. Final Score: Kerry 0-17; Tipperary 1-5.

Diarmuid Murphy

Aidan O'Mahony (0-1)	Marc Ó'Sé	Tom O'Sullivan
Tomás Ó'Sé (0-1)	Seamus Moynihan (0-1)	Mossie Lyons

Darragh Ó'Sé   Kieran Donaghy (0-2)

Declan O'Sullivan (0-1)	Eoin Brosnan	Paul Galvin (0-1)
Darran O'Sullivan	Bryan Sheehan (0-7)	Colm Cooper (0-1)

Substitutes: Mike Frank Russell (0-1) for Darran O'Sullivan, Eamonn Fitzmaurice (0-1) for Galvin, Ronan O'Connor for Brosnan, Tommy Griffin for Donaghy, Killian Young for Tom O'Sullivan.

Game 3 - Munster Final versus Cork in Killarney on July 9. Final Score: Kerry 0-10; Cork 0-10.

Diarmuid Murphy

Aidan O'Mahony	Mike McCarthy	Marc Ó'Sé

Tomás Ó'Sé	Seamus Moynihan	Mossie Lyons

Darragh Ó'Sé	Kieran Donaghy

Paul Galvin (0-1)	Declan O'Sullivan (0-1)	Eoin Brosnan

Colm Cooper (0-1)	Bryan Sheehan (0-6)	Paul O'Connor

Substitutes: Tom O'Sullivan for Lyons, Darran O'Sullivan (0-1) for O'Connor, Tommy Griffin for Tomás Ó'Sé.

Game 4 - Munster Final replay versus Cork in Cork on July 16. Final Score: Cork 1-12; Kerry 0-9.

Diarmuid Murphy

Tom O'Sullivan	Mike McCarthy	Marc Ó'Sé

Tomás Ó'Sé	Seamus Moynihan	Aidan O'Mahony

Darragh Ó'Sé (0-2)	Eoin Brosnan

Paul Galvin (0-1)	Eamonn Fitzmaurice	Declan O'Sullivan

Colm Cooper (0-1)	Bryan Sheehan (0-2)	Darran O'Sullivan (0-1)

Substitutes: Tommy Griffin for Fitzmaurice, Mossie Lyons for O'Mahony, Sean O'Sullivan (0-1) for Declan O'Sullivan, Mike Frank Russell (0-1) for Sheehan, Paul O'Connor for Galvin.

Game 5 - Qualifier versus Longford in Killarney on July 29. Final Score: Kerry 4-11; Longford 1-11.

Diarmuid Murphy

Marc Ó'Sé	Mike McCarthy	Tom O'Sullivan

Tomás Ó'Sé	Seamus Moynihan	Aidan O'Mahony

Darragh Ó'Sé (0-1)	Tommy Griffin (0-1)

Darran O'Sullivan	Eoin Brosnan (3-0)	Paul Galvin (0-1)

Colm Cooper (1-3)	Kieran Donaghy (0-1)	Mike Frank Russell (0-2)

Substitutes: Declan O'Sullivan for Darran O'Sullivan, Mossie Lyons for Tomás Ó'Sé, Bryan Sheehan (0-1) for Griffin, Eamonn Fitzmaurice for Moynihan, Sean O'Sullivan (0-1) for Galvin.

Game 6 - All-Ireland quarter-final versus Armagh in Croke Park on August 5. Final Score: Kerry 3-15; Armagh 1-13.

Diarmuid Murphy

| Marc Ó'Sé (0-2) | Mike McCarthy | Tom O'Sullivan |

| Tomás Ó'Sé (0-1) | Seamus Moynihan | Aidan O'Mahony |

Darragh Ó'Sé   Tommy Griffin

| Sean O'Sullivan (0-2) | Eoin Brosnan (1-0) | Paul Galvin (0-1) |

| Colm Cooper (0-3) | Kieran Donaghy (1-0) Mike Frank Russell (0-2) |

Substitutes: Darran O'Sullivan (1-0) for Sean O'Sullivan, Declan O'Sullivan (0-1) for Griffin, Bryan Sheehan (0-2) for Russell, Eamonn Fitzmaurice (0-1) for Brosnan.

Game 7 - All-Ireland semi-final versus Cork in Croke Park on August 20. Final Score: Kerry 0-16; Cork 0-10.

Diarmuid Murphy

| Marc Ó'Sé | Mike McCarthy | Tom O'Sullivan |

| Tomás Ó'Sé (0-1) | Seamus Moynihan | Aidan O'Mahony |

Darragh Ó'Sé   Tommy Griffin

| Sean O'Sullivan (0-2) | Eoin Brosnan | Paul Galvin (0-1) |

| Colm Cooper (0-4) | Kieran Donaghy (0-1) Mike Frank Russell (0-6) |

Substitutes: Declan O'Sullivan (0-1) for Brosnan, Darran O'Sullivan for Sean O'Sullivan, Eamonn Fitzmaurice for Griffin.

Game 8 - All-Ireland Final versus Mayo in Croke Park on September 17. Final Score: Kerry 4-15; Mayo 3-5.

Diarmuid Murphy

| Marc Ó'Sé | Mike McCarthy | Tom O'Sullivan |

| Tomás Ó'Sé | Seamus Moynihan (0-1) | Aidan O'Mahony (0-2) |

Darragh Ó'Sé   Tommy Griffin

Sean O'Sullivan (0-1)   Declan O'Sullivan (1-2)   Paul Galvin (0-1)

Colm Cooper (1-2)   Kieran Donaghy (1-2)   Mike Frank Russell (0-2)

Substitutes: Eoin Brosnan (1-1) for Tomás Ó'Sé, Darran O'Sullivan for Sean O'Sullivan, Eamonn Fitzmaurice for Griffin, Bryan Sheehan (0-1) for Cooper, Brendan Guiney for O'Mahony.

Scorers for the Year: Bryan Sheehan (0-26), Colm Cooper (2-17), Eoin Brosnan (5-1), Mike Frank Russell (0-14), Kieran Donaghy (2-6), Declan O'Sullivan (1-9), Paul Galvin (0-9), Sean O'Sullivan (0-7), Darran O'Sullivan (1-2), Tomás Ó'Sé (0-3), Aidan O'Mahony (0-3), Eamonn Fitzmaurice (0-3), Darragh Ó'Sé (0-3), Marc Ó'Sé (0-2), Seamus Moynihan (0-2), Paul O'Connor (0-1), Tommy Griffin (0-1).

Total Scored: 11-109

Appearances:

8 - Diarmuid Murphy, Marc O'Se, Tom O'Sullivan, Tomás Ó'Sé, Seamus Moynihan, Aidan O'Mahony, Darragh Ó'Sé, Paul Galvin, Declan O'Sullivan, Colm Cooper, Darran O'Sullivan, Eoin Brosnan, Tommy Griffin.

7 - Mike McCarthy, Kieran Donaghy, Eamonn Fitzmaurice, Bryan Sheehan.

6 - Mike Frank Russell

5 - Mossie Lyons, Sean O'Sullivan.

4 - None

3 - Paul O'Connor

2 - Ronan O'Connor

1 - Killian Young, Brendan Guiney.

2006 - GAA Winners:

All-Irelands: Senior Football: Kerry **Minor Football:** Roscommon
Under-21 Football: Mayo

National Leagues: Football: Kerry   Hurling: Kilkenny

Senior Hurling: Kilkenny

Kerry Juniors also take All-Ireland honours with this team: S. Og Ciardabhain, S. Hegarty, J. Costello, D. Doyle, D. O'Sullivan, B. Hickey, J. King, JP Brosnan, A. Garnett, N. Fleming, M. Murphy, C. Daly, R. McAuliffe, S. Wallace, J. Buckley. Subs: K. Foley, F. O'Sullivan, F. Griffin.

Kerry Co. Champions: Football: South Kerry   Hurling: Ballyduff

2006 Football All-Stars:

Stephen Cluxton (Dublin), **Marc Ó'Sé(Kerry),** Barry Owens (Fermanagh), Karl Lacey (Donegal); **Seamus Moynihan (Kerry),** Ger Spillane (Cork), **Aidan O'Mahony (Kerry),** Nicholas Murphy (Cork), **Darragh Ó'Sé (Kerry), Paul Galvin (Kerry),** Alan Brogan (Dublin), Alan Dillon (Mayo), Conor Mortimer (Mayo), **Kieran Donaghy (Kerry),** Ronan Clarke (Armagh).

2006 - In The News:

- Steve Staunton is appointed the new manager of the Republic of Ireland football team and will be mentored by Bobby Robson as International Football Consultant.
- The Gaelic Athletic Association, FAI and IRFU announce that a deal has been reached which will allow soccer and rugby to be played in Croke Park.
- Postal workers stage a 20 day wildcat strike disrupting most of Belfast's delivery service.
- The 25th anniversary of the Stardust Disaster, in which 48 young people died, is remembered by the families of the survivors.
- Rioting in Dublin as Republican protestors condemn the right for a "Love Ulster" (Unionist) parade in the city.
- The last ever competitive rugby international takes place at the oldest rugby venue in the world, Lansdowne Road, after 128 years of use, before the ground is redeveloped.
- Up to 120,000 people line the streets of Dublin to mark the 90th anniversary of the 1916 Easter Rising.
- The 2006 census takes place in the Republic of Ireland in April. CSO preliminary 2006 census findings indicate that the population of the Republic of Ireland is 4,234,925, an increase of 8.6% since 2002 and at its highest since the 1861 census. The total population for the island now stands at just under 6 million (estimates).
- Prince Philip of the United Kingdom meets President Mary McAleese and Taoiseach Bertie Ahern on a visit to Dublin.
- Fianna Fáil celebrates its 80th anniversary with a day of celebrations at the Mansion House, Dublin.

- The members of the Northern Ireland Assembly are recalled 3 1/2 years after the assembly was suspended, with a view to electing an executive, and having the suspension lifted.
- Armed Gardaí forcibly remove thirty Afghan refugees who had sought sanctuary in St. Patrick's cathedral, Dublin after a one week hunger-strike.
- Belfast City Airport is renamed George Best Belfast City Airport on what would have been George Best's 60th birthday.
- Australian Prime Minister John Howard formally addresses Dáil Éireann.
- The state funeral of the former Taoiseach Charles Haughey takes place in Dublin in June.
- Irish government announces plans to spend €3.8 billion on scientific research over 7 years.
- President Mary McAleese and leading representatives of all political parties in Ireland, north and south, mark the 90th anniversary of the Battle of the Somme at the Irish National War Memorial Gardens, Dublin.
- On July 7, Dublin Airport is evacuated for the second time in a week when an abandoned suspect package is found.
- Ireland is one of many countries affected by the 2006 European heat wave. July 2006 is the warmest month since records began in both the Republic and Northern Ireland.
- 150th anniversary of the birth of John Redmond, Leader of the Irish Parliamentary Party.
- Mary Harney resigns as leader of the Progressive Democrats. She has led the party since October 1993, with Michael McDowell becoming leader.
- Northern Ireland overtake the Republic of Ireland in the FIFA rankings for the first time.
- Loyalist Michael Stone attempts to bomb the Northern Ireland Assembly on the day nominations for first and deputy first ministers are scheduled.

2007

Summary: Played five championship games, won 72nd Munster title, won 35th All-Ireland title.

Game 1 - versus Waterford in Dungarvan on June 3. Final Score: Kerry 2-15; Waterford 0-4.

Diarmuid Murphy

Padraig Reidy	Tom O'Sullivan	Marc Ó'Sé (0-1)
Tomás Ó'Sé (0-1)	Aidan O'Mahony	Killian Young

Darragh Ó'Sé   Michael Quirke

Declan O'Sullivan	Eoin Brosnan (2-2)	Paul Galvin (0-2)
Colm Cooper (0-5)	Kieran Donaghy	Mike Frank Russell (0-1)

Substitutes: Paul O'Connor (0-2) for Russell, Darran O'Sullivan for Declan O'Sullivan, Sean O'Sullivan (0-1) for Galvin, Seamus Scanlon for Quirke, Mossie Lyons for Young.

Game 2 - Munster Final versus Cork in Killarney on July 1. Final Score: Kerry 1-15; Cork 1-13.

Diarmuid Murphy

Padraig Reidy	Tom O'Sullivan	Marc Ó'Sé
Tomás Ó'Sé	Aidan O'Mahony	Killian Young

Darragh Ó'Sé   Michael Quirke

Declan O'Sullivan (0-3)	Eoin Brosnan (0-1)	Paul Galvin
Colm Cooper (1-2)	Kieran Donaghy (0-2)	Mike Frank Russell (0-6)

Substitutes: Sean O'Sullivan (0-1) for Galvin, Tommy Griffin for Quirke, Darran O'Sullivan for Brosnan, Bryan Sheehan for Declan O'Sullivan.

Game 3 - All-Ireland quarter-final versus Monaghan in Croke Park on August 12. Final Score: Kerry 1-12; Monaghan 1-11.

Diarmuid Murphy

Marc Ó'Sé	Tom O'Sullivan	Padraig Reidy

Tomás Ó'Sé (0-1)	Aidan O'Mahony	Killian Young (0-1)
Darragh Ó'Sé		Seamus Scanlon
Declan O'Sullivan (1-0)	Eoin Brosnan (0-1)	Paul Galvin
Colm Cooper (0-3)	Kieran Donaghy	Mike Frank Russell (0-4)

Substitutes: Sean O'Sullivan for Galvin, Bryan Sheehan (0-2) for Russell, Tommy Griffin for Reidy, Darran O'Sullivan for Brosnan.

Game 4 - All-Ireland semi-final versus Dublin in Croke Park on August 26. Final Score: Kerry 1-15; Dublin 0-16.

Diarmuid Murphy

Padraig Reidy	Tom O'Sullivan	Marc Ó'Sé
Tomás Ó'Sé (0-1)	Aidan O'Mahony	Killian Young
Darragh Ó'Sé		Seamus Scanlon
Declan O'Sullivan (1-3)	Eoin Brosnan (0-2)	Paul Galvin (0-2)
Colm Cooper (0-3)	Kieran Donaghy	Bryan Sheehan (0-3)

Substitutes: Tommy Griffin for Darragh Ó'Sé, Darragh Ó'Sé for Tommy Griffin, Sean O'Sullivan (0-1) for Galvin, Darran O'Sullivan for Brosnan.

Game 5 - All-Ireland Final versus Cork in Croke Park on September 16. Final Score: Kerry 3-13; Cork 1-9.

Diarmuid Murphy

Padraig Reidy	Tom O'Sullivan	Marc Ó'Sé
Tomás Ó'Sé (0-1)	Aidan O'Mahony (0-1)	Killian Young
Darragh Ó'Sé		Seamus Scanlon (0-1)
Paul Galvin (0-1)	Declan O'Sullivan (0-1)	Eoin Brosnan
Colm Cooper (1-5)	Kieran Donaghy (2-0)	Bryan Sheehan (0-2)

Substitutes: Sean O'Sullivan (0-1) for Galvin, Darran O'Sullivan for Brosnan, Tommy Griffin for Young, Mike Frank Russell for Sheehan, Mossie Lyons for Padraig Reidy.

Scorers for the Year: Colm Cooper (2-18), Declan O'Sullivan (2-7), Eoin Brosnan (2-6), Mike Frank Russell (0-11), Kieran Donaghy (2-2), Bryan Sheehan (0-7), Paul Galvin (0-5), Sean O'Sullivan (0-4), Tomás Ó'Sé (0-4), Paul O'Connor (0-2), Marc Ó'Sé (0-1), Aidan O'Mahony (0-1), Killian Young (0-1), Seamus Scanlon (0-1).

Total Scored: 8-70

Appearances:

5 - Diarmuid Murphy, Padraig Reidy, Tom O'Sullivan, Marc Ó'Sé, Tomás Ó'Sé, Aidan O'Mahony, Killian Young, Darragh Ó'Sé, Declan O'Sullivan, Eoin Brosnan, Paul Galvin, Colm Cooper, Kieran Donaghy, Darran O'Sullivan, Sean O'Sullivan.

4 - Tommy Griffin, Seamus Scanlon, Bryan Sheehan, Mike Frank Russell.

3 - None

2 - Mossie Lyons, Michael Quirke.

1 - Paul O'Connor.

2007 - GAA Winners:

All-Irelands: Senior Football: Kerry **Minor Football:** Galway **Under-21 Football:** Cork

National Leagues: Football: Donegal   Hurling: Waterford

Senior Hurling: Kilkenny

Kerry Co. Champions: Football: Feale Rangers   Hurling: Lixnaw

2007 Football All-Stars:

Stephen Cluxton (Dublin), **Marc Ó'Sé (Kerry),** Kevin McCloy (Derry), Graham Canty (Cork), **Tomás Ó'Sé (Kerry), Aidan O'Mahony (Kerry),** Barry Cahill (Dublin), Ciarán Whelan (Dublin), **Darragh Ó'Sé (Kerry),** Stephen Bray (Meath), **Declan O'Sullivan (Kerry),** Alan Brogan (Dublin), **Colm Cooper (Kerry),** Paddy Bradley (Derry), Tomás Freeman (Monaghan).

2007 - In The News:

- Elections take place for the suspended Northern Ireland Assembly.
- Docklands railway station is opened in its temporary location, the first new station in Dublin's city centre since Tara Street Station in 1891.
- President Mary McAleese dissolves the 29ᵗʰ Dáil.
- The 2007 election results saw Fine Gael win seats at the expense of the smaller parties and independents. The proportion of votes increased significantly for Fine Gael only, with slight increases for both the Green Party and Sinn Féin, despite their disappointing seat totals. Negotiations began for the formation of the new government, with Bertie Ahern stating that his preferred option was for a coalition of Fianna Fáil, the Progressive Democrats, and like-minded Independents. The Fine Gael leader, Enda Kenny, did not rule out forming an alternative government, stating that he would talk to all parties except Fianna Fáil and Sinn Féin. Fianna Fáil hold 78 seats, Fine Gael have 51 seats, Labour 20, Green Party have 6, Sinn Féin 4, Progressive Democrats 2, and Independent TD's number 5. The election for Taoiseach took place in the Dáil on 14 June with Bertie Ahern becoming Taoiseach again. The government is a formation of a FF/Green/PD alliance.
- Kerry return the following members to the 30ᵗʰ Dáil:
  Kerry South: John O'Donoghue (FF); Tom Sheahan (FG); Jackie Healy-Rae (Independent).
  Kerry North: Jimmy Deenihan (FG); Martin Ferris (Sinn Fein); Tom McEllistrim (FF).
- Direct rule from Westminster is ended as the Northern Ireland Executive takes control of the affairs of Northern Ireland.
- Meetings of the North/South Ministerial Council include the Democratic Unionist Party (DUP) for the first time.

2008

Summary: Played seven championship games, lost All-Ireland final.

Game 1 - versus Clare in Killarney on June 15. Final Score: Kerry 1-14; Clare 0-5.

Diarmuid Murphy

Marc Ó'Sé   Tom O'Sullivan   Padraig Reidy

Tomás Ó'Sé (0-1)   Aidan O'Mahony (0-2)   Tommy Griffin

Darragh Ó'Sé (0-1)   Seamus Scanlon

Paul Galvin (0-1)   Declan O'Sullivan (0-1)   Eoin Brosnan (0-1)

Colm Cooper (1-0)   Tommy Walsh (0-1)   Bryan Sheehan (0-5)

Substitutes: Darran O'Sullivan (0-1) for Declan O'Sullivan, Kieran Donaghy for Walsh, Daniel Bohane for Griffin, Michael Quirke for Darragh Ó'Sé, Sean O'Sullivan for Sheehan.

Game 2 - Munster Final versus Cork in Cork on July 6. Final Score: Cork 1-16; Kerry 1-11.

Diarmuid Murphy

Marc Ó'Sé   Tom O'Sullivan   Padraig Reidy

Tomás Ó'Sé (0-1)   Aidan O'Mahony   Killian Young

Darragh Ó'Sé (0-1)   Seamus Scanlon

Donnacha Walsh (1-1)   Eoin Brosnan   Sean O'Sullivan (0-2)

Colm Cooper (0-3)   Kieran Donaghy   Bryan Sheehan (0-3)

Substitutes: Darran O'Sullivan for D. Walsh, Tommy Griffin for Brosnan, Tommy Walsh for S. O'Sullivan.

Game 3 - Qualifier in Croke Park August 3. Score: Kerry 1-13; Monaghan 0-13.

Diarmuid Murphy

Marc Ó'Sé   Tom O'Sullivan   Padraig Reidy

Tomás Ó'Sé	Aidan O'Mahony (0-1)	Killian Young
Darragh Ó'Sé	Seamus Scanlon (0-1)	
Donnacha Walsh	Declan O'Sullivan	Bryan Sheehan (0-5)
Colm Cooper (0-2)	Kieran Donaghy (1-2)	Tommy Walsh (0-2)

Substitutes: Eoin Brosnan for D. Walsh, Tommy Griffin for Scanlon, Darran O'Sullivan for T. Walsh, Sean O'Sullivan for D. O'Sullivan, Tommy Walsh for Donaghy.

Game 4 - All-Ireland quarter-final versus Galway in Croke Park on August 9. Final Score: Kerry 1-21; Galway 1-16.

Diarmuid Murphy

Padraig Reidy	Marc Ó'Sé	Tom O'Sullivan
Tomás Ó'Sé	Aidan O'Mahony (0-1)	Killian Young
Darragh Ó'Sé (0-1)	Seamus Scanlon	
Donnacha Walsh (1-0)	Declan O'Sullivan (0-4)	Bryan Sheehan (0-7)
Colm Cooper (0-3)	Kieran Donaghy (0-1)	Tommy Walsh (0-3)

Substitutes: Tommy Griffin for Reidy, Eoin Brosnan for Donnacha Walsh, Daniel Bohane for Scanlon, Darran O'Sullivan (0-1) for Tommy Walsh, Kieran O'Leary for Donaghy.

Game 5 - All-Ireland semi-final versus Cork in Croke Park on August 24. Final Score: Kerry 1-13; Cork 3-7 (Draw).

Diarmuid Murphy

Marc Ó'Sé	Tommy Griffin	Tom O'Sullivan
Tomás Ó'Sé (0-1)	Aidan O'Mahony	Killian Young
Darragh Ó'Sé	Seamus Scanlon	
Donnacha Walsh	Declan O'Sullivan	Bryan Sheehan (0-4)
Colm Cooper (0-3)	Kieran Donaghy (1-1)	Tommy Walsh (0-2)

Substitutes: Eoin Brosnan (0-1) for Donnacha Walsh, Darran O'Sullivan (0-1) for Tommy Walsh, Sean O'Sullivan for Declan O'Sullivan.

Game 6 - All-Ireland semi-final replay versus Cork in Croke Park on August 30. Final Score: Kerry 3-14; Cork 2-13.

Diarmuid Murphy

Marc Ó'Sé   Tommy Griffin   Tom O'Sullivan

Killian Young   Aidan O'Mahony   Tomás Ó'Sé (0-1)

Seamus Scanlon (0-2)   Michael Quirke

Eoin Brosnan (0-1)   Declan O'Sullivan (1-0)   Bryan Sheehan

Colm Cooper (1-8)   Kieran Donaghy   Tommy Walsh (1-2)

Substitutes: Darran O'Sullivan for Michael Quirke, Sean O'Sullivan for Sheehan, David Moran for Brosnan, Daniel Bohane for Walsh, Michael Quirke for Donaghy.

Game 7 - All-Ireland Final versus Tyrone in Croke Park on September 21. Final Score: Tyrone 1-15; Kerry 0-14.

Diarmuid Murphy

Marc Ó'Sé   Tom O'Sullivan   Padraig Reidy

Tomás Ó'Sé (0-1)   Aidan O'Mahony   Killian Young

Darragh Ó'Sé (0-1)   Seamus Scanlon

Eoin Brosnan   Declan O'Sullivan (0-2)   Bryan Sheehan (0-2)

Colm Cooper (0-6)   Kieran Donaghy   Tommy Walsh (0-1)

Substitutes: Darran O'Sullivan (0-1) for Brosnan, Tommy Griffin for Scanlon, Paul Galvin for Walsh, David Moran for Sheehan.

Scorers for the Year: Colm Cooper (2-25), Bryan Sheehan (0-26), Tommy Walsh (1-11), Declan O'Sullivan (1-7), Kieran Donaghy (2-4), Donnacha Walsh (2-1), Tomás Ó'Sé (0-5), Darragh Ó'Sé (0-4), Aidan O'Mahony (0-4), Darran O'Sullivan (0-4), Eoin Brosnan (0-3), Seamus Scanlon (0-3), Sean O'Sullivan (0-2), Paul Galvin (0-1).

Total Scored: 8-100

Appearances:

7 - Diarmuid Murphy, Tommy Griffin, Marc Ó'Sé, Tom O'Sullivan, Tomás Ó'Sé, Aidan O'Mahony, Seamus Scanlon, Eoin Brosnan, Bryan Sheehan, Colm Cooper, Kieran Donaghy, Tommy Walsh, Darran O'Sullivan.

6 - Killian Young, Darragh Ó'Sé, Declan O'Sullivan.

5 - Padraig Reidy, Sean O'Sullivan.

4 - Donnacha Walsh.

3 - Daniel Bohane.

2 - Michael Quirke, Paul Galvin, David Moran.

1 - Kieran O'Leary.

2008 - GAA Winners:

All-Irelands: Senior Football: Tyrone   **Minor   Football:**   Tyrone **Under-21 Football:** Kerry

Kerry's Winning Under-21 Team: T. Mac an tSaoir, C. O'Mahoney, M. Moloney, S. Enright, A. O'Sullivan, K. Young, G. Duffy, D. Moran, A. O'Sullivan, K. O'Leary, J. Buckley, M. O'Donoghue, P. Curran, T. Walsh, P. O'Connor. Subs: K. Brennan, E. Hickson; B. Looney, J. Doolan; E. O'Neill.

National Leagues: Football: Derry   Hurling: Tipperary

Senior Hurling: Kilkenny

Kerry Co. Champions: Football: Mid-Kerry   Hurling: Kilmoyley

2008 Football All-Stars:

Gary Connaughton (Westmeath), Conor Gormley (Tyrone), Justin McMahon (Tyrone), John Keane (Westmeath), David Harte (Tyrone), **Tomás Ó'Sé (Kerry),** Phillip Jordan (Tyrone), Enda McGinley (Tyrone), Shane Ryan (Dublin), Brian Dooher (Tyrone), **Declan O'Sullivan (Kerry),** Sean Cavanagh (Tyrone), **Colm Cooper (Kerry), Kieran Donaghy (Kerry),** Ronan Clarke (Armagh).

2008 - In The News:

- Aer Lingus end their service from Shannon to London's Heathrow Airport.
- Ireland is the 22nd nation to recognize Kosovo's independence.
- Taoiseach Bertie Ahern resigns and Brian Cowen is elected the seventh leader of Fianna Fáil.
- Patrick Hillery, Ireland's sixth President, dies at age 84.
- Ireland rejects the Lisbon Treaty in a referendum by a margin of 53% to 47%.
- The 2008 Kerry bogslides was a natural disaster that occurred in the Maghanknockane area of Lyrecrompane in August and September. The first bogslide extended to over four kilometres destroying an estimated 10 hectares (25 acres) of bog, engulfing two bridges, and leading to the closure of a section of road. It was reported that it could take anything up to six months to fix the road. The plot of land owned by Moss Moore, which inspired John B. Keane's play "The Field", escaped the disaster by only a couple of kilometres. Comparisons were drawn with the occurrence of an earthquake as it was claimed that a 30 metres (100 ft) wide section was missing from the hill. The second bogslide was blamed on heavy rain overnight which led to a "small slippage" of bog material. The slippage happened between two bridges, Harris and Scanlon, on a tributary of the Smerlagh River and again forced the closure of a local road.
- The Irish economy had officially entered recession in January of 2008, the first time since 1983.
- All Irish pork products are recalled following an announcement that animal feed used may contain between 80 and 200 more times dioxins than the recognised safety limit. Six days later Irish pork is confirmed safe and returns to the market.
- 2008 Irish road traffic deaths are at the lowest level recorded since statistics began.

2009

Summary: Played 8 championship games; won 36th All-Ireland title.

Game 1 - versus Cork in Killarney on June 7. Final Score: Kerry 0-13; Cork 1-10 (Draw).

Diarmuid Murphy

Marc Ó'Sé	Tom O'Sullivan	Padraig Reidy
Tomás Ó'Sé	Tommy Griffin	Aidan O'Mahony

Tadgh Kennelly (0-1)   Michael Quirke

Paul Galvin	Declan O'Sullivan	Donnacha Walsh (0-2)
Colm Cooper (0-3)	Tommy Walsh (0-1)	Darran O'Sullivan

Subs: Darragh Ó'Sé (0-1) for T. Walsh, Bryan Sheehan (0-5) for Darran O'Sullivan, Darran O'Sullivan for D. Walsh, David Moran for Quirke, Barry John Walsh for Darran O'Sullivan, Sean O'Sullivan for Kennelly.

Game 2 - Replay versus Cork in Cork on June 13. Final Score: Cork 1-17; Kerry 0-12.

Diarmuid Murphy

Marc Ó'Sé	Tom O'Sullivan	Padraig Reidy
Tomás Ó'Sé (0-1)	Aidan O'Mahony	Killian Young

Darragh Ó'Sé (0-1)   Tommy Griffin

Paul Galvin	Declan O'Sullivan (0-2)	Tadgh Kennelly (0-1)
Colm Cooper (0-4)	Tommy Walsh	Bryan Sheehan (0-2)

Subs: David Moran for M. Ó'Sé, Darran O'Sullivan (0-1) for Sheehan, Aidan O'Shea for Reidy, Donnacha Walsh for Tommy Walsh, Eoin Brosnan for Darragh Ó'Sé.

Game 3 - Qualifier versus Longford in Longford on July 11. Score: Kerry 1-12; Longford 0-11.

Diarmuid Murphy

Killian Young	Tommy Griffin	Tom O'Sullivan

Tomás Ó'Sé (0-1)	Marc Ó'Sé	Aidan O'Shea

Darragh Ó'Sé		Seamus Scanlon

Donnacha Walsh (0-1)	Declan O'Sullivan (0-1)	Sean O'Sullivan (0-2)

Colm Cooper (0-5)	Kieran Donaghy	Tommy Walsh (1-2)

Subs: Darran O'Sullivan for Declan O'Sullivan, Barry John Walsh for Donaghy, Michael Quirke for Scanlon, David Moran for Sean O'Sullivan, Bryan Sheehan for Darragh Ó'Sé.

Game 4 - Qualifier versus Sligo in Tralee on July 18. Score: Kerry 0-14; Sligo 1-10.

	Diarmuid Murphy	

Marc Ó'Sé	Tommy Griffin	Tom O'Sullivan

Tomás Ó'Sé	Mike McCarthy	Aidan O'Mahony

Darragh Ó'Sé (0-1)		Seamus Scanlon

Paul Galvin (0-3)	Declan O'Sullivan (0-4)	Donnacha Walsh (0-1)

Colm Cooper (0-2)	Tommy Walsh (0-1)	Sean O'Sullivan (0-1)

Subs: Padraig Reidy for Marc Ó'Sé, Darran O'Sullivan for Donnacha Walsh, Michael Quirke for Scanlon, Bryan Sheehan (0-1) for Sean O'Sullivan, Daniel Bohane for O'Mahony.

Game 5 - Qualifier versus Antrim in Tullamore on July 26. Score: Kerry 2-12; Antrim 0-10.

	Diarmuid Murphy	

Marc Ó'Sé	Tommy Griffin	Tom O'Sullivan

Killian Young	Mike McCarthy	Aidan O'Mahony

Darragh Ó'Sé		Seamus Scanlon

Paul Galvin (1-2)	Tadgh Kennelly	Darran O'Sullivan

Tommy Walsh (1-2)	Declan O'Sullivan (0-1)	Sean O'Sullivan (0-1)

Subs: Colm Cooper (0-4) for Sean O'Sullivan, Tomás Ó'Sé for O'Mahony, Donnacha Walsh for Tadgh Kennelly, Paul O'Connor (0-2) for Darran O'Sullivan, Michael Quirke for Scanlon.

Game 6 - All-Ireland quarter-final versus Dublin in Croke Park on August 3. Score: Kerry 1-24; Dublin 1-7.

Diarmuid Murphy

Marc Ó'Sé	Tommy Griffin	Tom O'Sullivan (0-1)
Tomás Ó'Sé (0-2)	Mike McCarthy	Killian Young
Darragh Ó'Sé		Seamus Scanlon (0-1)
Paul Galvin (0-2)	Declan O'Sullivan (0-3)	Donnacha Walsh (0-1)
Colm Cooper (1-7)	Tommy Walsh	Darran O'Sullivan (0-3)

Subs: Tadgh Kennelly (0-2) for Tommy Walsh, Paul O'Connor (0-2) for Donnacha Walsh, Sean O'Sullivan for Darran O'Sullivan, Aidan O'Mahony for Killian Young, Michael Quirke for Darragh Ó'Sé.

Game 7 - All-Ireland semi-final versus Meath in Croke Park on August 30. Score: Kerry 2-8; Meath 1-7.

Diarmuid Murphy

Marc Ó'Sé	Tommy Griffin	Tom O'Sullivan
Tomás Ó'Sé	Mike McCarthy	Killian Young
Darragh Ó'Sé		Seamus Scanlon
Paul Galvin	Tadgh Kennelly (0-2)	Donnacha Walsh
Colm Cooper (0-3)	Declan O'Sullivan	Darran O'Sullivan (1-1)

Subs: Tommy Walsh (1-2) for Donnacha Walsh, Paul O'Connor for Colm Cooper, Michael Quirke for Darragh Ó'Sé, Aidan O'Mahony for Killian Young, Bryan Sheehan for Declan O'Sullivan.

Game 8 - All-Ireland Final versus Cork in Croke Park on September 20. Score: Kerry 0-16; Cork 1-9.

Diarmuid Murphy

Marc Ó'Sé   Tommy Griffin   Tom O'Sullivan

Tomás Ó'Sé (0-2)   Mike McCarthy   Killian Young

Darragh Ó'Sé   Seamus Scanlon

Paul Galvin   Declan O'Sullivan (0-1)   Tadgh Kennelly (0-2)

Colm Cooper (0-6)   Tommy Walsh (0-4)   Darran O'Sullivan

Subs: Donnacha Walsh for Tadgh Kennelly, Michael Quirke for Darragh Ó'Sé, Kieran Donaghy for Darran O'Sullivan, David Moran for Tommy Walsh, Aidan O'Mahony for Killian Young.

Scorers for the Year: Colm Cooper (1-34), Tommy Walsh (3-12), Declan O'Sullivan (0-12), Paul Galvin (1-7), Darran O'Sullivan (1-6), Tadgh Kennelly (0-8), Bryan Sheehan (0-8), Tomás Ó'Sé (0-5), Donnacha Walsh (0-5), Paul O'Connor (0-4), Sean O'Sullivan (0-4), Darragh Ó'Sé (0-3), David Moran (0-1), Tom O'Sullivan (0-1), Seamus Scanlon (0-1).

Total Scored: 6-111

Appearances:

8 - Diarmuid Murphy, Tommy Griffin, Marc Ó'Sé, Tom O'Sullivan, Tomás Ó'Sé, Darragh Ó'Sé, Colm Cooper, Declan O'Sullivan, Darran O'Sullivan, Tommy Walsh, Donnacha Walsh.

7 - Paul Galvin, Aidan O'Mahony, Michael Quirke.

6 - Killian Young, Seamus Scanlon, Tadgh Kennelly.

5 - Sean O'Sullivan, Mike McCarthy, Bryan Sheehan.

4 - David Moran.

3 - Paul O'Connor, Padraig Reidy.

2 - Kieran Donaghy, Aidan O'Shea, B.J. Walsh.

1 - Daniel Bohane, Eoin Brosnan.

2009 - GAA Winners:

All-Irelands: Senior Football: Kerry   **Minor   Football:**   Armagh
Under-21 Football: Cork

National Leagues: Football: Kerry   Hurling: Kilkenny

Senior Hurling: Kilkenny

Kerry Co. Champions: Football: South Kerry   Hurling: Kilmoyley

2009 All-Stars:

Diarmuid Murphy (Kerry), Karl Lacey (Donegal), Michael Shields (Cork), **Tom O'Sullivan (Kerry), Tomás Ó'Sé (Kerry),** Graham Canty (Cork), John Miskella (Cork), Dermot Earley (Kildare), **Seamus Scanlon (Kerry), Paul Galvin (Kerry),** Pearse O'Neill (Cork), **Tadgh Kennelly (Kerry),** Daniel Goulding (Cork), **Declan O'Sullivan (Kerry),** Stephen O'Neill (Tyrone).

2009 - In The News:

- Ireland begins the phase-out of incandescent light bulbs.
- Fr. Michael Mernagh completes a nine-day, 272 km atonement pilgrimage from Cobh to Dublin's Pro Cathedral in repentance of the Church's response to clerical child abuse.
- Dell announces the axing of almost 2,000 jobs at their Limerick facility.
- Anglo Irish Bank is nationalized when President Mary McAleese signs the Anglo Irish Bank Corporation Bill 2009.
- Waterford Crystal announces closure of its plant in Kilbarry, prompting a 50 day sit-in.
- A Supplementary Budget is delivered by Minister for Finance, Brian Lenihan, in April.
- Ireland's oldest brewery, built in 1650 and home to Beamish and Crawford since 1792, closes its doors on South Main Street in Cork.
- Ryan Tubridy is named new presenter of The Late Late Show, replacing Pat Kenny.
- The Leaving Certificate's English Paper 2 is postponed for 2 days after students in Co. Louth had already seen the paper.
- The "Special Group on Public Service Numbers and Expenditure Programmes" also called "An Bord Snip Nua" report is published

by UCD economist Colm McCarthy. It recommends €5.3bn in potential savings, including 17,300 public service job cuts and a 5% drop in social welfare.

- Draft legislation to establish the National Asset Management Agency is published. The Bill proposes to give NAMA extensive powers to take over land and development loans from banks in an effort to get them lending again and supporting economic recovery.

- Muhammed Ali vists Ennis, Co. Clare, the birthplace of his great-grandfather, Abe Grady.

- 21 people are injured when a Luas tram collides with a double-decker bus in Dublin's O'Connell Street.

- The Unemployment Rate rises from 8.3% at the start of 2009 to 12.5% in August.

- Ireland votes YES on the Lisbon Treaty by a margin of 67% to 33%.

Register of Players

Note that data is from 1928 onward only. There are many players on this list who also played before 1928, the first year the Sam Maguire trophy was presented to the All-Ireland winners.

The scoring data is also incomplete. What is presented below is believed accurate, but scorer details from some games in 1928, 1931, 1934, 1942, 1944, and 1946 amounting to 7 goals and 22 points are not available. Hence, players from those years may have greater individual totals than shown here.

Aherne, Darren; 1995; (1-1) in 1 appearance
Aherne, Pat; 1963; 1 appearance
Aherne, Roger; 1928; 1 appearance
Ashe, Mickey; 1959; 1 appearance
Ashe, Tom; 1949-1953; (4-9) in 9 appearances

Bailey, James; 1928-1929; 3 appearances
Barrett, JJ; 1962-1965; (1-3) in 8 appearances
Barrett, Joe; 1928-1934; 15 appearances
Barrett, Tim; 1957; 1 appearance
Barrett, Tony; 1964-1967; (2-2) in 5 appearances
Bohane, Daniel; 2008-2009; 4 appearances
Bowler, Teddy; 1965-1968; 5 appearances
Breen, Eamonn; 1990-1999; (1-10) in 25 appearances
Brennan, John; 1997; 1 appearance
Brick, Willie; 1934-1936; (1-3) in 3 appearances
Brosnan, Con; 1928-1932; (1-2) in 16 appearances
Brosnan, Eoin; 2001-2009; (15-42) in 53 appearances

Brosnan, Jim; 1949-1960; (3-23) in 27 appearances
Brosnan, Liam; 1998; 2 appearances
Brosnan, Mick; 1953; (0-1) in 1 appearance
Brosnan, Paddy Bawn; 1938-1952; (2-6) in 40 appearances
Brosnan, Sean; 1936-1944; (1-17) in 26 appearances
Brosnan, Tim; (1944-1947); 8 appearances
Buckley, Bobby; (1953-1956); (3-1) in 12 appearances
Bunyan, John; 1975; 3 appearances
Burke, Derry; 1945-1948; 3 appearances
Burke, John; 1961; (0-1) in 1 appearance
Burke, Paddy; 1946; (3-8) in 6 appearances
Burke, Sean; 1990-1997; (1-0) in 17 appearances
Burke, Tom; 1961; (0-7) in 2 appearances
Burke, Willie; 1945; 2 appearances
Burns, Killian; 1996-2000; (0-2) in 13 appearances
Burns, PJ; 1970; 1 appearance
Burrows, Seanie; 1965-1968; 10 appearances

Cahalane, James; 2003; 1 appearance
Callaghan, Bernie; 1963-1965; (5-39) in 11 appearances
Carmody, Jer; 1937; 4 appearances
Casey, Bill; 1938-1949; 29 appearances
Clarke, Brian; 1996-1999; (0-2) in 4 appearances
Clifford, Gary; 1961; (1-2) in 3 appearances
Clifford, J.; 1929; (1-1) in 1 appearance
Clifford, Johnny; 1943-1944; (1-1) in 6 appearances
Coffey, Kevin; 1958-1964; (0-2) in 19 appearances
Collins, Tom; 1956-1957; (0-1) in 2 appearances
Condon, Eddie; 1943-1944; 4 appearances
Conway, Alan; 1962; 1 appearance
Conway, Albie; 1945; 1 appearance
Conway, Dan Joe; 1928-1929; 2 appearances
Cooper, Colm; 2002-2009; (15-165) in 54 appearances
Costelloe, Tom; 1955; (2-2) in 3 appearances
Coughlan, C.; 1946; 1 appearance
Cronin, Gus; 1944-1948; (1-4) in 7 appearances
Cronesberry, Paddy; 1944; 1 appearance
Cronin, John; 1953-1956; (3-1) in 15 appearances
Cronin, John; 1991-1992; (1-5) in 4 appearances
Crowley, Derry; 1968-1974; 10 appearances
Crowley, DJ; 1967-1971; (2-14) in 16 appearances

Crowley, John; 1995-2004; (12-53) in 46 appearances
Culhane, Kieran; 1990-1993; 6 appearances
Culloty, Johnny; 1955-1971; (1-1) in 44 appearances

Daly, Donal; 1996-2002; (0-8) in 28 appearances
Deenihan, Jim; 1973-1981; 29 appearances
Dennehy, Pa; 1989-1995; (1-4) in 8 appearances
Dennehy, Pat; 1949; 1 appearance
Dillon, Bill; 1937-1944; (2-3) in 26 appearances
Donaghy, Kieran; 2005-2009; (6-12) in 24 appearances
Doran, Willie; 1963; 1 appearance
Dowd, Teddy; 1961; (0-1) in 3 appearances
Dowling, Eddie; 1944-1952; (2-2) in 23 appearances
Dowling, Jack; 1956-1961; 13 appearances
Dowling, John; 1951-1961; (1-22) in 26 appearances
Dowling, Pat; 1960; 3 appearances
Dowling, Tommy; 1950; 1 appearance
Doyle, Miko; 1929-1939; (5-21) in 33 appearances
Doyle, Tommy; 1977-1989; (0-25) in 41 appearances
Dunne, Eddie; 1944-1945; (2-2) in 3 appearances

Egan, John; 1973-1984; (14-59) in 41 appearances

Falvey, Jackie; 1942-1946; (1-3) in 5 appearances
Farrell, David; 1990-1991; (2-1) in 5 appearances
Farrell, Gene; 1995-1996; (0-5) in 6 appearances
Ferriter, M.; 1936-1937; (2-4) in 4 appearances
Finucane, Mick; 1947-1950; 5 appearances
Fitzgerald, Eamonn; 1928-1931; (0-1) in 6 appearances
Fitzgerald, Eamonn; 1972-1973; 7 appearances
Fitzgerald, G.; 1936-1937; (0-3) in 4 appearances
Fitzgerald, J.; 1944; (0-2) in 2 appearances
Fitzgerald, JB; 1940; (0-2) in 2 appearances
Fitzgerald, Liam; 1950-1951; 6 appearances
Fitzgerald, Maurice; 1988-2001; (12-205) in 45 appearances
Fitzgerald, Ned; 1955-1958; (0-4) in 3 appearances
Fitzgerald, Pop; 1957; (0-1) in 1 appearance
Fitzgerald, Tom; 1958; 2 appearances
Fitzmaurice, Eamonn; 1998-2006; (0-7) in 48 appearances
Fitzpatrick, PJ; 1966; (0-1) in 1 appearance
Flavin, Jack; 1932-1937; (0-4) in 3 appearances
Fleming, Mick; 1963-1970; (1-6) in 20 appearances

Fleming, Timmy; 1989-1994; (1-9) in 12 appearances
Foley, Johnny; 1953; 2 appearances

Galvin, Brendan; 1952; (0-1) in 1 appearance
Galvin, Enda; 2000-2002; 4 appearances
Galvin, Paul; 2003-2009; (1-32) in 36 appearances
Galwey, Mick; 1986-1989; 2 appearances
Garvey, Batt; 1945-1950; (6-24) in 20 appearances
Geaney, Con; 1931-1938; (2-9) in 15 appearances
Geaney, Dave; 1959-1966; (1-16) in 14 appearances
Geaney, Sean; 1990-1996; (3-4) in 8 appearances
Gleeson, Anthony; 1989-1996; 10 appearances
Gleeson, Mick; 1969-1973; (4-12) in 15 appearances
Godley, Pat; 1950-1951; (2-5) in 7 appearances
Griffin, Pat; 1963-1974; (2-42) in 29 appearances
Griffin, Tommy; 2000-2009; (0-1) in 35 appearances
Guiney, Brendan; 2004-2006; 3 appearances

Hanafin, Dermot Jnr; 1985-1993; (1-1) in 7 appearances
Hanafin, Dermot Snr; 1950-1953; (1-1) in 8 appearances
Hanrahan, Eddie; 1936; 2 appearances
Hartnett, Liam; 1989; 1 appearance
Hassett, Liam; 1995-2005; (4-37) in 42 appearances
Hassett, Mike; 1994-2001; (0-1) in 19 appearances
Hayes, Tim; 1932; (0-1) in 1 appearance
Healy, John; 1962; 1 appearance
Healy, Mick; 1929-1933; 3 appearances
Healy, Tadgh; 1937-1945; (0-1) in 27 appearances
Healy, Tim; 1949-1951; 3 appearances
Higgins, John; 1985-1987; 5 appearances
Higgins, Liam; 1969-1973; (2-20) in 16 appearances
Holly, Pat; 1943; (0-1) in 1 appearance

Kavanagh, Dan; 1944-1950; (5-11) in 21 appearances
Kavanagh, Donal; 1971-1973; (3-1) in 8 appearances
Kearney, Conor; 1993-1995; 4 appearances
Kelliher, Brian; 1946-1948; (1-1) in 2 appearances
Kelliher, Tom; 1967; (0-3) in 2 appearances
Kelliher, Brian; 1946-1948; (1-1) in 2 appearances
Kelly, Murt; 1936-1944; (7-52) in 28 appearances
Kelly, Paddy; 2004-2005; (0-1) in 5 appearances
Kelly, Sean; 1952-1954; (4-13) in 10 appearances

Kennedy, John; 1984-1989; (0-26) in 15 appearances
Kennedy, Paddy; 1936-1947; (4-22) in 44 appearances
Kennelly, Colm; 1952-1956; (0-1) in 16 appearances
Kennelly, Eddie; 1951; (1-0) in 1 appearance
Kennelly, Noel; 1998-2002; (1-18) in 20 appearances
Kennelly, Tadgh; 2009; (0-8) in 6 appearances
Kennelly, Tim; 1975-1983; (0-1) in 31 appearances
Kennington, Joe; 1942-1943; (0-1) in 5 appearances
Keohane, Joe; 1936-1948; 44 appearances
Kerins, Michael; 1957; 1 appearance
Kiely, T.; 1936; 1 appearance
Kinnerk, Bill; 1932-1938; 19 appearances
Kirby, Willie; 1997-2005; (0-12) in 26 appearances

Laide, Pa; 1990-1998; (2-14) in 14 appearances
Landers, Bill; 1933; 2 appearances
Landers, John Joe; 1928-1938; (11-20) in 29 appearances
Landers, Tim; 1931-1945; (8-20) in 20 appearances
Lane, Brendan; 1994; 1 appearance
Lawlor, Tom; 1942-1945; 2 appearances
Leen, JP; 1966; 1 appearance
Liston, Eoin; 1978-1993; (20-50) in 39 appearances
Locke, Sammy; 1929-1930; (0-5) in 3 appearances
Long, John; 1974-1977; (0-1) in 3 appearances
Long, Tom; 1956-1964; (5-22) in 26 appearances
Lovett, Declan; 1968; 1 appearance
Lucey, Jimmy; 1962-1965; (0-1) in 8 appearances
Lucey, Noel; (1962-1963); 5 appearances
Lucey, Vincent; 1963-1965; (2-8) in 6 appearances
Lynch, Brendan; 1968-1976; (3-87) in 32 appearances
Lynch, Ger; 1982-1988; (0-1) in 21 appearances
Lynch, Paudie; 1971-1983; (0-7) in 39 appearances
Lyne, Dinny; 1944-1948; 18 appearances
Lyne, Domo; 1986-1991; 2 appearances
Lyne, Jackie; 1944-1954; (5-12) in 34 appearances
Lyne, Mikey; 1937-1945; (0-9) in 6 appearances
Lyne, Tadghie; 1952-1960; (5-65) in 24 appearances
Lyons, Mossie; 2001-2007; 14 appearances
Lyons, Tim; 1956-1963; 24 appearances

MacGearailt, Aodhán; 1999-2003; (5-25) in 25 appearances

MacGearailt, Seamus; 1966-1974; (2-7) in 18 appearances
Maher, Willie; 1984-1991; (4-7) in 12 appearances
McAuliffe, Dan; 1955-1964; (5-39) in 21 appearances
McAuliffe, Mike; 1987-1989; (1-5) in 6 appearances
McAuliffe, Tony; 1938-1940; (3-6) in 9 appearances
McCarthy, Charlie; 1996; (0-1) in 4 appearances
McCarthy, Donal; 1990; (0-1) in 1 appearance
McCarthy, John; 1964; 1 appearance
McCarthy, Johnny; 1939; 1 appearance
McCarthy, Martin; 1942-1948; (1-0) in 11 appearances
McCarthy, Mike; 1999-2009; (0-1) in 52 appearances
McCarthy, Pat; 1975-1978; (0-3) in 12 appearances
McCarthy, Phil; 1944-1950; (1-2) in 5 appearances
McCarthy, Sean; 1937-1940; (6-2) in 7 appearances
McElligott, Bernard; 1993-1995; 2 appearances
McElligott, John L.; 1982-1983; 4 appearances
McElligott, Sean; 1990; (0-5) in 2 appearances
McElligott, Tom; 1946; 1 appearance
McEvoy, Donal; 1988; (1-1) in 1 appearance
McGlynn, John; 1999-2001; (0-5) in 4 appearances
McIntyre, PJ; 1968; 1 appearance
McKenna, M.; 1934; (1-1) in 4 appearances
McKenna, Pat; 1990; (0-2) in 1 appearance
McKenna, Toss; 1961; 1 appearance
McMahon, DJ; 1950; (1-0) in 2 appearances
McMahon, Garry; 1958-1962; (7-6) in 12 appearances
Moloney, Jerh; 1951; 1 appearance
Moran, David; 2008-2009; (0-1) in 6 appearances
Moran, Denis Ogie; 1975-1987; (0-42) in 46 appearances
Moriarty, Johnny; 1939-1944; 2 appearances
Moriarty, Murt; 1991; (1-0) in 2 appearances
Moriarty, Tom; 1949-1958; (0-3) in 15 appearances
Morris, Mick; 1964-1969; 16 appearances
Moynihan, Pat; 1966-1969; (0-7) in 4 appearances
Moynihan, Seamus; 1992-2006; (0-5) in 61 appearances
Mulvihill, John; 1978; (0-2) in 1 appearance
Murphy, Connie; 1988-1994; (1-2) in 15 appearances
Murphy, Diarmuid; 2004-2009; 41 appearances
Murphy, Donie; 1948-1955; 15 appearances
Murphy, Gerard; 1988; (0-1) in 2 appearances
Murphy, Gerard, 1999; (1-0) in 1 appearance

Murphy, J.; 1938; 1 appearance
Murphy, Jas.; 1949-1954; 16 appearances
Murphy, Mick; 1955-1958; (3-4) in 9 appearances
Murphy, Padraig; 1950-1952; 2 appearances
Murphy, Seamus; 1958-1970; (0-10) in 41 appearances
Murphy, Sean; 1951-1961; 28 appearances
Murphy, Tommy; 1937-1938; 2 appearances
Myers, Bill; 1937-1946; 29 appearances

Nelligan, Charlie; 1976-1991; 49 appearances
Nix, Morgan; 1988-1995; 12 appearances

O'Brien, JB; 1991; 1 appearance
O'Brien, Josie; 1967; 1 appearance
O'Brien, Peter; 1995; 2 appearances
O'Callaghan, Tommy; 1966; 2 appearances
Ó'Cinneide, Dara; 1995-2005; (11-149) in 54 appearances
O'Connell, Denis "Rory"; 1928-1930; 4 appearances
O'Connell, John; 1991-1996; 3 appearances
O'Connell, Mick; 1956-1974; (1-121) in 56 appearances
O'Connell, Moss; 1958-1959; 4 appearances
O'Connor, Charlie; 1946; (0-3); 2 appearances
O'Connor, Dee; 1929-1936; 19 appearances
O'Connor, F.; 1944; 1 appearance
O'Connor, Jack; 1928-1933; (1-0) in 2 appearances
O'Connor, JD; 1960-1967; (0-4) in 15 appearances
O'Connor, Michael; 1950; 1 appearance
O'Connor, Paul; 2006-2009; (0-7) in 7 appearances
O'Connor, Ronan; 2002-2006; (0-1) in 7 appearances
O'Connor, Sean; 1951; (2-1) in 4 appearances
O'Connor, Teddy; 1946-1952; (1-4) in 17 appearances
O'Connor, Tom Gega; 1937-1947; (7-47) in 35 appearances
O'Connor, Vincent; 1979-1987; (1-5) in 12 appearances
O'Donnell, Dom; 1964-1969; (4-1) in 5 appearances
O'Donnell, Tim; 1929-1937; (0-3) in 23 appearances
O'Donnell, Willie; 1942-1951; (8-23) in 18 appearances
O'Donoghue, Diarmuid; 1984; (0-1) in 1 appearance
O'Donoghue, Eamonn; 1967-1974; (1-16) in 24 appearances
O'Donoghue, Nicholas; 1946; 1 appearance
O'Donoghue, Paddy; 1942-1944; (2-1) in 2 appearances
O'Donoghue, Paud; 1964-1974; 34 appearances

O'Donovan, Ambrose; 1984-1992; (1-6) in 26 appearances
O'Dowd, Timmy; 1984-1987; (1-11) in 14 appearances
O'Driscoll, Bingo; 1994-1996; (2-10) in 8 appearances
O'Driscoll, Gene; 1962; (1-1) in 1 appearance
O'Driscoll, Ger; 1975-1980; (2-3) in 7 appearances
O'Driscoll, John; 1996; 2 appearances
O'Dwyer, Denis; 1996-2001; (1-4) in 18 appearances
O'Dwyer, Karl; 1992-1993; (0-5) in 3 appearances
O'Dwyer, Mick; 1957-1973; (6-129) in 48 appearances
O'Flaherty, Liam; 1991-1998; (0-1) in 18 appearances
O'Gorman, Jimmy; 1934-1940; (1-8) in 13 appearances
O'Gorman, Jimmy (B); 1940-1943; (8-16) in 13 appearances
O'Gorman, Michael; 1937; (2-1) in 1 appearance
O'Keeffe, Anthony; 1977; 1 appearance
O'Keeffe, Dan; 1931-1948; 66 appearances
O'Keeffe, Declan; 1996-2003; 39 appearances
O'Keeffe, Frank; 1946-1951; (5-1) in 7 appearances
O'Keeffe, Ger; 1973-1983; (0-1) in 28 appearances
O'Keeffe, John; 1970-1984; (0-9) in 49 appearances
O'Leary, Frank; 1963-1964; (1-7) in 6 appearances
O'Leary, Kieran; 2008; 1 appearance
O'Leary, Noel; 1992; 1 appearance
O'Leary, Peter; 1992-1995; 6 appearances
O'Leary, Tim; 1937-1938; (4-10) in 11 appearances
O'Mahony, Aidan; 2004-2009; (0-10) in 40 appearances
O'Mahony, Garry; 1954-1956; 7 appearances
O'Mahony, Noel; 1990-1994; (0-3) in 10 appearances
O'Mahony, Pat; 1978; (1-0) in 1 appearance
O'Mahony, Paudie; 1974-1978; 15 appearances
O'Neill, Donal; 1952-1958; 7 appearances
O'Neill, Frank; 1932; 1 appearance
O'Riordan, Jerry; 1962-1963; 4 appearances
Ó'Ruairc, Micheál; 1929-1930; (1-1) in 2 appearances
Ó'Sé, Darragh; 1994-2009; (1-31) in 81 appearances
Ó'Sé, Marc; 2002-2009; (0-8) in 53 appearances
Ó'Sé, Micheál; 1968-1973; 16 appearances
Ó'Sé, Páidí; 1974-1988; (0-8) in 53 appearances
Ó'Sé, Tomás; 1998-2009; (3-24) in 69 appearances
O'Shea, Aidan; 2009; 2 appearances
O'Shea, Barry; 1995-2002; 17 appearances
O'Shea, Batt; 1975; 1 appearance

O'Shea, Billy; 1992-1999; (2-11) in 19 appearances
O'Shea, Brendan; 1952-1954; 6 appearances
O'Shea, Derry; 1965-1966; (3-5) in 5 appearances
O'Shea, Dinny; 1955-1958; (1-0) in 9 appearances
O'Shea, Jack; 1977-1992; (11-55); 53 appearances
O'Shea, Jerome; 1952-1961; 25 appearances
O'Shea, John "Thorny"; 1965-1967; (0-10) in 3 appearances
O'Shea, Morgan; 1997; 2 appearances
O'Shea, Seamus; 1936; 1 appearance
O'Sullivan, Bernard; 1981; 1 appearance
O'Sullivan, Billy; 1992; 1 appearance
O'Sullivan, Carl; 1946; 1 appearance
O'Sullivan, Charlie; 1933-1943; (10-26) in 29 appearances
O'Sullivan, Darran; 2005-2009; (2-12) in 29 appearances
O'Sullivan, Declan; 2003-2009; (7-44) in 42 appearances
O'Sullivan, Denis; 1964-1968; (0-1) in 16 appearances
O'Sullivan, Donie; 1962-1974; (0-2) in 35 appearances
O'Sullivan, Gerald; 1946-1956; (4-15) in 24 appearances
O'Sullivan, Jas.; 1928; 2 appearances
O'Sullivan, Joe; 1929-1934; 15 appearances
O'Sullivan, Mickey; 1971-1978; (4-17) in 17 appearances
O'Sullivan, Paud; 1928-1929; 2 appearances
O'Sullivan, Sean; 2002-2009; (1-30) in 34 appearances
O'Sullivan, Teddy; 1947-1950; (2-6) in 8 appearances
O'Sullivan, Tim; 1961-1964; (0-7) in 7 appearances
O'Sullivan, Tom; 2000-2009; (0-1) in 65 appearances
O'Sullivan, William; 1928; 1 appearance

Palmer, Micksie; 1950-1955; (1-1) in 21 appearances
Pierce, Jimmy; 1942-1943; 2 appearances
Powell, Eugene; 1938; (0-3) in 2 appearances
Power, Ger; 1973-1988; (14-34) in 52 appearances
Prendergast, Tom; (1966-1973); (1-6) in 23 appearances
Prendiville, Ray; 1975; (1-0) in 1 appearance

Quill, Declan; 2001-2005; (0-9) in 14 appearances
Quirke, Michael; 2004-2009; 12 appearances

Raymond, Mick; 1939-1942; 4 appearances
Regan, Martin; 1931-1938; (7-14) in 16 appearances
Reidy, Brendan; 1932-1937; 2 appearances
Reidy, Padraig; 2007-2009; 13 appearances

Riordan, Johnny; 1928-1931; 10 appearances
Roche, Ned; 1953-1958; 18 appearances
Roche, Seamus; 1962-1963; (1-0) in 3 appearances
Russell, Mike Frank; 1997-2007; (8-130) in 56 appearances
Russell, Paul; 1928-1934; (3-10) in 20 appearances
Ryan, Dan; 1928-1938; 4 appearances
Ryan, Jackie; 1928-1934; (4-50) in 19 appearances

Saunders, John; 1967-1972; (0-5) in 3 appearances
Savage, Ken; 1989; 2 appearances
Savage, Niall; 1991; 1 appearance
Scanlon, Seamus; 2002-2009; (0-7) in 26 appearances
Sexton, P.; 1942; 1 appearance
Shanahan, Paddy Batt; 1950; 2 appearances
Shannon, Joe; 1988-1990; (0-2) in 4 appearances
Sheehan, Bryan; 2005-2009; (0-71) in 29 appearances
Sheehan, JJ; 1951-1955; (2-7) in 11 appearances
Sheehan, John; 2002-2004; (0-2) in 11 appearances
Sheehan, Tim; 1967-1968; (0-1) in 3 appearances
Sheehy, Brian; 1961; (1-0) in 3 appearances
Sheehy, John Joe; 1928-1930; (4-22) in 8 appearances
Sheehy, Mike; 1974-1987; (29-205) in 49 appearances
Sheehy, Niall; 1958-1965; 26 appearances
Sheehy, Paudie; 1951-1962; (6-56) in 35 appearances
Sheehy, Sean Óg; 1962-1963; (1-0) in 7 appearances
Slattery, Pat; 1990; 2 appearances
Spillane, Jerome; 1952; 1 appearance
Spillane, Mick; 1978-1989; 33 appearances
Spillane, Pat; 1975-1991; (19-123) in 56 appearances
Spillane, Tom; 1948-1955; (0-1) in 5 appearances
Spillane, Tom; 1981-1991; (1-13) in 27 appearances
Spring, Dan; 1934-1940; (6-10) in 13 appearances
Stack, Bob; 1928-1932; (0-4) in 16 appearances
Stack, Gerard; 1954; 3 appearances
Stack, John; 1929; (0-1) in 1 appearance
Stack, Stephen; 1986-1998; 16 appearances
Sweeney, Ned; 1928-1930; (3-3) in 8 appearances

Teahan, Ger; 1938-1947; 10 appearances
Twiss, Ian; 2002; (0-2) in 2 appearances

Walsh, Barry; 1977; (2-8) in 3 appearances

Walsh, Barry John; 2009; 2 appearances
Walsh, Denis; 1942-1943; 3 appearances
Walsh, Donnacha; 2008-2009; (2-6) in 12 appearances
Walsh, Eddie; 1938-1947; 38 appearances
Walsh, Jack; 1928-1934; 20 appearances
Walsh, Jackie; 1972-1976; (0-1) in 6 appearances
Walsh, Johnny; 1932-1944; (3-11) in 37 appearances
Walsh, Sean; 1976-1987; (6-22) in 41 appearances
Walsh, Tommy; 2008-2009; (4-23) in 15 appearances
Whitty, Paddy; 1928-1936; (0-6) in 19 appearances

Young, Killian; 2006-2009; (0-1) in 18 appearances